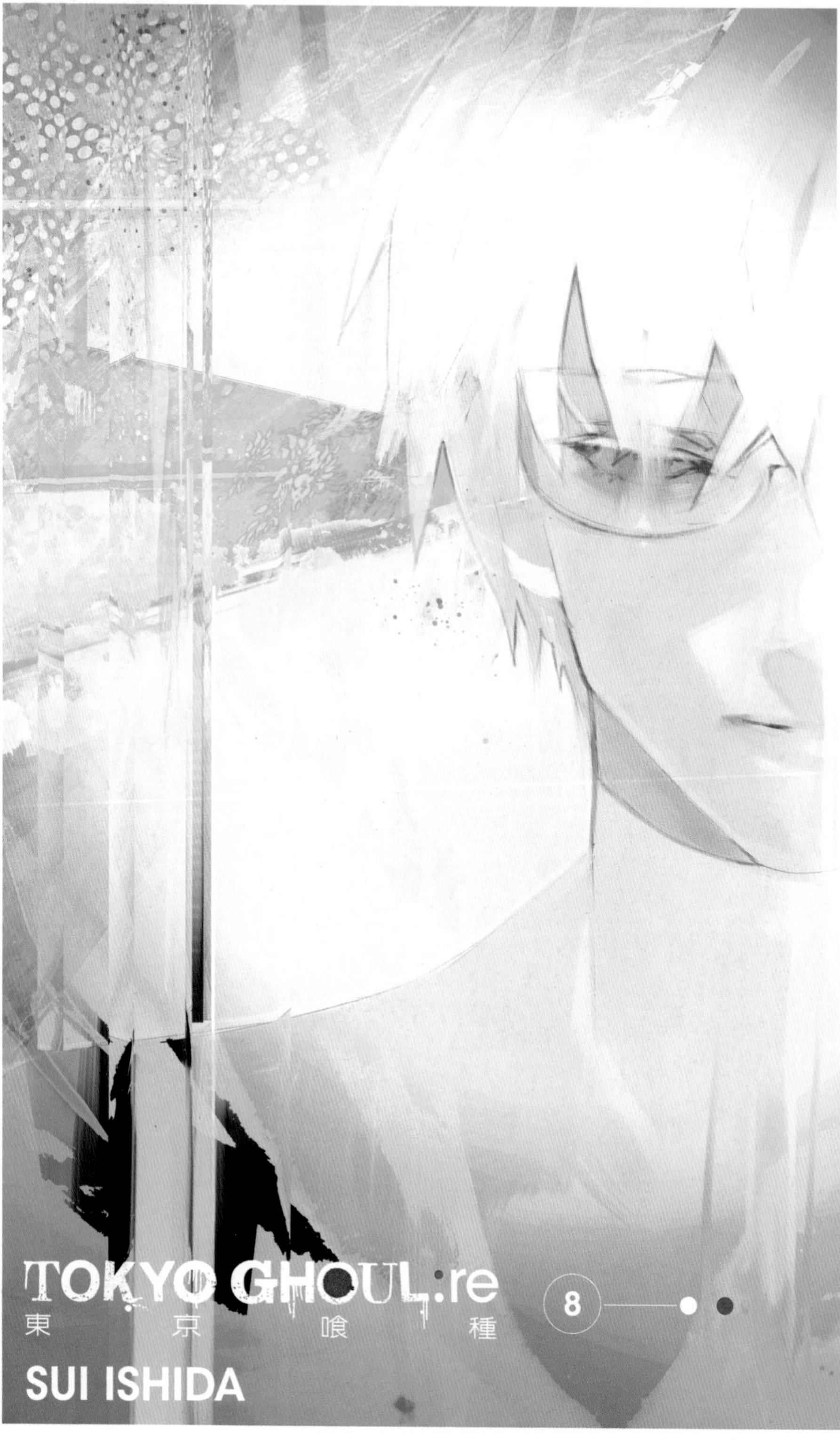
TOKYO GHOUL:re
東京喰種
8
SUI ISHIDA

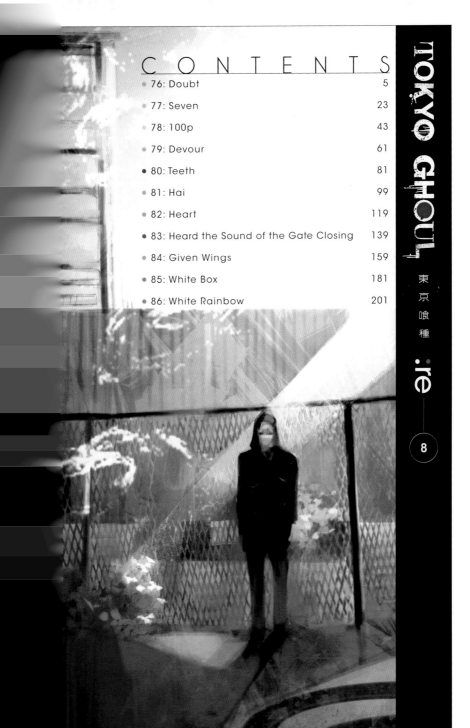

CONTENTS

TOKYO GHOUL

東京喰種

:re

8

CCG Ghoul Investigators

Tokyo Ghoul : re

The CCG is the only organization in the world that investigates and solves Ghoul-related crimes. Founded by the Washu family, the CCG developed and evolved Quinques, a type of weapon derived from Ghouls' Kagune. Quinx, an advanced, next-generation technology where humans are implanted with Quinques, is currently under development.

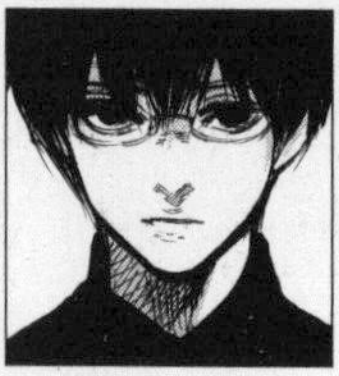

Ken Kaneki
金木 研

Half-Ghoul and former mentor of the Qs Squad. Recently regained his memory investigating the Aogiri Tree with Furuta. He has a particular reason for attempting to break into Cochlea.

Mado Squad

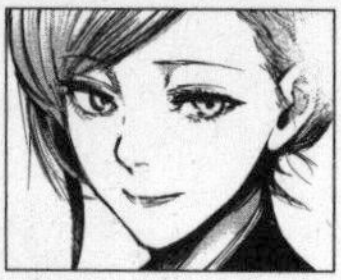

Akira Mado
真戸 暁

Assistant Special Investigator
Mentor to Haise. Takes after her father. Determined to eradicate Ghouls. Investigating the Aogiri Tree. Concerned about Fueguchi.

Qs (Quinx)

Investigators implanted with Quinques. They all live together in a house called the **Chateau** under Urie's new mentorship.

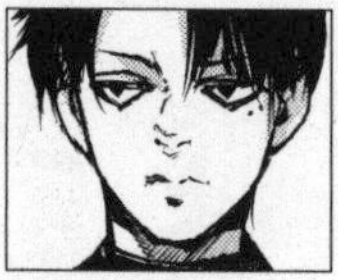

Kuki Urie
瓜江久生

Rank 1 Investigator
New Quinx Squad Leader. His father, a special investigator, was killed by a Ghoul. Urie seeks to avenge his death. He is demonstrating leadership after the death of Shirazu Ginshi.

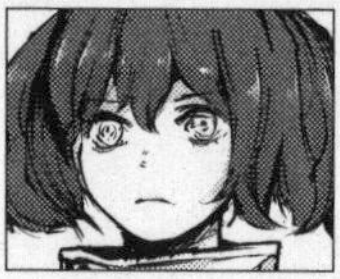

Saiko Yonebayashi
米林才子

Rank 2 Investigator
Supporting Urie while playing with her subordinates. By far the most suitable Quinx Procedure candidate, but she is very bad at time management and a sucker for games and snacks.

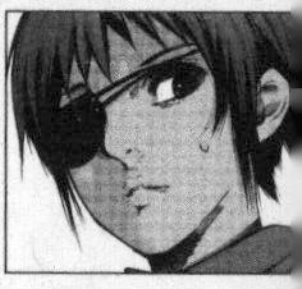

Toru Mutsuki
六月 透

Rank 1 Investigator
Both his parents wer killed by a Ghoul. Assigned female at birth, he transitionec after undergoing th Quinx procedure. Abducted by Torso during the Rushima Operation.

Suzuya Squad

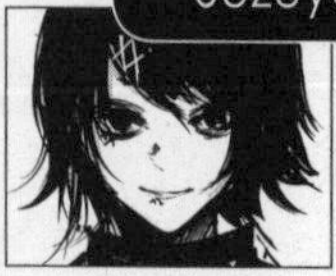

Juzo Suzuya
鈴屋什造

Special Investitgator
Promoted to special investigator at 22, a record previously only held by Kisho Arima. A maverick who fights with knives hidden in his prosthetic leg.

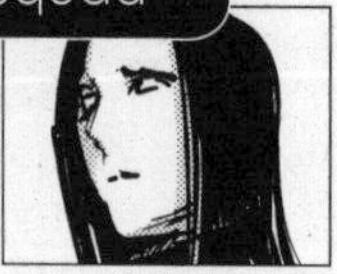

Hanbeh Abarai
阿原半兵衛

Rank 1 Investigator
Suzuya's right-hand man.

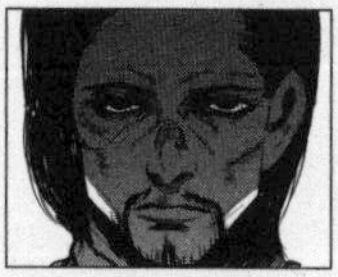

Yoshitoki Washu
阿原半兵衛

CCG Bureau Chief
Supervisor of the Quinx project. A member of the CCG's founding family, but he still has an approachable side. Commander of the Rushima Operation.

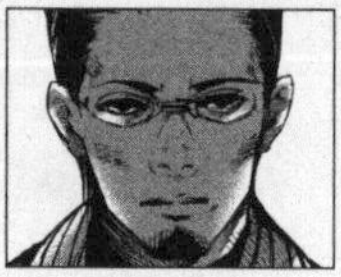

Matsuri Washu
和修 政

Special Investitgator
Yoshitoki's son. A Washu supremacist. Is skeptical of Quinxes. Deputy Commander of the Rushima Operation.

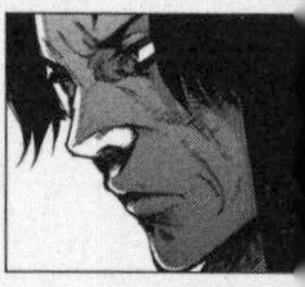

Itsuki Marude
丸手 斎

Special Investigator
Heads Counter-measure II. Deputy Commander of the Rushima Operation.

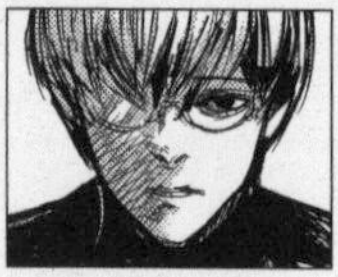

Kisho Arima
有馬貴将

Special Investigator
An undefeated investigator respected by many at the CCG.

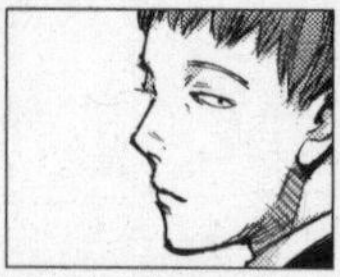

Take Hirako
有馬貴将

Senior Investigator
Kisho Arima's former partner. A reticent investigator.

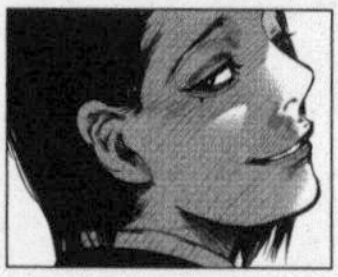

Nimura Furuta
旧多二福

Rank 1 Investigator
Former subordinate of the late Shiki Kijima. Has many secrets.

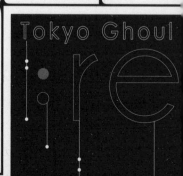

Tokyo Ghoul :re

Tokyo Ghoul :re

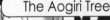

Ghouls

They appear human, but have a unique predation organ called Kagune and can only survive by feeding on human flesh. They are the nemesis of humanity. Besides human flesh, the only other thing they can ingest is coffee. Ghouls can only be wounded by a Kagune or a Quinque made from a Kagune. One of the most prominent Ghoul factions is the Aogiri Tree, a hostile organization that is increasing its strength.

The Aogiri Tree

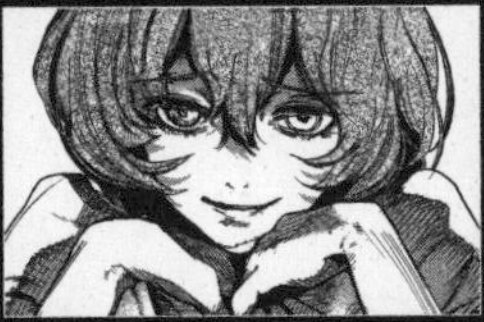

Eto/Sen Takatsuki
エト／高槻泉
Founder of the Aogiri Tree. Also a remarkable author with many fans. Revealed herself as a Ghoul after announcing her final novel.

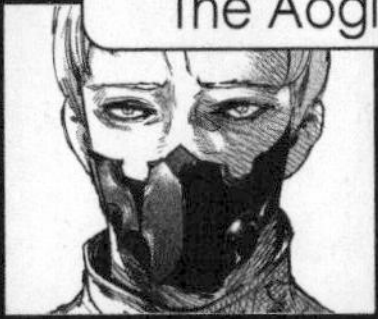

Tatara
タタラ
A leading member of the Aogiri Tree. Related to the former head of the Chì shé lián. A Chinese Ghoul.

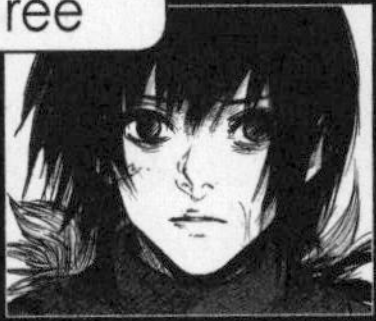

Ayato
アヤト
A leading member of the Aogiri Tree. A Rate SS Ghoul known as the Rabbit.

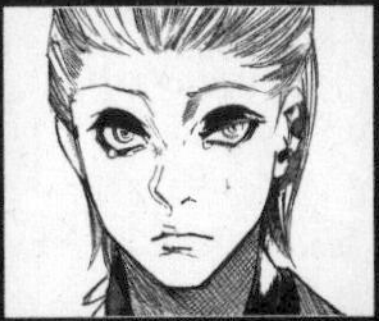

Naki
ナキ
Member of the Aogiri Tree. Current leader of the White Suits. A Rate S, but frequently loses control.

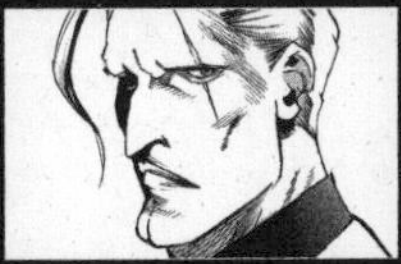

Shosei
承正
Member of the Aogiri Tree and the White Suits. Joined after being beaten by Naki during Jason's leadership.

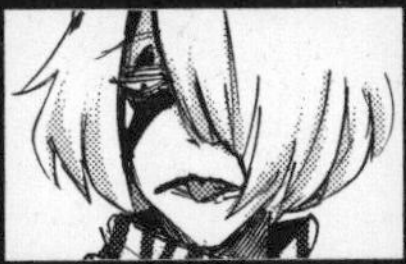

Hohguro
ホオグロ
Member of the Aogiri Tree and the White Suits. Joined after tying with Shosei.

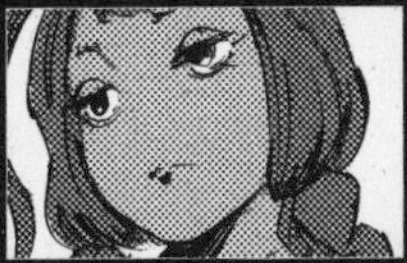

Miza
ミザ
Member of the Aogiri Tree. Controlled the 18th Ward as the head of the Blades. Known as Triple Blade.

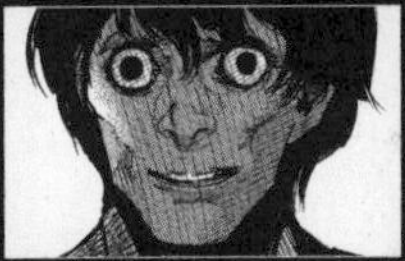

Torso (Karao Saeki)
トルソー
Rate A Ghoul. Abused his position as a taxi driver to prey on women with scars. Obsessed with Toru Mutsuki.

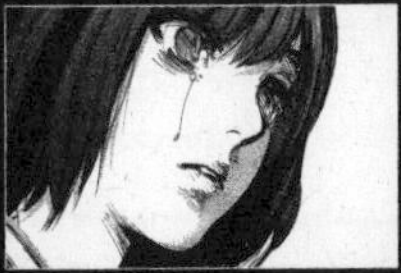

Hinami Fueguchi
フエグチヒナミ
Member of the Aogiri Tree. Captured by Haise Sasaki and sent to Cochlea, but has since been freed.

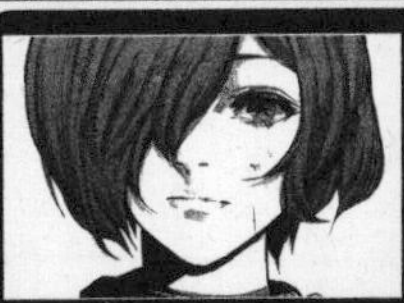

Touka
トーカ
Manager of café :re. Infiltrated Cochlea to save Hinami.

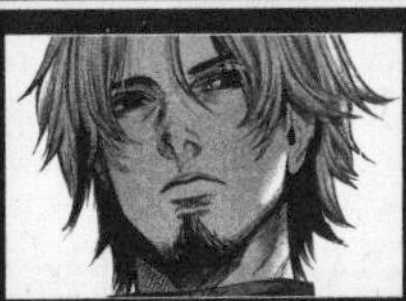

Renji Yomo
四方蓮示
Barista at café :re. Infiltrated Cochlea with Touka.

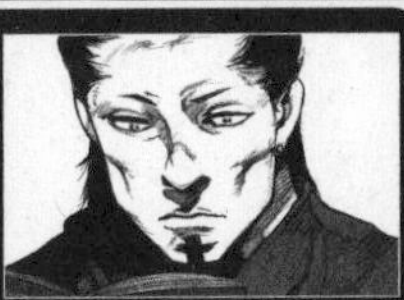

Banjo
バンジョー
Ayato's assistant.

So far in :re

T • K Y • G H • U L

Haise Sasaki and the four Qs who fight using Ghoul abilities are recognized for their role in the Tsukiyama family eradication operation and assigned to individual cases. The CCG discovers the Aogiri's stronghold, Rushima Island. Meanwhile, Sen Takatsuki reveals herself as a Ghoul at the press conference for her final novel, *King Bileygr*. The rift between humans, Ghouls and the CCG over the One-Eyed King grows ever deeper. Haise, assigned to defend Cochlea, attempts to free Hinami, but is no match for Arima and his Quinque, the Owl...

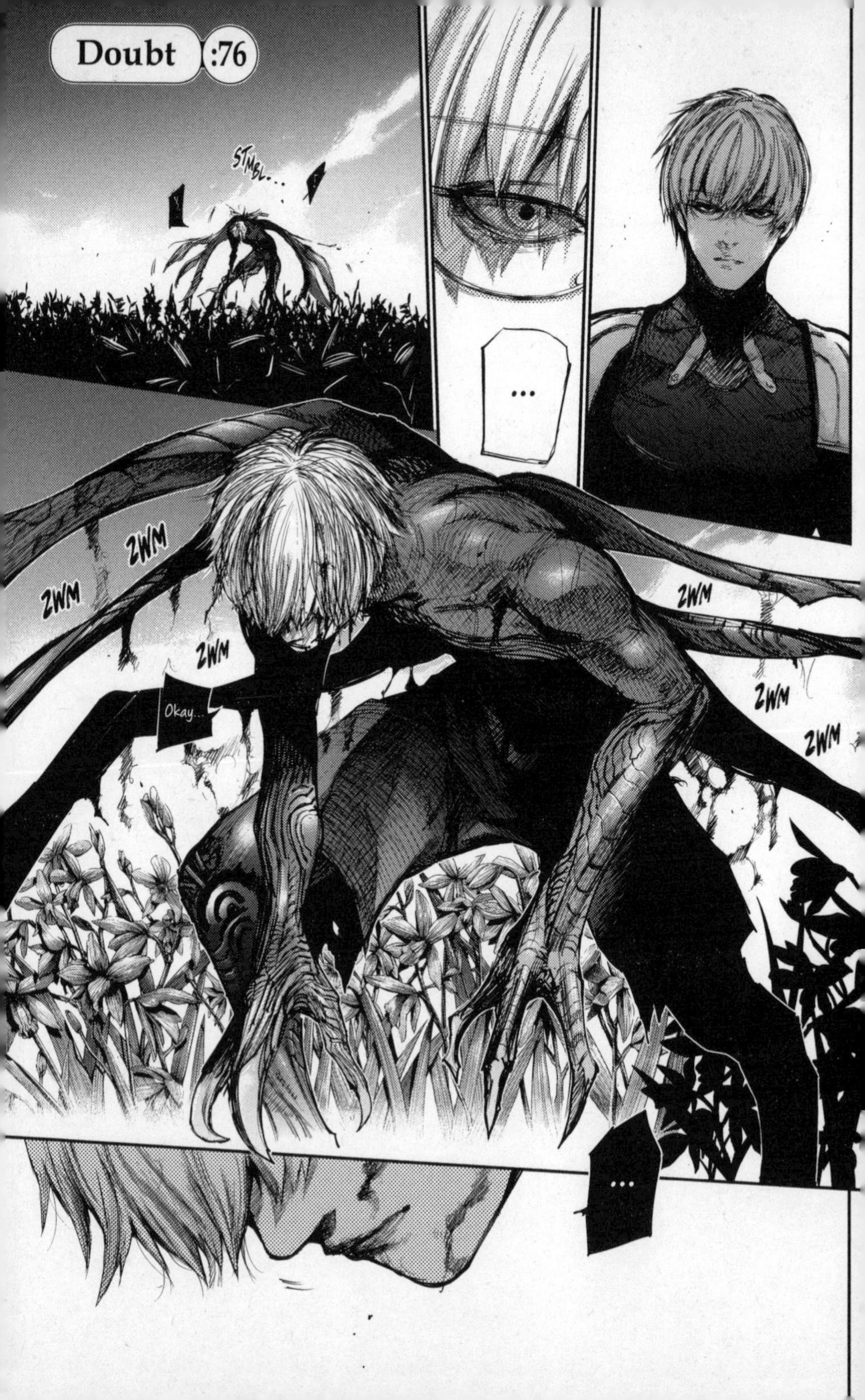
Doubt :76
...
STMBL...
ZWM
ZWM
ZWM
ZWM
Okay...
ZWM
ZWM
ZWM
...

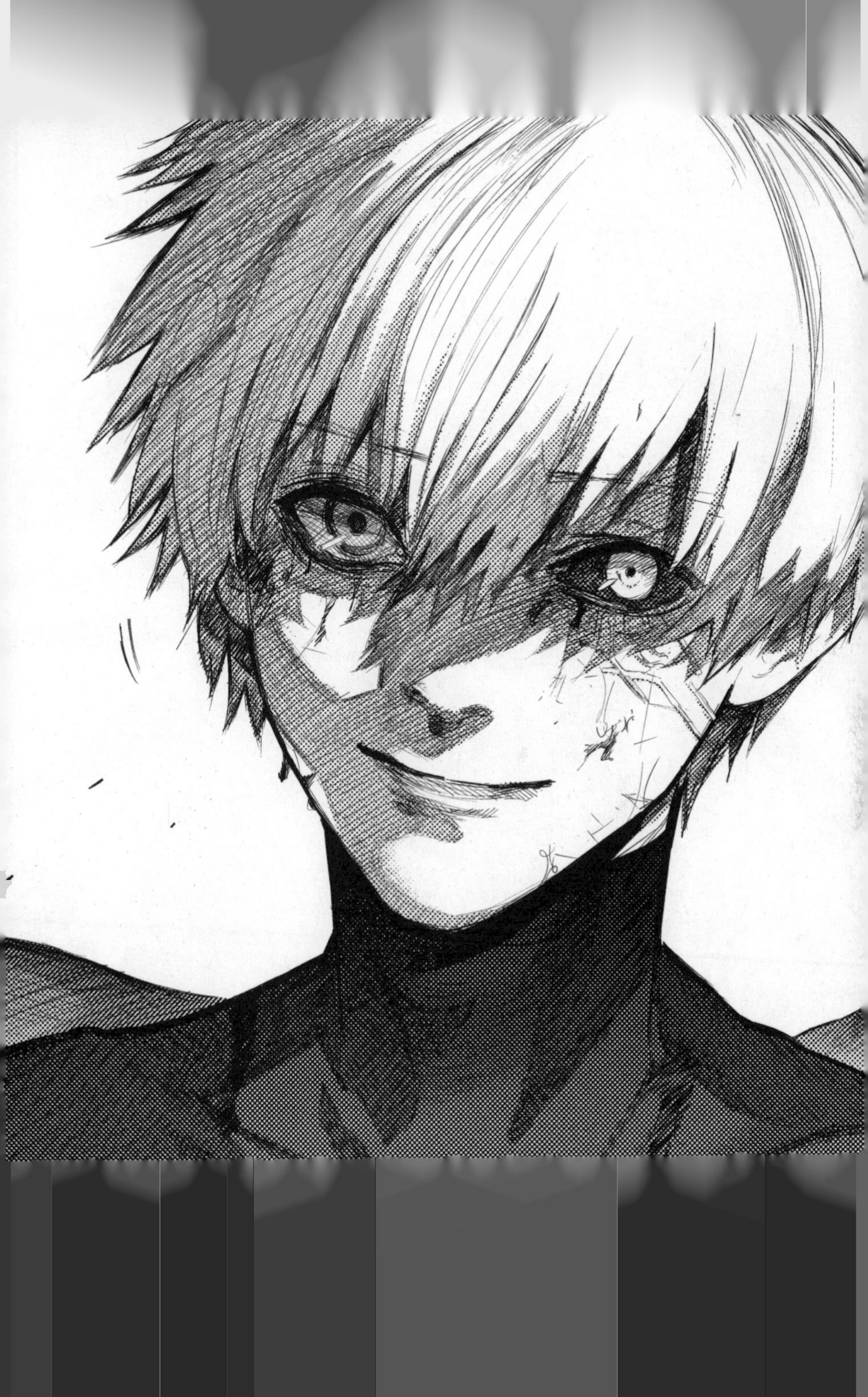

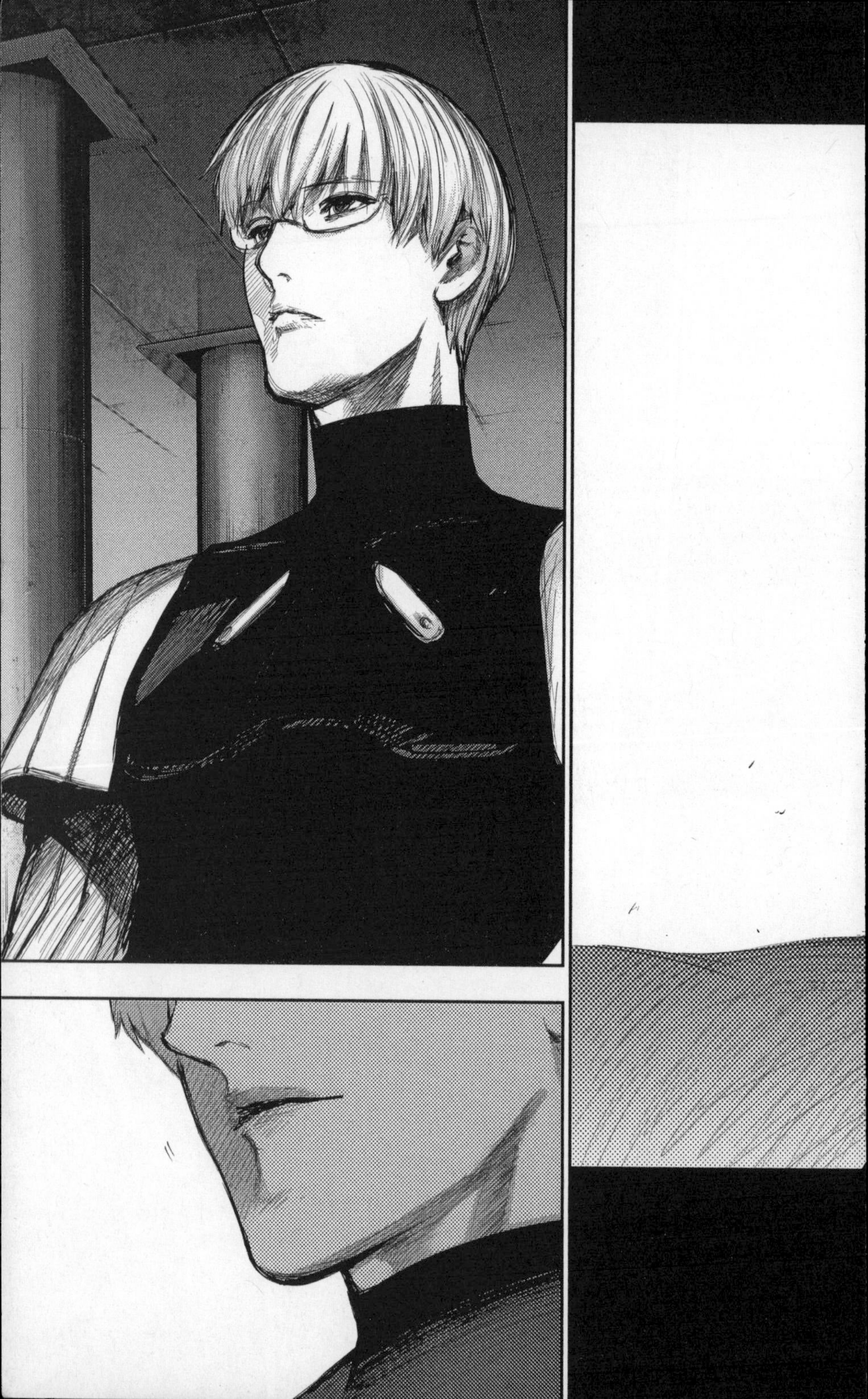

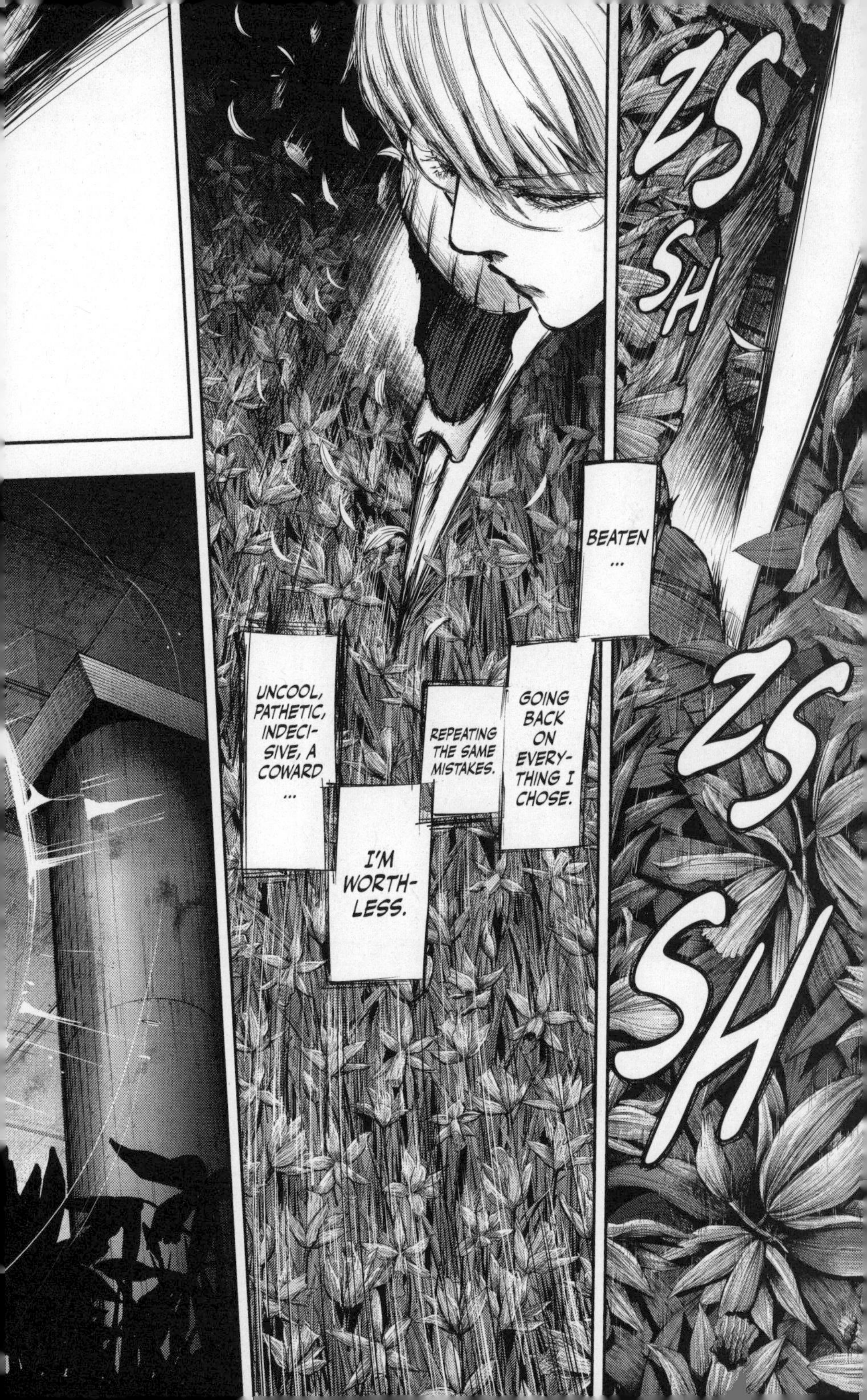
ZSSH
BEATEN...
GOING BACK ON EVERYTHING I CHOSE.
REPEATING THE SAME MISTAKES.
UNCOOL, PATHETIC, INDECISIVE, A COWARD...
I'M WORTHLESS.
ZSSH

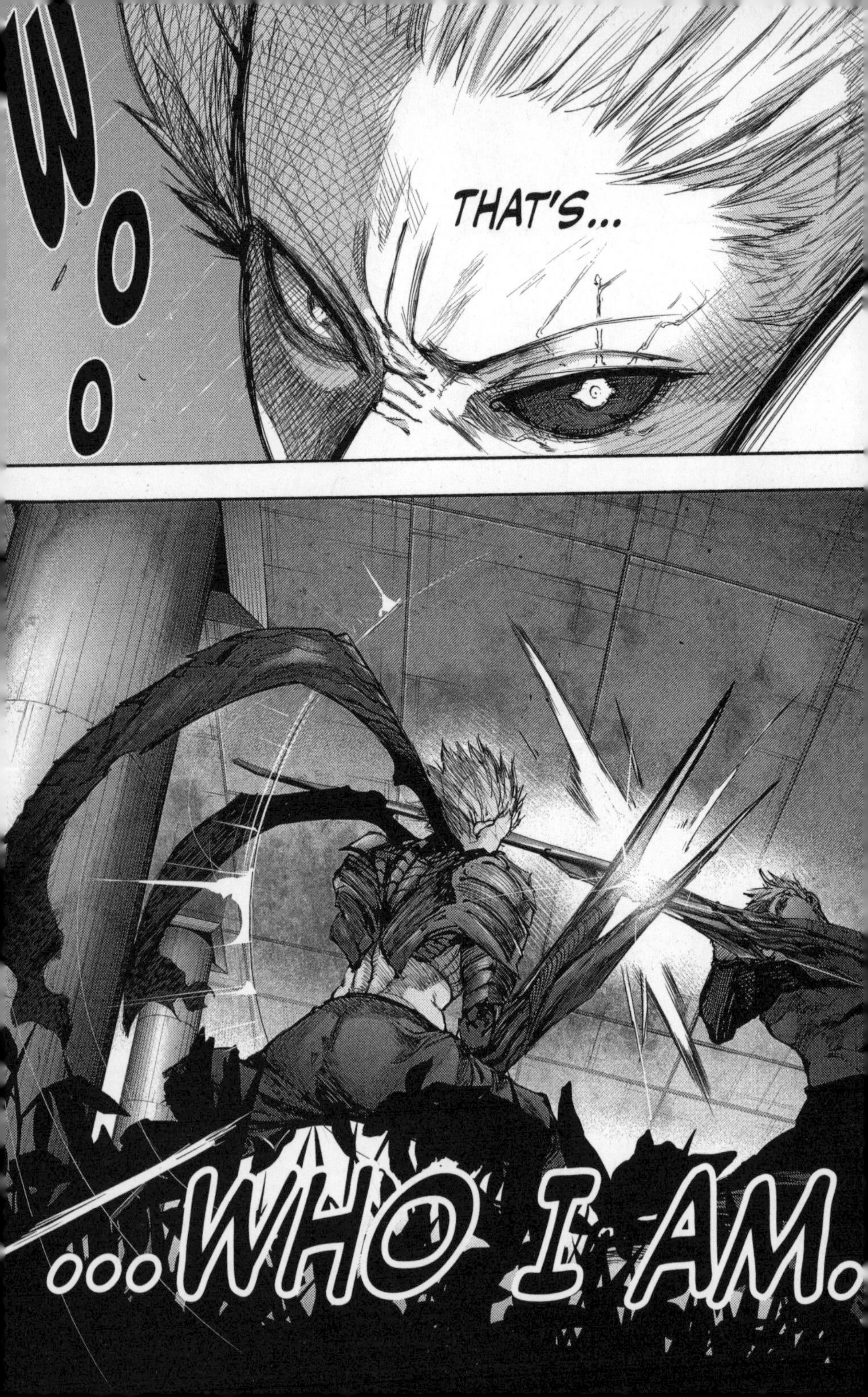
THAT'S...
...WHO I AM.

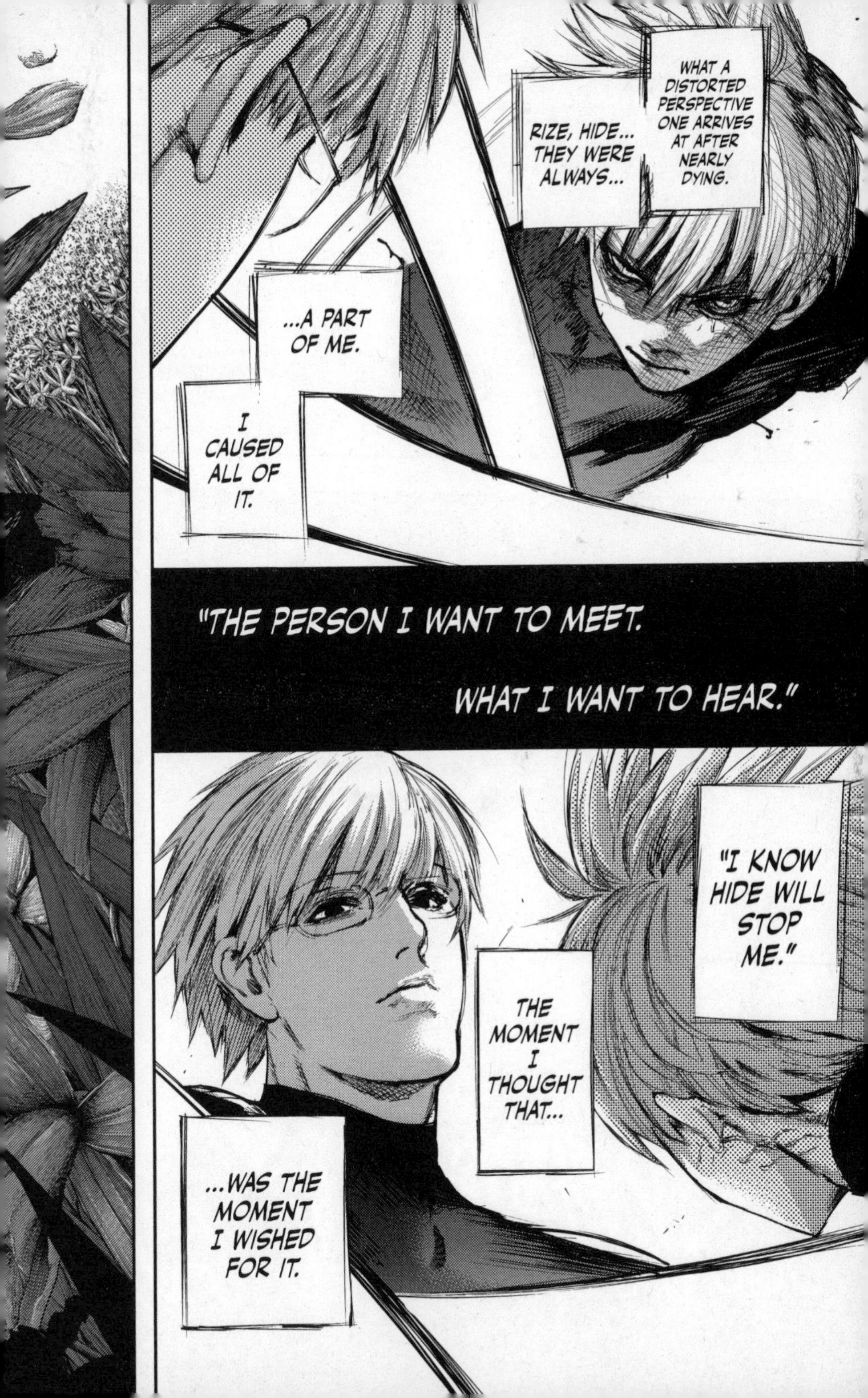
WHAT A DISTORTED PERSPECTIVE ONE ARRIVES AT AFTER NEARLY DYING.
RIZE, HIDE... THEY WERE ALWAYS...
...A PART OF ME.
I CAUSED ALL OF IT.
"THE PERSON I WANT TO MEET.
WHAT I WANT TO HEAR."
"I KNOW HIDE WILL STOP ME."
THE MOMENT I THOUGHT THAT...
...WAS THE MOMENT I WISHED FOR IT.

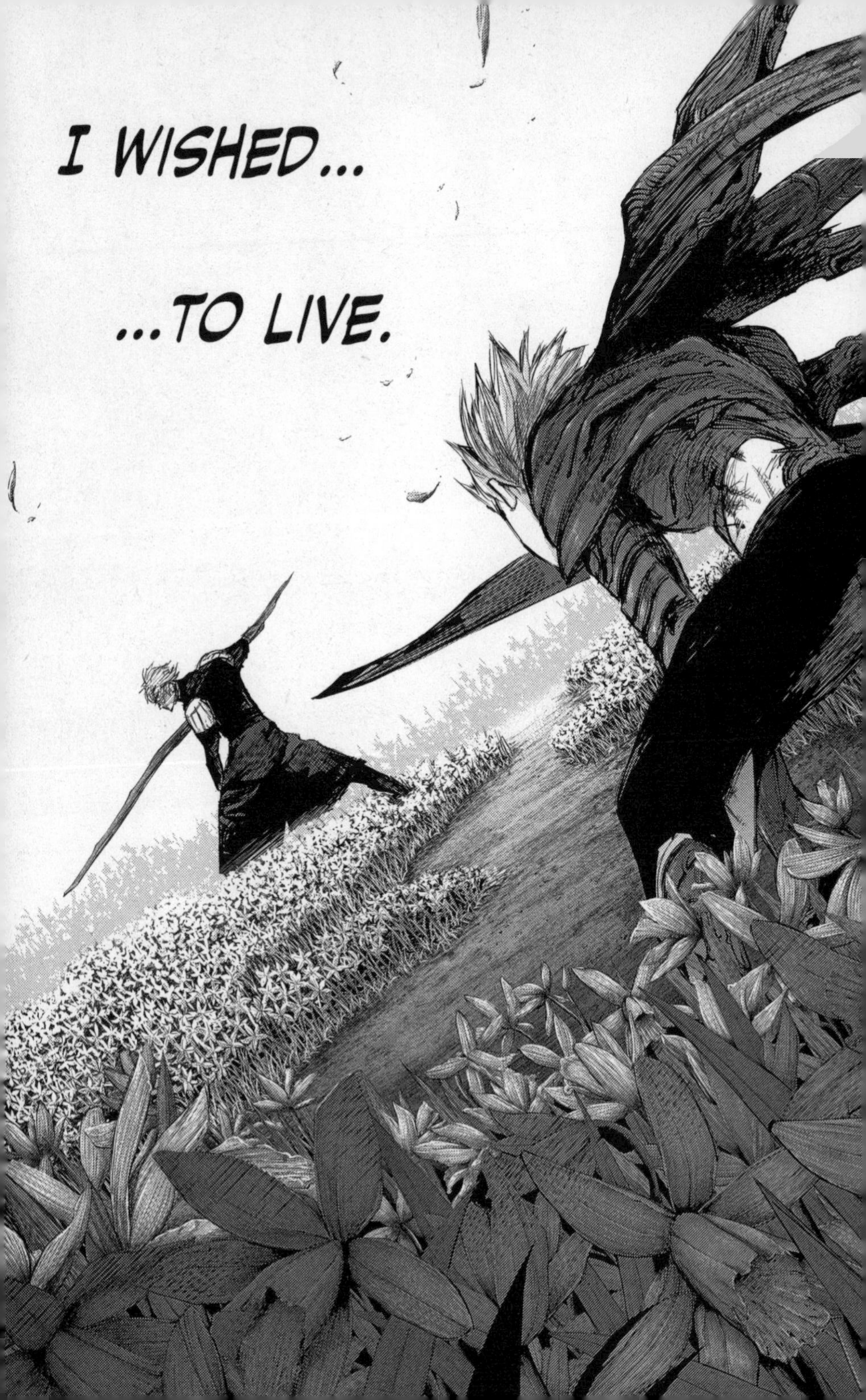
I WISHED...
...TO LIVE.

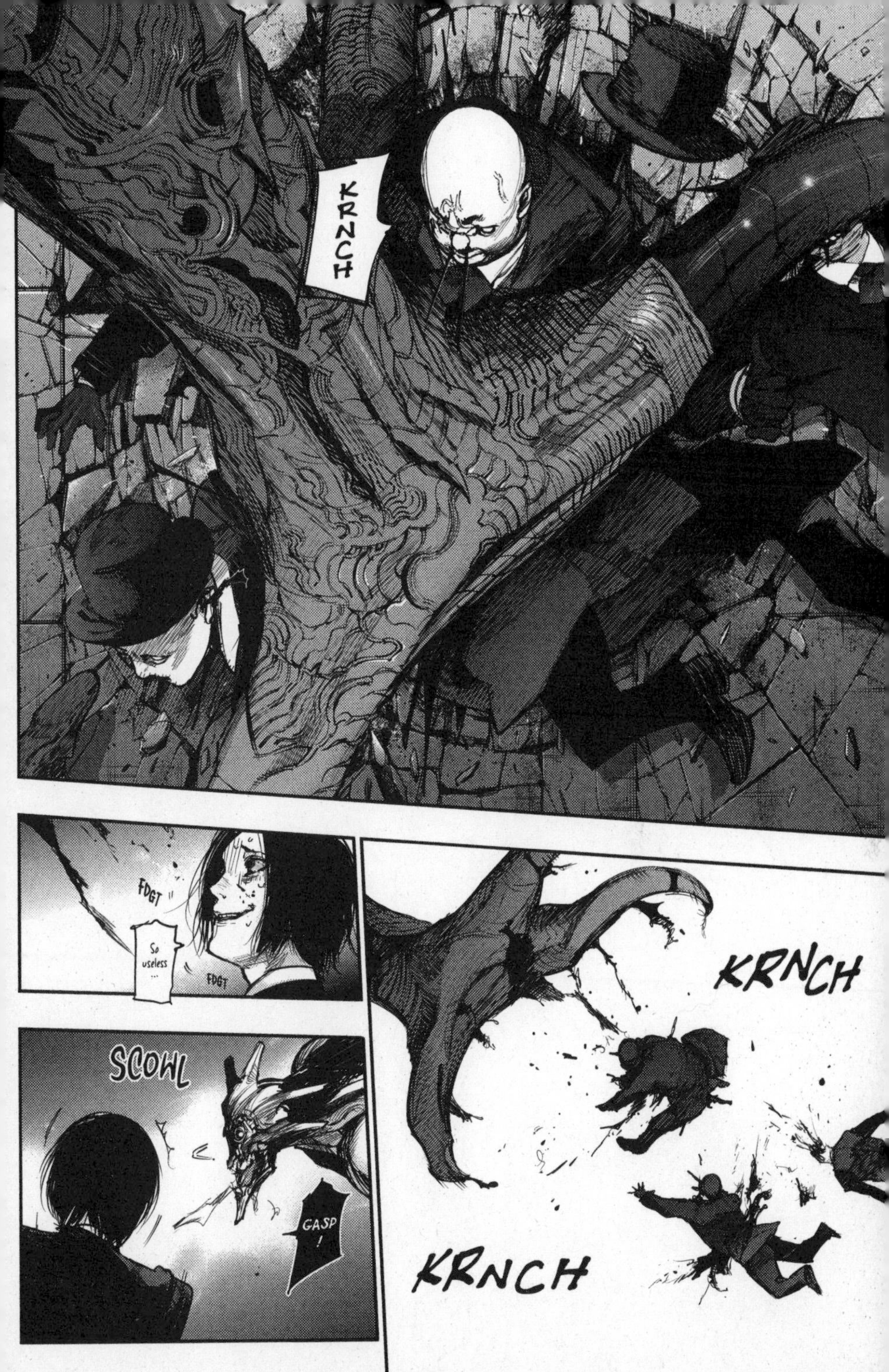
KRNCH
KRNCH
KRNCH
FDGT
So useless...
FDGT
SCOWL
GASP!

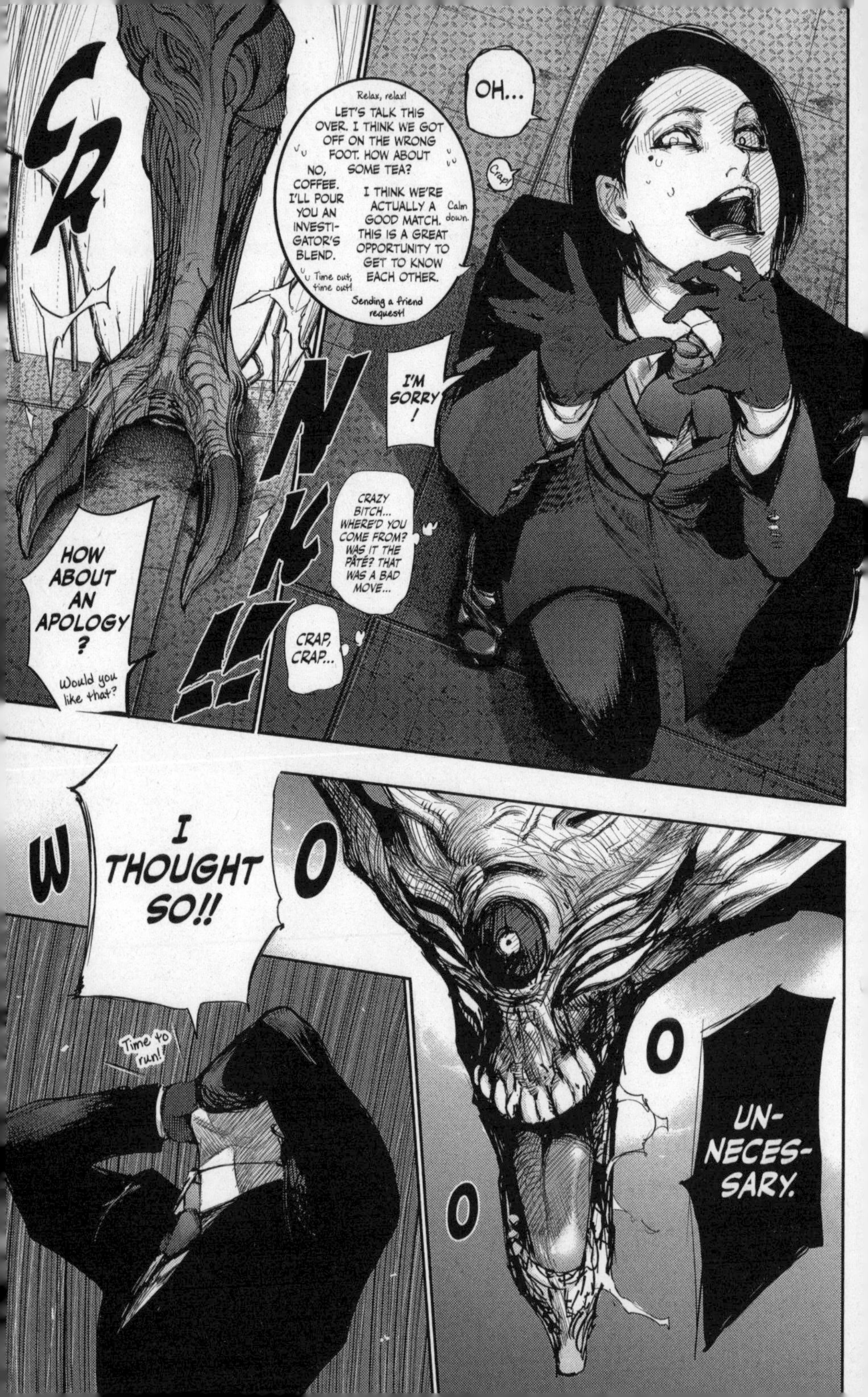
OH...
Crap!
Relax, relax!
LET'S TALK THIS OVER. I THINK WE GOT OFF ON THE WRONG FOOT. HOW ABOUT SOME TEA?
I THINK WE'RE ACTUALLY A GOOD MATCH. THIS IS A GREAT OPPORTUNITY TO GET TO KNOW EACH OTHER.
NO, COFFEE. I'LL POUR YOU AN INVESTIGATOR'S BLEND.
Time out, time out!
Sending a friend request!
Calm down.
I'M SORRY!
CRAZY BITCH... WHERE'D YOU COME FROM? WAS IT THE PÂTÉ? THAT WAS A BAD MOVE...
CRAP, CRAP...
CRNK!!
HOW ABOUT AN APOLOGY?
Would you like that?
UN-NECES-SARY.
I THOUGHT SO!!
WOOOO
Time to run!

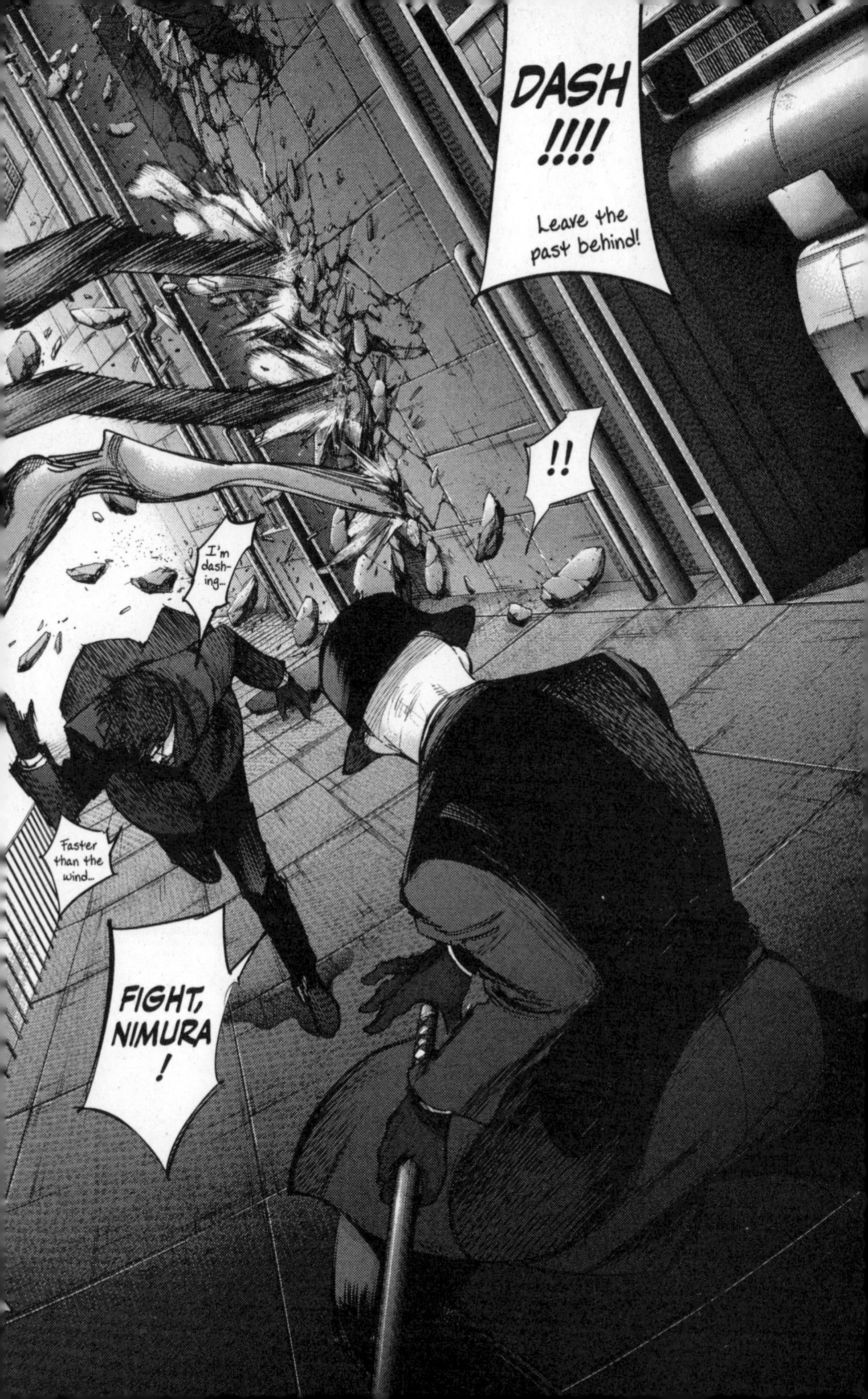
DASH !!!!
Leave the past behind!
!!
I'm dashing...
Faster than the wind...
FIGHT, NIMURA!

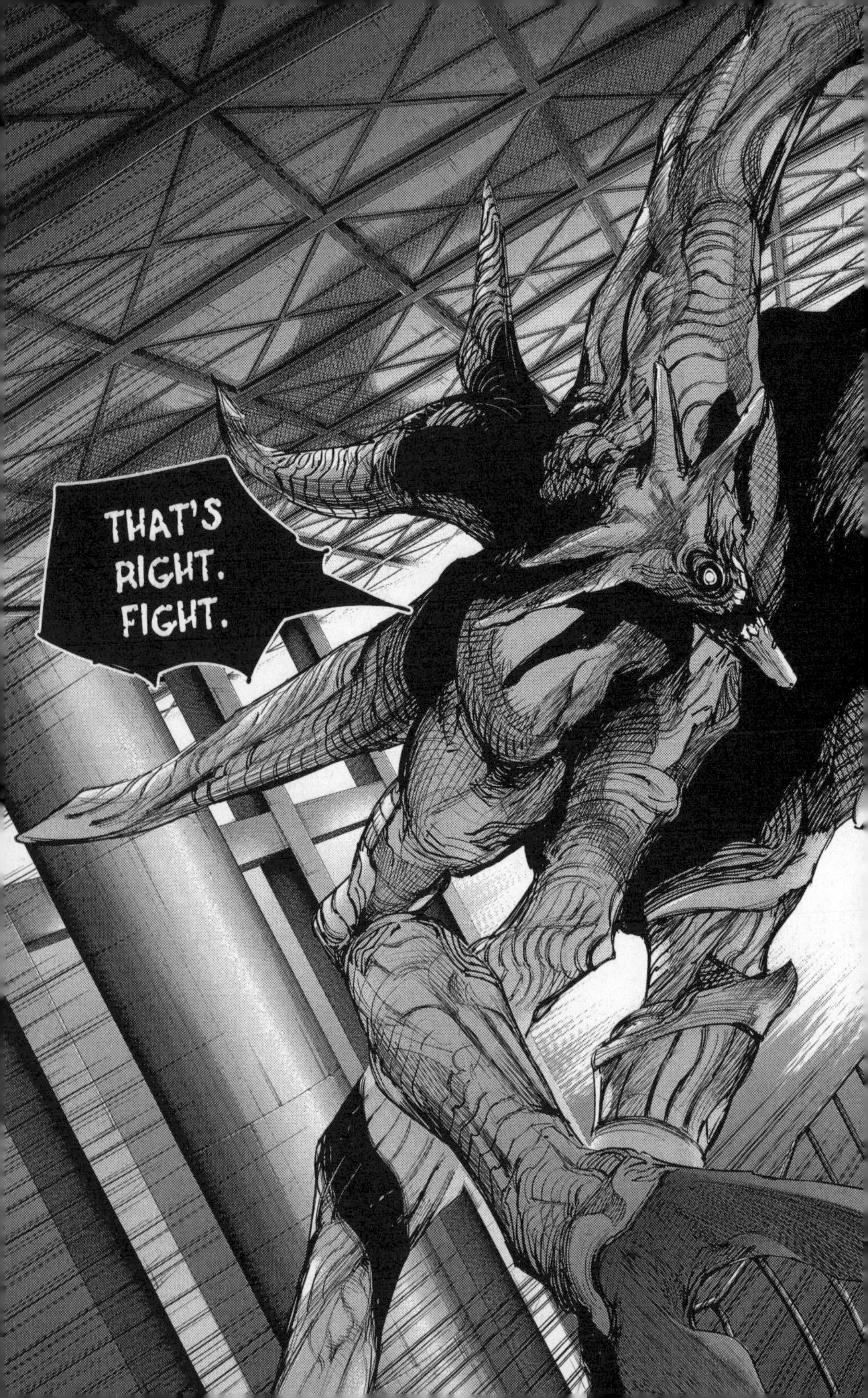
THAT'S RIGHT. FIGHT.

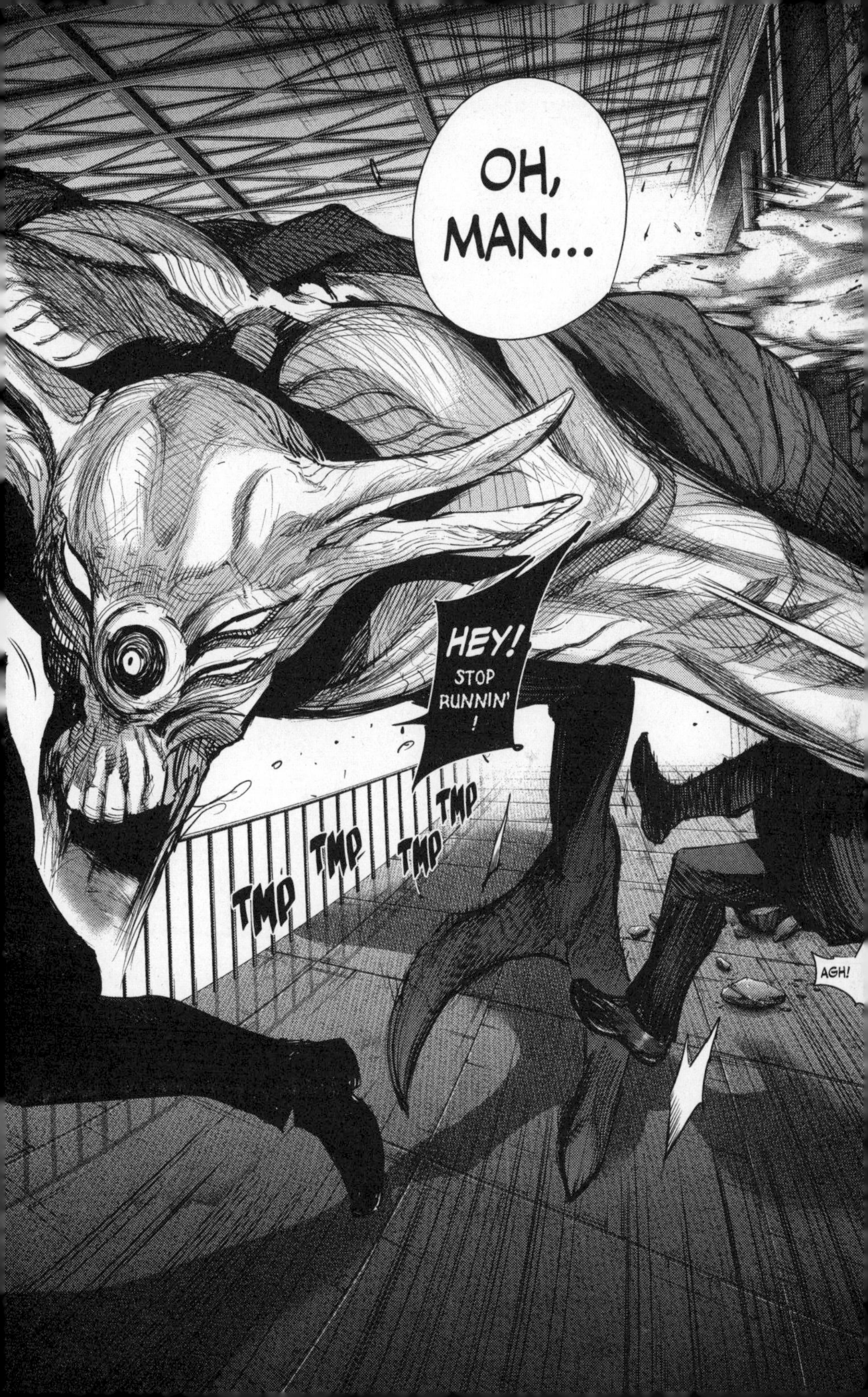
OH, MAN...
HEY! STOP RUNNIN'!
TMP TMP TMP TMP
AGH!

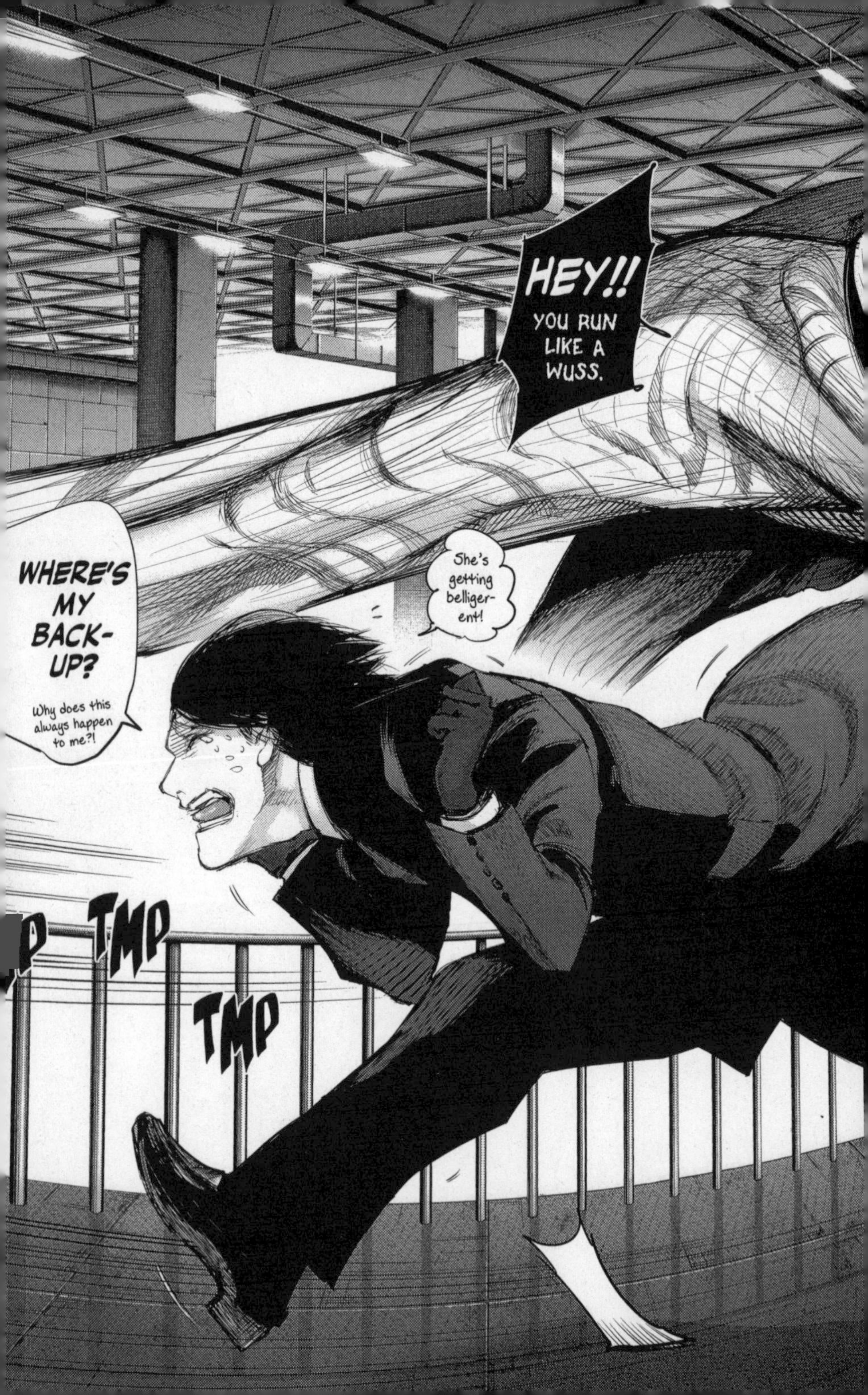
HEY!! YOU RUN LIKE A WUSS.
She's getting belliger-ent!
WHERE'S MY BACK-UP?
Why does this always happen to me?!
TMP
TMP

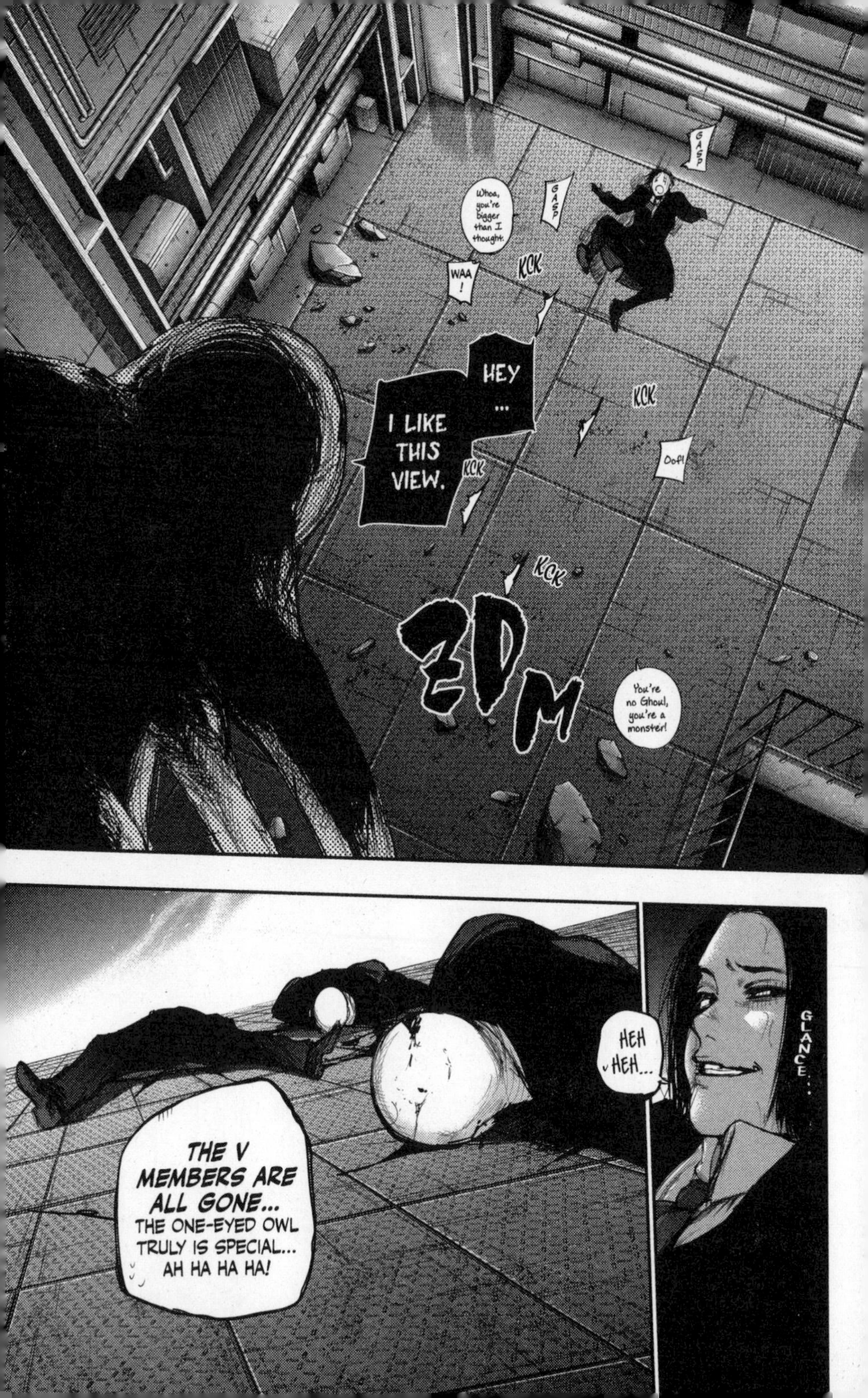
GASP
GASP
Whoa, you're bigger than I thought.
KCK
WAA!
HEY ...
KCK
I LIKE THIS VIEW.
Oof!
KCK
KCK
You're no Ghoul, you're a monster!
ZDM
GLANCE...
HEH HEH...
THE V MEMBERS ARE ALL GONE... THE ONE-EYED OWL TRULY IS SPECIAL... AH HA HA HA!

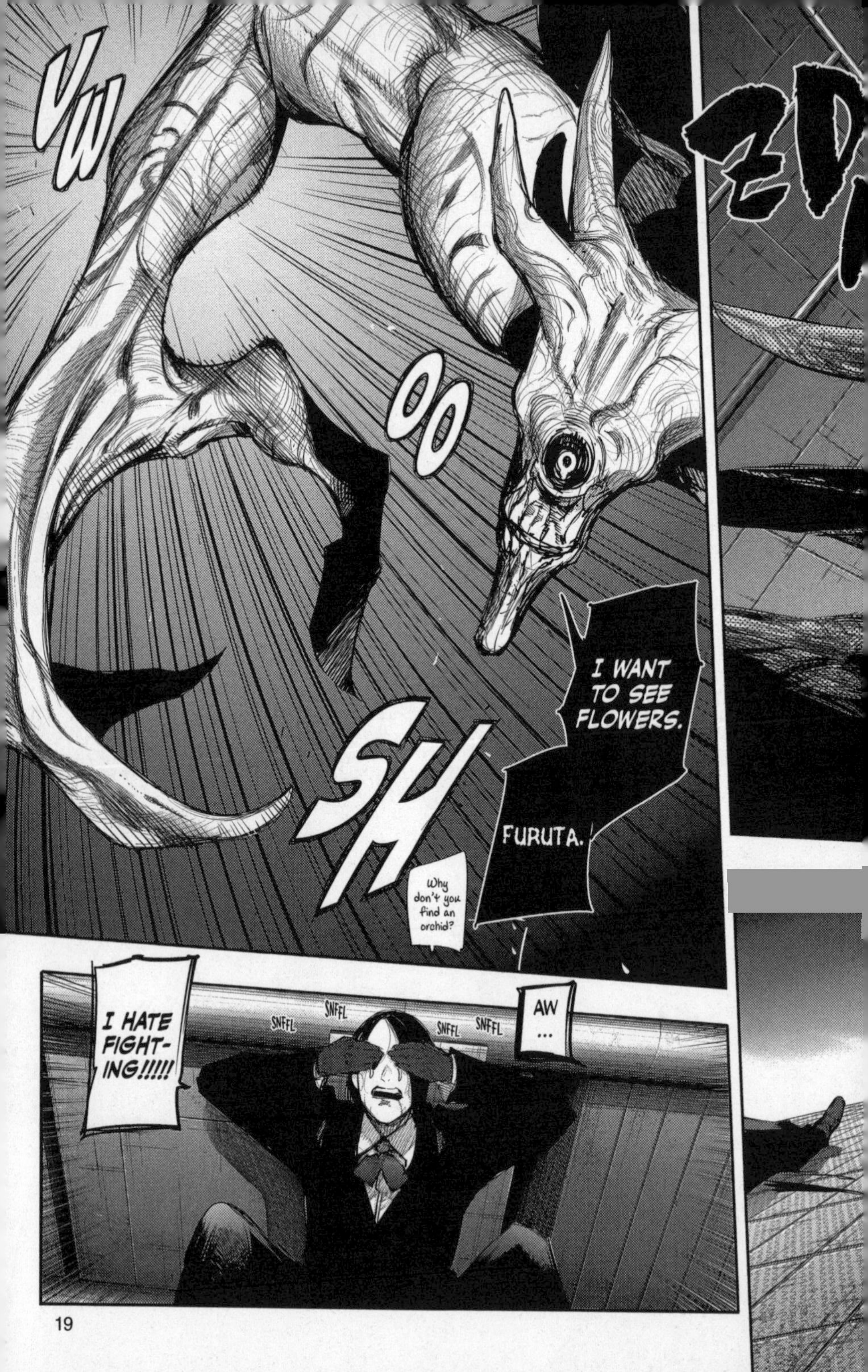
ZD
VW
OO
I WANT TO SEE FLOWERS.
FURUTA.
SH
Why don't you find an orchid?
AW ...
SNFFL
SNFFL
SNFFL
SNFFL
I HATE FIGHT-ING!!!!!

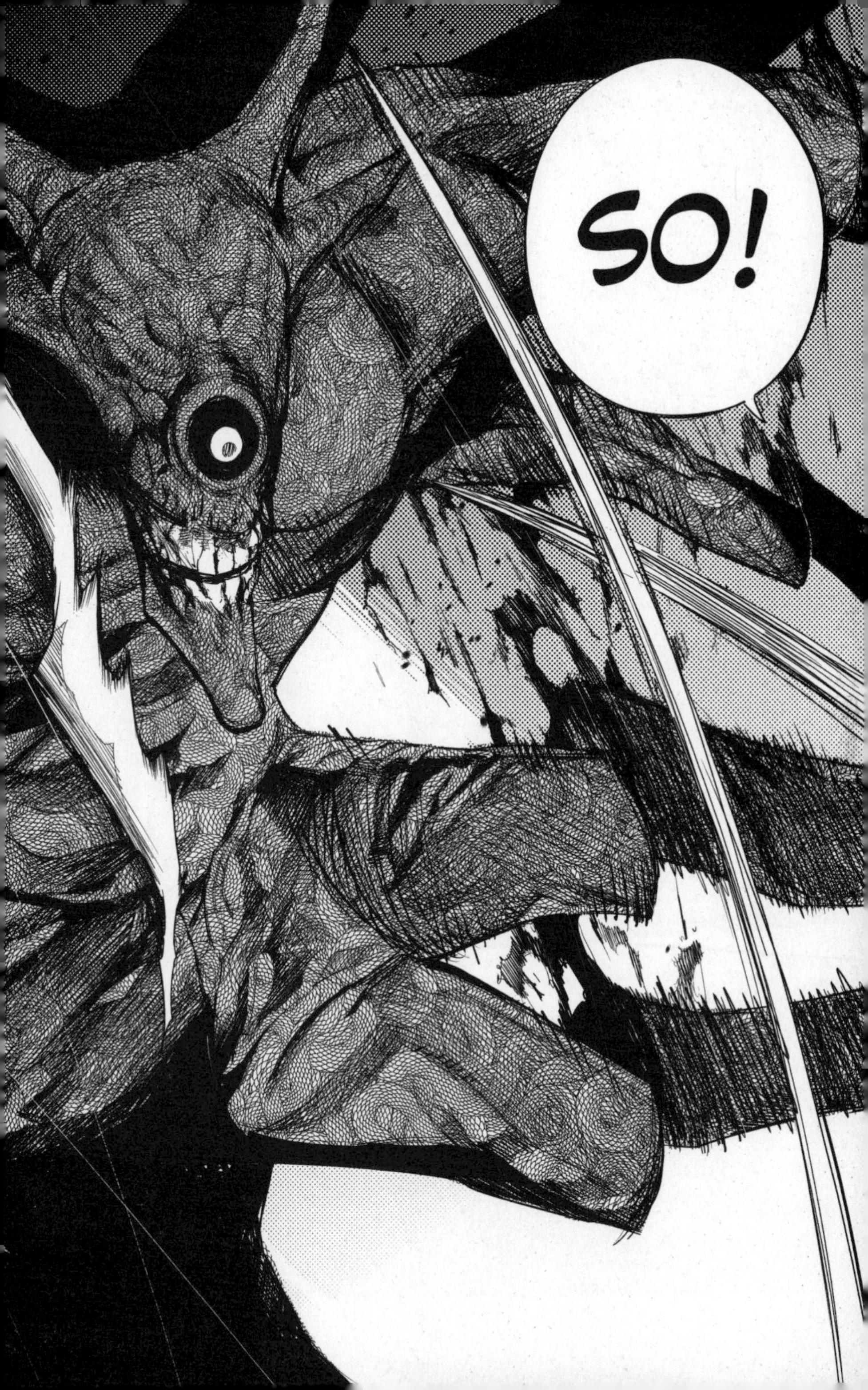
SO!

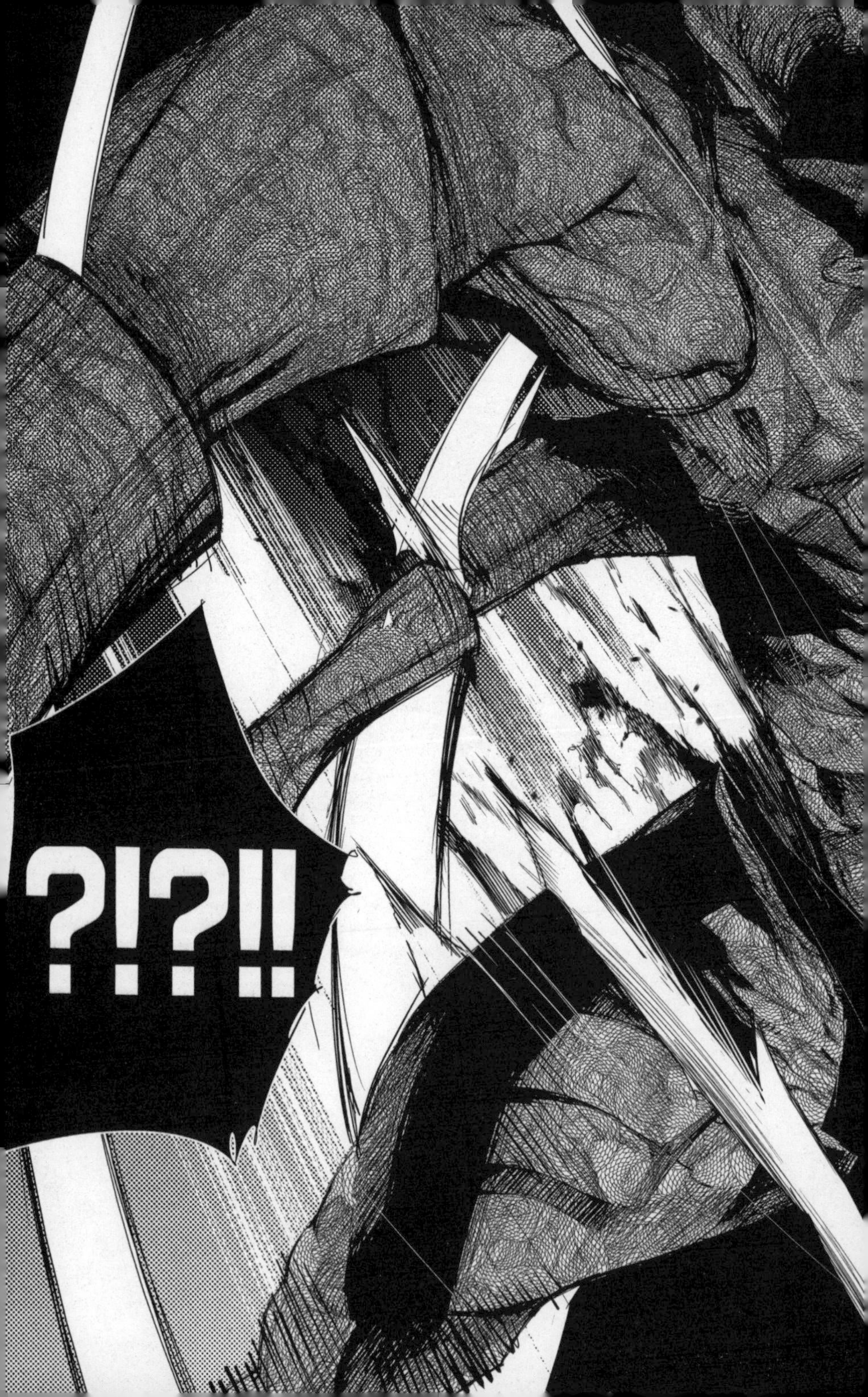
?!?!!

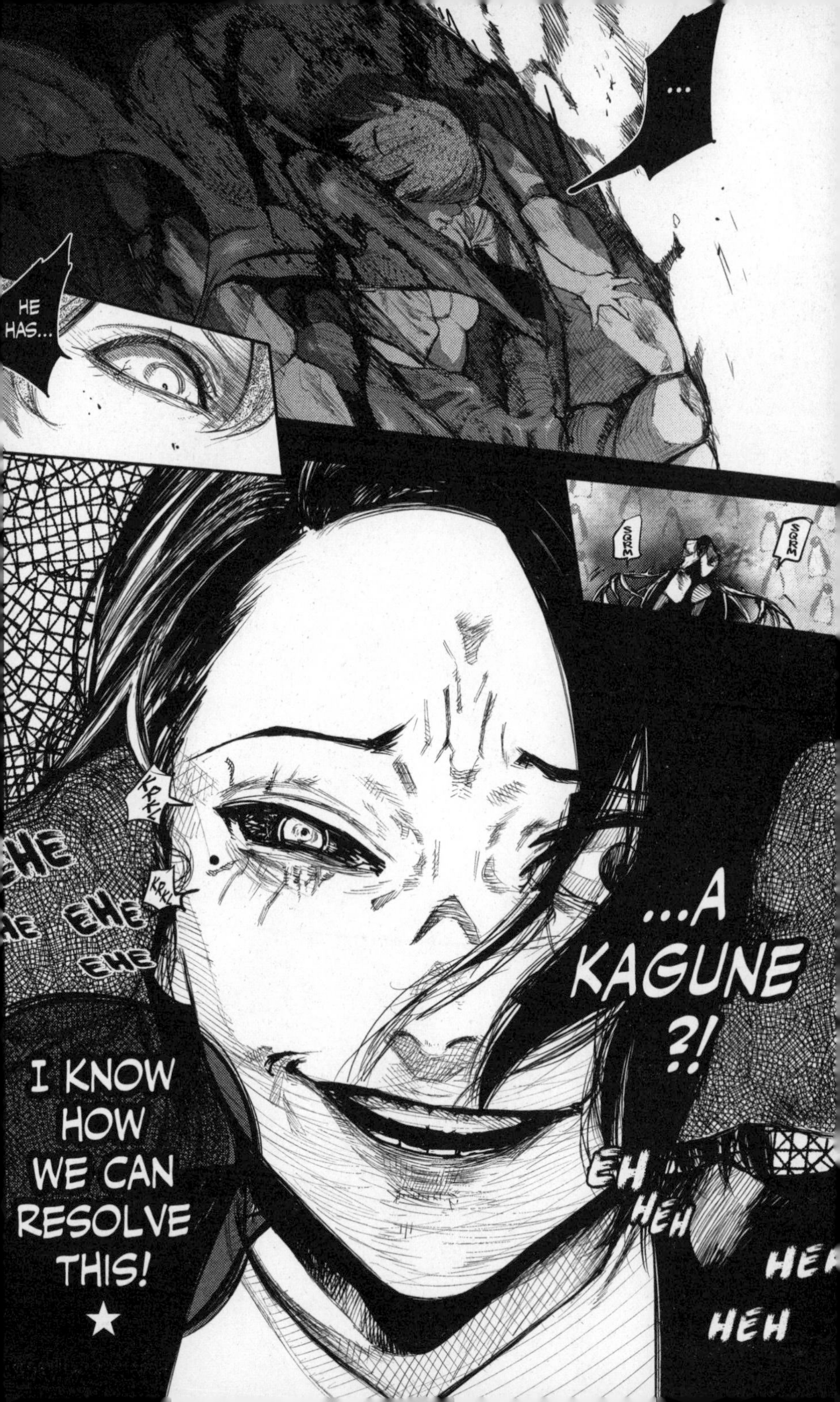
...
HE HAS...
SQRM
SQRM
...A KAGUNE ?!
KRKL
KRKL
EH HEH HEH
EHE EHE
I KNOW HOW WE CAN RESOLVE THIS! ★

Seven :77

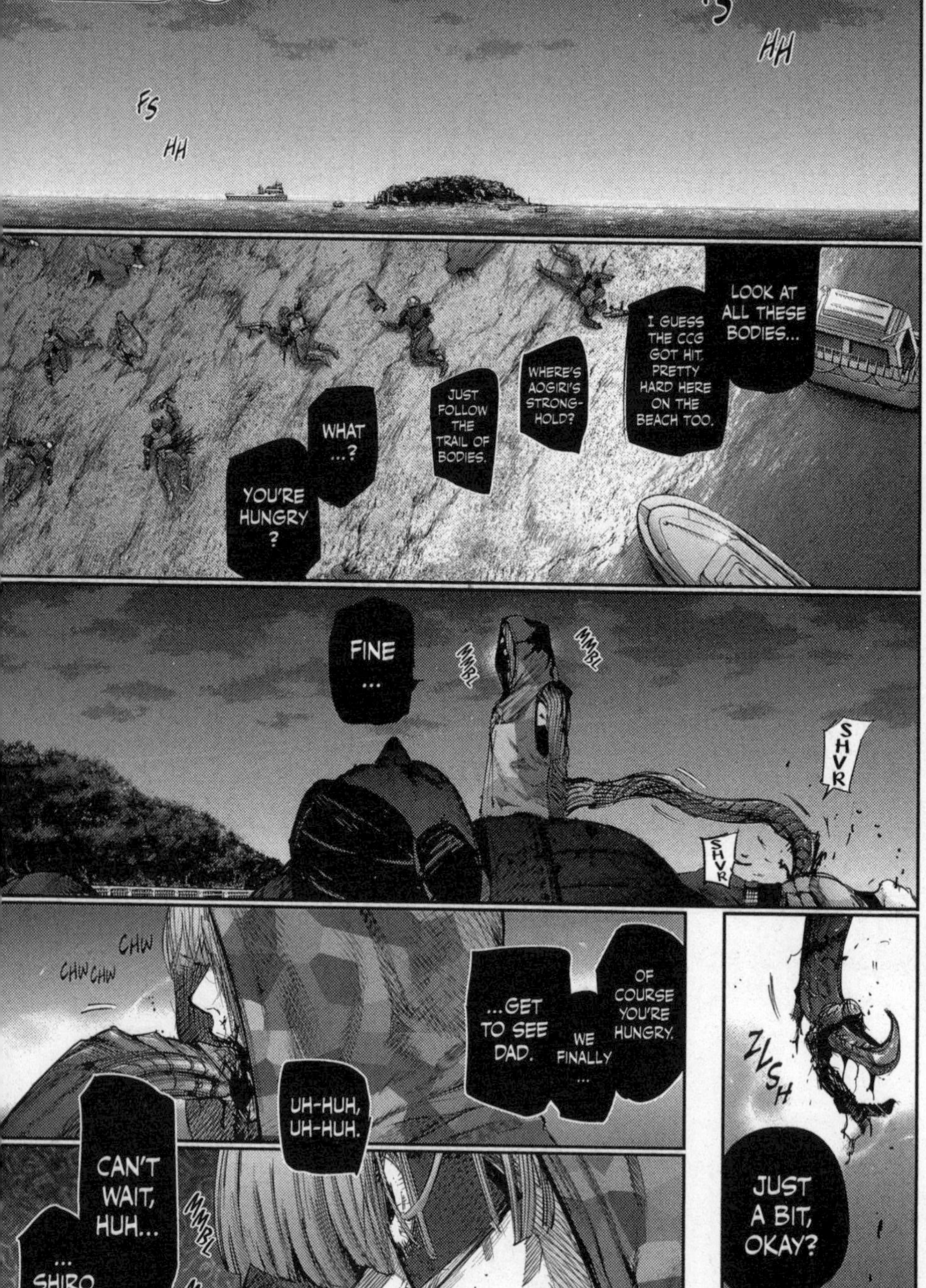

FS
HH
FS
HH
LOOK AT ALL THESE BODIES...
I GUESS THE CCG GOT HIT PRETTY HARD HERE ON THE BEACH TOO.
WHERE'S AOGIRI'S STRONG-HOLD?
JUST FOLLOW THE TRAIL OF BODIES.
WHAT ...?
YOU'RE HUNGRY ?
SHVR
SHVR
MMBL
FINE ...
MMBL
ZVSH
JUST A BIT, OKAY?
OF COURSE YOU'RE HUNGRY.
WE FINALLY ...
...GET TO SEE DAD.
UH-HUH, UH-HUH.
CHN
CHN CHN
CAN'T WAIT, HUH...
... SHIRO ?
MMBL
MMBL
MMBL

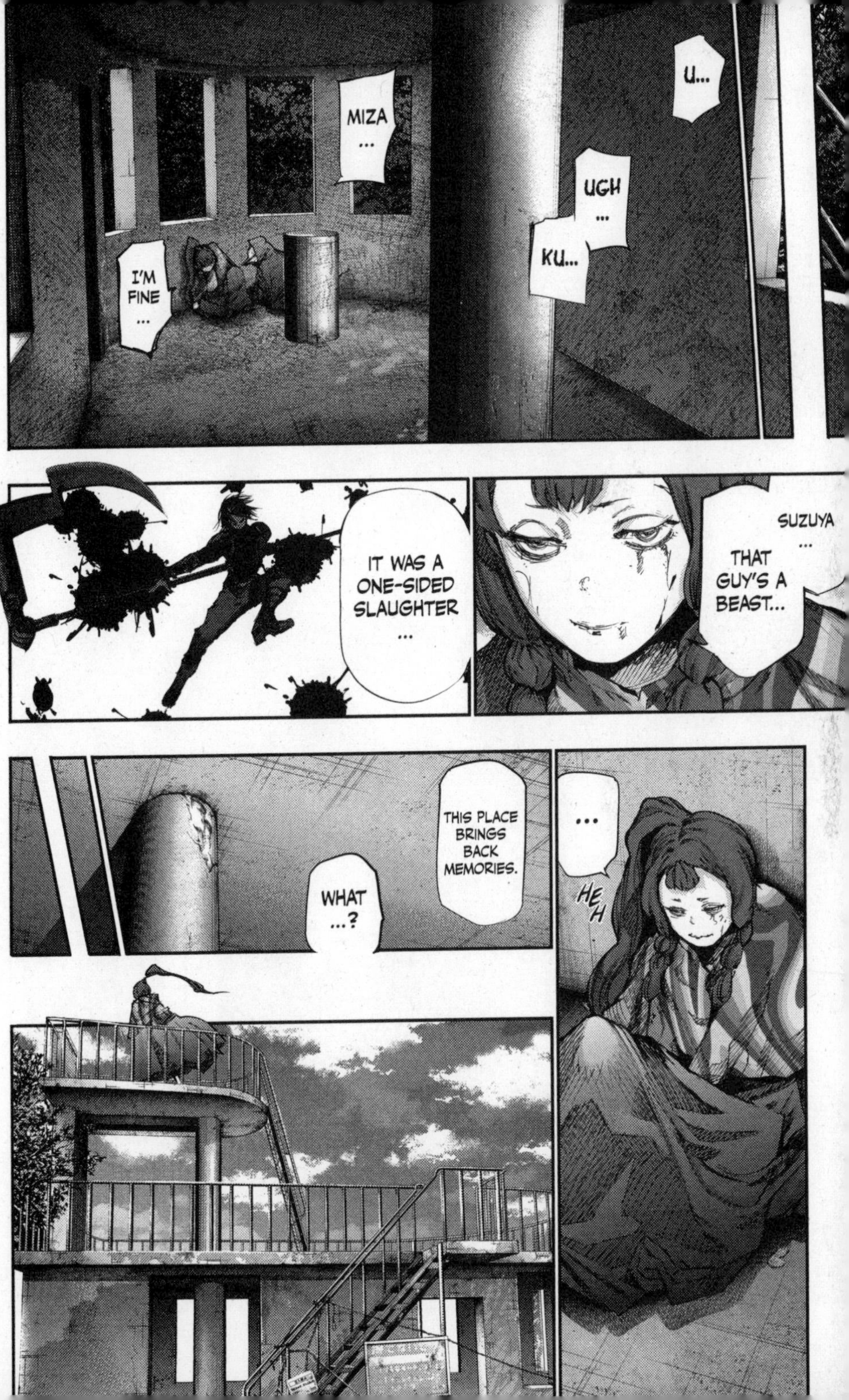
U...
UGH...
KU...
MIZA...
I'M FINE...
SUZUYA... THAT GUY'S A BEAST...
IT WAS A ONE-SIDED SLAUGHTER...
...
HEH
THIS PLACE BRINGS BACK MEMORIES.
WHAT...?

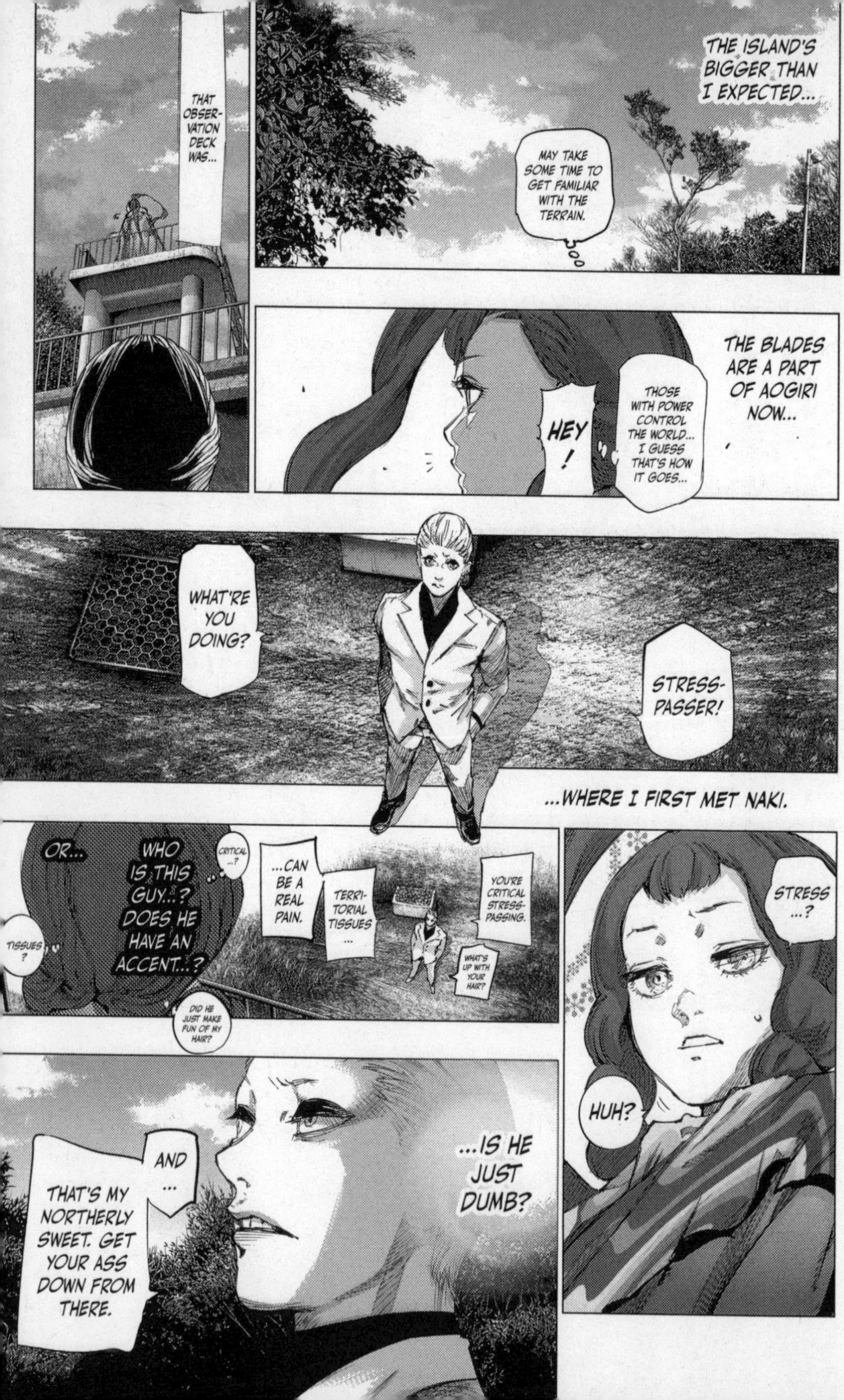
THE ISLAND'S BIGGER THAN I EXPECTED...
MAY TAKE SOME TIME TO GET FAMILIAR WITH THE TERRAIN.
THE BLADES ARE A PART OF AOGIRI NOW...
THOSE WITH POWER CONTROL THE WORLD... I GUESS THAT'S HOW IT GOES...
HEY!
THAT OBSERVATION DECK WAS...
STRESS-PASSER!
WHAT'RE YOU DOING?
...WHERE I FIRST MET NAKI.
STRESS...?
HUH?
YOU'RE CRITICAL STRESS-PASSING.
WHAT'S UP WITH YOUR HAIR?
TERRITORIAL TISSUES...
...CAN BE A REAL PAIN.
CRITICAL...?
WHO IS THIS GUY...? DOES HE HAVE AN ACCENT...?
TISSUES?
DID HE JUST MAKE FUN OF MY HAIR?
OR...
...IS HE JUST DUMB?
AND...
THAT'S MY NORTHERLY SWEET. GET YOUR ASS DOWN FROM THERE.

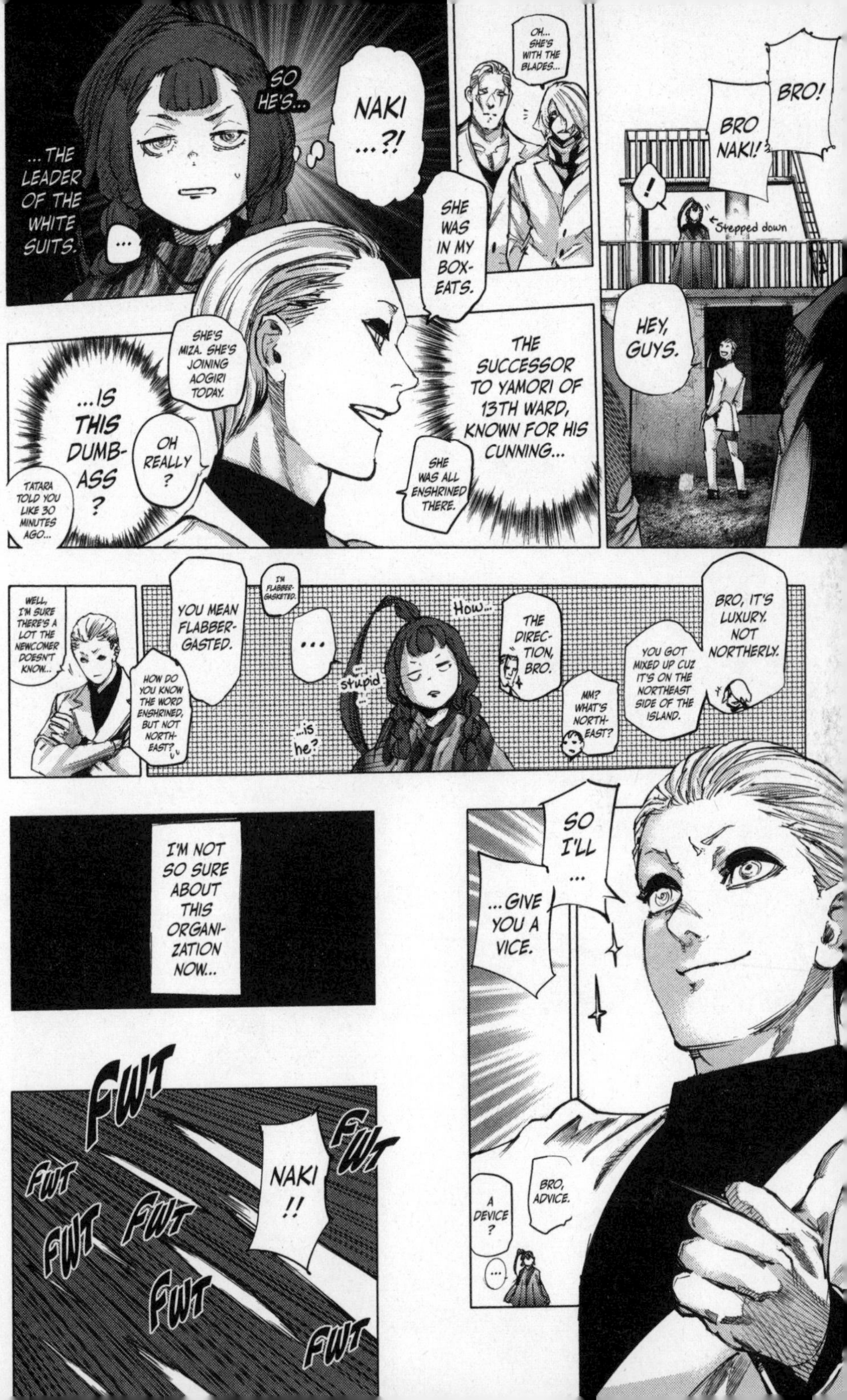
BRO!
BRO NAKI!
!
Stepped down
HEY, GUYS.
OH... SHE'S WITH THE BLADES...
SHE WAS IN MY BOX-EATS.
NAKI ...?!
SO HE'S...
...THE LEADER OF THE WHITE SUITS.
...
THE SUCCESSOR TO YAMORI OF 13TH WARD, KNOWN FOR HIS CUNNING...
SHE'S MIZA. SHE'S JOINING AOGIRI TODAY.
OH REALLY?
...IS THIS DUMB-ASS?
TATARA TOLD YOU LIKE 30 MINUTES AGO...
SHE WAS ALL ENSHRINED THERE.
BRO, IT'S LUXURY. NOT NORTHERLY.
YOU GOT MIXED UP CUZ IT'S ON THE NORTHEAST SIDE OF THE ISLAND.
MM? WHAT'S NORTH-EAST?
THE DIREC-TION, BRO.
How...
I'M FLABBER-GASKETED.
...
...stupid...
...is he?
YOU MEAN FLABBER-GASTED.
HOW DO YOU KNOW THE WORD ENSHRINED, BUT NOT NORTH-EAST?
WELL, I'M SURE THERE'S A LOT THE NEWCOMER DOESN'T KNOW...
SO I'LL...
...GIVE YOU A VICE.
BRO, ADVICE.
A DEVICE?
...
I'M NOT SO SURE ABOUT THIS ORGANI-ZATION NOW...
FWT
FWT
NAKI!!
FWT
FWT
FWT
FWT
FWT

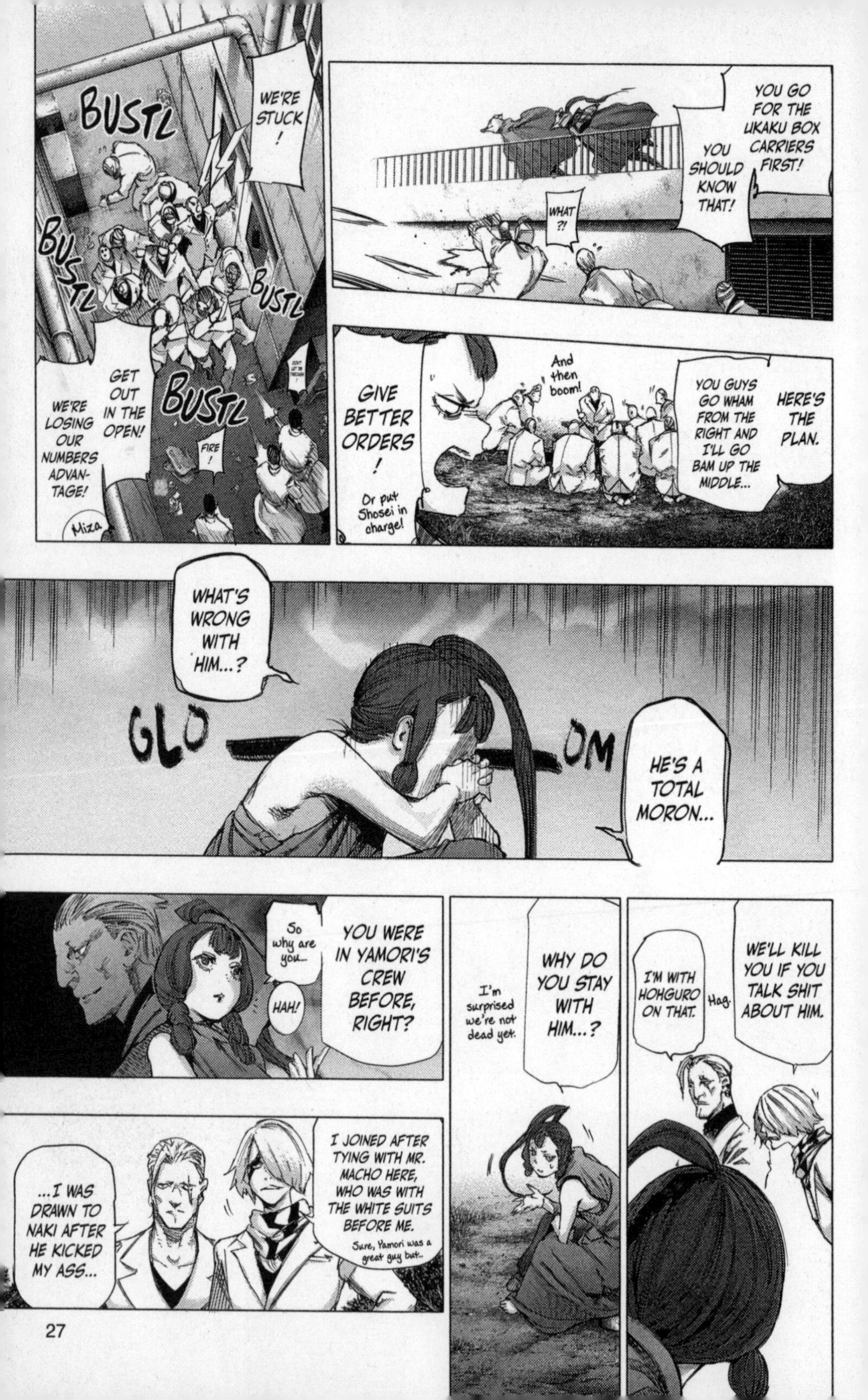
YOU GO FOR THE UKAKU BOX CARRIERS FIRST!
YOU SHOULD KNOW THAT!
WHAT?!
HERE'S THE PLAN.
YOU GUYS GO WHAM FROM THE RIGHT AND I'LL GO BAM UP THE MIDDLE...
And then boom!
GIVE BETTER ORDERS!
Or put Shosei in charge!
WE'RE STUCK!
BUSTL
BUSTL
BUSTL
BUSTL
FIRE!
GET OUT IN THE OPEN!
WE'RE LOSING OUR NUMBERS ADVANTAGE!
Miza
WHAT'S WRONG WITH HIM...?
GLO OM
HE'S A TOTAL MORON...
WE'LL KILL YOU IF YOU TALK SHIT ABOUT HIM.
Hag.
I'M WITH HOHGURO ON THAT.
WHY DO YOU STAY WITH HIM...?
I'm surprised we're not dead yet.
YOU WERE IN YAMORI'S CREW BEFORE, RIGHT?
So why are you...
HAH!
I JOINED AFTER TYING WITH MR. MACHO HERE, WHO WAS WITH THE WHITE SUITS BEFORE ME.
Sure, Yamori was a great guy but..
...I WAS DRAWN TO NAKI AFTER HE KICKED MY ASS...

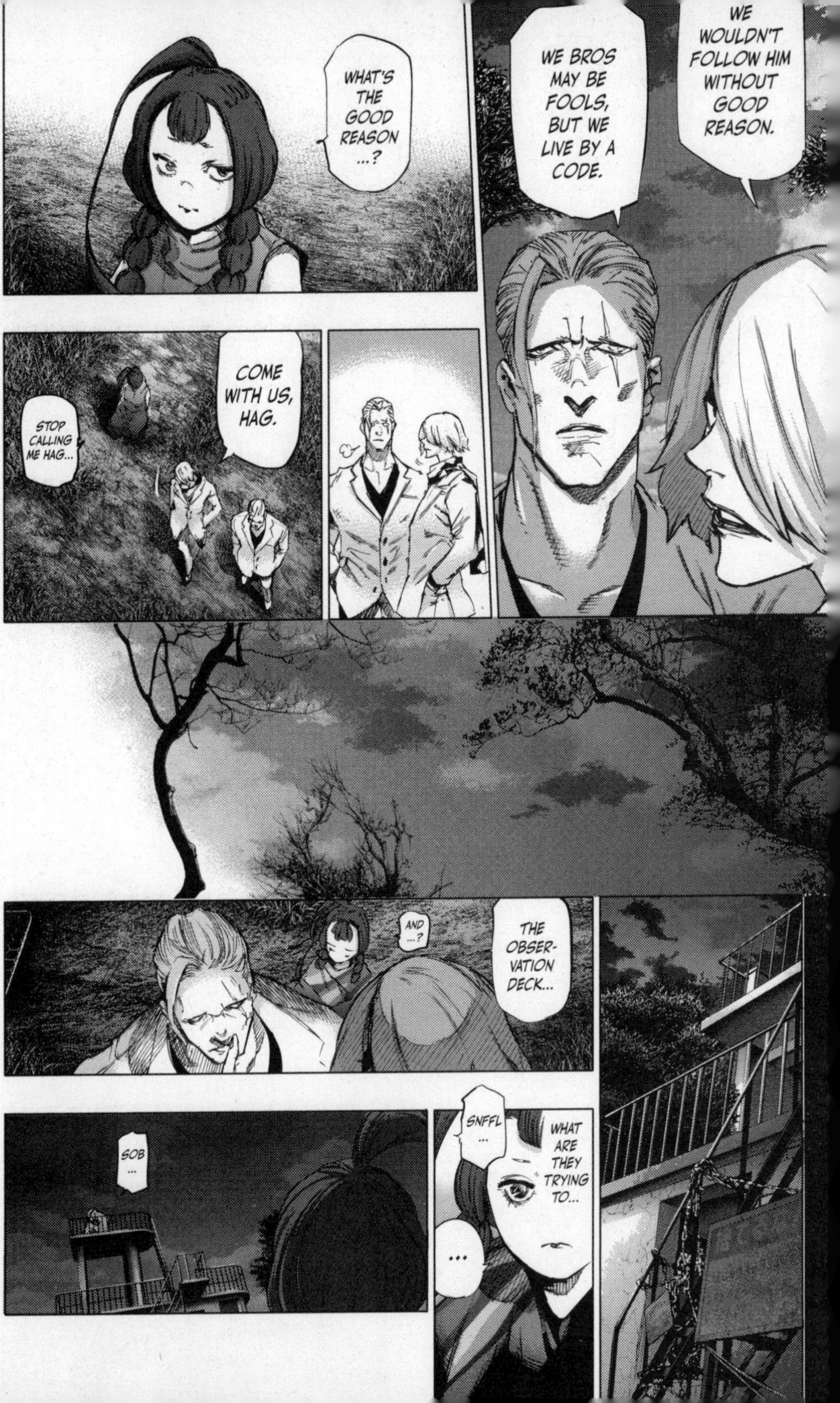
WE WOULDN'T FOLLOW HIM WITHOUT GOOD REASON.
WE BROS MAY BE FOOLS, BUT WE LIVE BY A CODE.
WHAT'S THE GOOD REASON ...?
COME WITH US, HAG.
STOP CALLING ME HAG...
THE OBSER-VATION DECK...
AND ...?
WHAT ARE THEY TRYING TO...
SNFFL ...
...
SOB ...

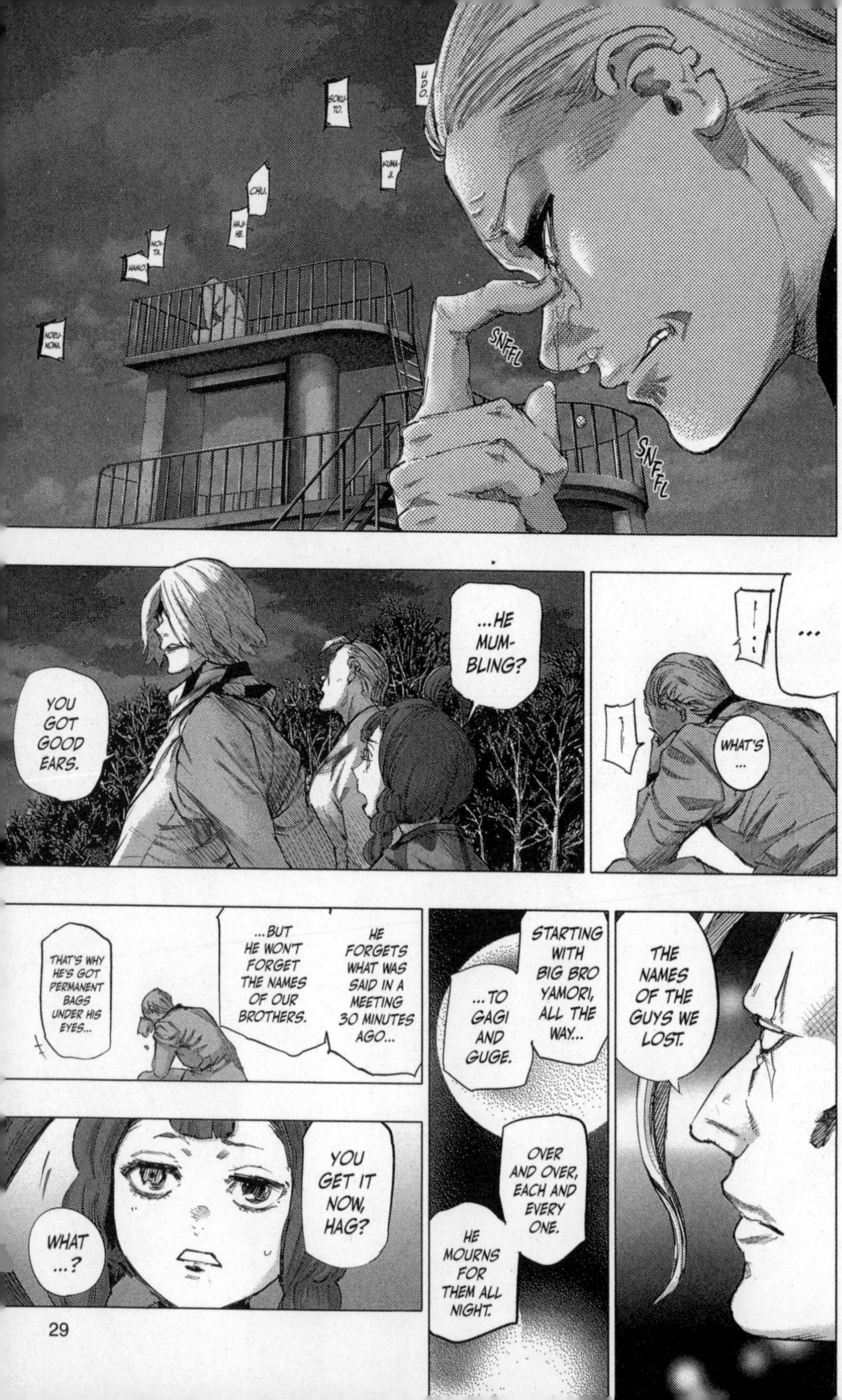
UDO.
SOKU-TO.
KUMA-JI.
CHU.
HAJI-HE.
NOI-TA.
HAMO.
NORU-NOMA.
SNFFL
SNFFL
...
!
!
WHAT'S ...
...HE MUMBLING?
YOU GOT GOOD EARS.
THE NAMES OF THE GUYS WE LOST.
STARTING WITH BIG BRO YAMORI, ALL THE WAY...
...TO GAGI AND GUGE.
OVER AND OVER, EACH AND EVERY ONE.
HE MOURNS FOR THEM ALL NIGHT.
HE FORGETS WHAT WAS SAID IN A MEETING 30 MINUTES AGO...
...BUT HE WON'T FORGET THE NAMES OF OUR BROTHERS.
THAT'S WHY HE'S GOT PERMANENT BAGS UNDER HIS EYES...
YOU GET IT NOW, HAG?
WHAT ...?

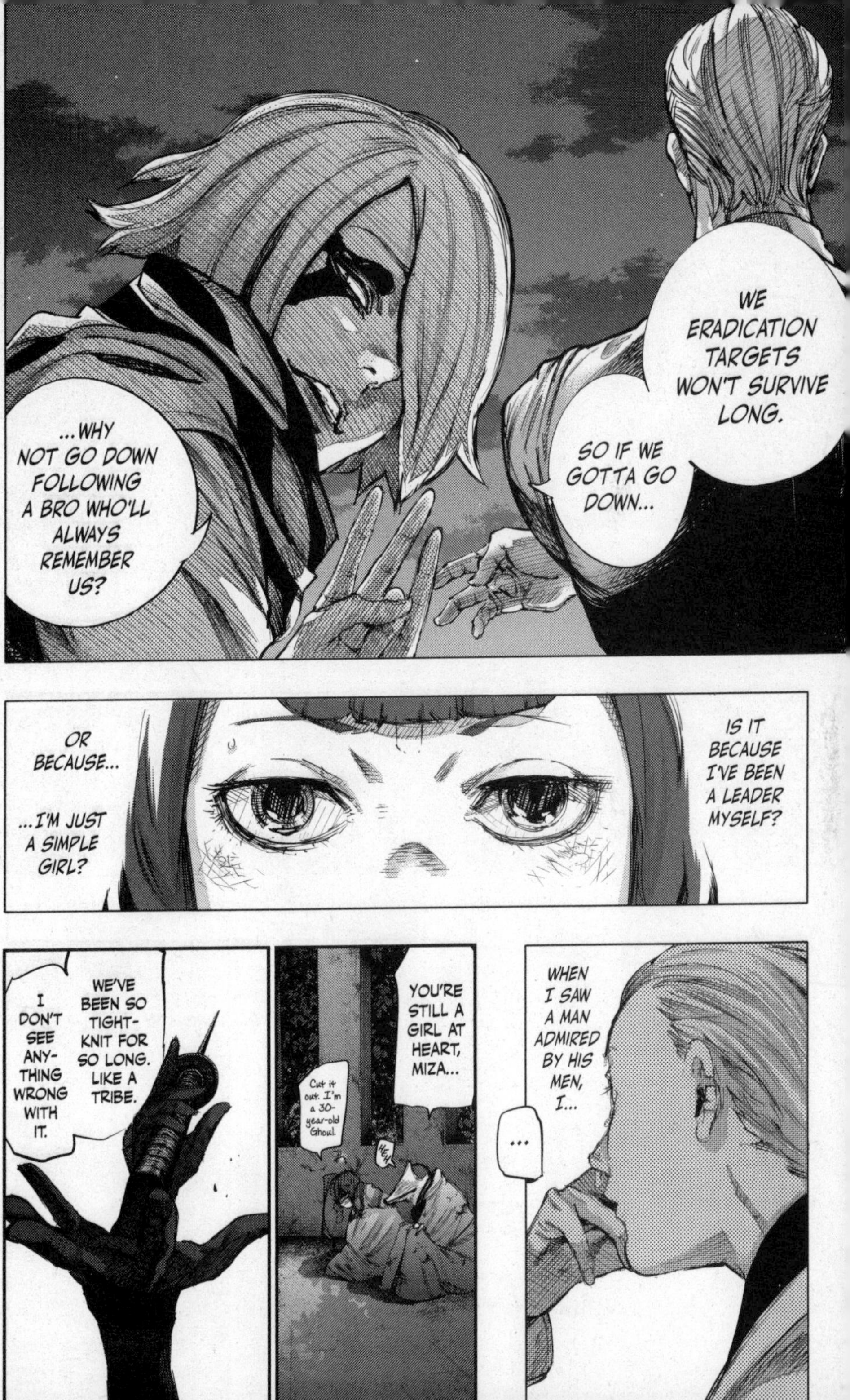
WE ERADICATION TARGETS WON'T SURVIVE LONG.
SO IF WE GOTTA GO DOWN...
...WHY NOT GO DOWN FOLLOWING A BRO WHO'LL ALWAYS REMEMBER US?
IS IT BECAUSE I'VE BEEN A LEADER MYSELF?
OR BECAUSE...
...I'M JUST A SIMPLE GIRL?
WHEN I SAW A MAN ADMIRED BY HIS MEN, I...
...
YOU'RE STILL A GIRL AT HEART, MIZA...
Cut it out. I'm a 30-year-old Ghoul.
HEH
WE'VE BEEN SO TIGHT-KNIT FOR SO LONG. LIKE A TRIBE.
I DON'T SEE ANYTHING WRONG WITH IT.

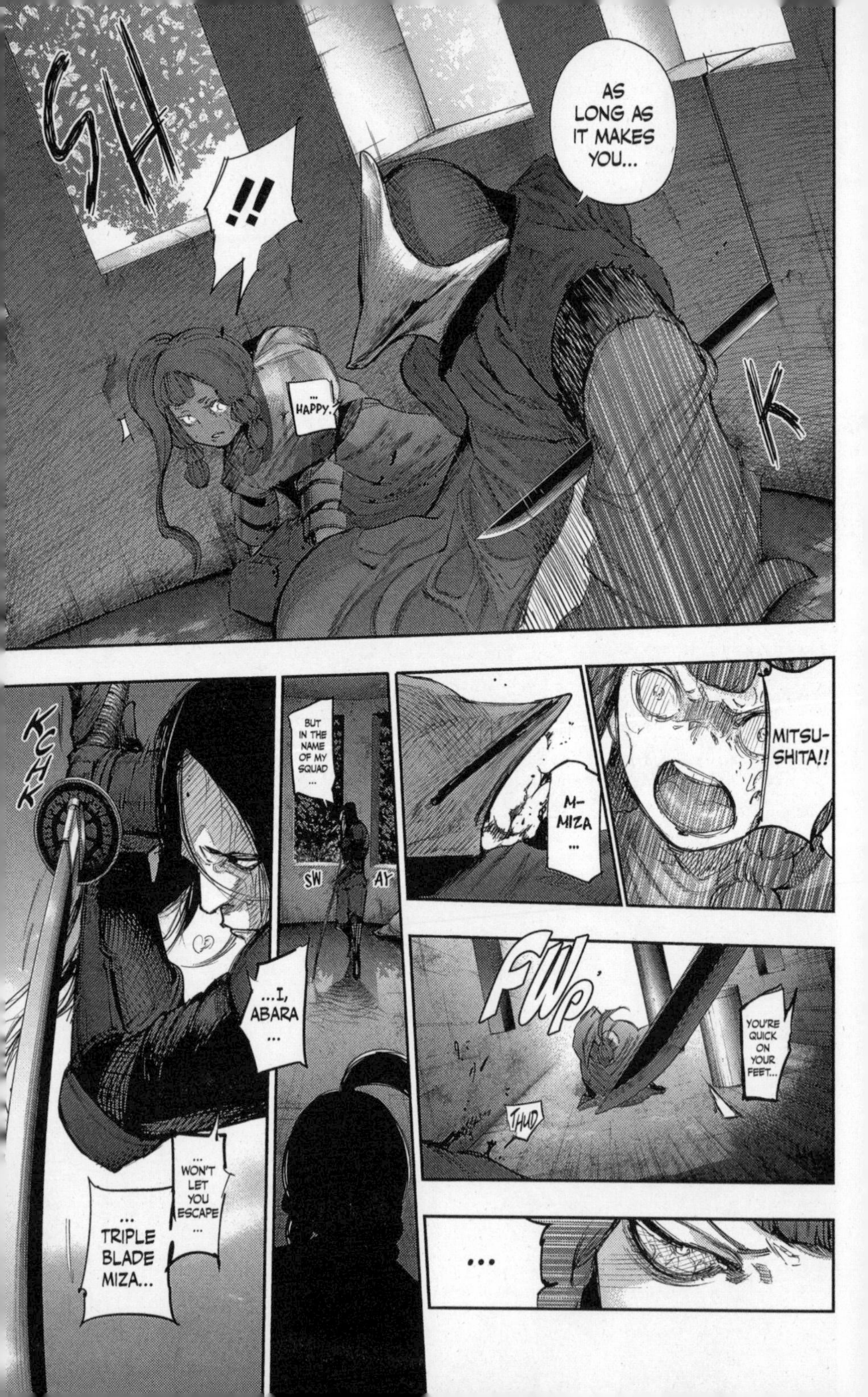
AS LONG AS IT MAKES YOU...
SH
!!
K
...HAPPY.
MITSU-SHITA!!
M-MIZA...
FWP
YOU'RE QUICK ON YOUR FEET...
THUD
...
BUT IN THE NAME OF MY SQUAD...
SW AY
KCHK
...I, ABARA...
...WON'T LET YOU ESCAPE...
...TRIPLE BLADE MIZA...

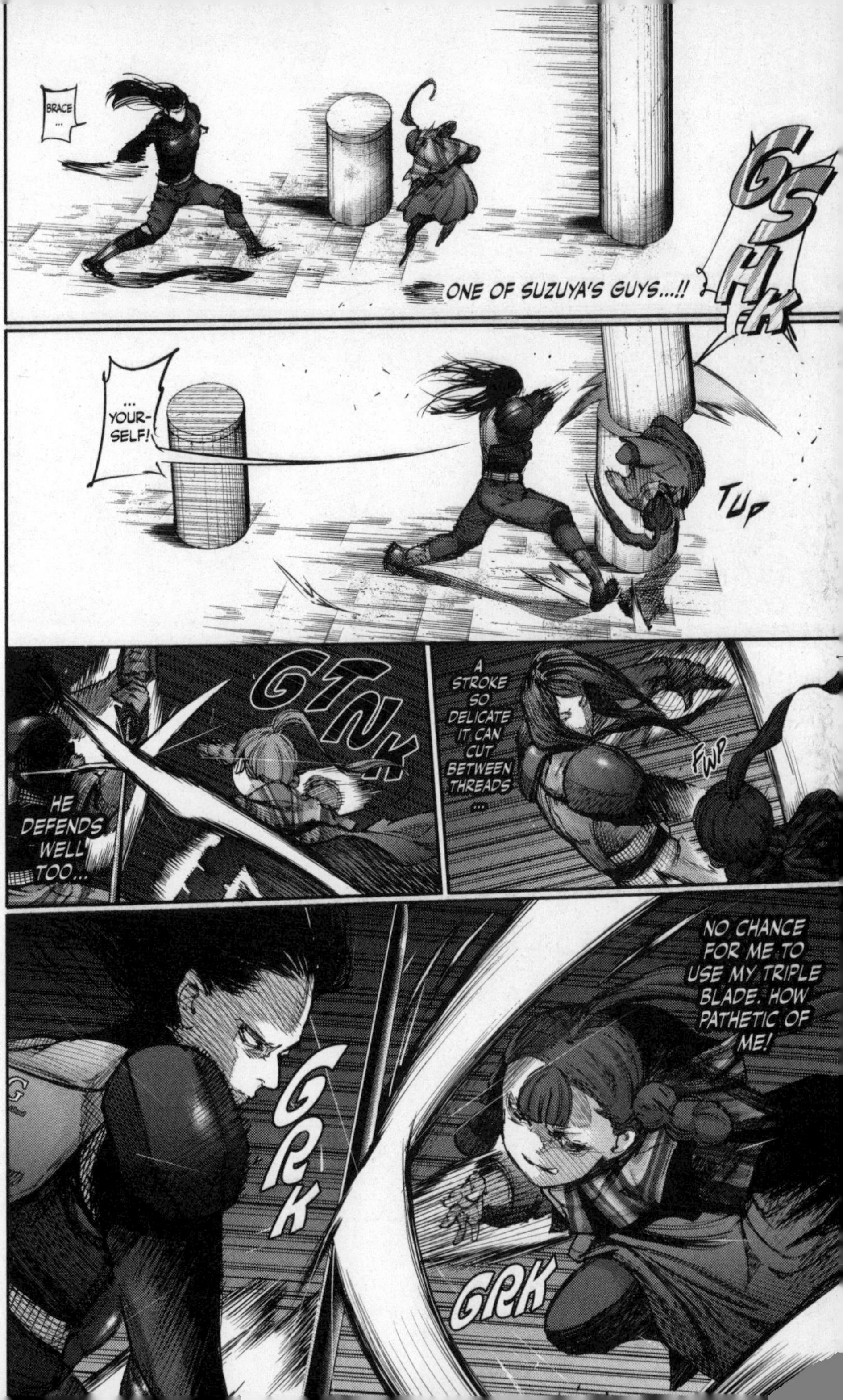
GSHK
BRACE ...
ONE OF SUZUYA'S GUYS...!!
... YOUR-SELF!
TUP
A STROKE SO DELICATE IT CAN CUT BETWEEN THREADS ...
FWP
GTNK
HE DEFENDS WELL TOO...
NO CHANCE FOR ME TO USE MY TRIPLE BLADE. HOW PATHETIC OF ME!
GRK
GRK

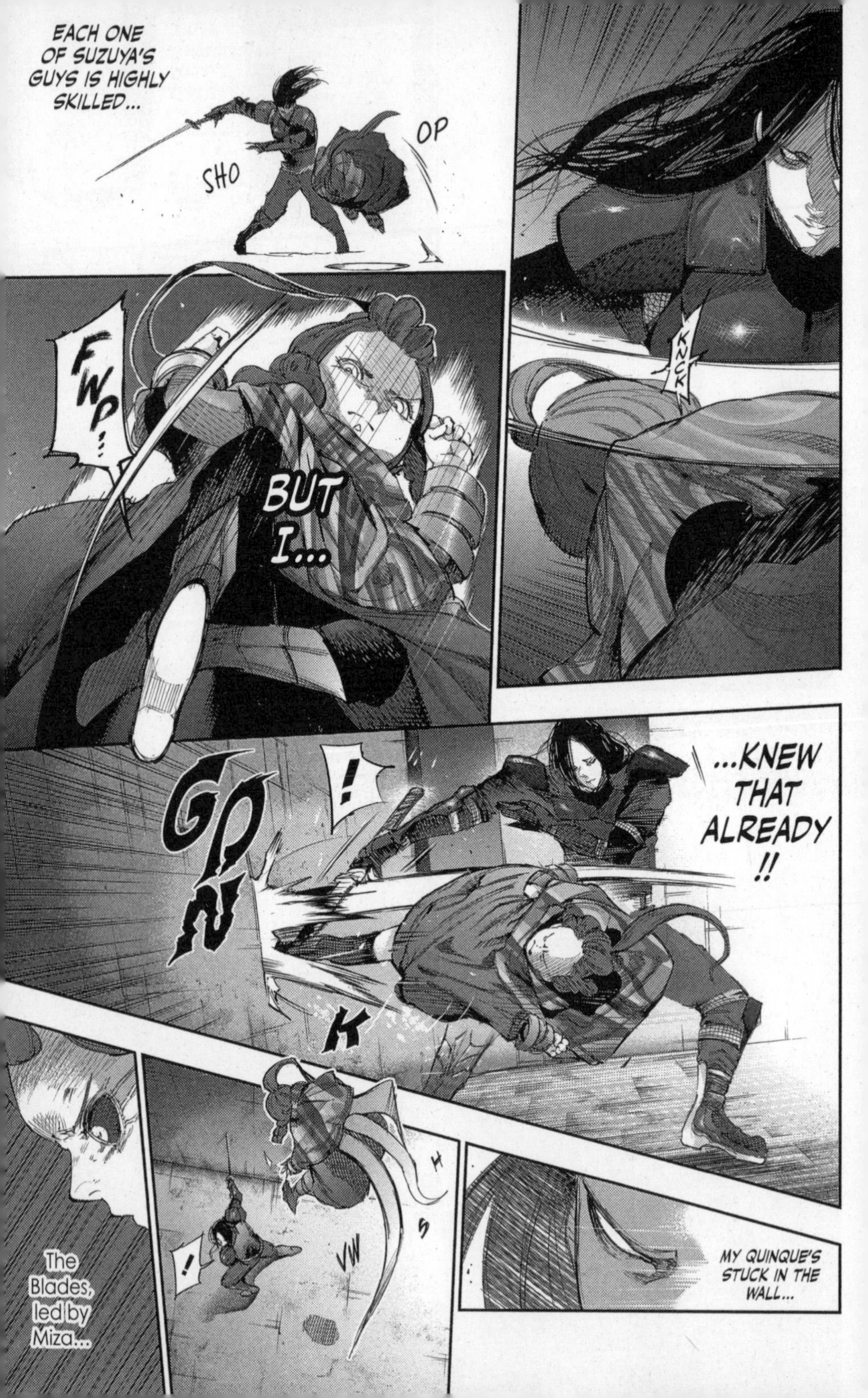
KNCK
EACH ONE OF SUZUYA'S GUYS IS HIGHLY SKILLED...
SHO
OP
FWP!!
BUT I...
...KNEW THAT ALREADY!!
!
GDN
K
MY QUINQUE'S STUCK IN THE WALL...
H
S
VW
!
The Blades, led by Miza...

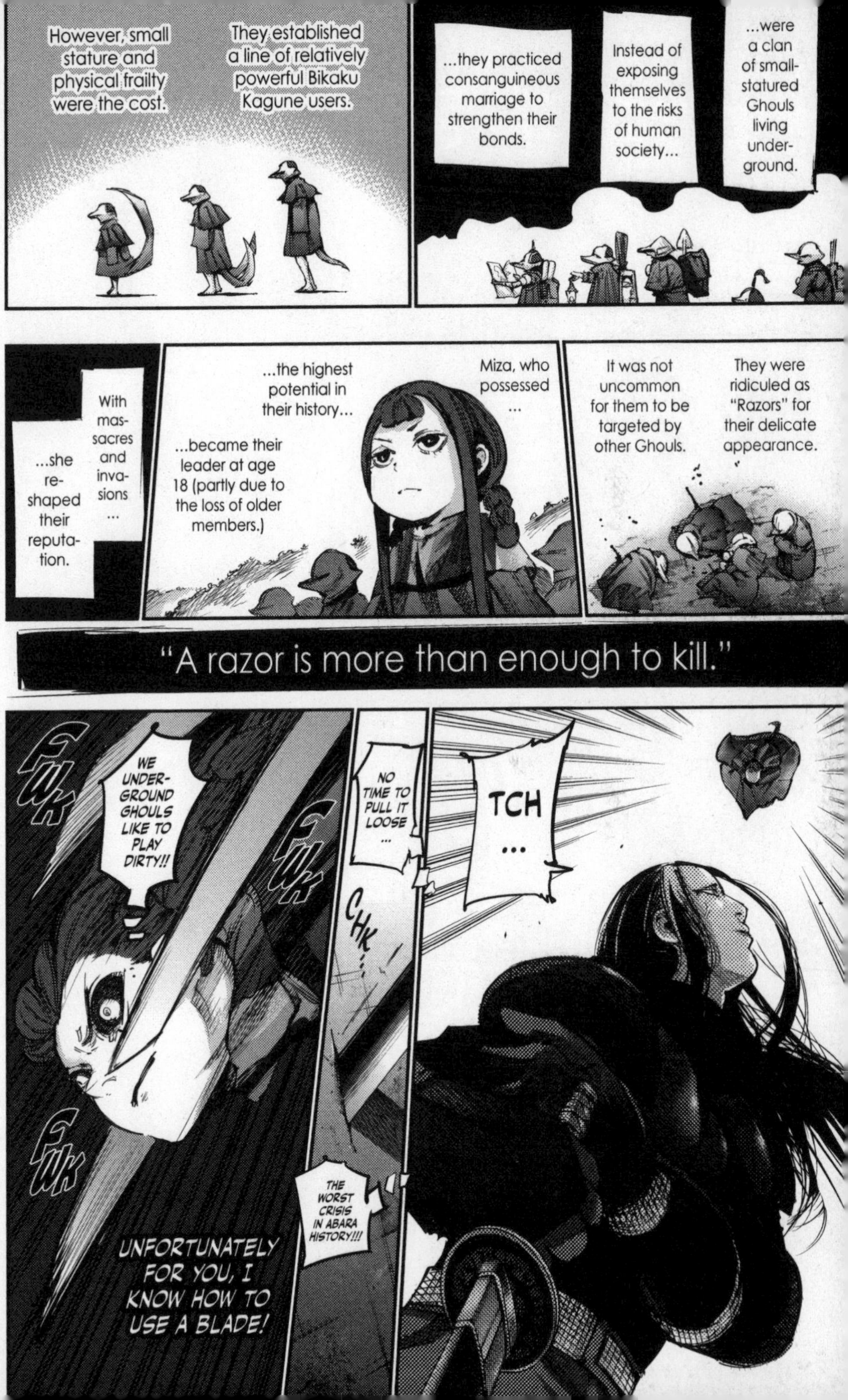
...were a clan of small-statured Ghouls living underground.
Instead of exposing themselves to the risks of human society...
...they practiced consanguineous marriage to strengthen their bonds.
They established a line of relatively powerful Bikaku Kagune users.
However, small stature and physical frailty were the cost.
They were ridiculed as "Razors" for their delicate appearance.
It was not uncommon for them to be targeted by other Ghouls.
Miza, who possessed...
...the highest potential in their history...
...became their leader at age 18 (partly due to the loss of older members.)
With massacres and invasions...
...she reshaped their reputation.
"A razor is more than enough to kill."
TCH...
NO TIME TO PULL IT LOOSE...
CHK
THE WORST CRISIS IN ABARA HISTORY!!!
WE UNDERGROUND GHOULS LIKE TO PLAY DIRTY!!
FWK
FWK
FWK
UNFORTUNATELY FOR YOU, I KNOW HOW TO USE A BLADE!

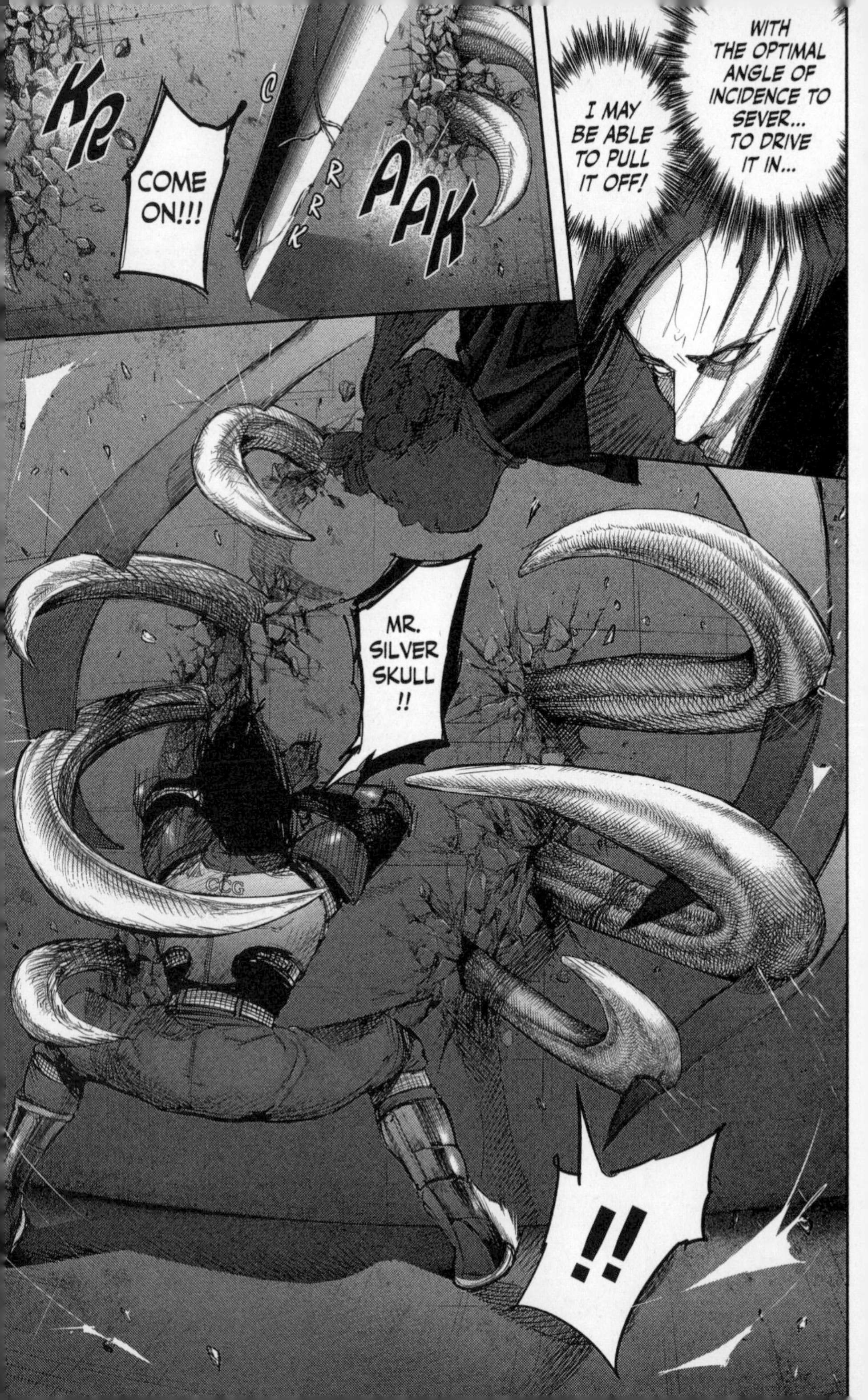
WITH THE OPTIMAL ANGLE OF INCIDENCE TO SEVER... TO DRIVE IT IN...
I MAY BE ABLE TO PULL IT OFF!
AAK
CRRRK
COME ON!!!
KR
MR. SILVER SKULL !!
CCG
!!

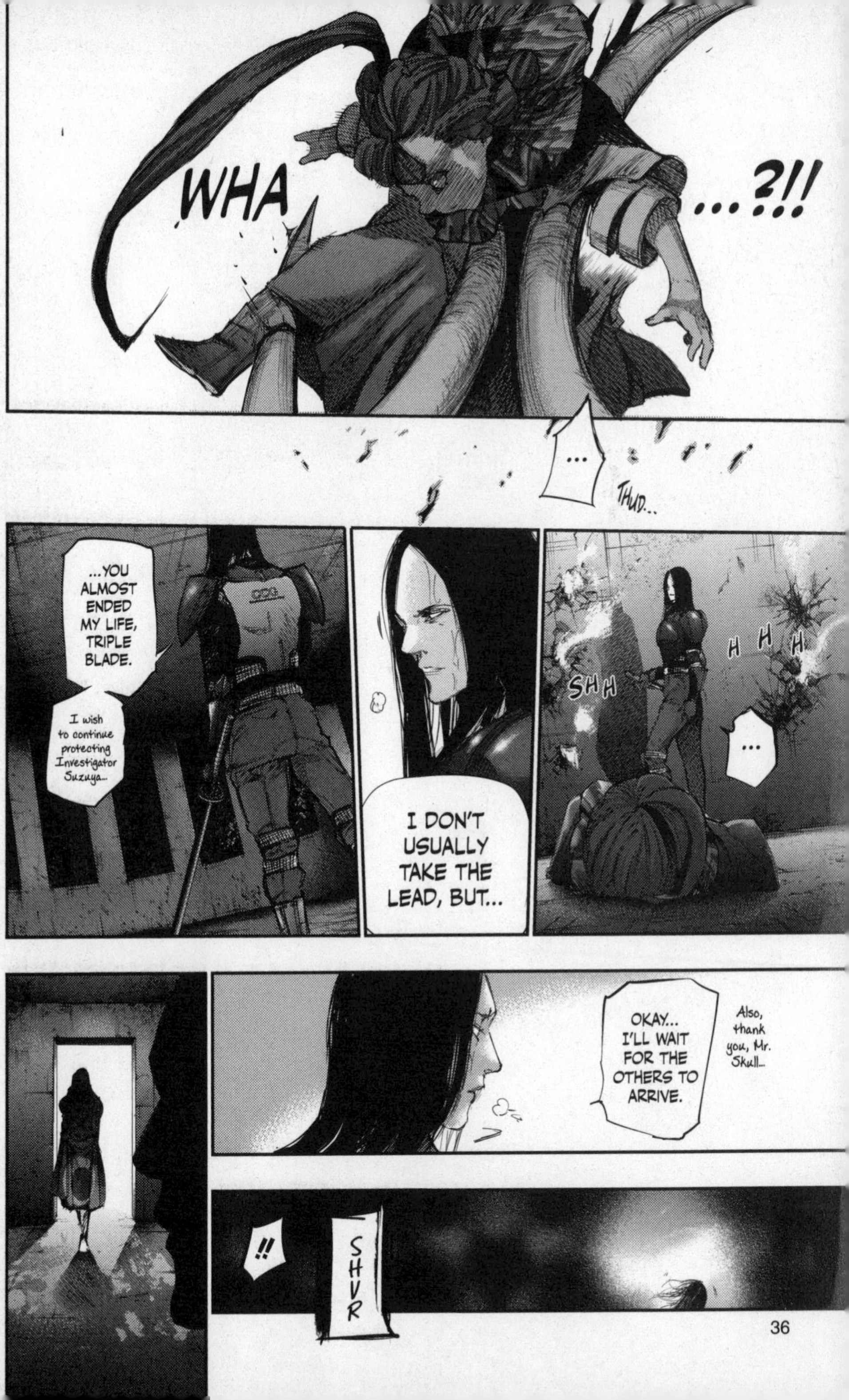
WHA ...?!!
...
THUD...
SHH
H H H
...
I DON'T USUALLY TAKE THE LEAD, BUT...
...YOU ALMOST ENDED MY LIFE, TRIPLE BLADE.
I wish to continue protecting Investigator Suzuya...
OKAY... I'LL WAIT FOR THE OTHERS TO ARRIVE.
Also, thank you, Mr. Skull...
SHVR
!!

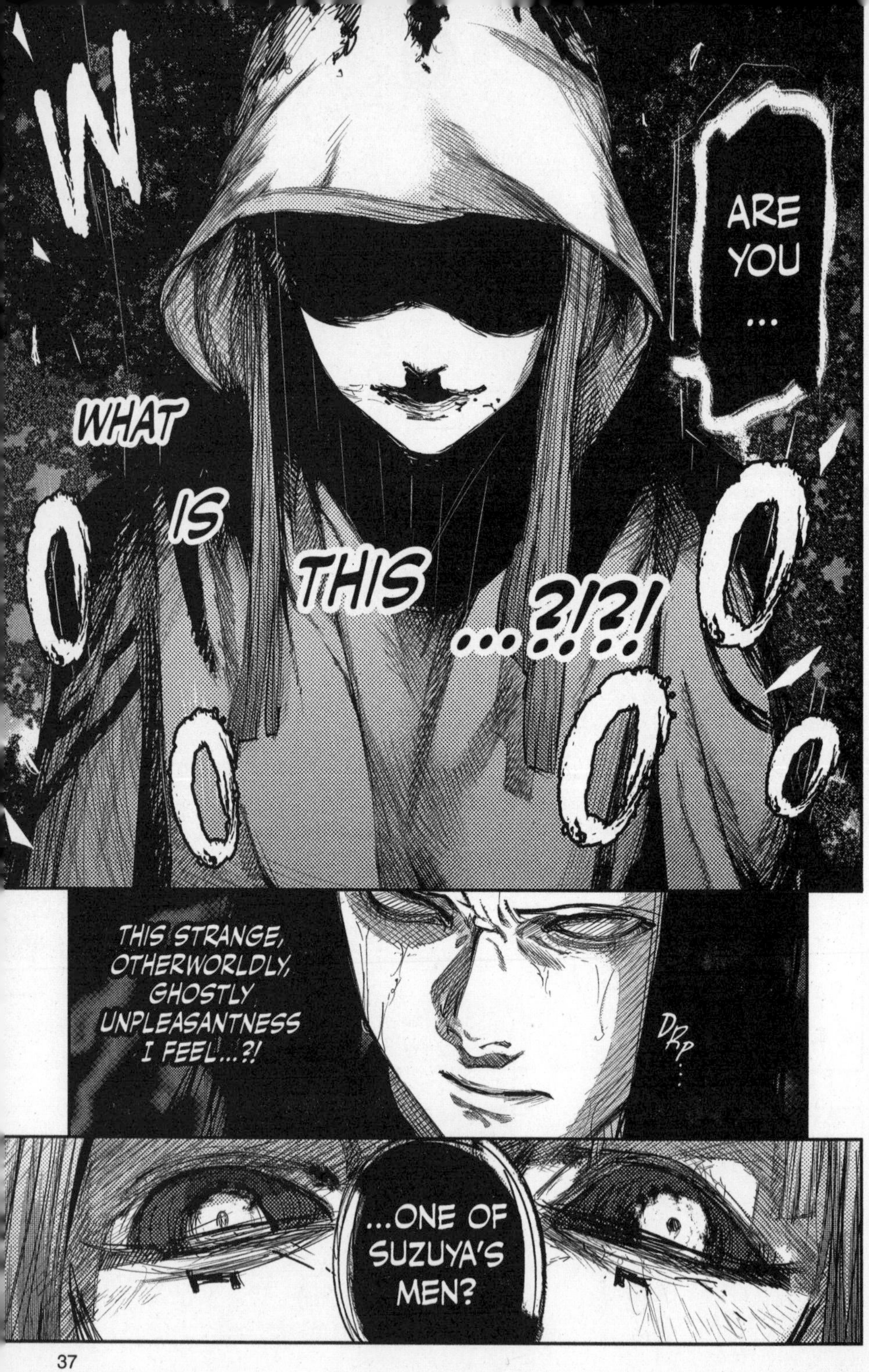
ARE YOU ...
WHAT IS THIS ...?!?!
THIS STRANGE, OTHERWORLDLY, GHOSTLY UNPLEASANTNESS I FEEL...?!
DRP...
...ONE OF SUZUYA'S MEN?

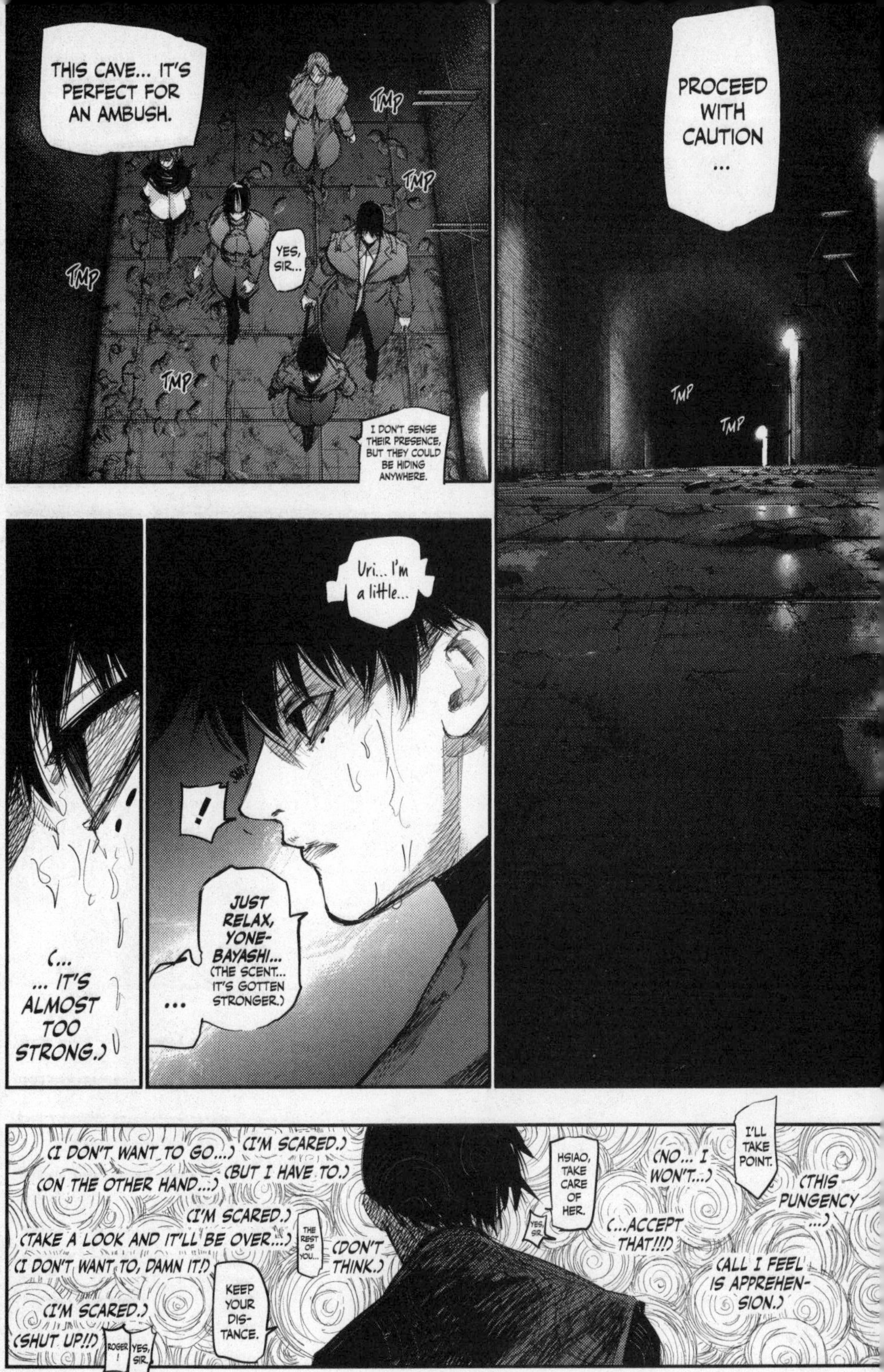
PROCEED WITH CAUTION ...
TMP
TMP
THIS CAVE... IT'S PERFECT FOR AN AMBUSH.
TMP
TMP
YES, SIR...
TMP
TMP
I DON'T SENSE THEIR PRESENCE, BUT THEY COULD BE HIDING ANYWHERE.
Uri... I'm a little...
!
JUST RELAX, YONE-BAYASHI...
(THE SCENT... IT'S GOTTEN STRONGER.)
...
(... ... IT'S ALMOST TOO STRONG.)
I'LL TAKE POINT.
(THIS PUNGENCY ...)
(NO... I WON'T...)
HSIAO, TAKE CARE OF HER.
YES, SIR.
(...ACCEPT THAT!!!)
(ALL I FEEL IS APPREHEN-SION.)
THE REST OF YOU...
(DON'T THINK.)
KEEP YOUR DIS-TANCE.
ROGER!
YES, SIR.
(I'M SCARED.)
(I DON'T WANT TO GO...)
(BUT I HAVE TO.)
(ON THE OTHER HAND...)
(I'M SCARED.)
(TAKE A LOOK AND IT'LL BE OVER...)
(I DON'T WANT TO, DAMN IT!)
(I'M SCARED.)
(SHUT UP!!)

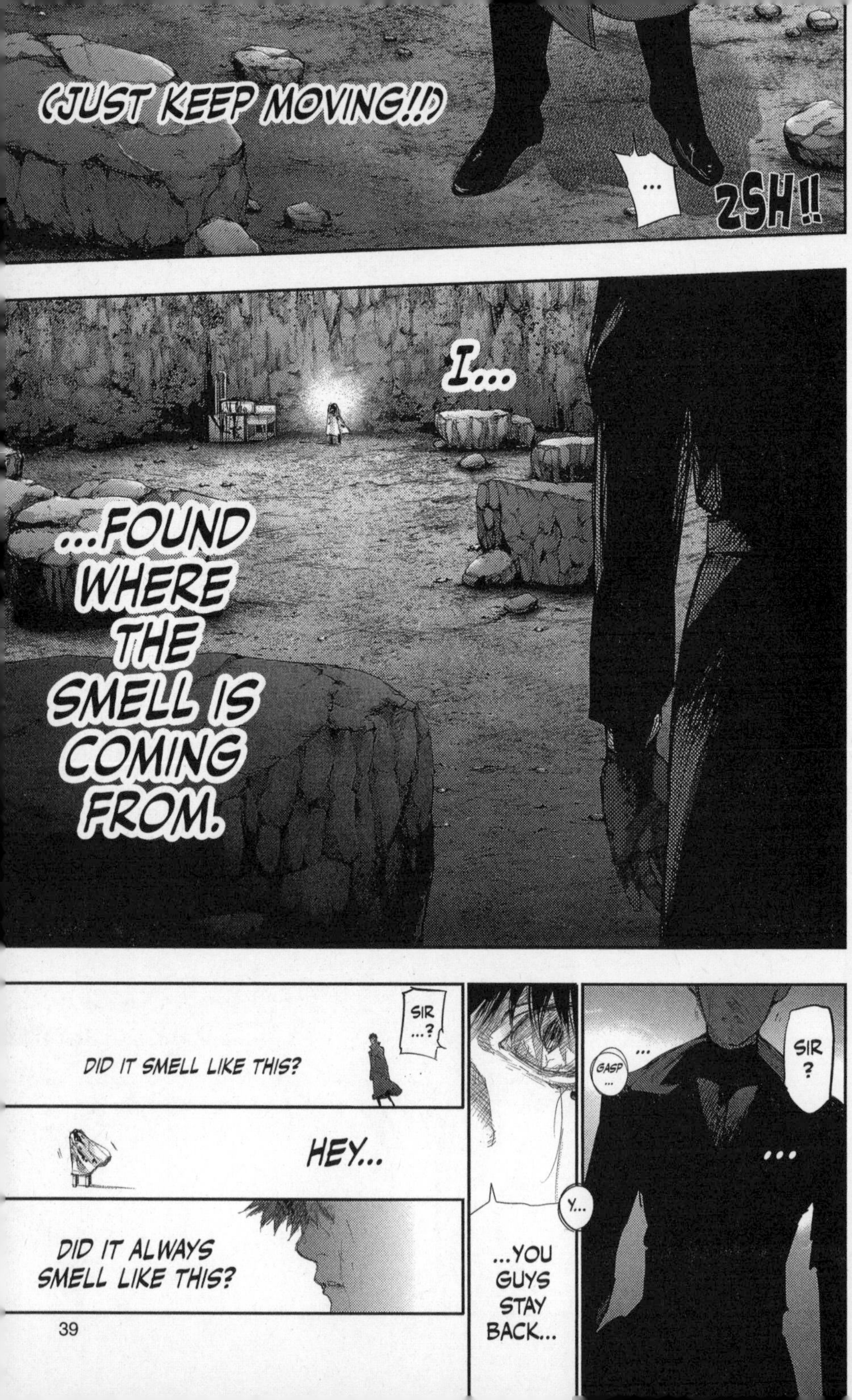

(JUST KEEP MOVING!!)
...
ZSH!!
I...
...FOUND WHERE THE SMELL IS COMING FROM.
SIR?
...
GASP...
...
Y...
...YOU GUYS STAY BACK...
SIR...?
DID IT SMELL LIKE THIS?
HEY...
DID IT ALWAYS SMELL LIKE THIS?

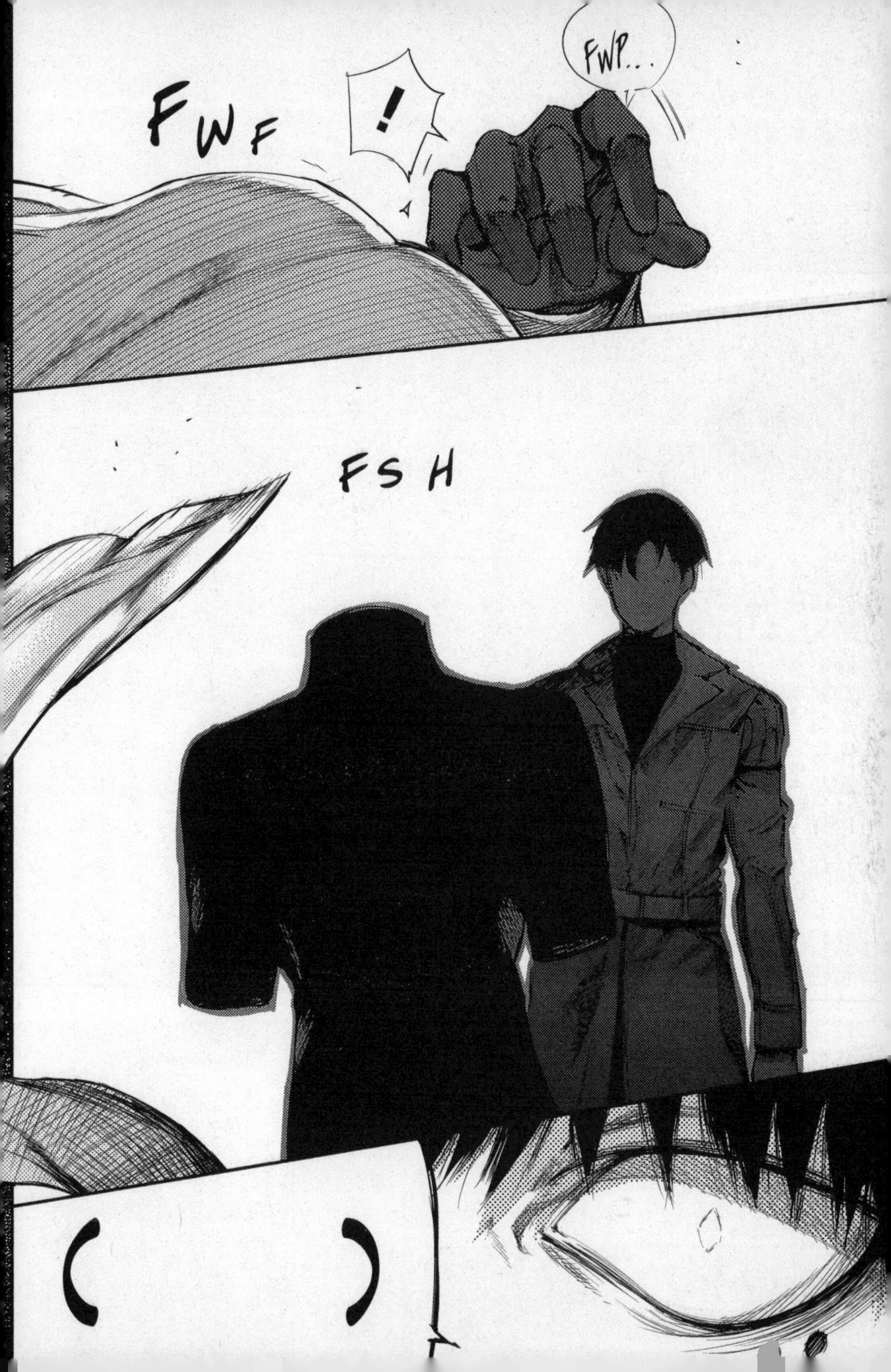
FWP...
!
FWF
FSH

Tsukiyama at work ①

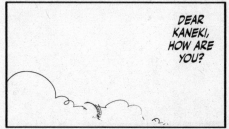

DEAR KANEKI, HOW ARE YOU?
I'M WORKING ON A FARM FOR A LIVING.
TILLING THE SOIL HAS BECOME MY LIFE'S WORK...
HEY THERE, FALLEN NOBILITY.
You're really doing this, huh?
HELLO, HORI!
LOOK AT MY GARDEN!
HERE ARE MY ROSES (FLOWERS).
MARIGOLDS (FLOWERS).
BLUE LESCHENAULTIAS (FLOWERS).
OVER THERE ARE MY GAZANIAS (FLOWERS).
And...
GROW SOMETHING WE CAN EAT!
Typical Ghoul...

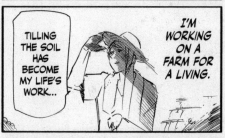

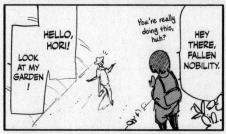

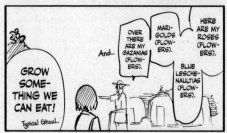

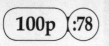

MY FAMILY WAS KILLED BY GHOULS.

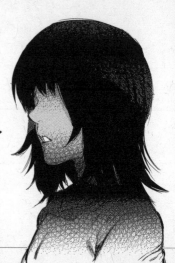

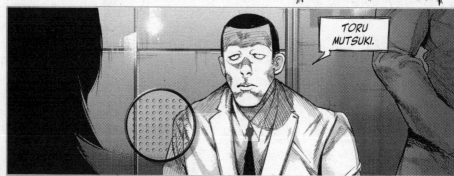

TORU MUTSUKI.

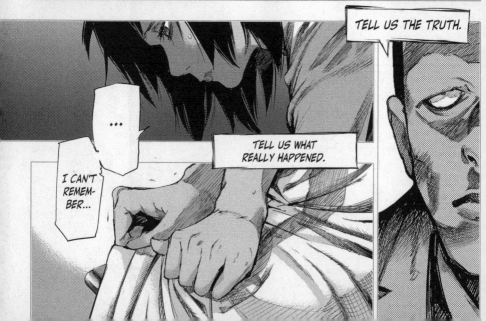

TELL US THE TRUTH.

...

TELL US WHAT REALLY HAPPENED.

I CAN'T REMEMBER...

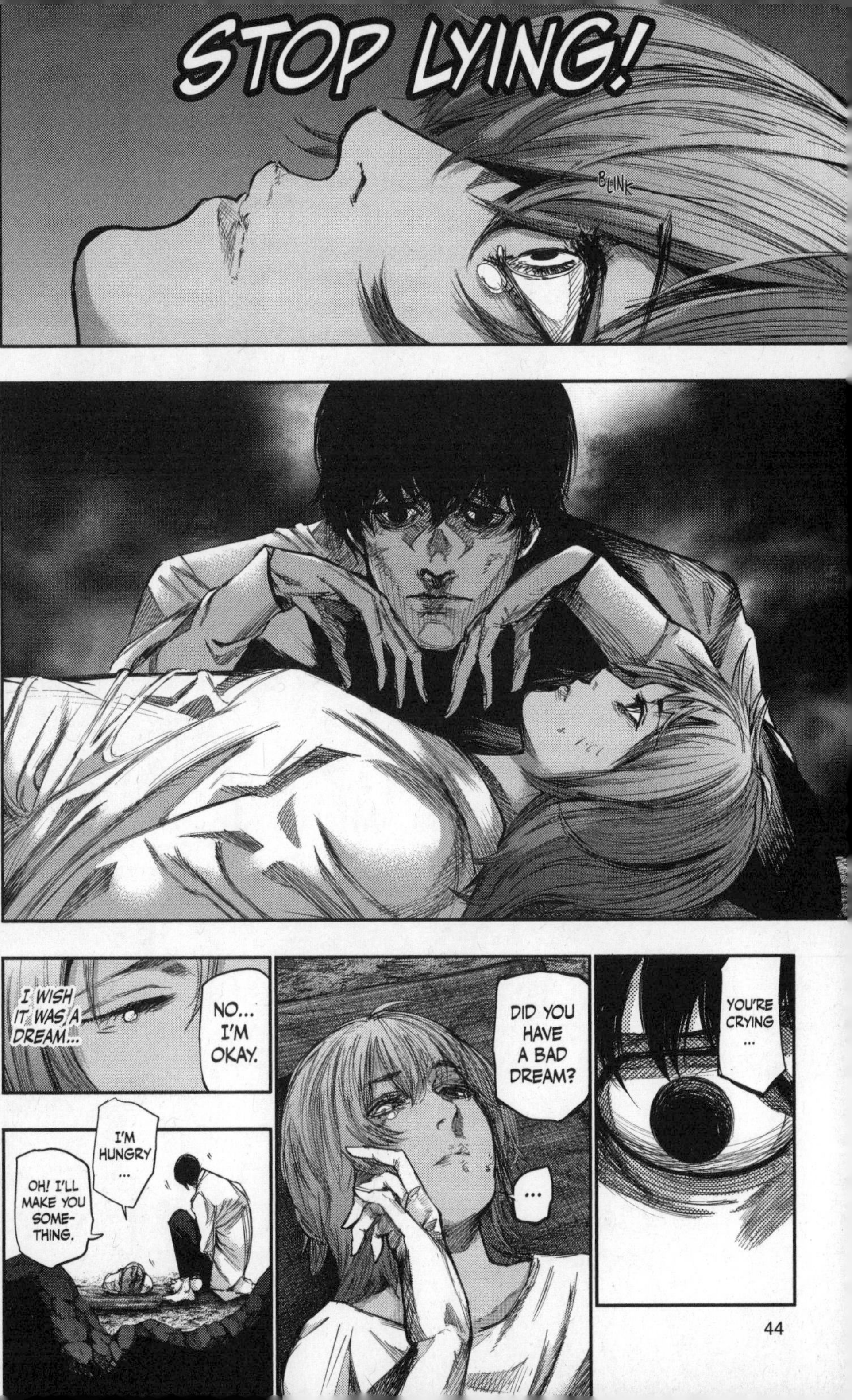
STOP LYING!
BLINK
YOU'RE CRYING ...
DID YOU HAVE A BAD DREAM?
...
NO... I'M OKAY.
I WISH IT WAS A DREAM...
I'M HUNGRY ...
OH! I'LL MAKE YOU SOME- THING.

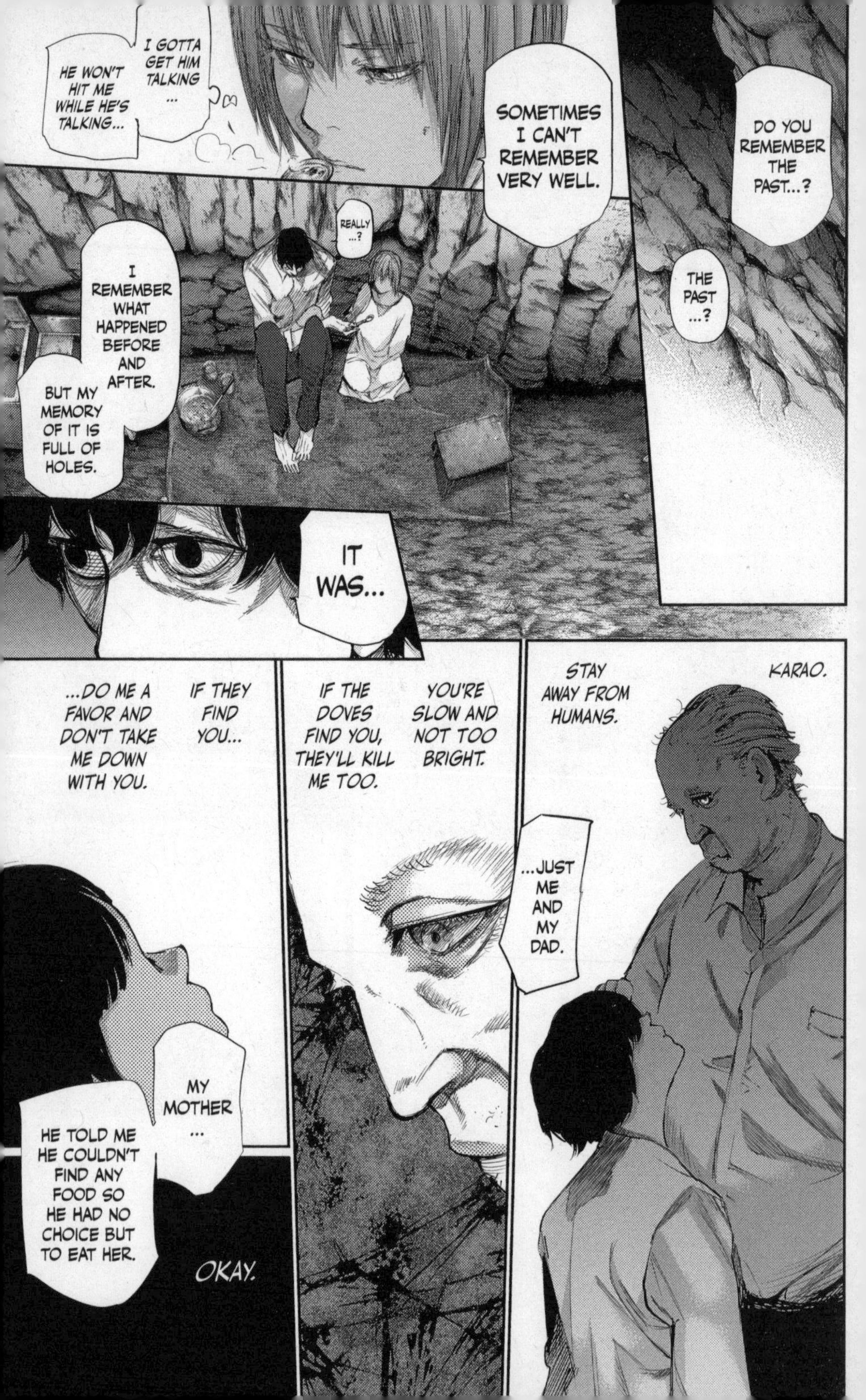
DO YOU REMEMBER THE PAST...?
THE PAST...?
SOMETIMES I CAN'T REMEMBER VERY WELL.
I GOTTA GET HIM TALKING...
HE WON'T HIT ME WHILE HE'S TALKING...
REALLY...?
I REMEMBER WHAT HAPPENED BEFORE AND AFTER.
BUT MY MEMORY OF IT IS FULL OF HOLES.
IT WAS...
KARAO.
STAY AWAY FROM HUMANS.
...JUST ME AND MY DAD.
YOU'RE SLOW AND NOT TOO BRIGHT.
IF THE DOVES FIND YOU, THEY'LL KILL ME TOO.
IF THEY FIND YOU...
...DO ME A FAVOR AND DON'T TAKE ME DOWN WITH YOU.
MY MOTHER...
HE TOLD ME HE COULDN'T FIND ANY FOOD SO HE HAD NO CHOICE BUT TO EAT HER.
OKAY.

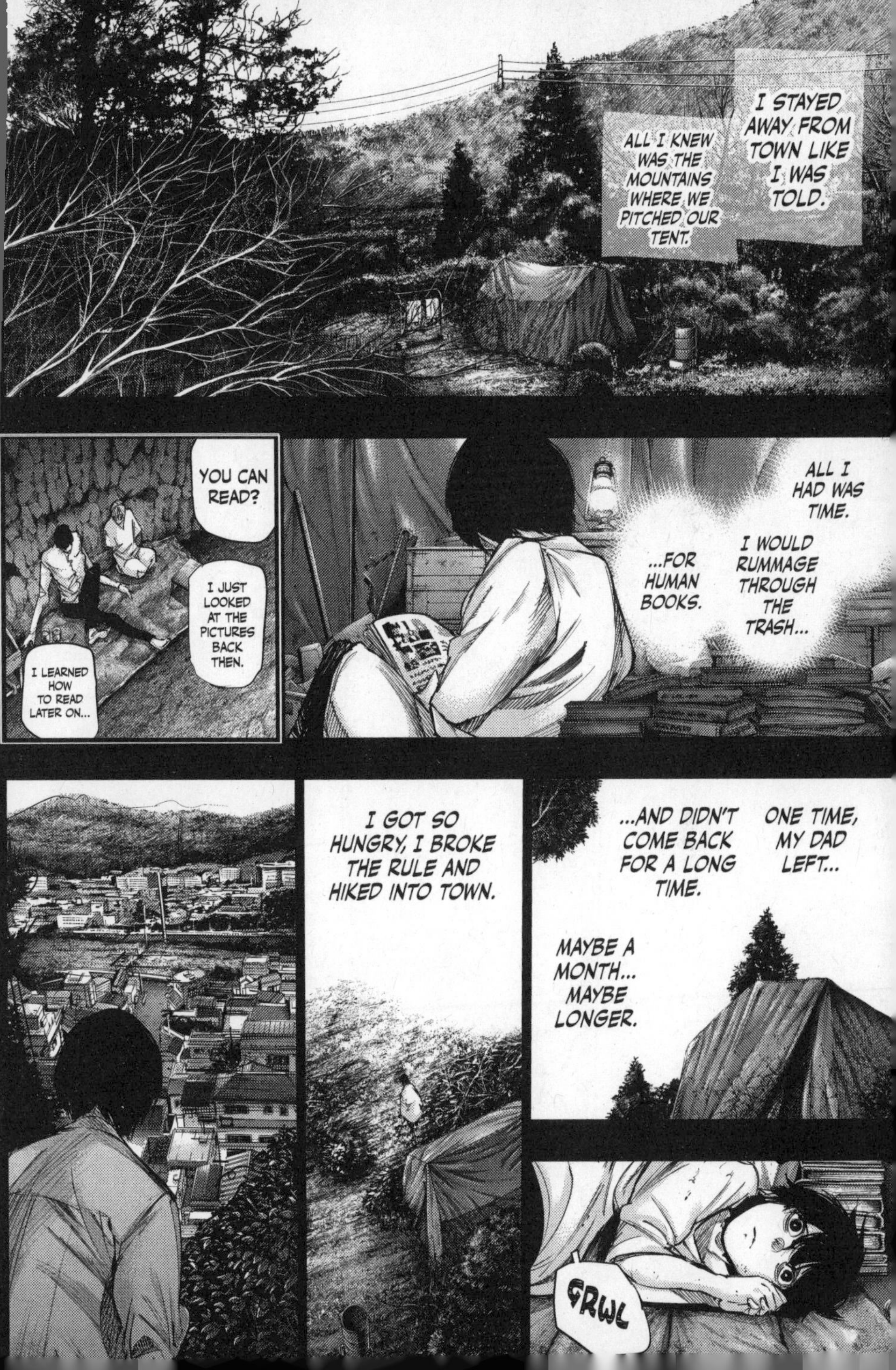
I STAYED AWAY FROM TOWN LIKE I WAS TOLD.
ALL I KNEW WAS THE MOUNTAINS WHERE WE PITCHED OUR TENT.
ALL I HAD WAS TIME.
I WOULD RUMMAGE THROUGH THE TRASH...
...FOR HUMAN BOOKS.
YOU CAN READ?
I JUST LOOKED AT THE PICTURES BACK THEN.
I LEARNED HOW TO READ LATER ON...
ONE TIME, MY DAD LEFT...
...AND DIDN'T COME BACK FOR A LONG TIME.
MAYBE A MONTH... MAYBE LONGER.
GRWL
I GOT SO HUNGRY, I BROKE THE RULE AND HIKED INTO TOWN.

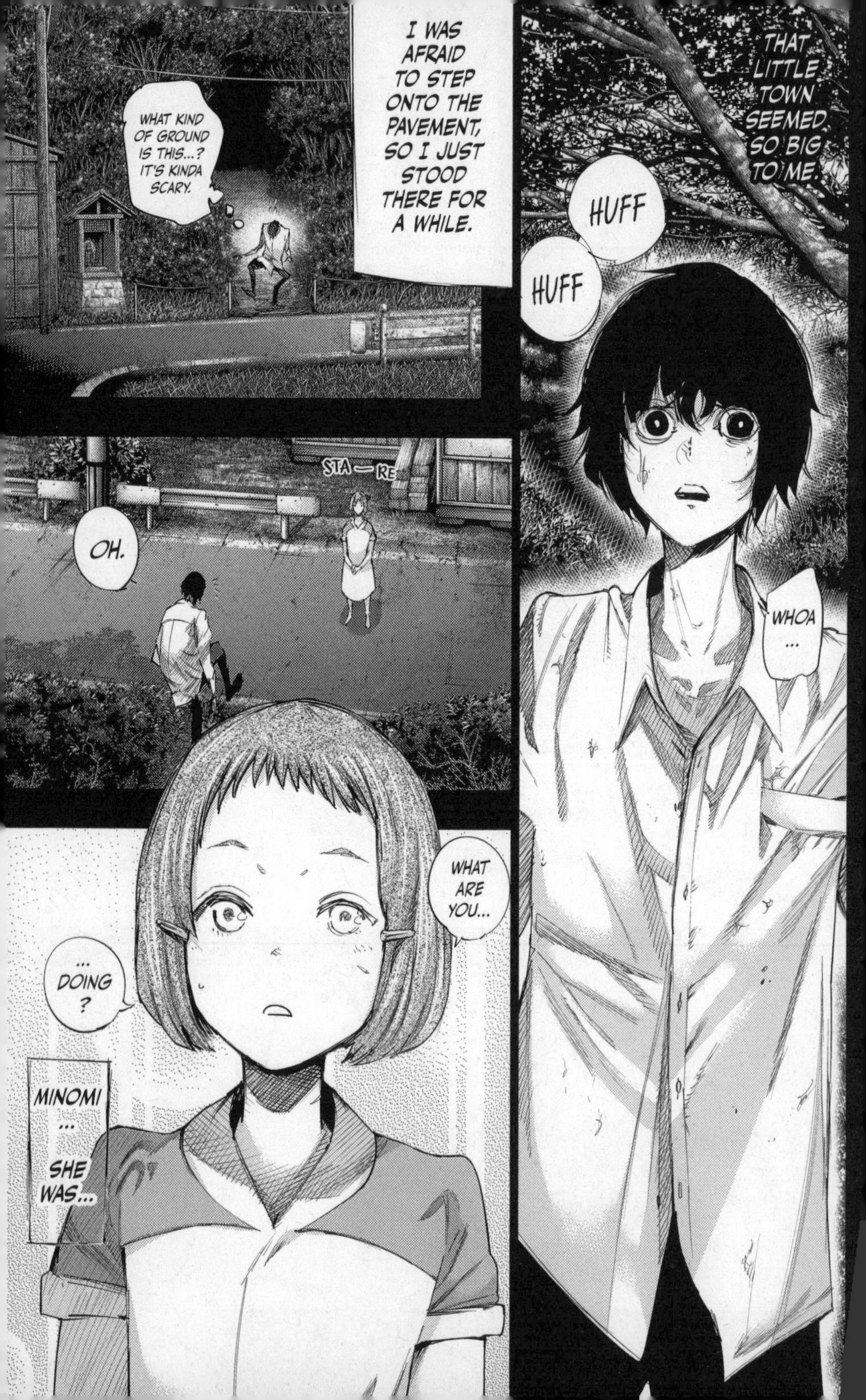
THAT LITTLE TOWN SEEMED SO BIG TO ME.
HUFF
HUFF
WHOA...
I WAS AFRAID TO STEP ONTO THE PAVEMENT, SO I JUST STOOD THERE FOR A WHILE.
WHAT KIND OF GROUND IS THIS...? IT'S KINDA SCARY.
STA—RE
OH.
WHAT ARE YOU...
...DOING?
MINOMI... SHE WAS...

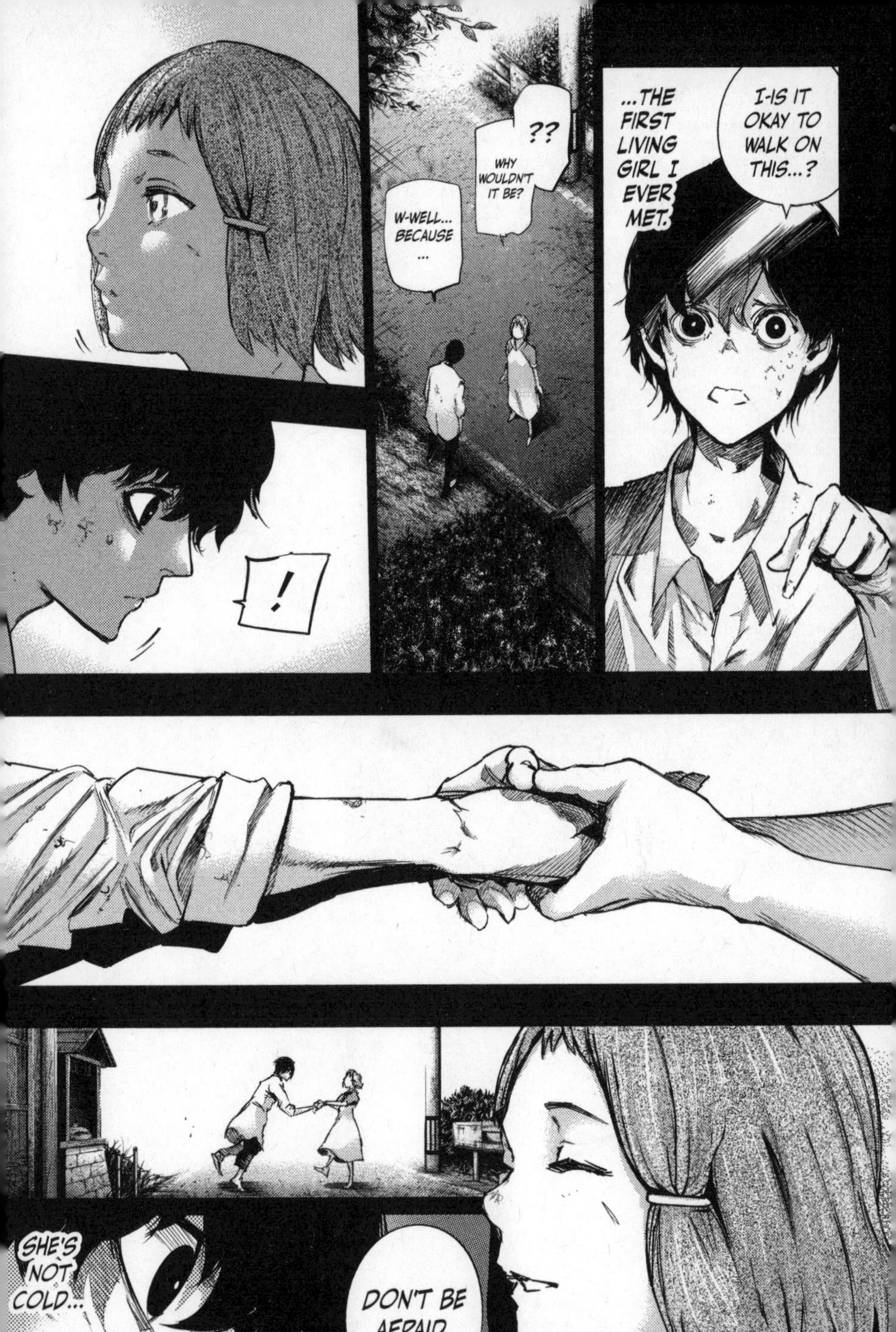
I-IS IT OKAY TO WALK ON THIS...?
...THE FIRST LIVING GIRL I EVER MET.
??
WHY WOULDN'T IT BE?
W-WELL... BECAUSE ...
!
DON'T BE AFRAID.
SHE'S NOT COLD...

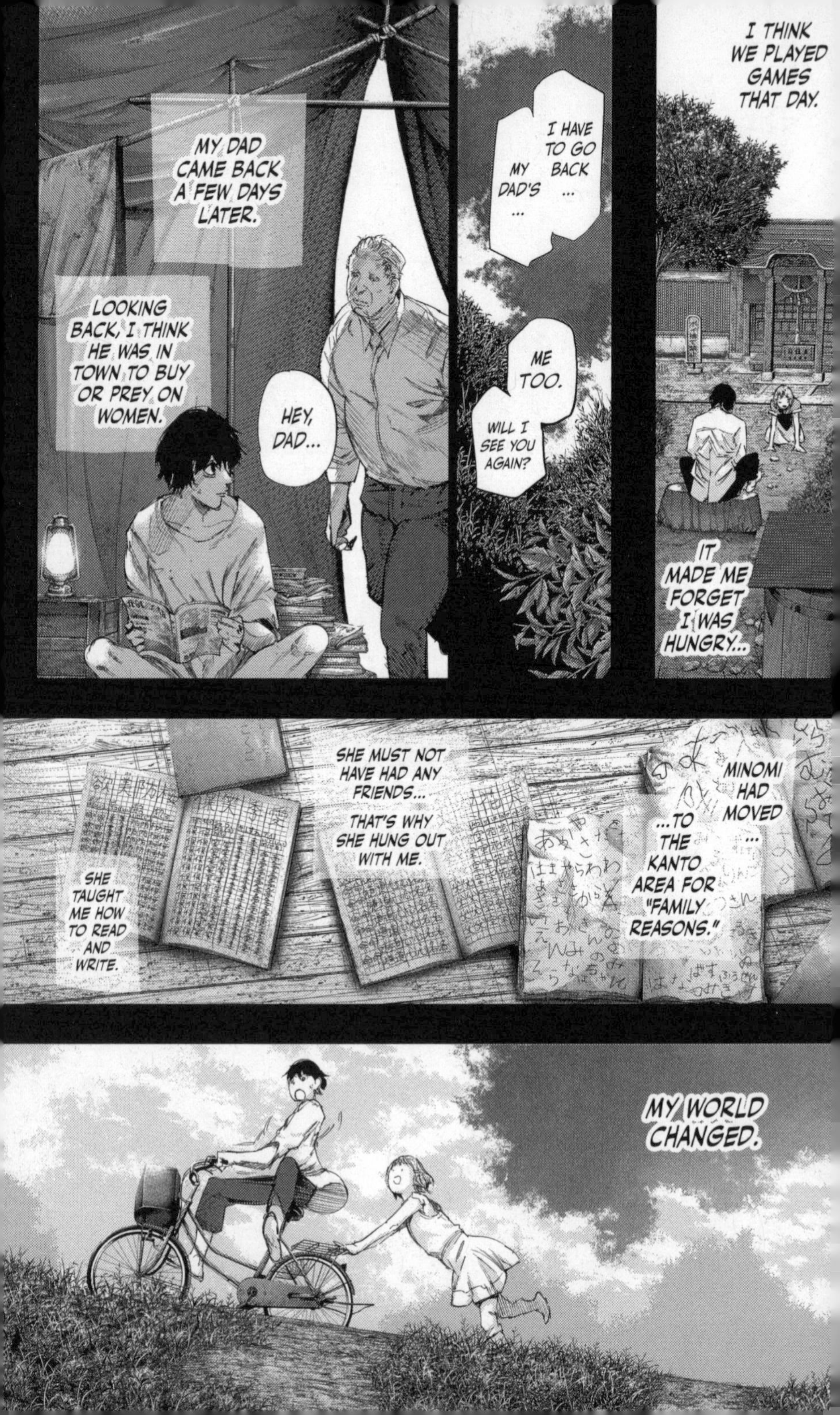
I THINK WE PLAYED GAMES THAT DAY.
IT MADE ME FORGET I WAS HUNGRY...
I HAVE TO GO BACK ...
MY DAD'S ...
ME TOO.
WILL I SEE YOU AGAIN?
MY DAD CAME BACK A FEW DAYS LATER.
LOOKING BACK, I THINK HE WAS IN TOWN TO BUY OR PREY ON WOMEN.
HEY, DAD...
MINOMI HAD MOVED ...
...TO THE KANTO AREA FOR "FAMILY REASONS."
SHE MUST NOT HAVE HAD ANY FRIENDS...
THAT'S WHY SHE HUNG OUT WITH ME.
SHE TAUGHT ME HOW TO READ AND WRITE.
MY WORLD CHANGED.

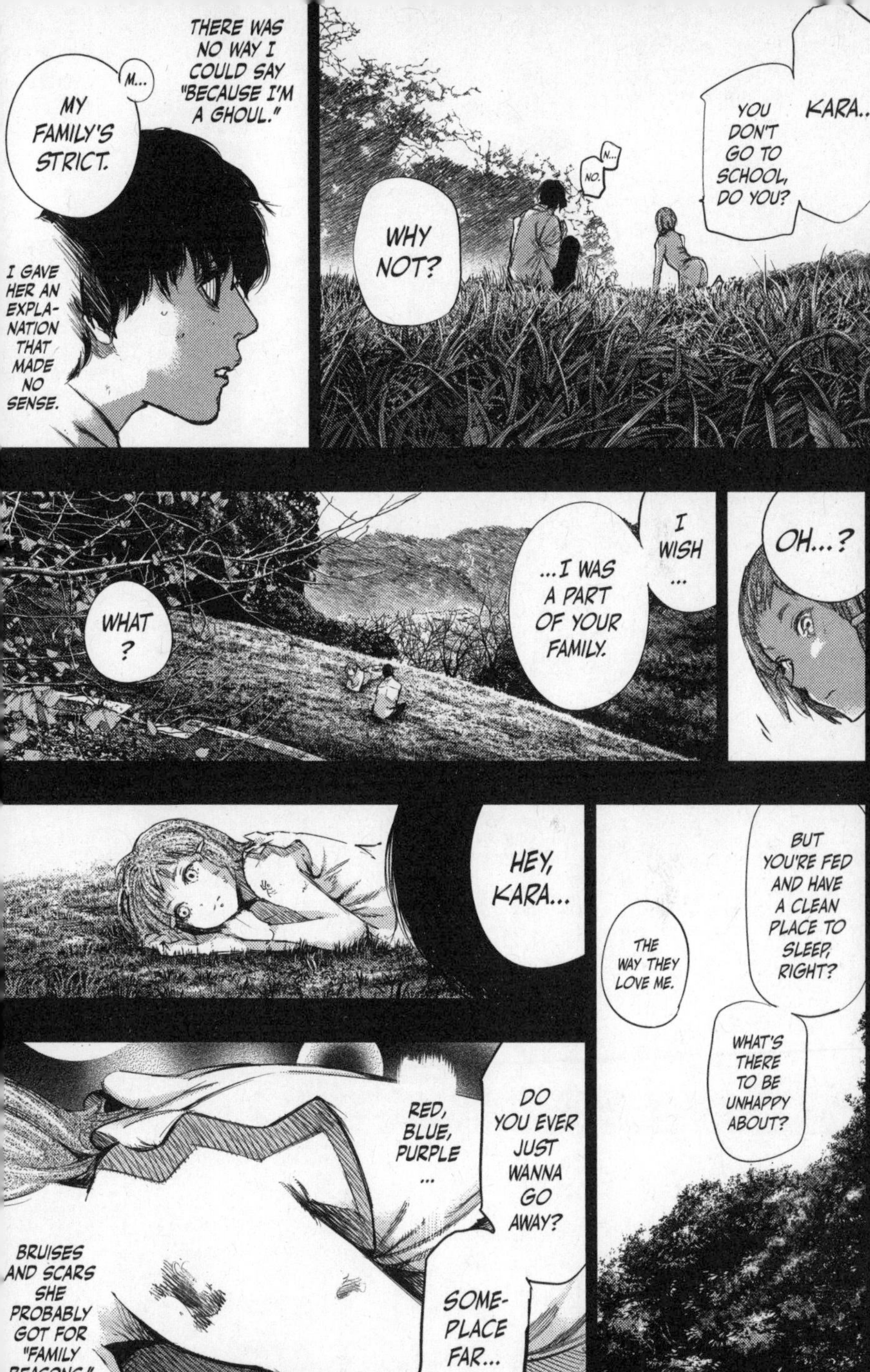
KARA...
YOU DON'T GO TO SCHOOL, DO YOU?
N...
NO.
WHY NOT?
M...
MY FAMILY'S STRICT.
THERE WAS NO WAY I COULD SAY "BECAUSE I'M A GHOUL."
I GAVE HER AN EXPLANATION THAT MADE NO SENSE.
OH...?
I WISH...
...I WAS A PART OF YOUR FAMILY.
WHAT?
BUT YOU'RE FED AND HAVE A CLEAN PLACE TO SLEEP, RIGHT?
THE WAY THEY LOVE ME.
WHAT'S THERE TO BE UNHAPPY ABOUT?
HEY, KARA...
DO YOU EVER JUST WANNA GO AWAY?
RED, BLUE, PURPLE...
SOME-PLACE FAR...
BRUISES AND SCARS SHE PROBABLY GOT FOR "FAMILY REASONS."

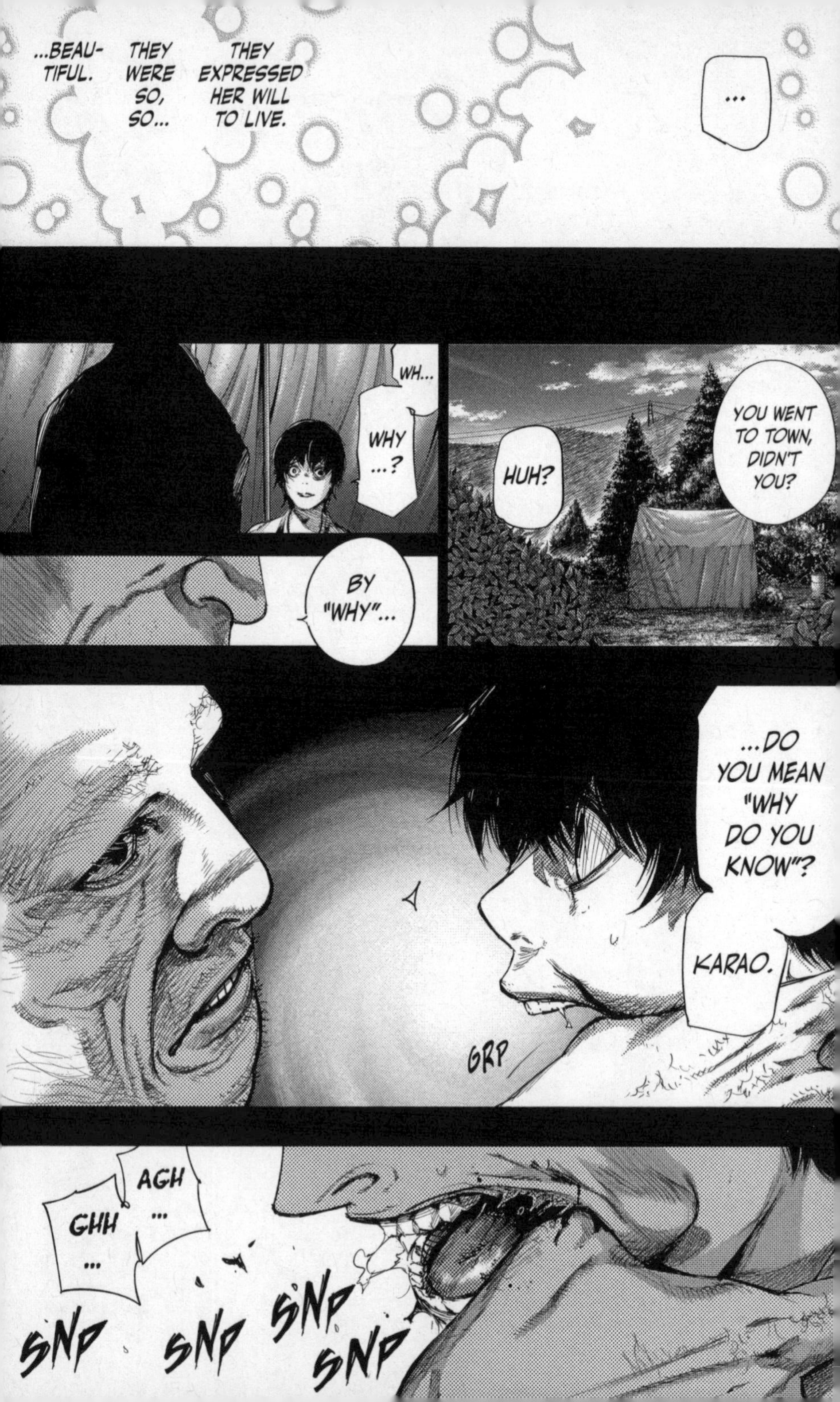
...
THEY EXPRESSED HER WILL TO LIVE.
THEY WERE SO, SO...
...BEAUTIFUL.
YOU WENT TO TOWN, DIDN'T YOU?
HUH?
WH...
WHY ...?
BY "WHY"...
...DO YOU MEAN "WHY DO YOU KNOW"?
KARAO.
GRP
AGH ...
GHH ...
SNP
SNP
SNP
SNP
SNP

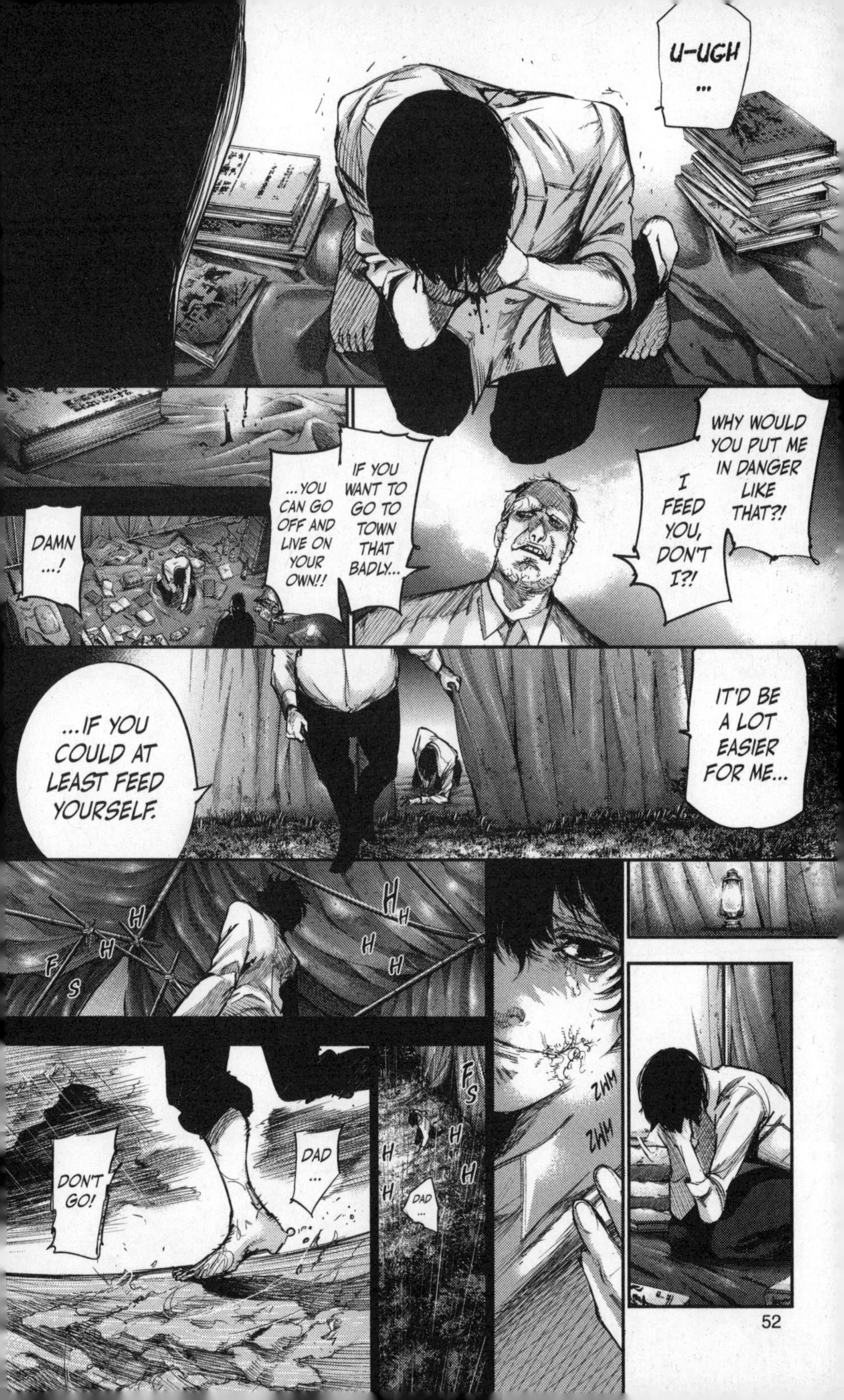
U-UGH ...
WHY WOULD YOU PUT ME IN DANGER LIKE THAT?!
I FEED YOU, DON'T I?!
IF YOU WANT TO GO TO TOWN THAT BADLY...
...YOU CAN GO OFF AND LIVE ON YOUR OWN!!
DAMN ...!
IT'D BE A LOT EASIER FOR ME...
...IF YOU COULD AT LEAST FEED YOURSELF.
ZWM
ZWM
HH
H
H
H
FSH
FS
H
H
H
H
DAD ...
DAD ...
DON'T GO!

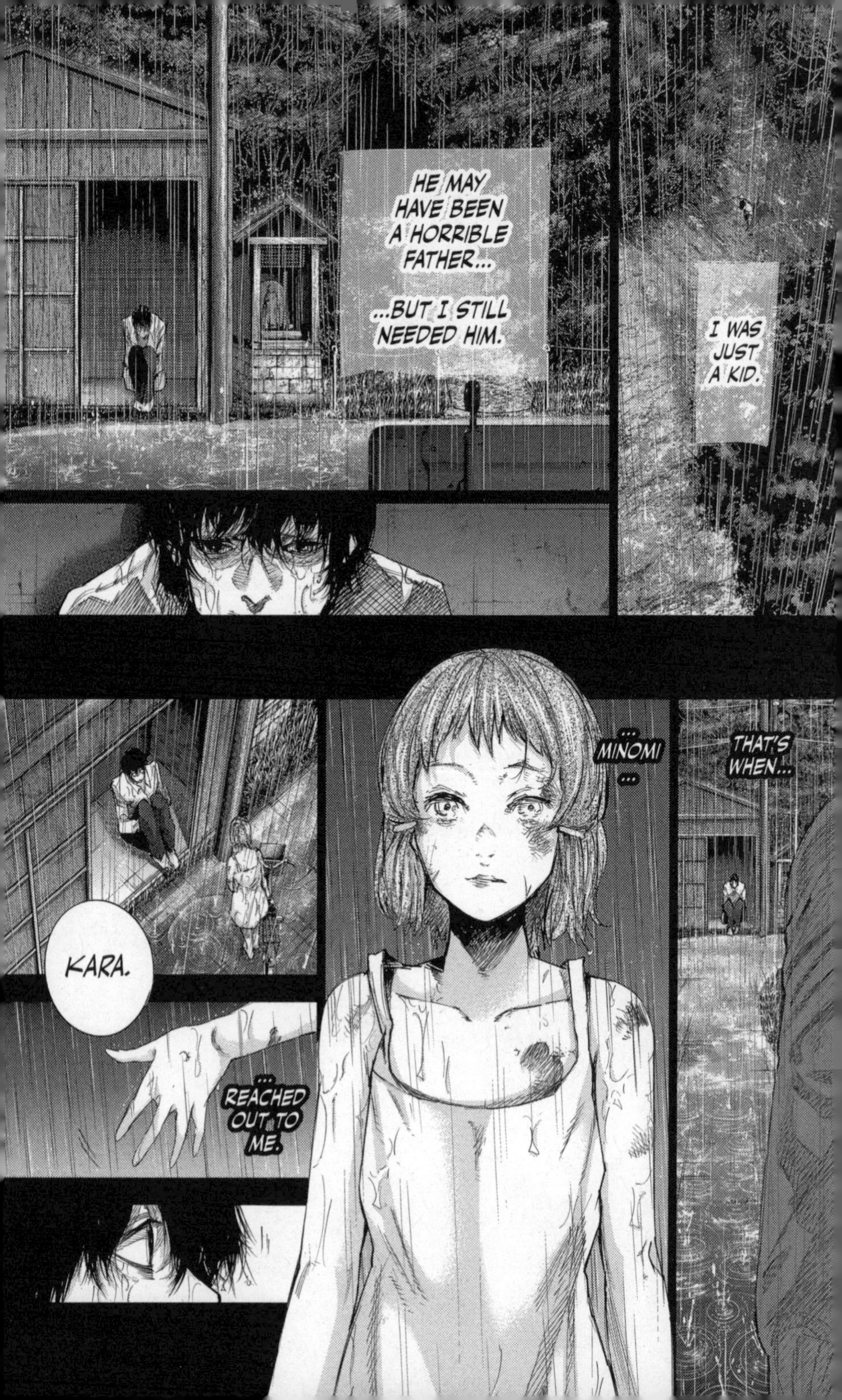
I WAS JUST A KID.
HE MAY HAVE BEEN A HORRIBLE FATHER...
...BUT I STILL NEEDED HIM.
THAT'S WHEN...
...MINOMI...
KARA.
...REACHED OUT TO ME.

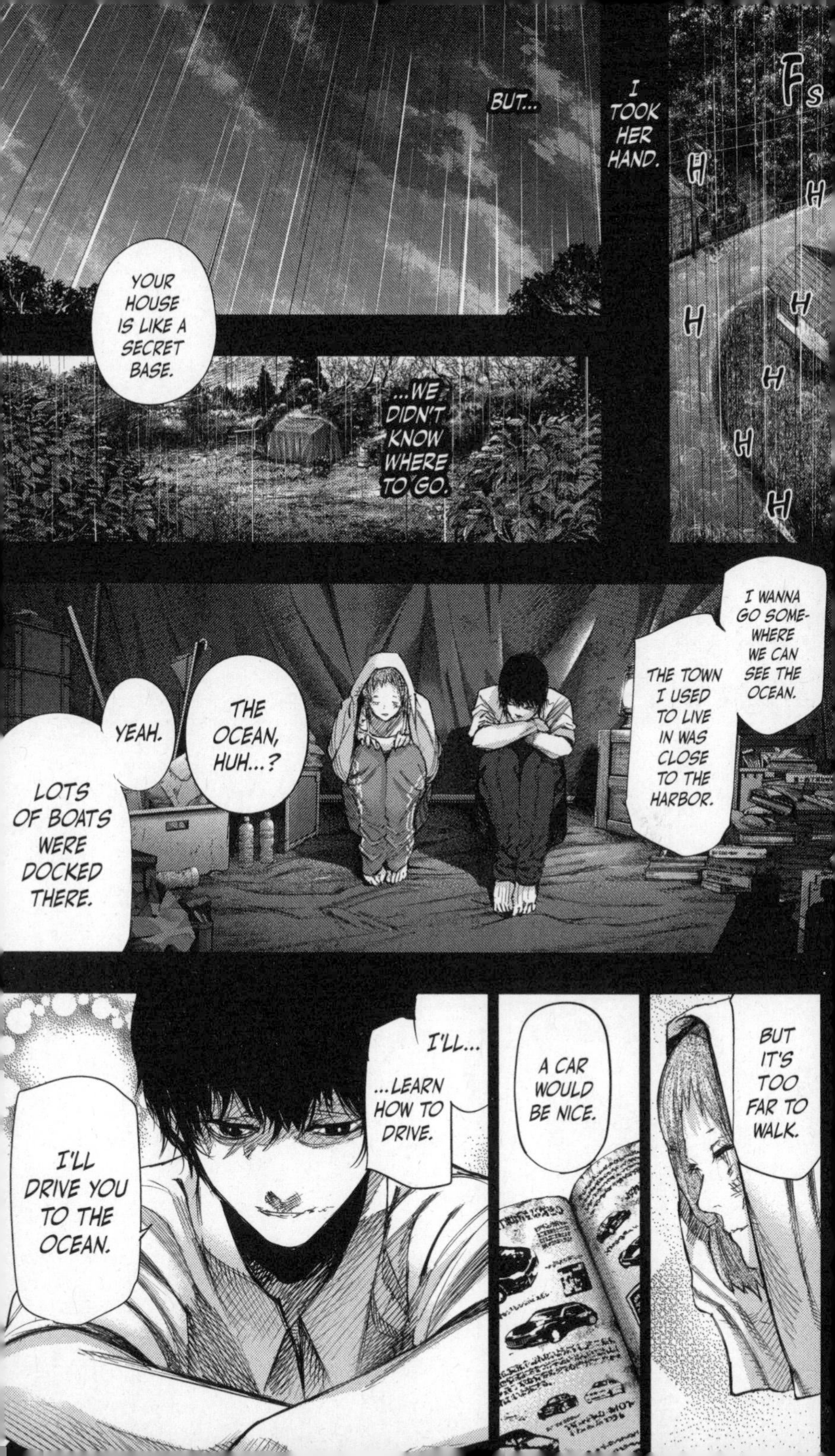
I TOOK HER HAND.
FsHHHHHHH
BUT...
...WE DIDN'T KNOW WHERE TO GO.
YOUR HOUSE IS LIKE A SECRET BASE.
I WANNA GO SOMEWHERE WE CAN SEE THE OCEAN.
THE TOWN I USED TO LIVE IN WAS CLOSE TO THE HARBOR.
THE OCEAN, HUH...?
YEAH.
LOTS OF BOATS WERE DOCKED THERE.
BUT IT'S TOO FAR TO WALK.
A CAR WOULD BE NICE.
I'LL...
...LEARN HOW TO DRIVE.
I'LL DRIVE YOU TO THE OCEAN.

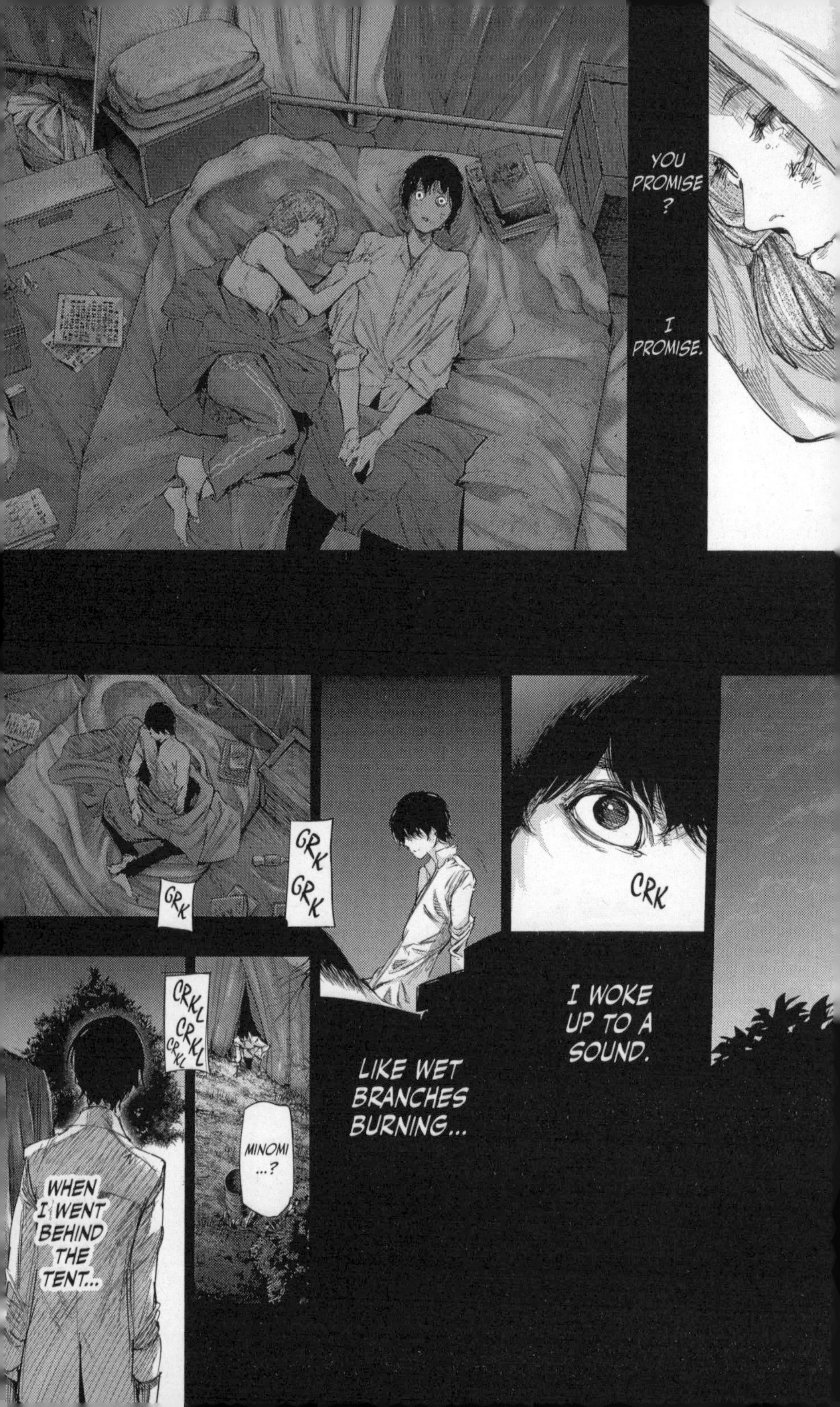
YOU PROMISE?
I PROMISE.
CRK
I WOKE UP TO A SOUND.
GRK GRK
LIKE WET BRANCHES BURNING...
GRK
CRKL CRKL CRKL
MINOMI...?
WHEN I WENT BEHIND THE TENT...

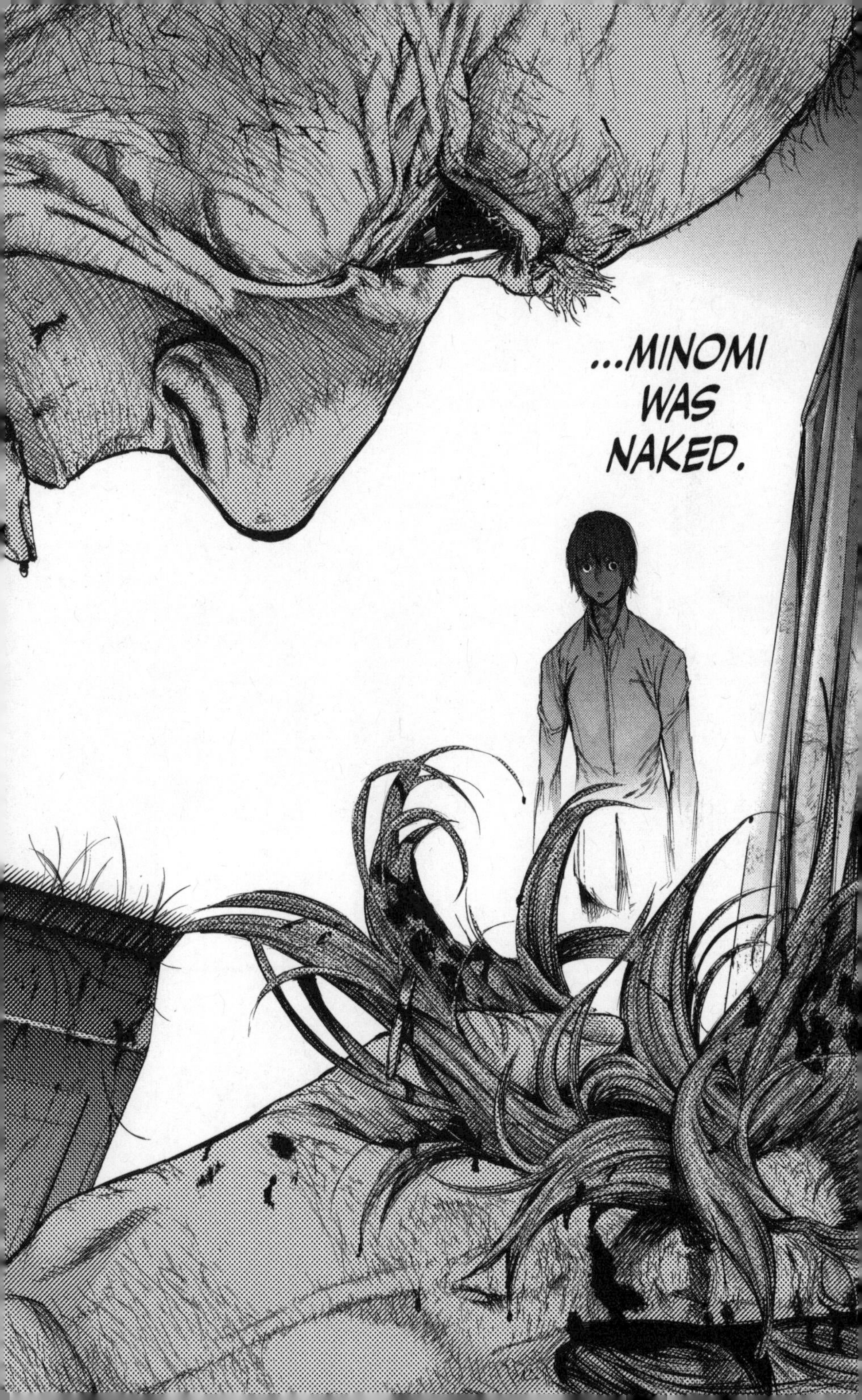
...MINOMI WAS NAKED.

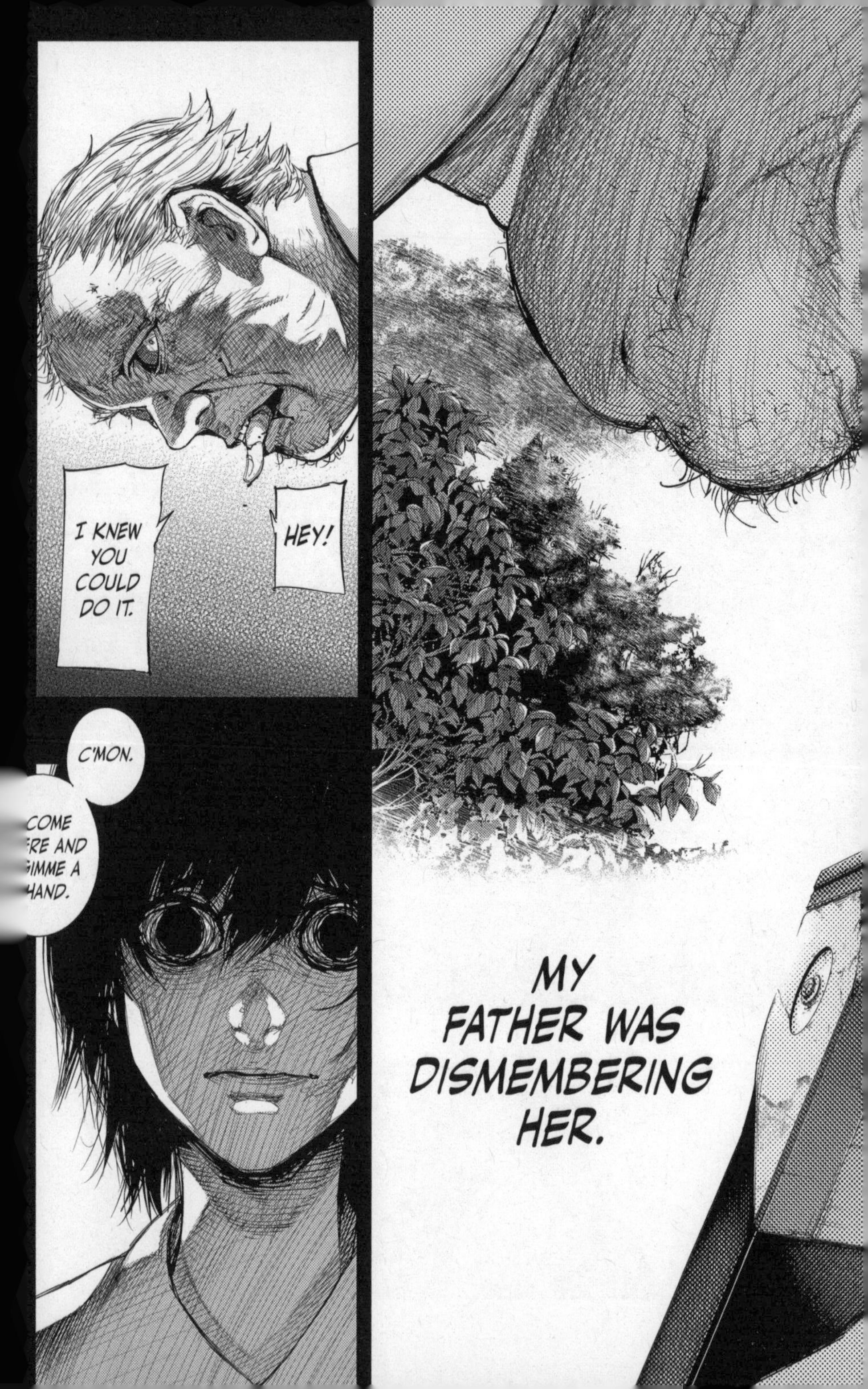

MY FATHER WAS DISMEMBERING HER.
HEY!
I KNEW YOU COULD DO IT.
C'MON.
COME ERE AND GIMME A HAND.

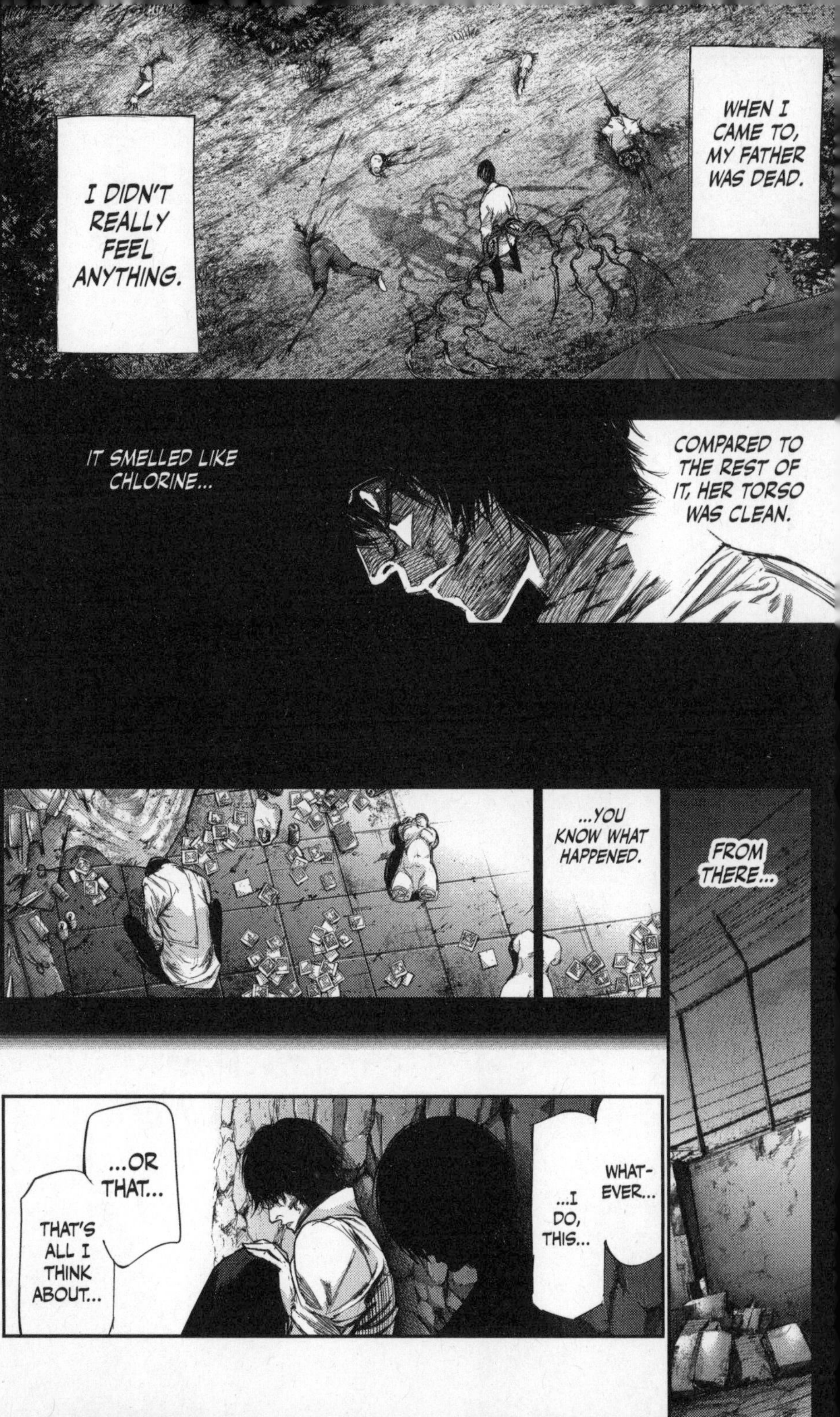
WHEN I CAME TO, MY FATHER WAS DEAD.
I DIDN'T REALLY FEEL ANYTHING.
COMPARED TO THE REST OF IT, HER TORSO WAS CLEAN.
IT SMELLED LIKE CHLORINE...
FROM THERE...
...YOU KNOW WHAT HAPPENED.
WHAT-EVER...
...I DO, THIS...
...OR THAT...
THAT'S ALL I THINK ABOUT...

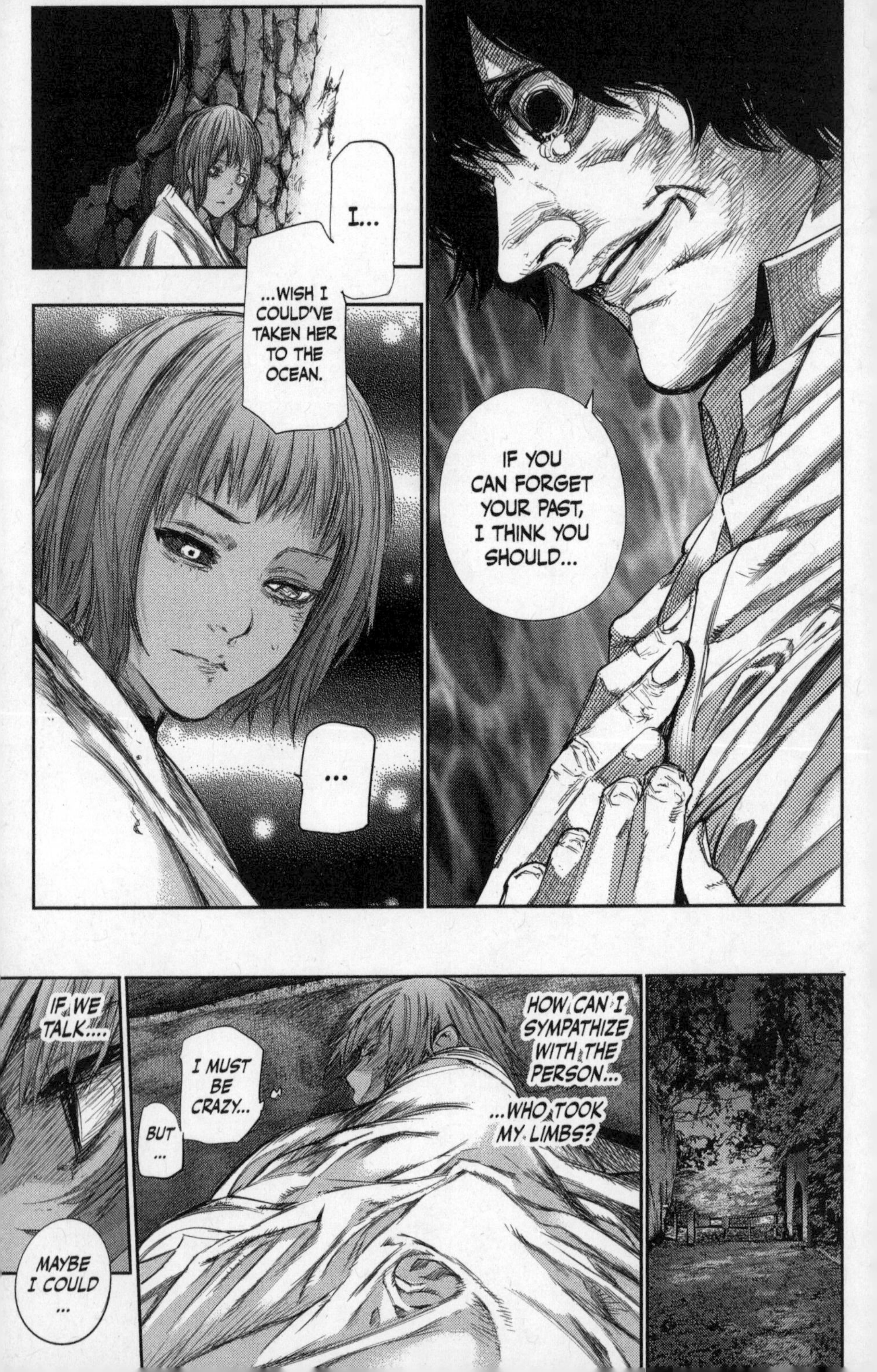
IF YOU CAN FORGET YOUR PAST, I THINK YOU SHOULD...
I...
...WISH I COULD'VE TAKEN HER TO THE OCEAN.
...
HOW CAN I SYMPATHIZE WITH THE PERSON...
...WHO TOOK MY LIMBS?
I MUST BE CRAZY...
BUT ...
IF WE TALK....
MAYBE I COULD ...

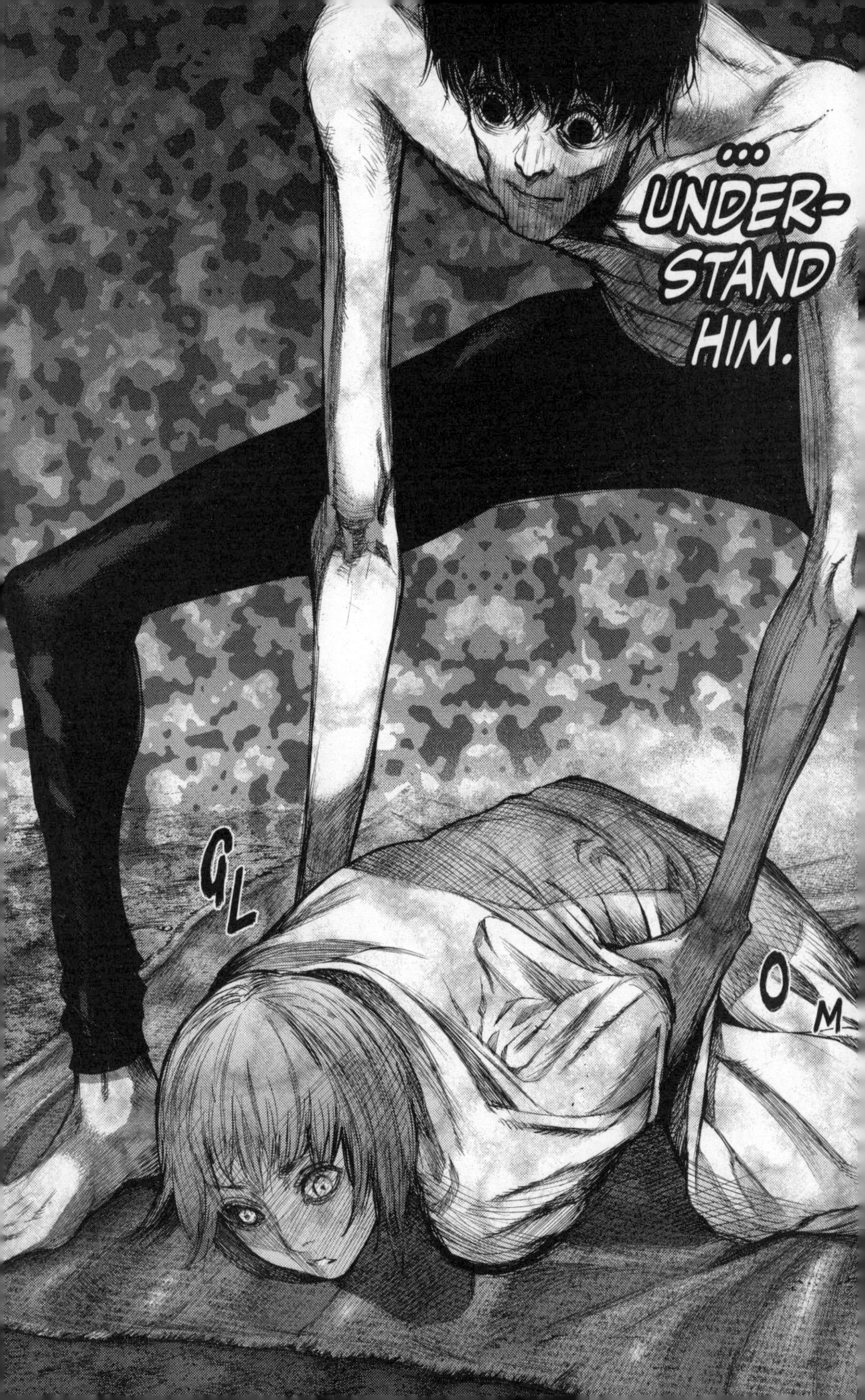
...UNDER-
STAND
HIM.
GL
OM

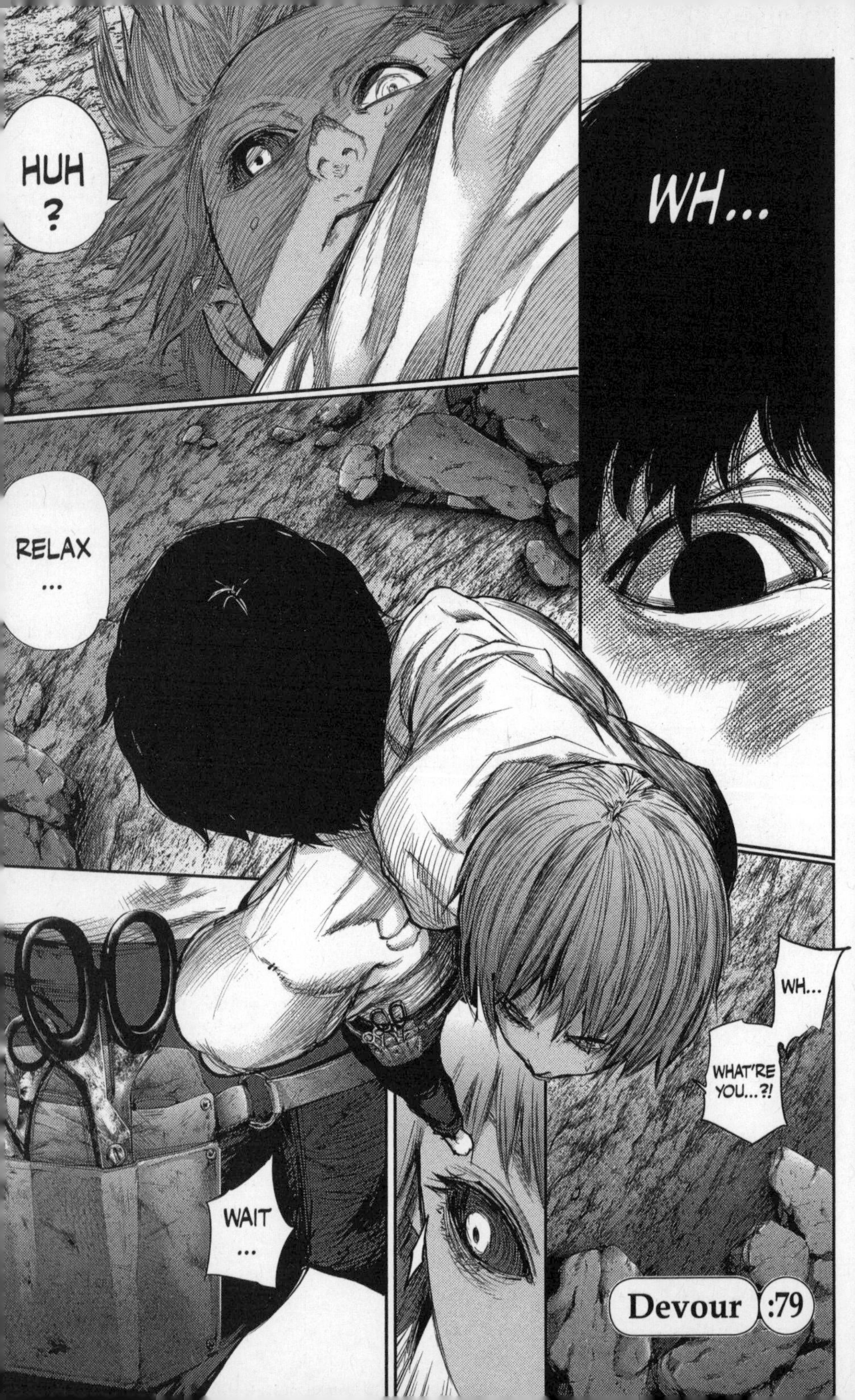
WH...
HUH ?
RELAX ...
WH...
WHAT'RE YOU...?!
Devour :79
WAIT ...

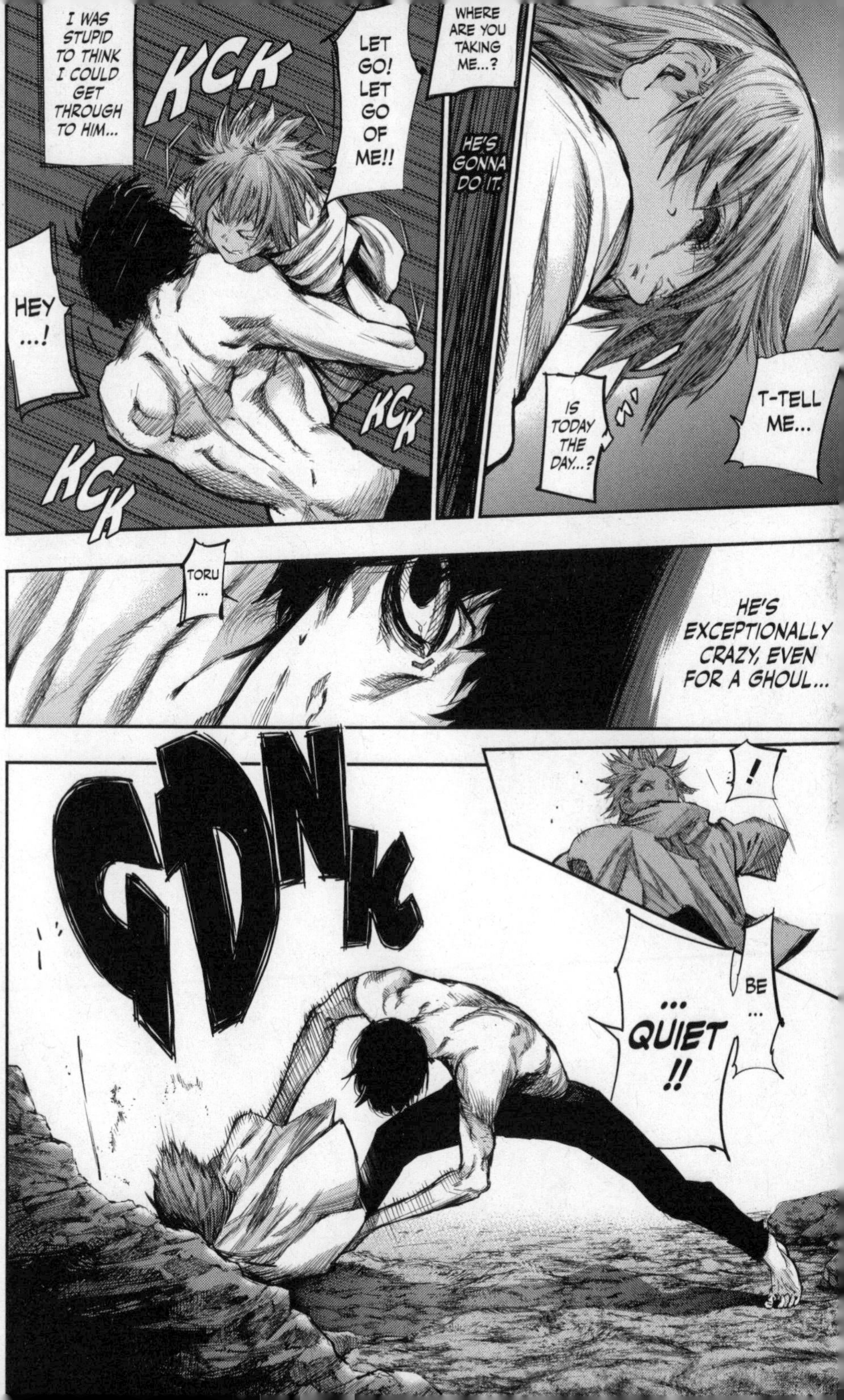
T-TELL ME...
IS TODAY THE DAY...?
WHERE ARE YOU TAKING ME...?
HE'S GONNA DO IT.
LET GO! LET GO OF ME!!
KCK
I WAS STUPID TO THINK I COULD GET THROUGH TO HIM...
HEY ...!
KCK
KCK
HE'S EXCEPTIONALLY CRAZY, EVEN FOR A GHOUL...
TORU ...
!
BE ...
... QUIET !!
GDNK

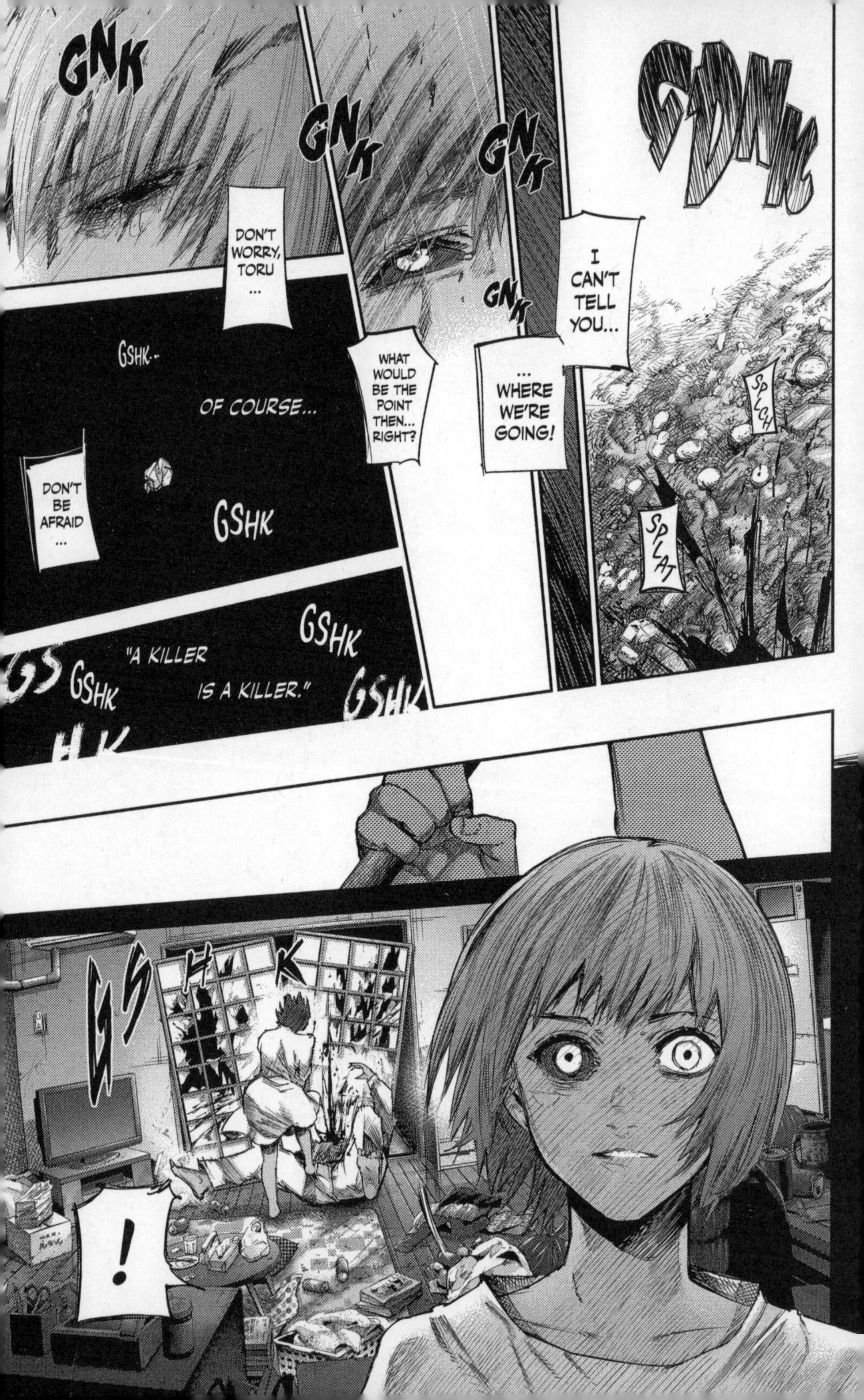
GDNK
I CAN'T TELL YOU...
... WHERE WE'RE GOING!
SPLCH
SPLAT
GNK
GNK
GNK
WHAT WOULD BE THE POINT THEN... RIGHT?
GNK
DON'T WORRY, TORU ...
GSHK..
OF COURSE...
DON'T BE AFRAID ...
GSHK
GSHK
"A KILLER
IS A KILLER."
GSHK
GSHK
GSHK
!

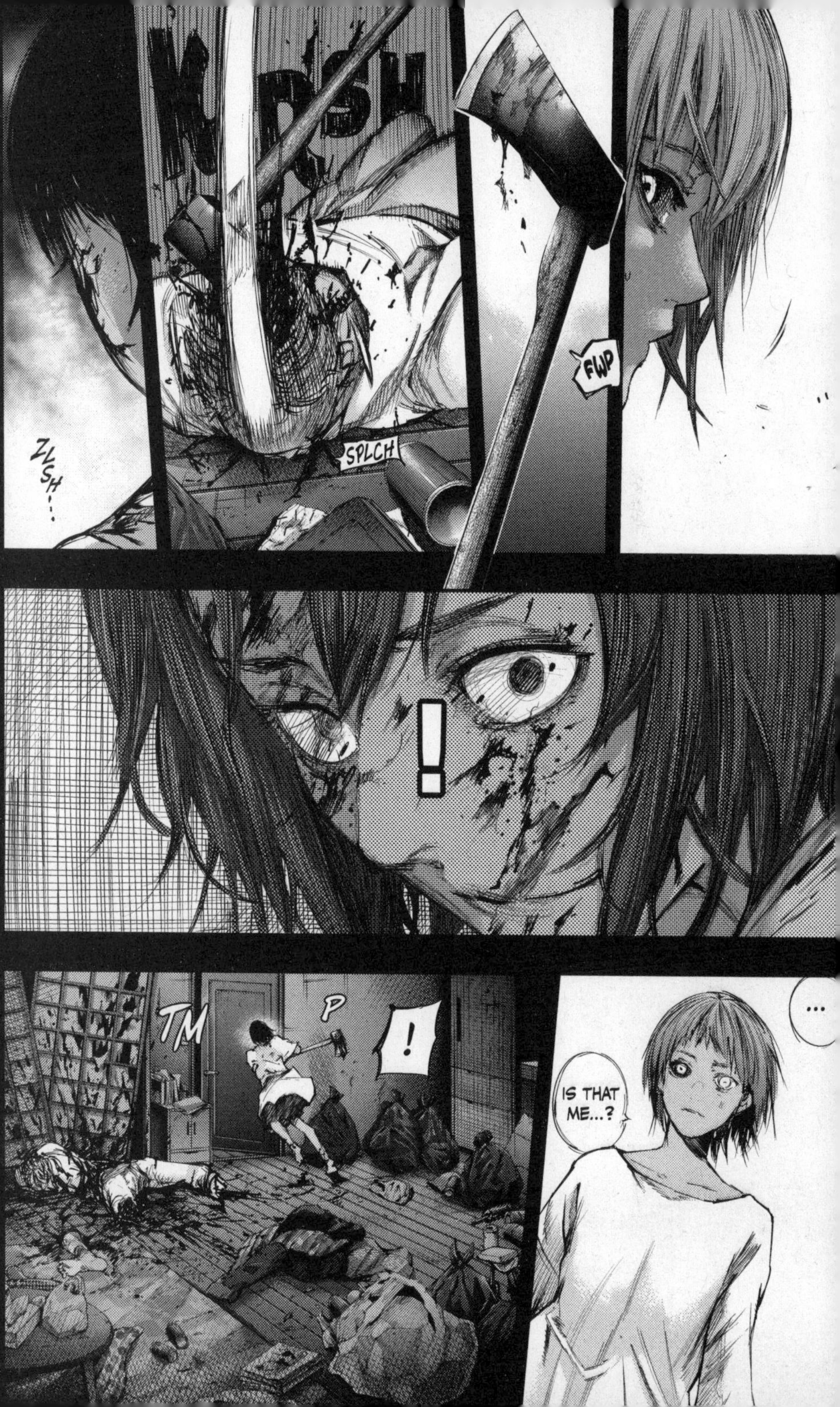
FWP
SPLCH
ZLSH...
!
...
IS THAT ME...?
!
P
TM

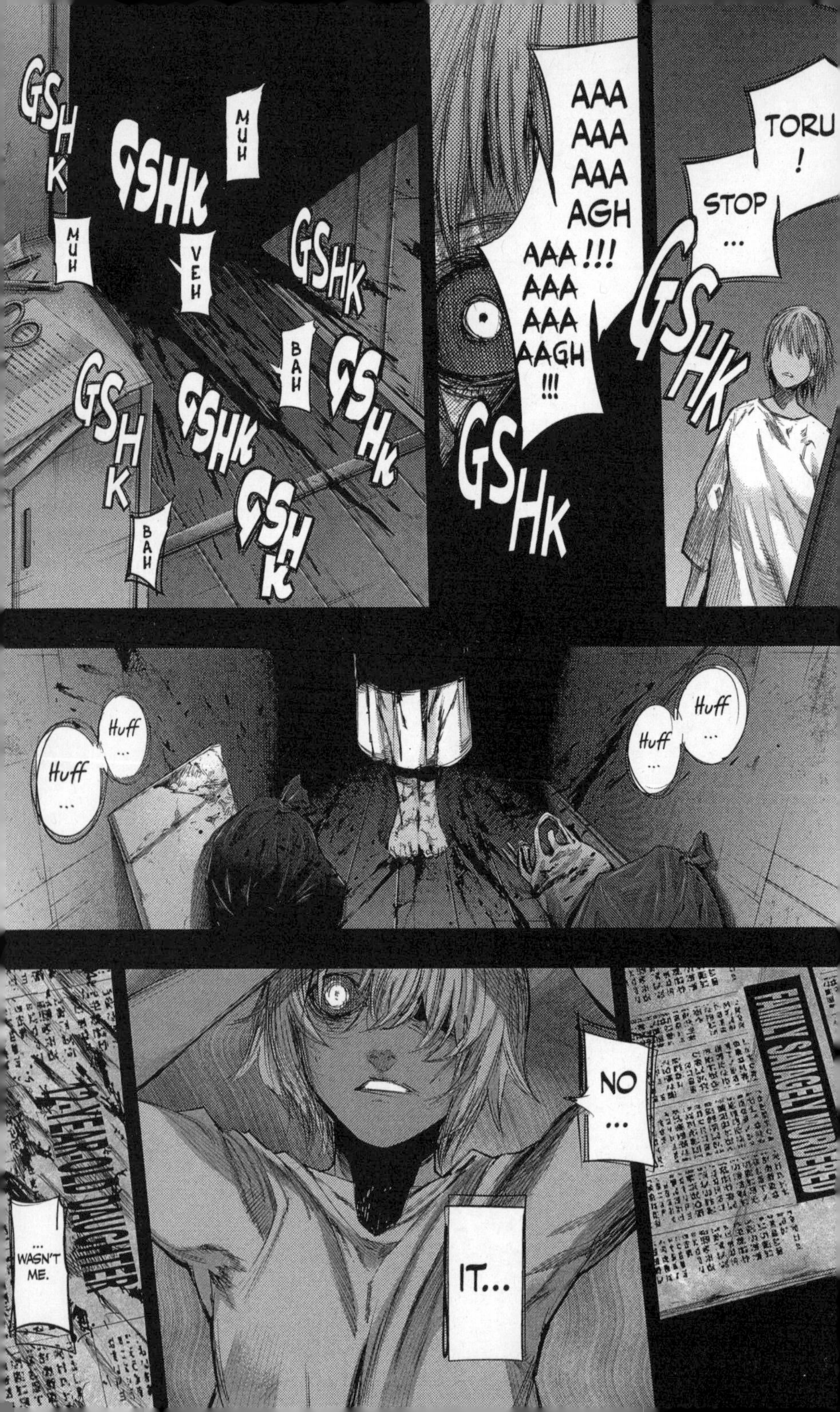
TORU!
STOP...
GSHK
AAAAAAAAAAGH!!!
AAAAAAAAAAAGH!!!
GSHK
MUH
GSHK
GSHK
VEH
MUH
GSHK
BAH
GSHK
GSHK
GSHK
GSHK
BAH
Huff...
Huff...
Huff...
Huff...
FAMILY SAVAGELY MURDERED
NO...
IT...
17-YEAR-OLD DAUGHTER
...WASN'T ME.

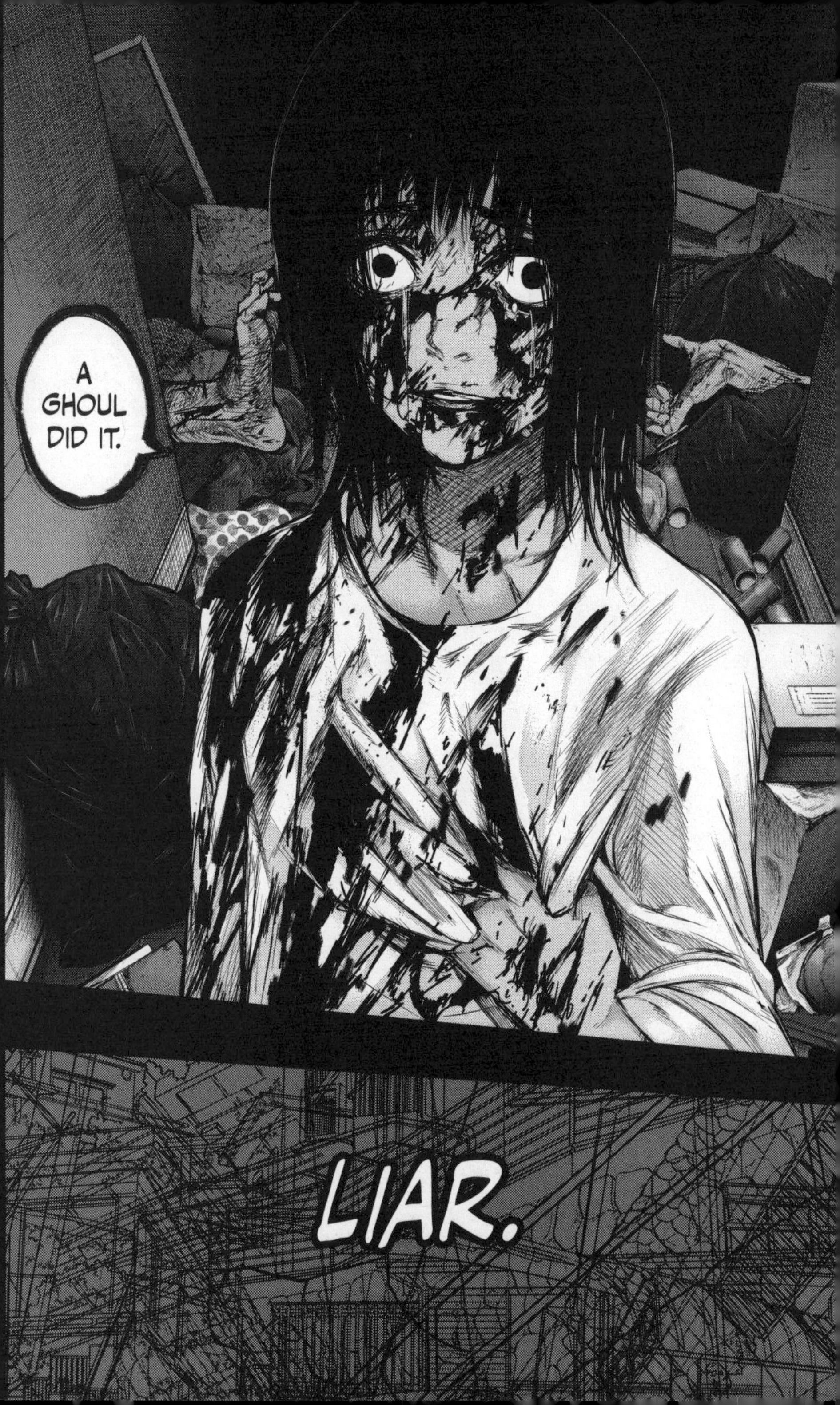
A GHOUL DID IT.
LIAR.

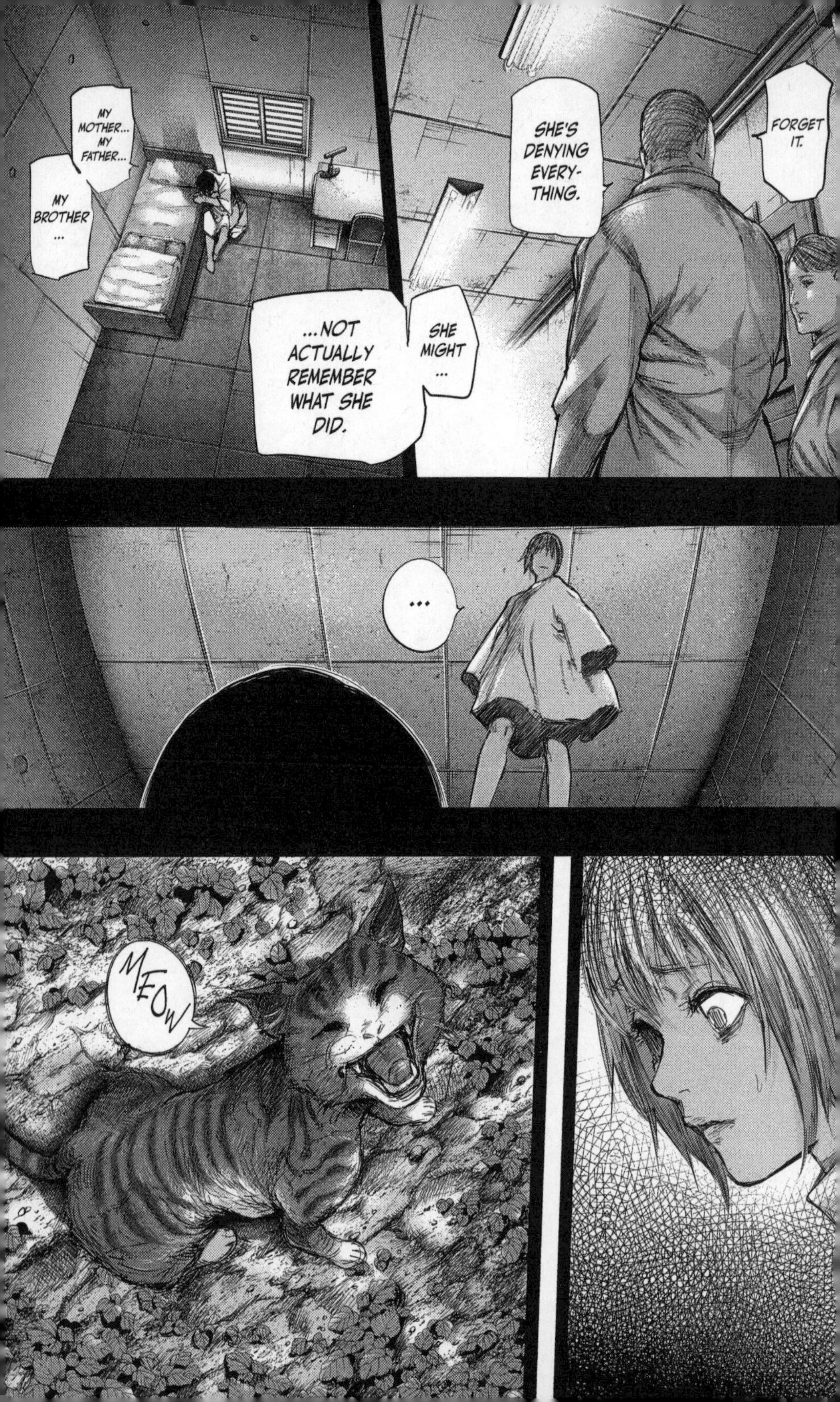
FORGET IT.
SHE'S DENYING EVERYTHING.
SHE MIGHT...
...NOT ACTUALLY REMEMBER WHAT SHE DID.
MY MOTHER... MY FATHER...
MY BROTHER...
...
MEOW

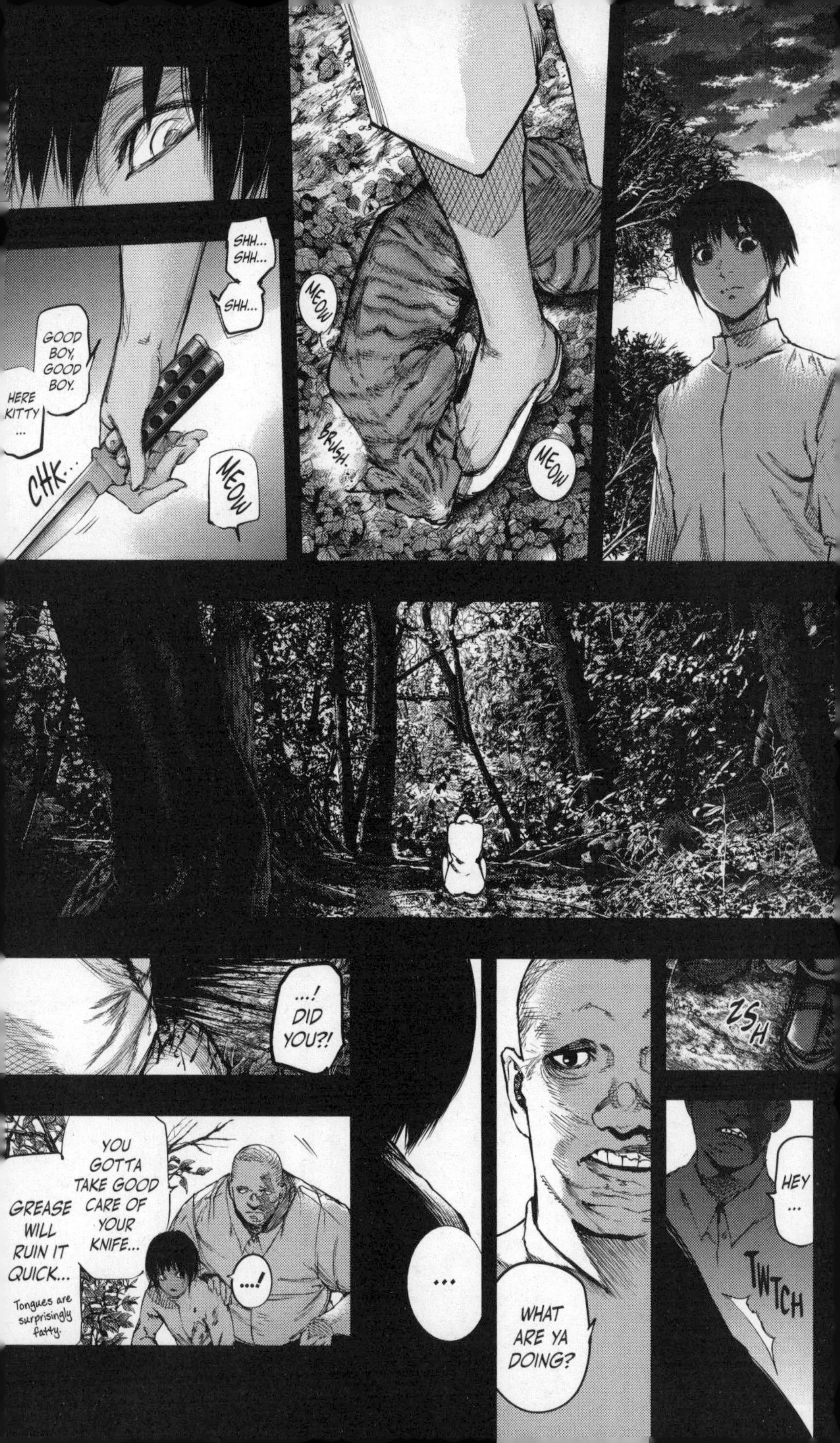
MEOW
BRUSH.
MEOW
SHH... SHH...
SHH...
GOOD BOY, GOOD BOY.
HERE KITTY ...
CHK...
MEOW
ZSH
HEY ...
TWTCH
WHAT ARE YA DOING?
...
...! DID YOU?!
YOU GOTTA TAKE GOOD CARE OF YOUR KNIFE...
GREASE WILL RUIN IT QUICK...
...!
Tongues are surprisingly fatty.

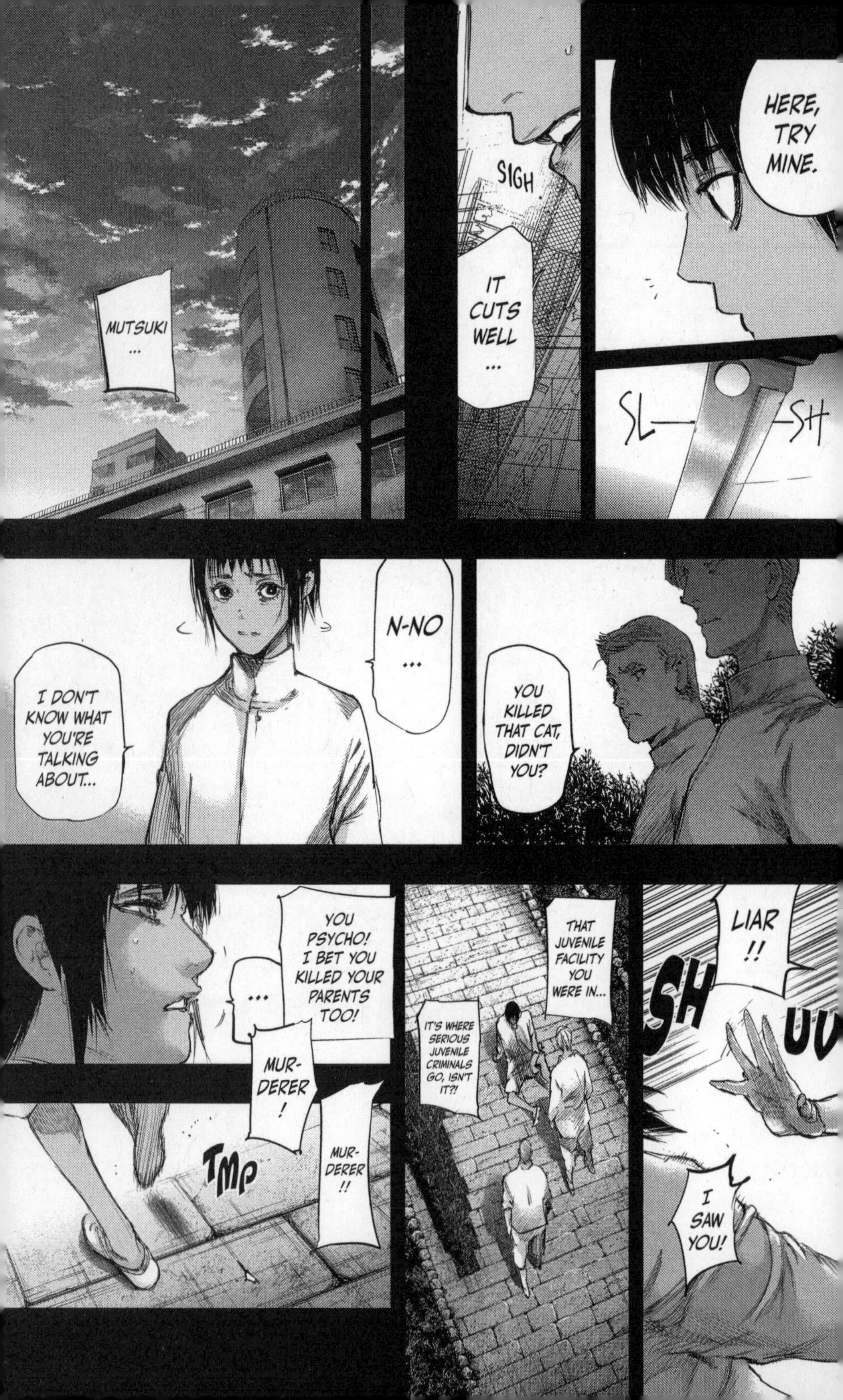
HERE, TRY MINE.
SL—SH
SIGH
IT CUTS WELL...
MUTSUKI...
YOU KILLED THAT CAT, DIDN'T YOU?
N-NO...
I DON'T KNOW WHAT YOU'RE TALKING ABOUT...
LIAR!!
SHUU
I SAW YOU!
THAT JUVENILE FACILITY YOU WERE IN...
IT'S WHERE SERIOUS JUVENILE CRIMINALS GO, ISN'T IT?!
YOU PSYCHO! I BET YOU KILLED YOUR PARENTS TOO!
...
MUR-DERER!
TMP
MUR-DERER!!

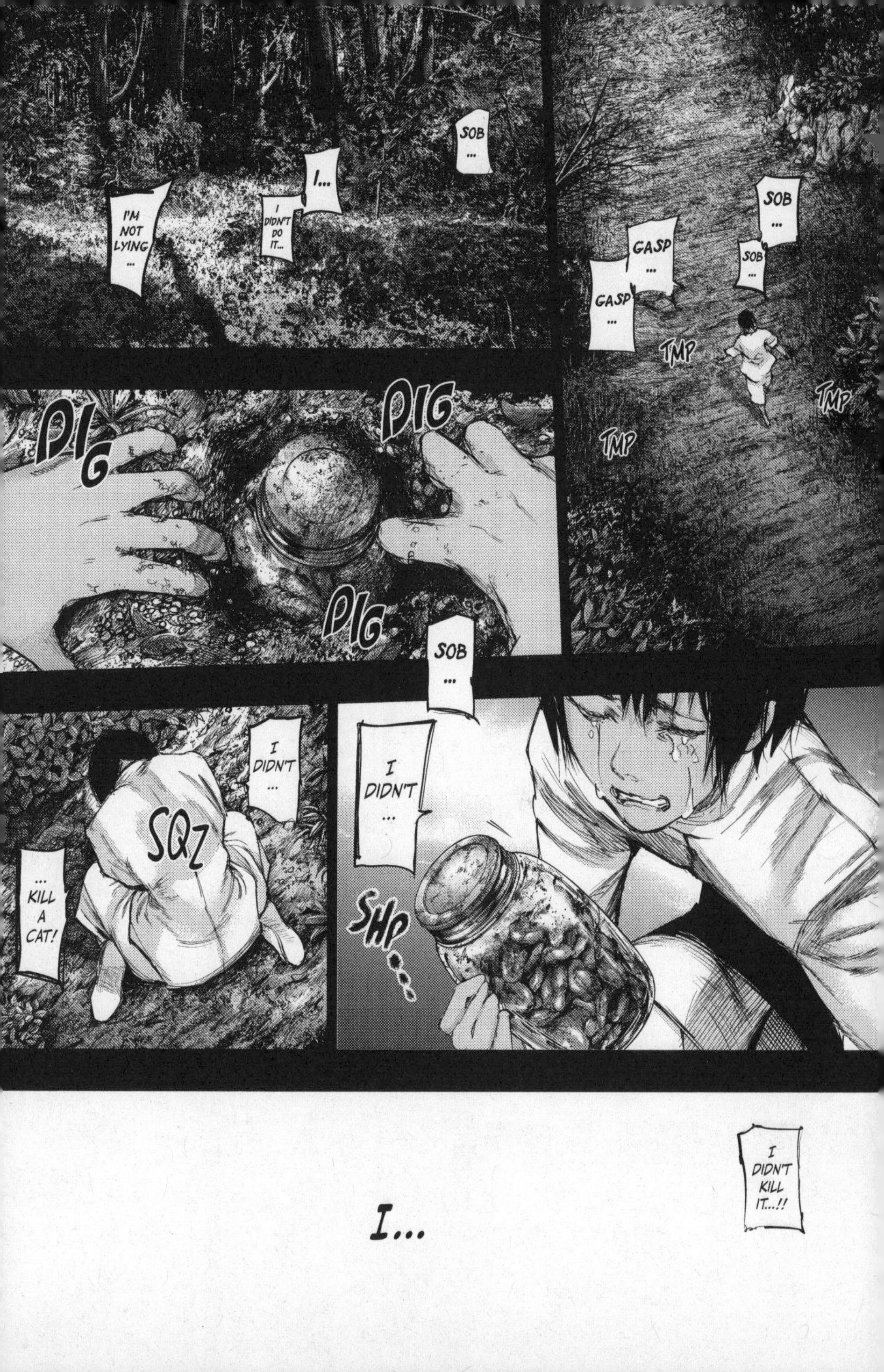
SOB...
SOB...
GASP...
GASP...
TMP
TMP
TMP
SOB...
I...
I DIDN'T DO IT...
I'M NOT LYING...
DIG
DIG
DIG
SOB...
I DIDN'T...
SHP...
I DIDN'T...
SQZ
...KILL A CAT!
I DIDN'T KILL IT...!!
I...

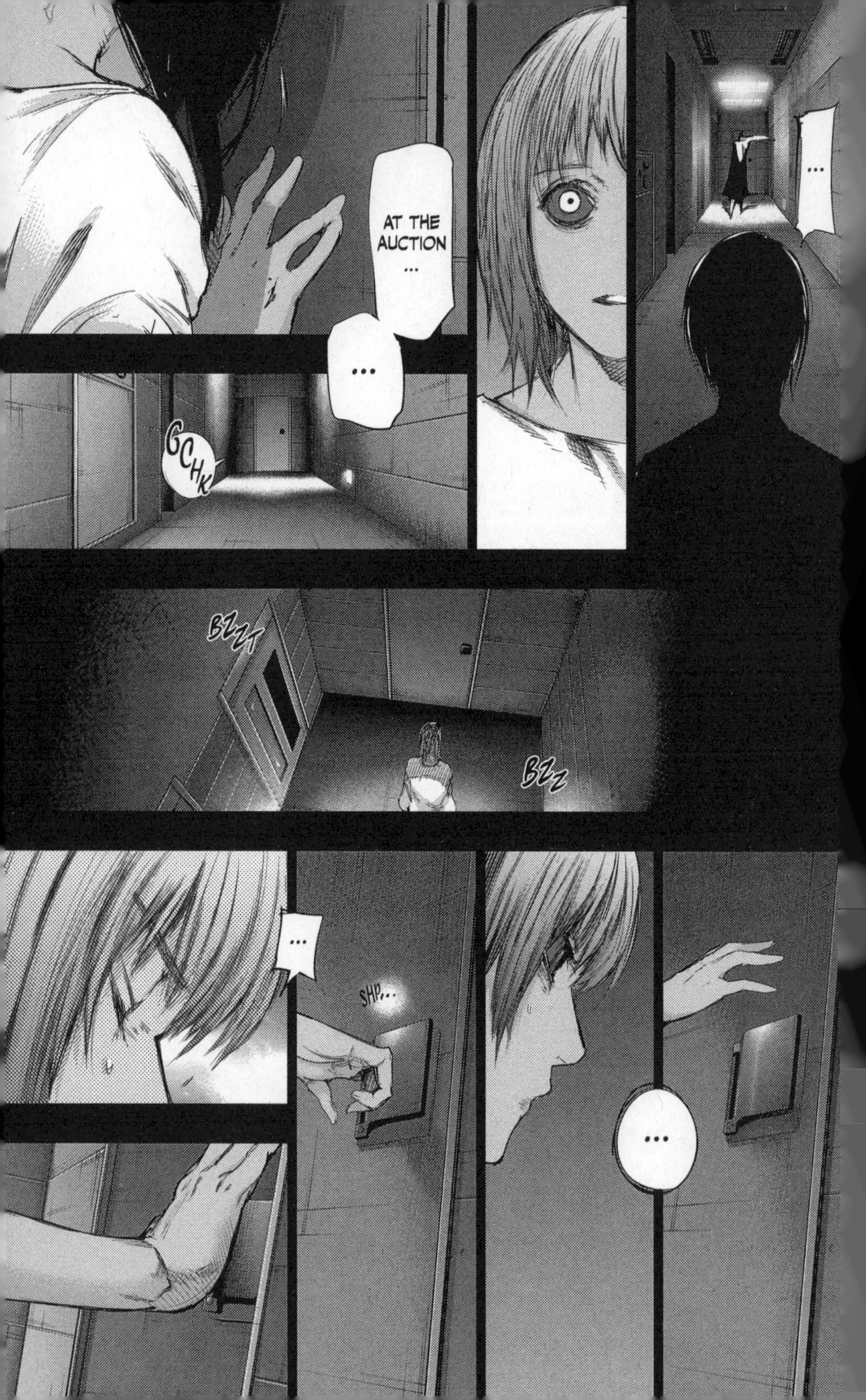
...
AT THE AUCTION ...
...
GCHK
BZZZT
BZZ
...
SHP...
...

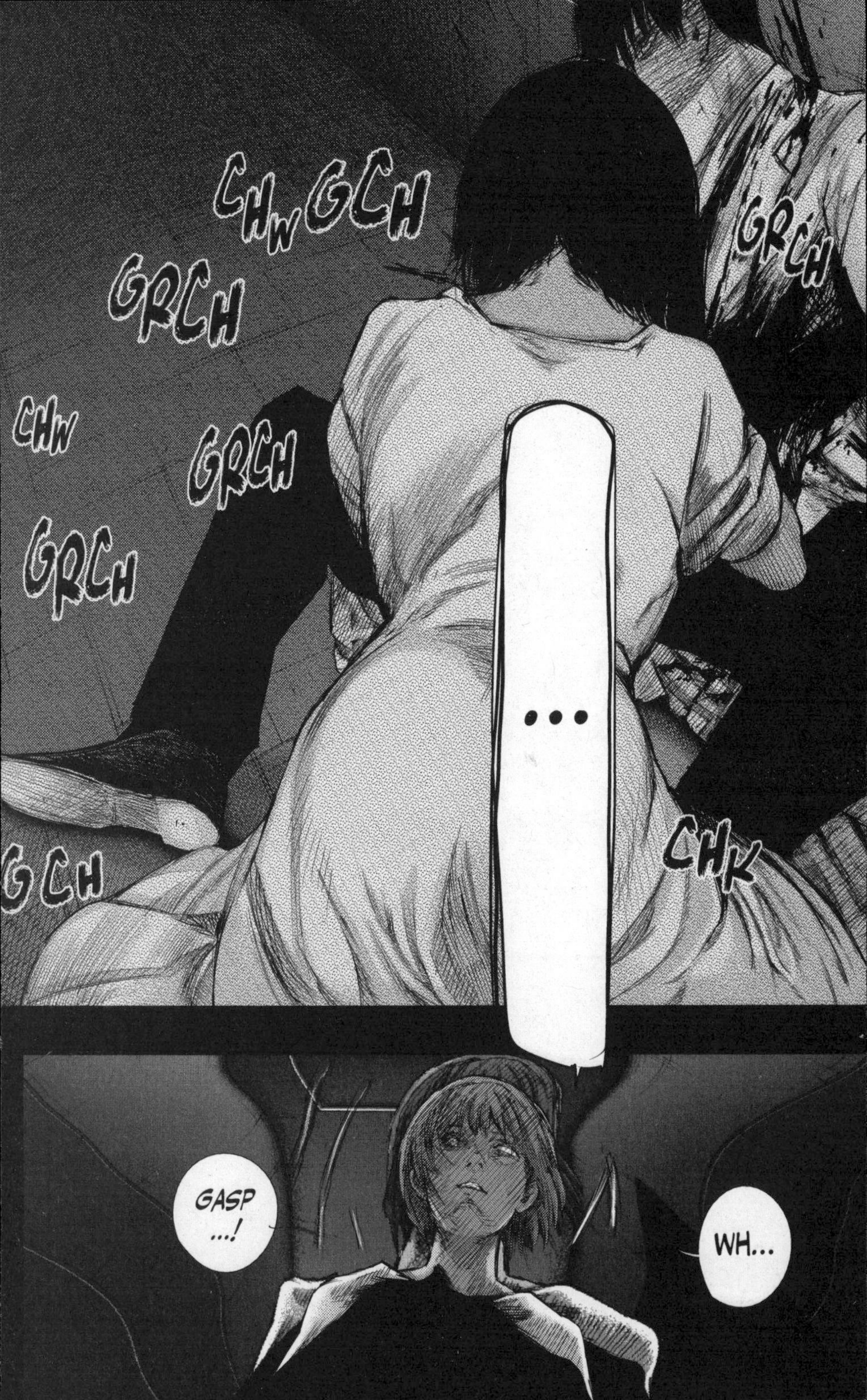
GRCH
CHWGCH
GRCH
CHW
GRCH
GRCH
...
CHK
GCH
WH...
GASP ...!

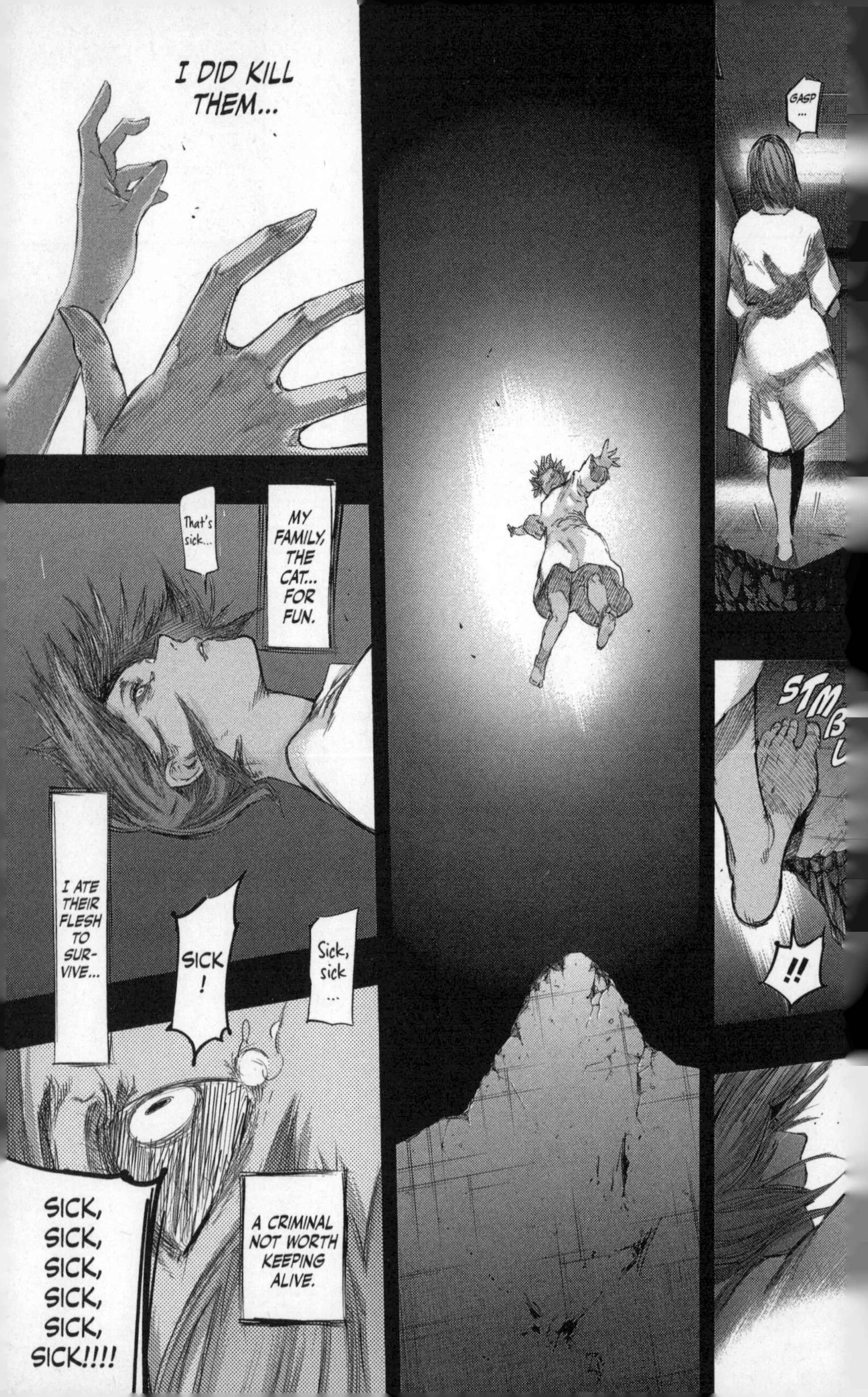
GASP...
STMBL
!!
I DID KILL THEM...
MY FAMILY, THE CAT... FOR FUN.
That's sick...
Sick, sick...
SICK!
I ATE THEIR FLESH TO SUR-VIVE...
A CRIMINAL NOT WORTH KEEPING ALIVE.
SICK, SICK, SICK, SICK, SICK, SICK!!!!

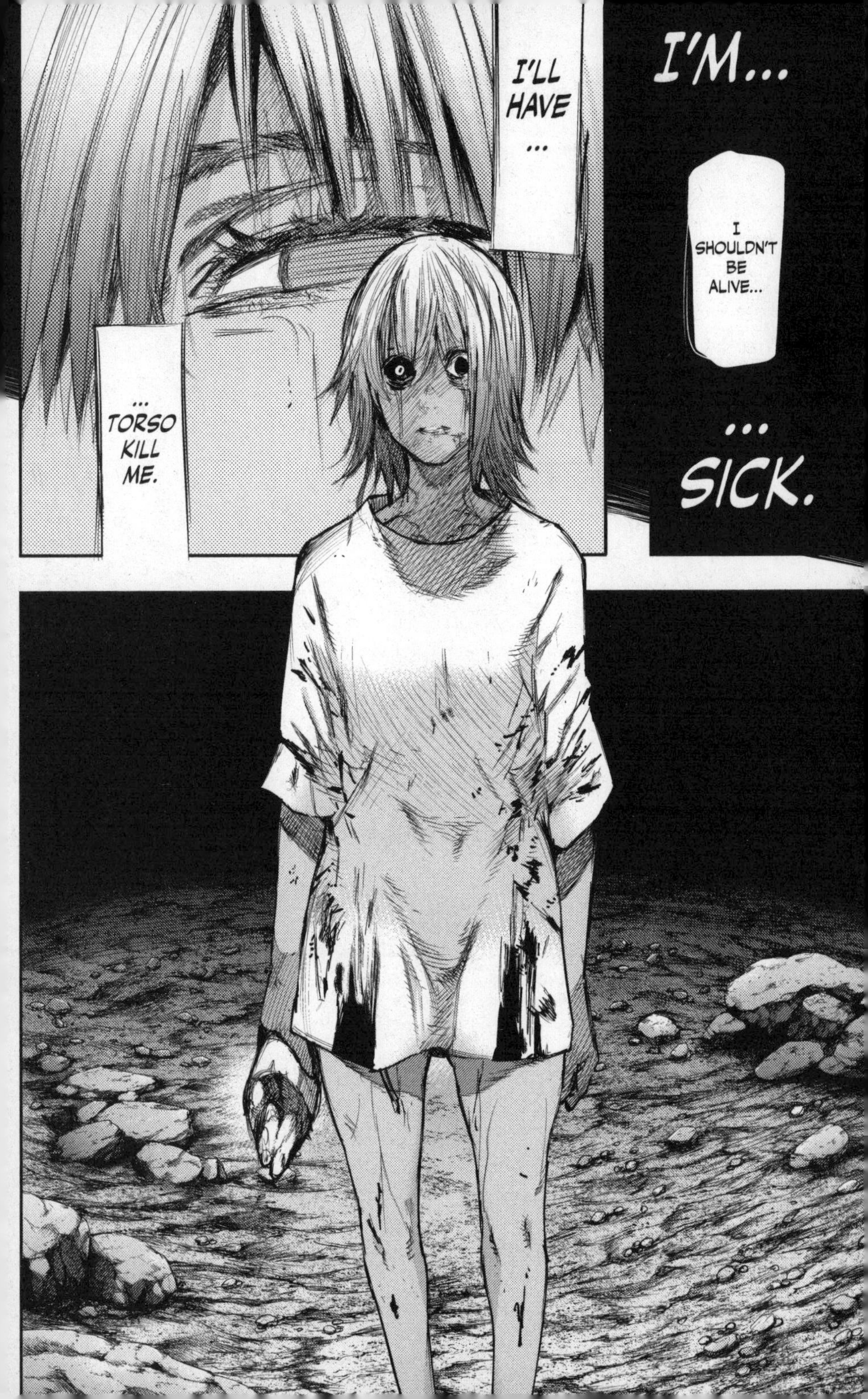
I'M...
I SHOULDN'T BE ALIVE...
...SICK.
I'LL HAVE ...
... TORSO KILL ME.

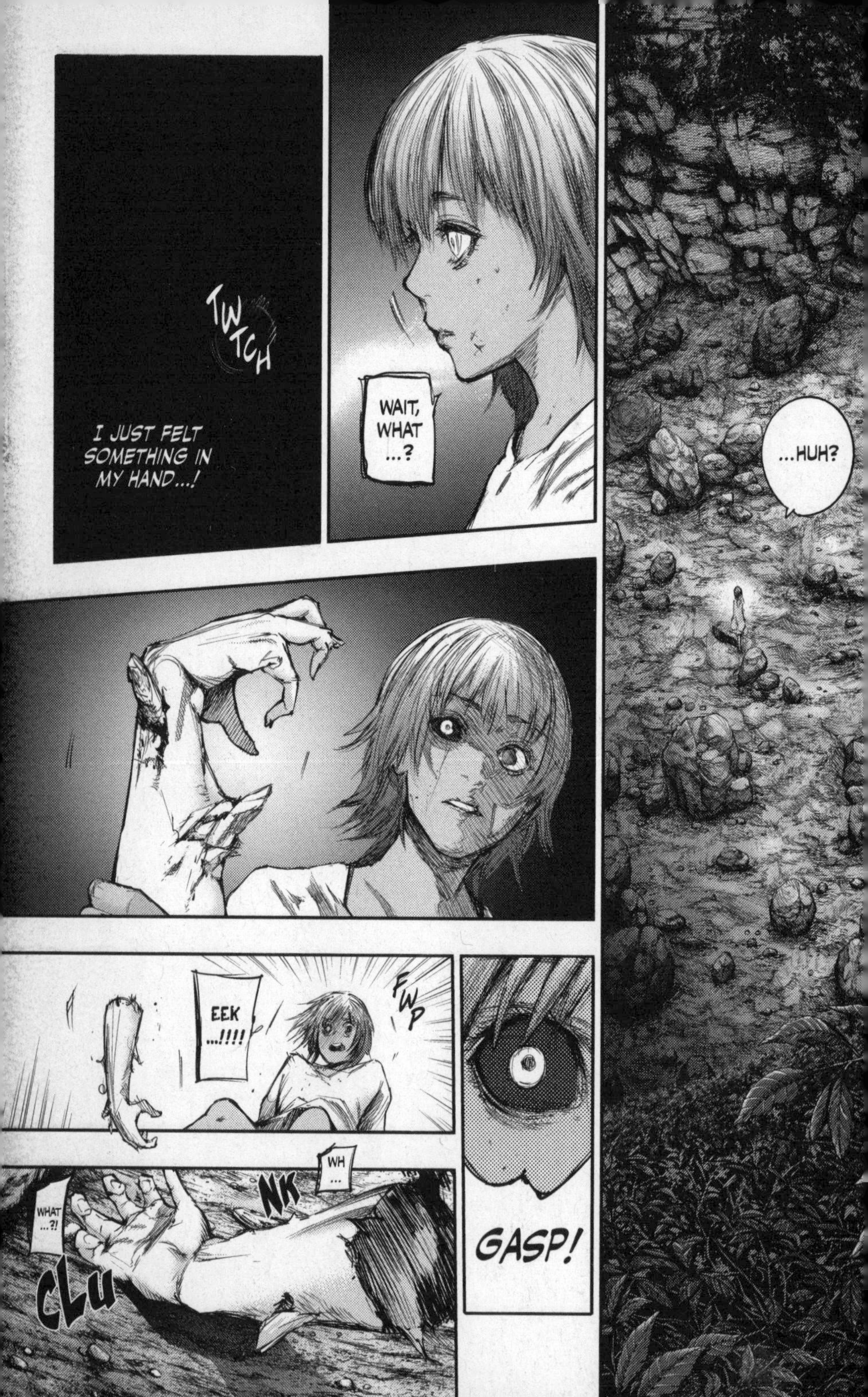
...HUH?
WAIT, WHAT ...?
TWITCH
I JUST FELT SOMETHING IN MY HAND...!
GASP!
FWP
EEK ...!!!!
WH ...
NK
WHAT ...?!
CLU

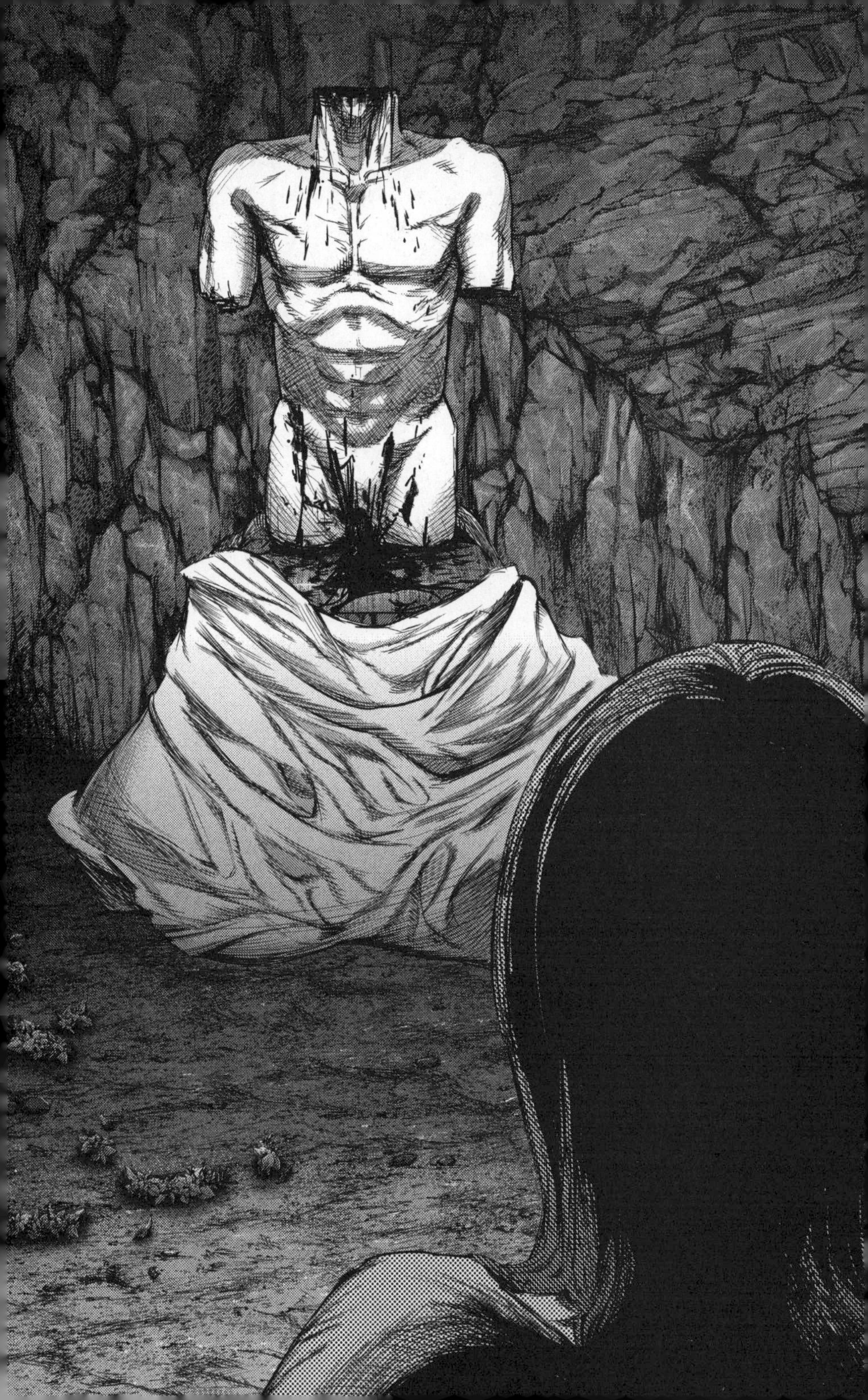

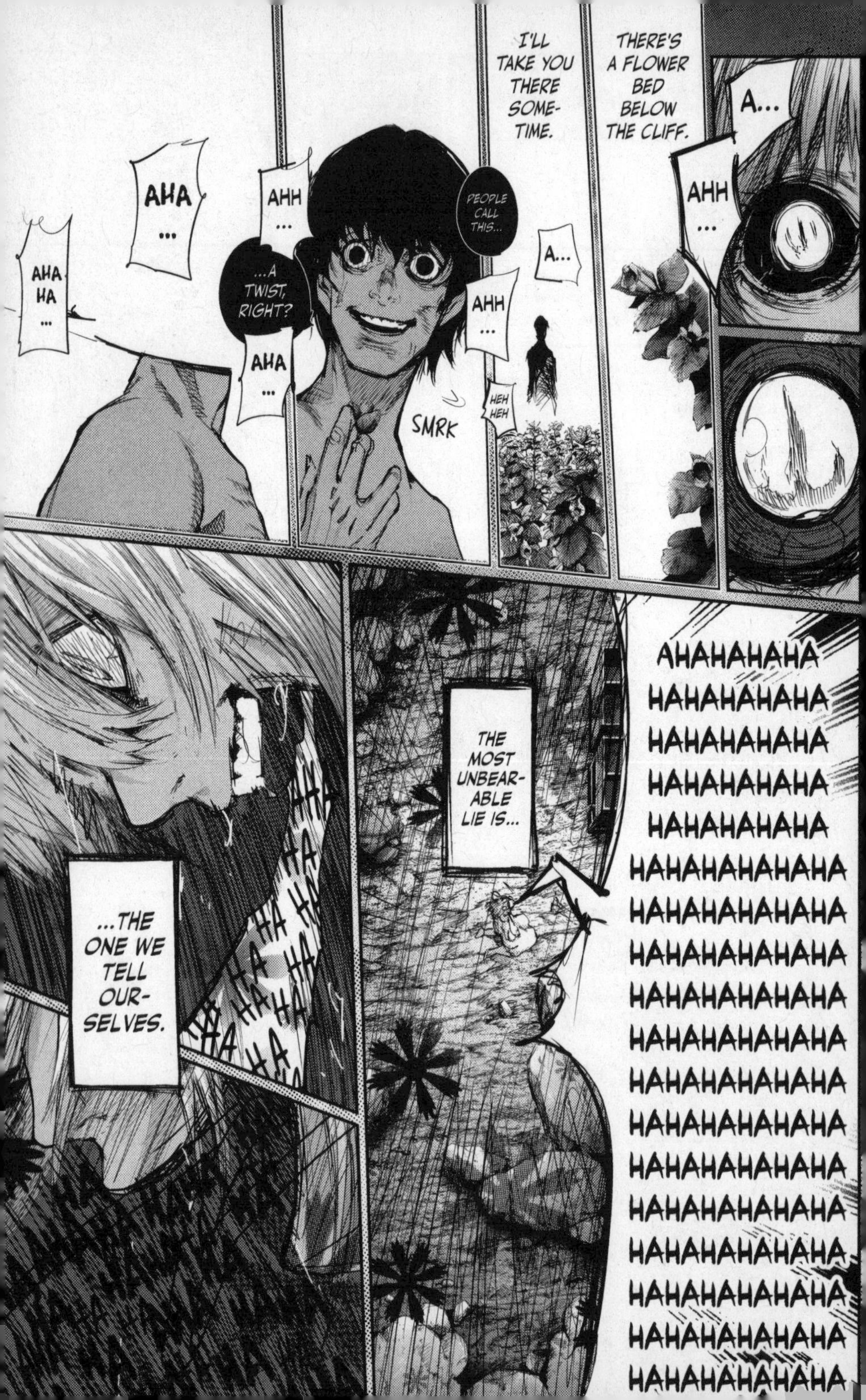
A...
AHH ...
THERE'S A FLOWER BED BELOW THE CLIFF.
I'LL TAKE YOU THERE SOME-TIME.
A...
AHH ...
HEH HEH
PEOPLE CALL THIS...
...A TWIST, RIGHT?
AHH ...
AHA ...
SMRK
AHA ...
AHA HA ...
AHAHAHAHA
HAHAHAHAHA
HAHAHAHAHA
HAHAHAHAHA
HAHAHAHAHA
HAHAHAHAHAHA
HAHAHAHAHAHA
HAHAHAHAHAHA
HAHAHAHAHAHA
HAHAHAHAHAHA
HAHAHAHAHAHA
HAHAHAHAHAHA
HAHAHAHAHAHA
HAHAHAHAHAHA
HAHAHAHAHAHA
HAHAHAHAHAHA
HAHAHAHAHAHA
HAHAHAHAHAHA
THE MOST UNBEARABLE LIE IS...
...THE ONE WE TELL OUR-SELVES.

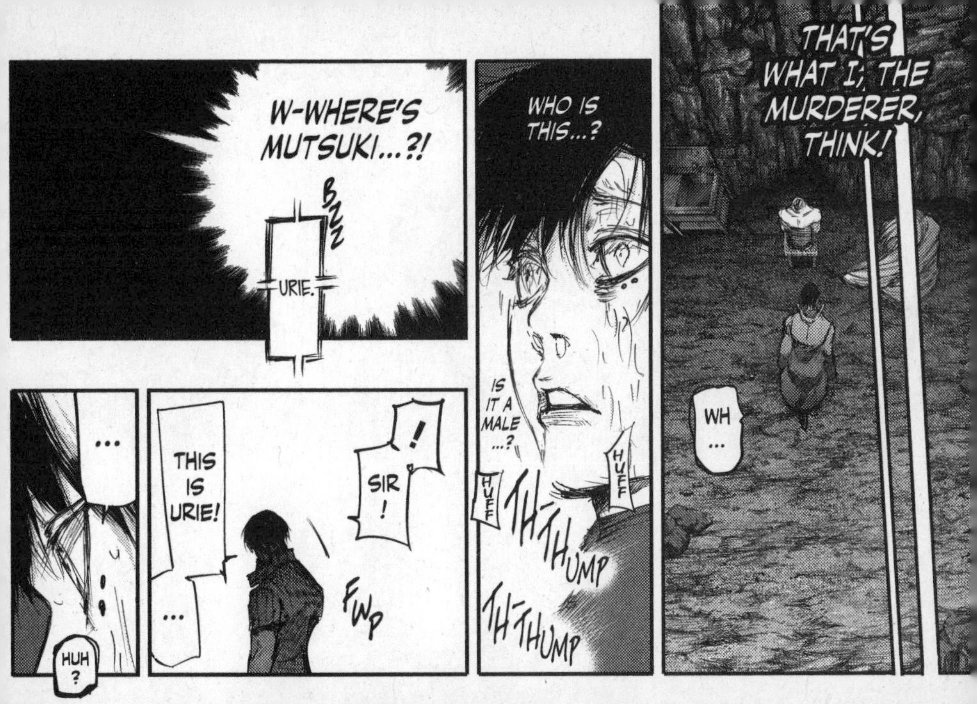
THAT'S WHAT I, THE MURDERER, THINK!
WH ...
WHO IS THIS...?
IS IT A MALE ...?
HUFF
HUFF
THTHUMP
THTHUMP
W-WHERE'S MUTSUKI...?!
BZZ
URIE.
!
SIR!
THIS IS URIE!
...
FWP
...
HUH ?

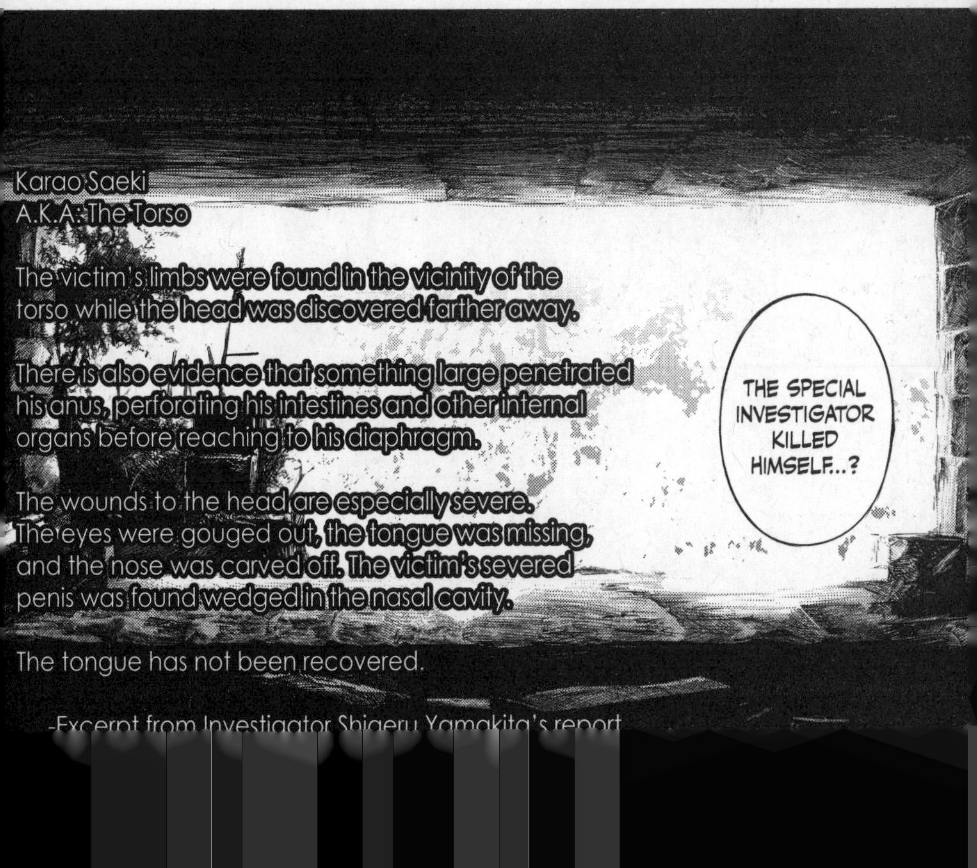
THE SPECIAL INVESTIGATOR KILLED HIMSELF...?

Karao Saeki
A.K.A: The Torso

The victim's limbs were found in the vicinity of the torso while the head was discovered farther away.

There is also evidence that something large penetrated his anus, perforating his intestines and other internal organs before reaching to his diaphragm.

The wounds to the head are especially severe. The eyes were gouged out, the tongue was missing, and the nose was carved off. The victim's severed penis was found wedged in the nasal cavity.

The tongue has not been recovered.

-Excerpt from Investigator Shigeru Yamakita's report

Tsukiyama at work ②

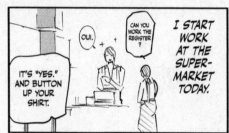

I START WORK AT THE SUPER-MARKET TODAY.
CAN YOU WORK THE REGISTER?
OUI.
IT'S "YES." AND BUTTON UP YOUR SHIRT.
SO THIS IS A CASH REGIS-TER...!
TAKE THE MONEY... RETURN CORRECT CHANGE...
IT'S THE PANDORA'S BOX OF SUPER-MARKETS ...
GULP
AND I WAS PUT IN CHARGE OF IT...!!
FANTASTIC CRAZY SYSTEM!!
CLK CLK CLK CLK CLK
210
THEY FIRED ME FOR BEING TOO LOUD.
OH.
THAT'S A VALID REASON.
CAMERAS

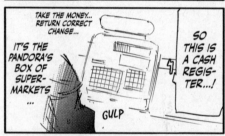

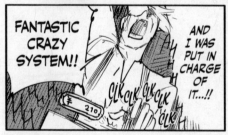

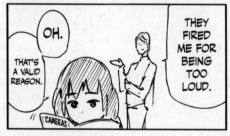

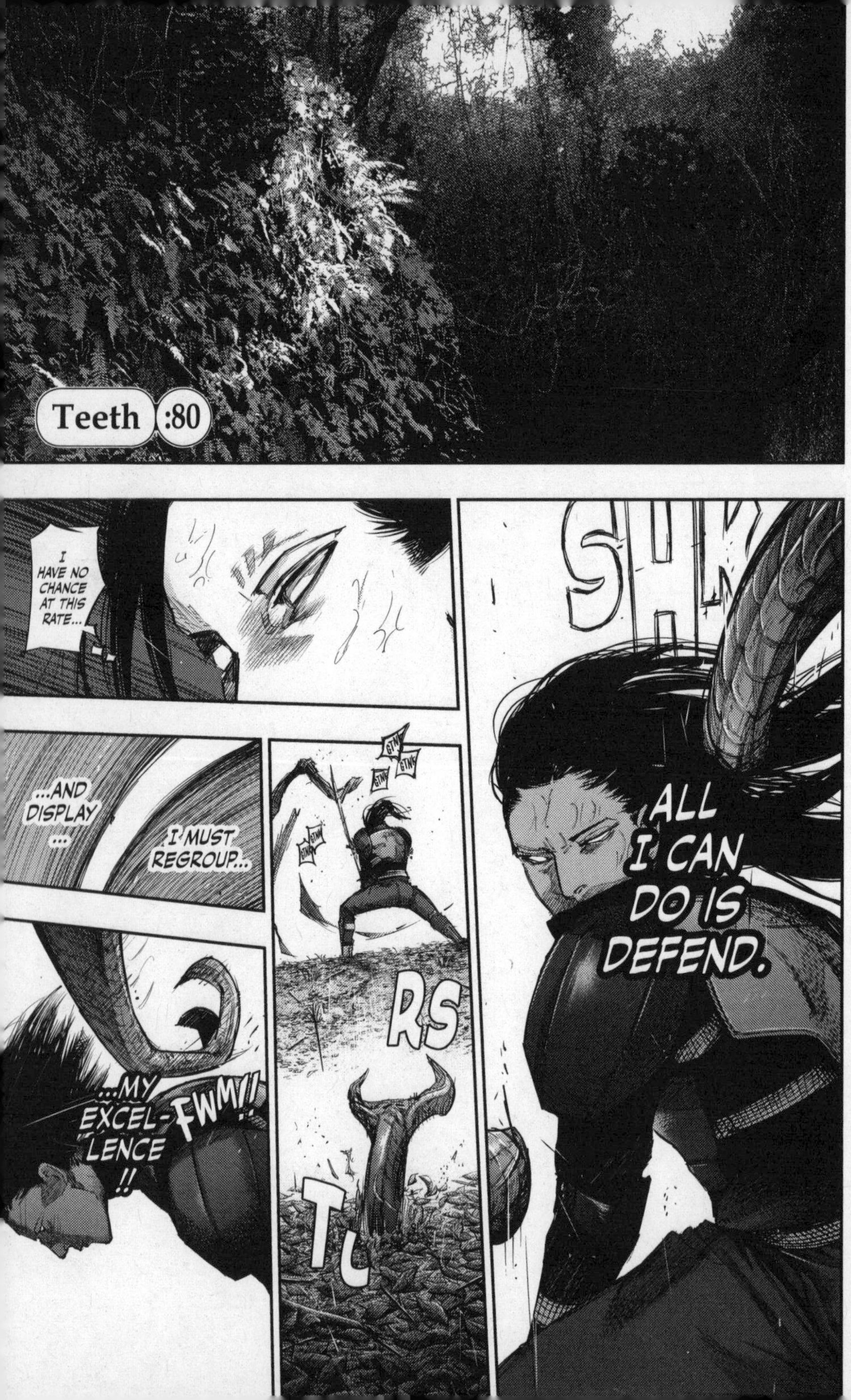
Teeth :80
SHK
ALL I CAN DO IS DEFEND.
I HAVE NO CHANCE AT THIS RATE...
GTNK
GTNK
GTNK
GTNK
GTNK
RS
TU
I MUST REGROUP...
...AND DISPLAY...
...MY EXCEL-LENCE!!
FWM!!

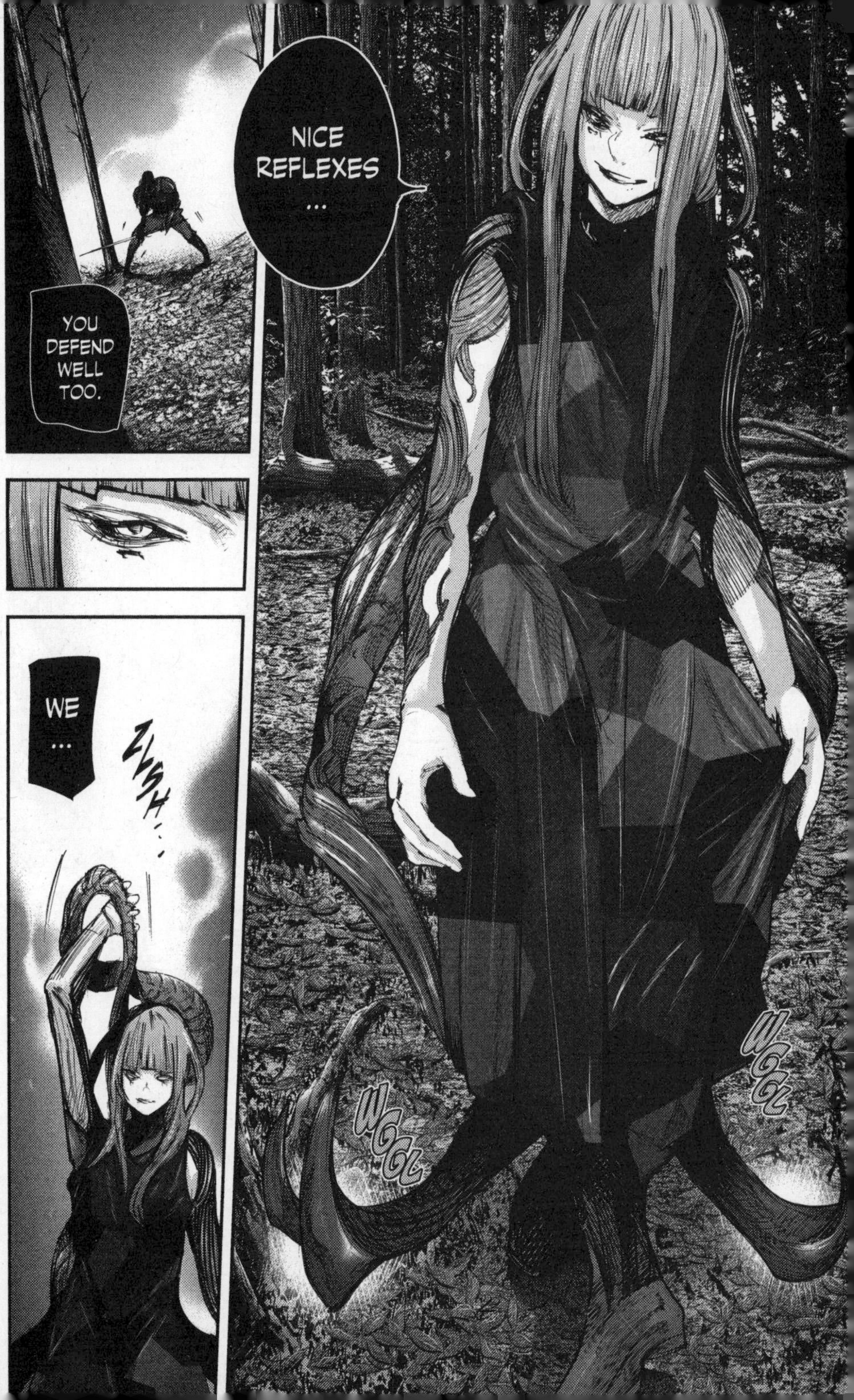
NICE REFLEXES ...
WGGL
WGGL
YOU DEFEND WELL TOO.
WE ...
ZLSH

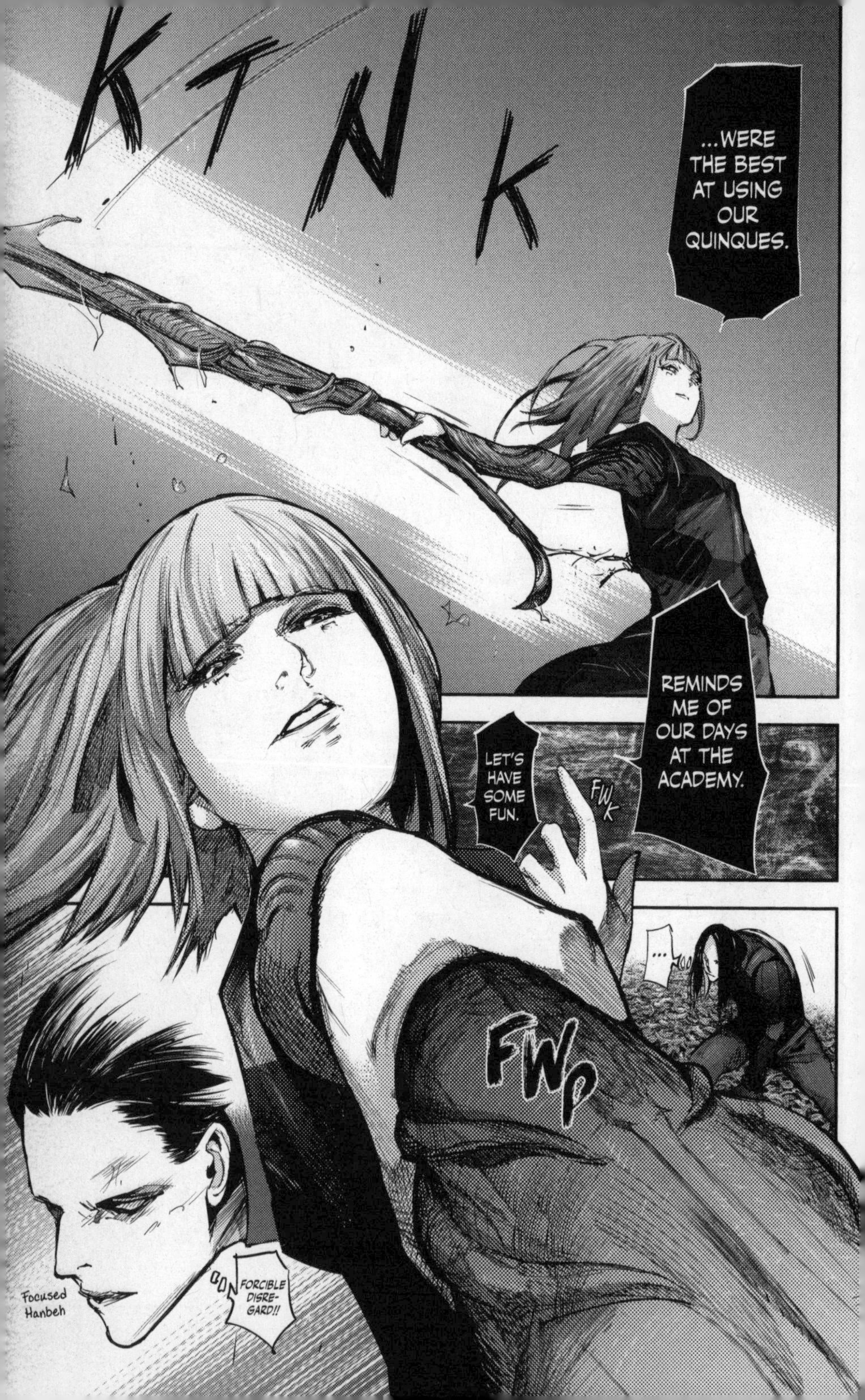
KTNK
...WERE THE BEST AT USING OUR QUINQUES.
REMINDS ME OF OUR DAYS AT THE ACADEMY.
LET'S HAVE SOME FUN.
FWK
...
FWP
FORCIBLE DISRE-GARD!!
Focused Hanbeh

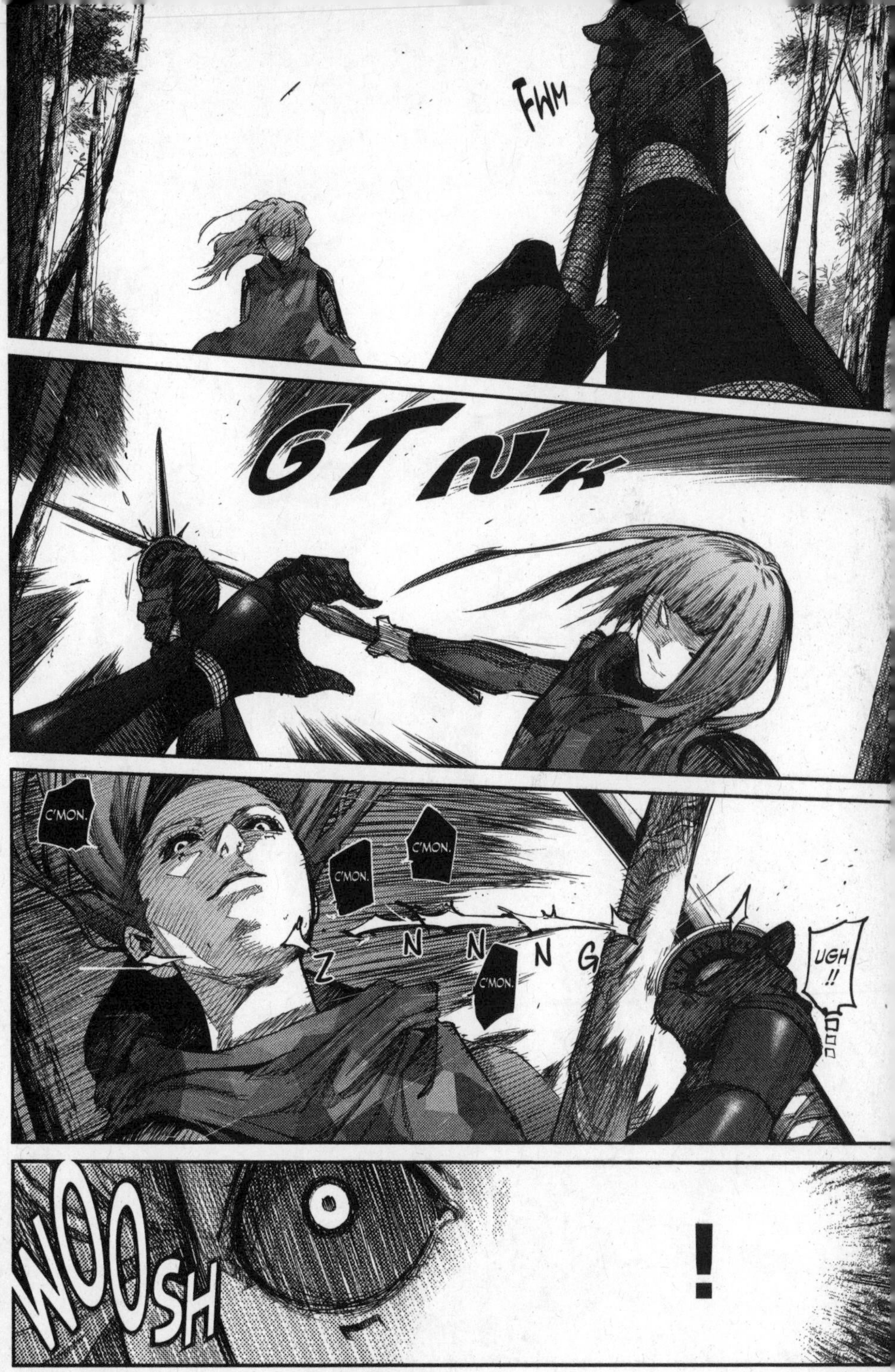
FWM
GTNK
UGH!!
C'MON.
C'MON.
C'MON.
ZNNNG
C'MON.
!
WOOSH

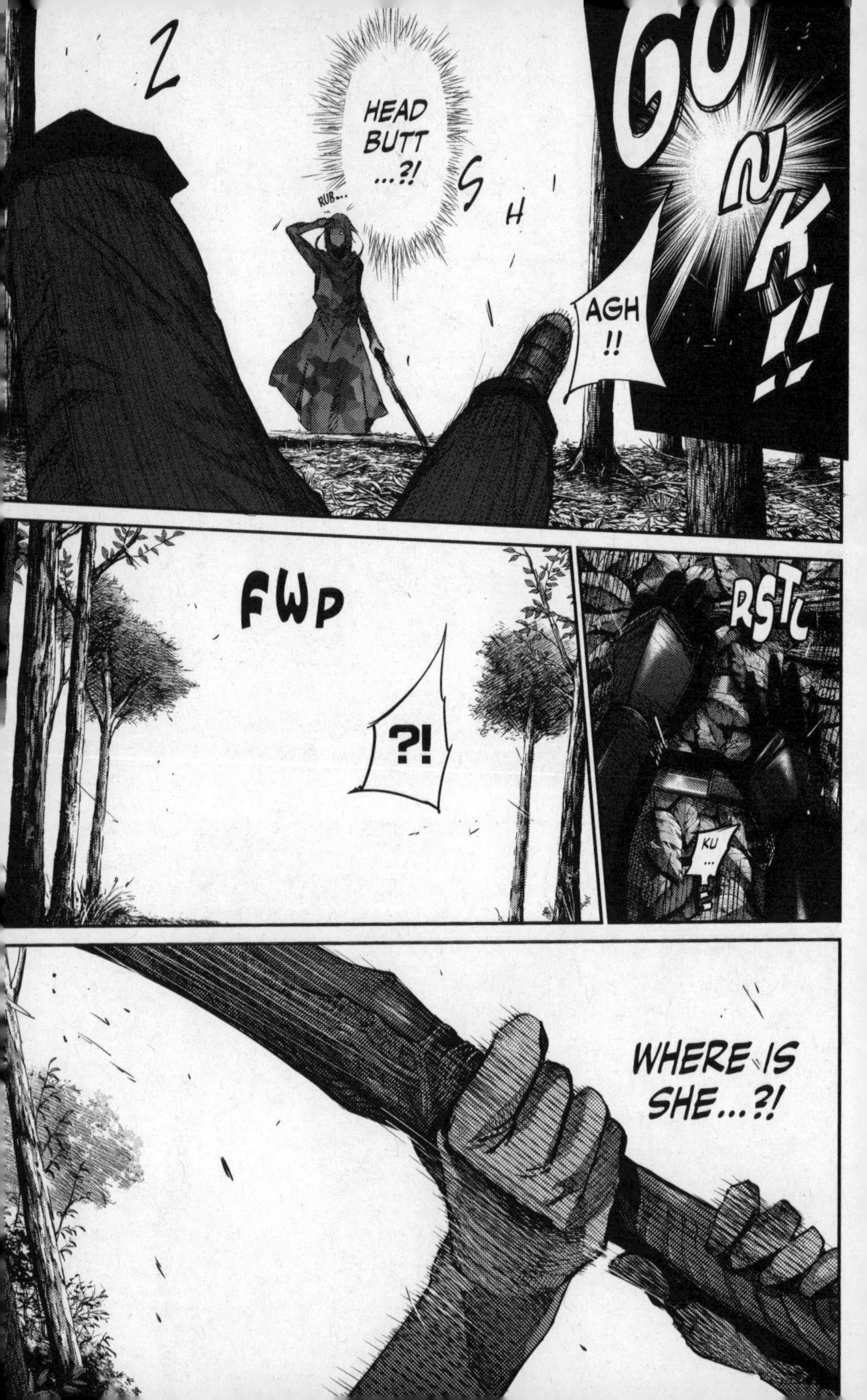
GONK!!
AGH!!
Z
HEAD BUTT ...?!
RUB...
SH
RSTL
KU...
FWP
?!
WHERE IS SHE...?!

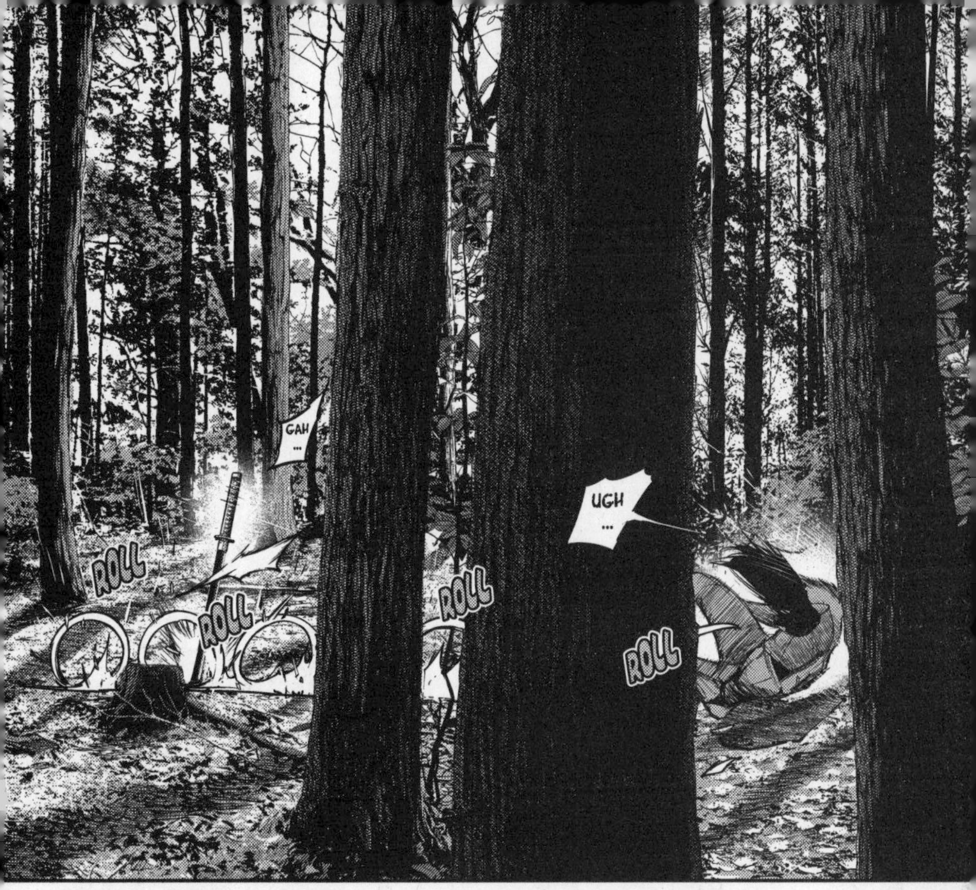
UGH ...
ROLL
ROLL
GAH ...
ROLL
ROLL

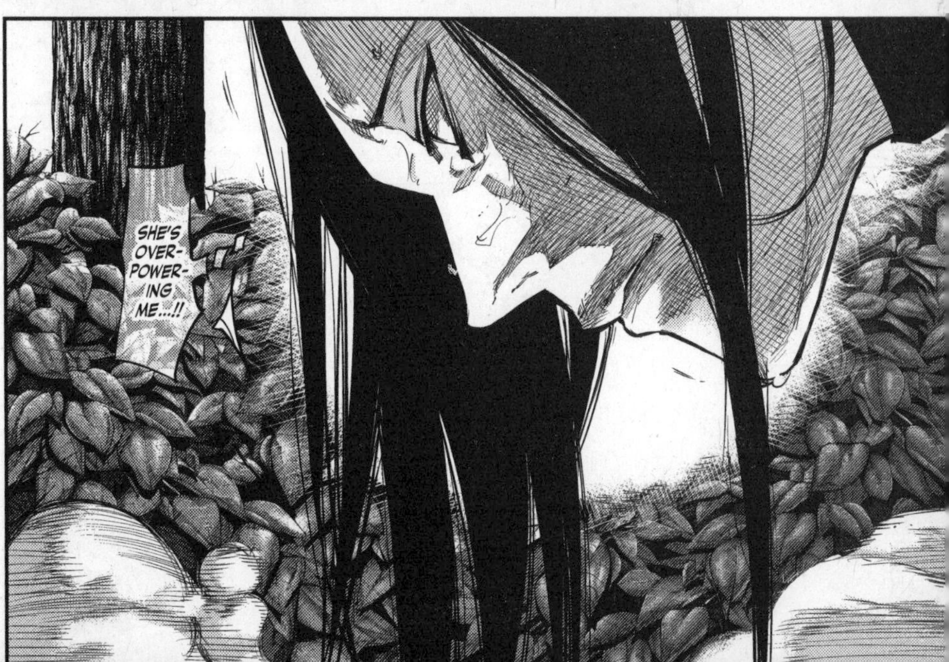
SHE'S OVER-POWER-ING ME...!!

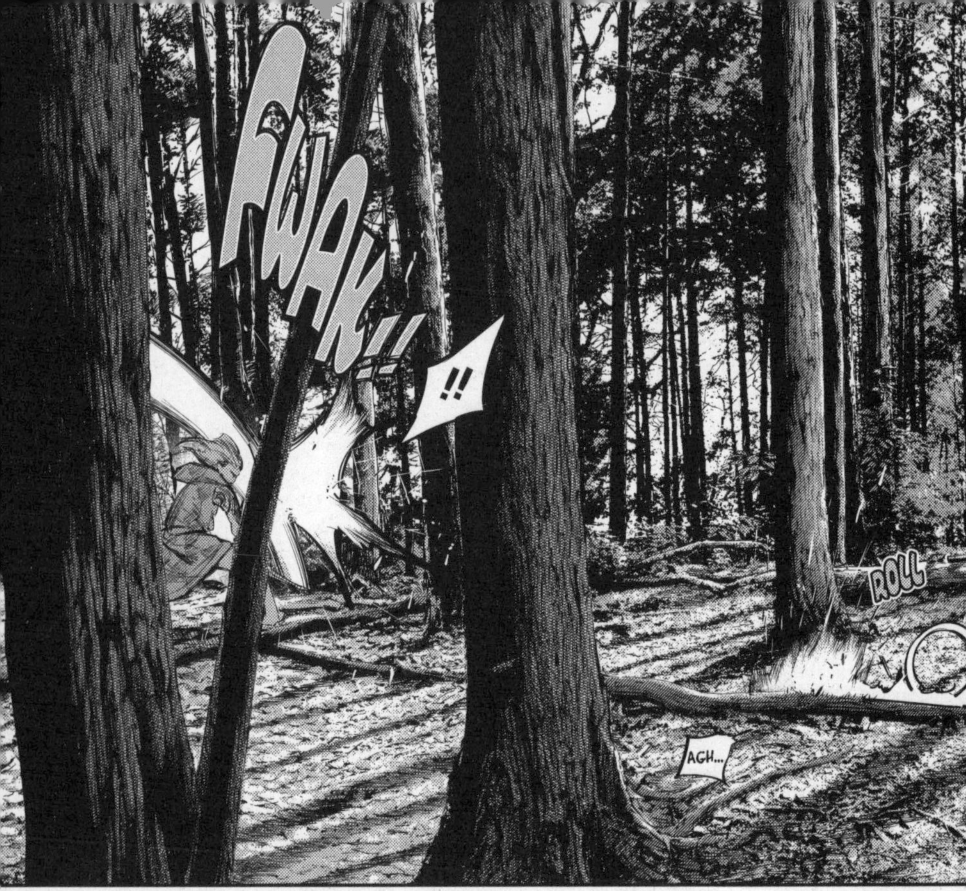
FWAK!!
!!
ROLL
AGH...
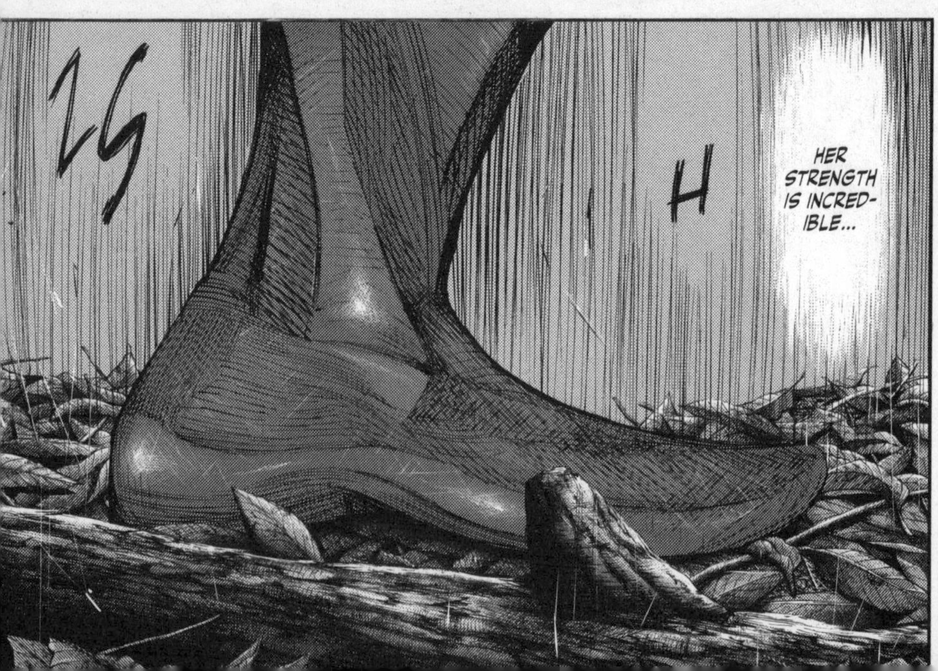
ZSH
HER STRENGTH IS INCREDIBLE...

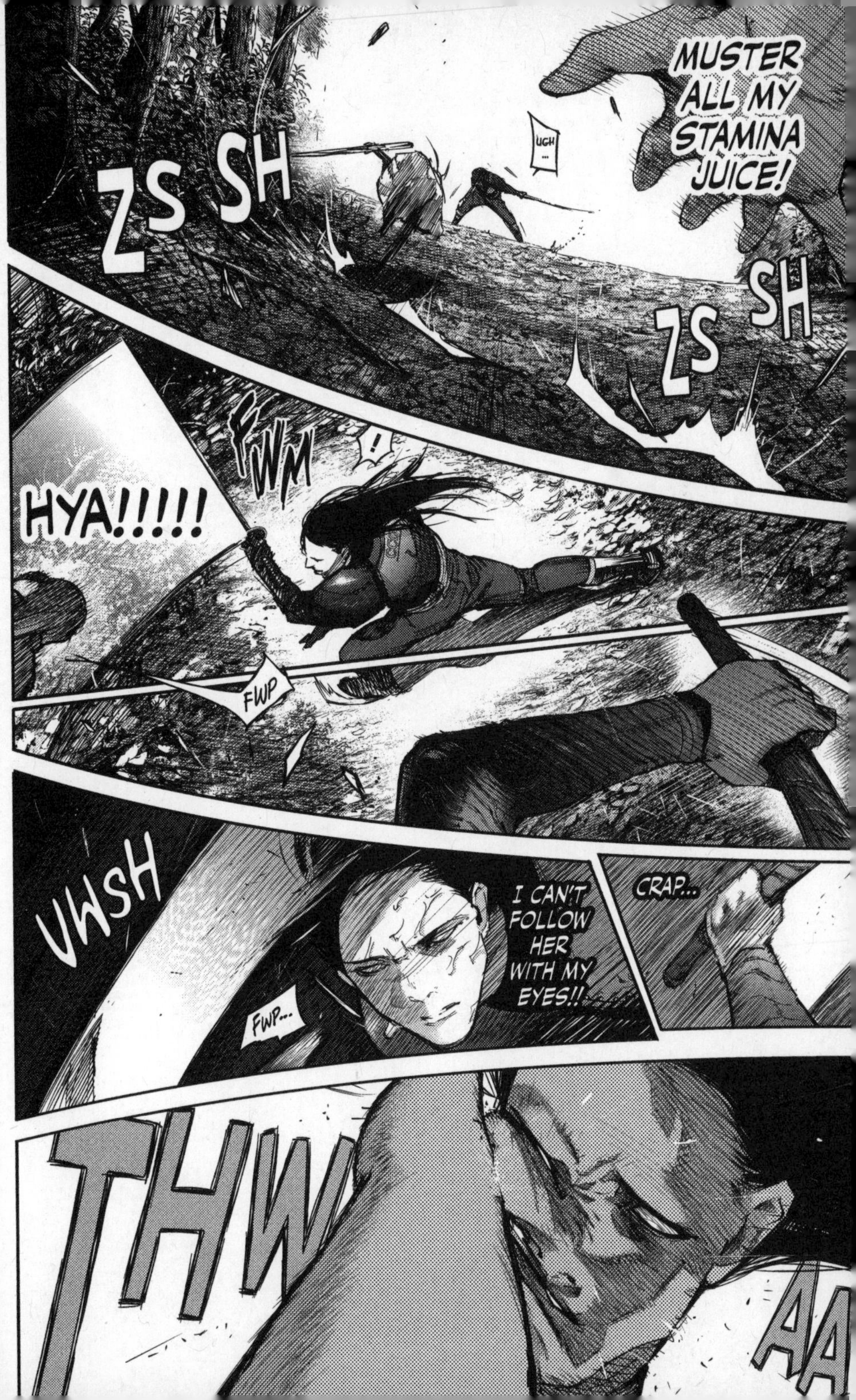
MUSTER ALL MY STAMINA JUICE!
UGH...
ZS SH
ZS SH
!
FWM
HYA!!!!!
FWP
CRAP...
I CAN'T FOLLOW HER WITH MY EYES!!
UWSH
FWP...
AA
THW

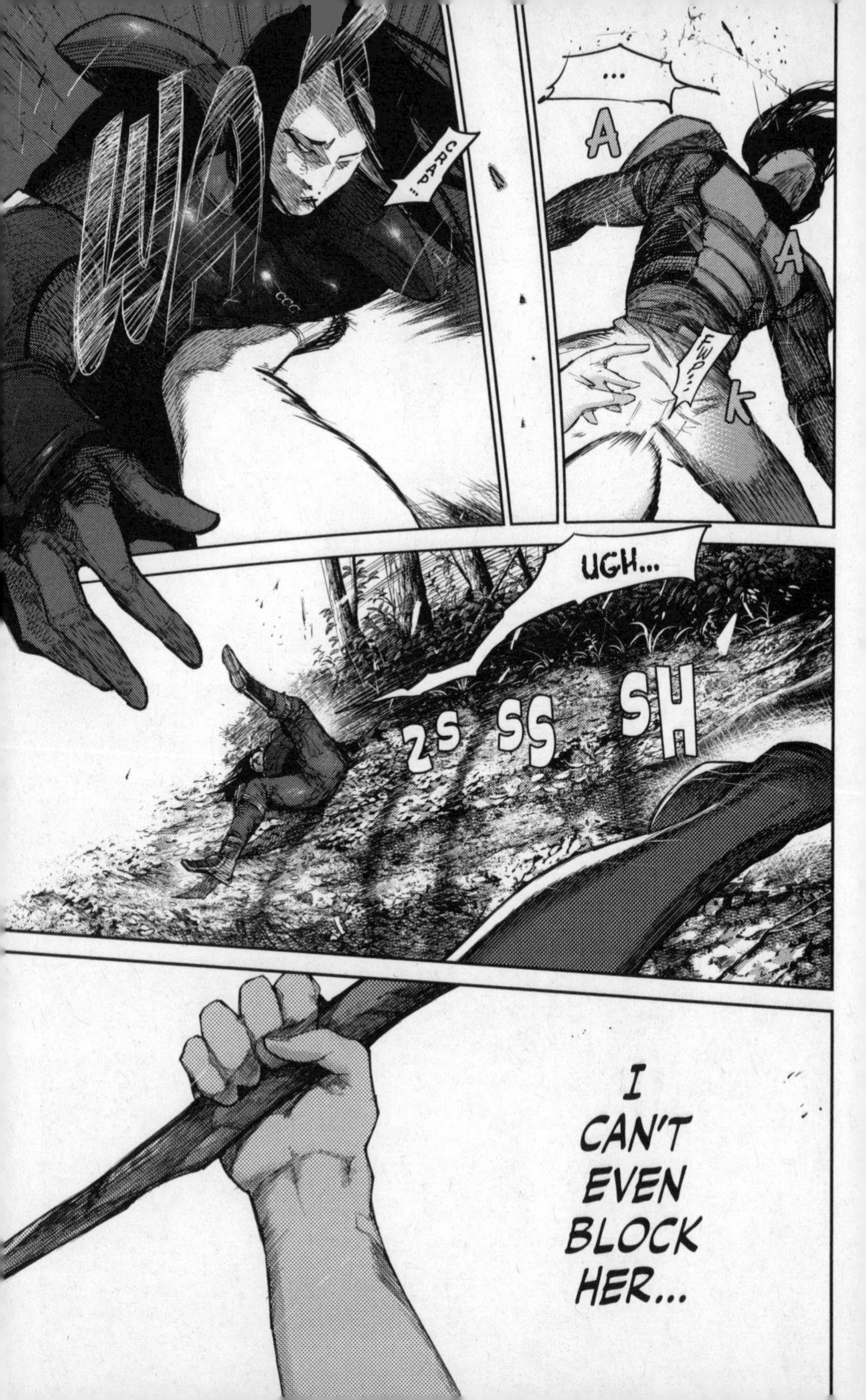
...
A
A
FWP...
K
CRAP...
UGH...
ZS SS SH
I CAN'T EVEN BLOCK HER...

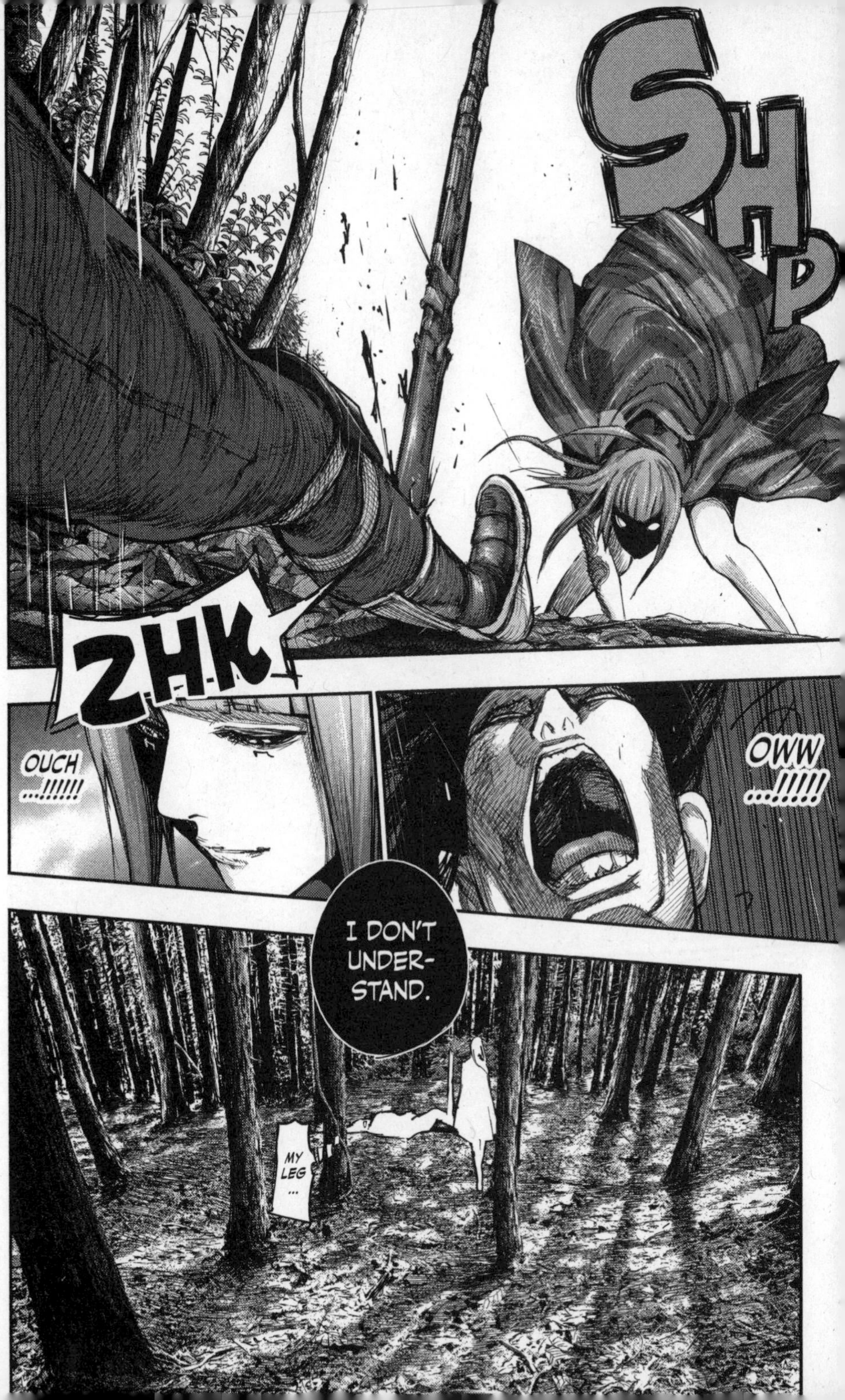
SHP
ZHK
OWW ...!!!!!
OUCH ...!!!!!!
I DON'T UNDER-STAND.
MY LEG ...

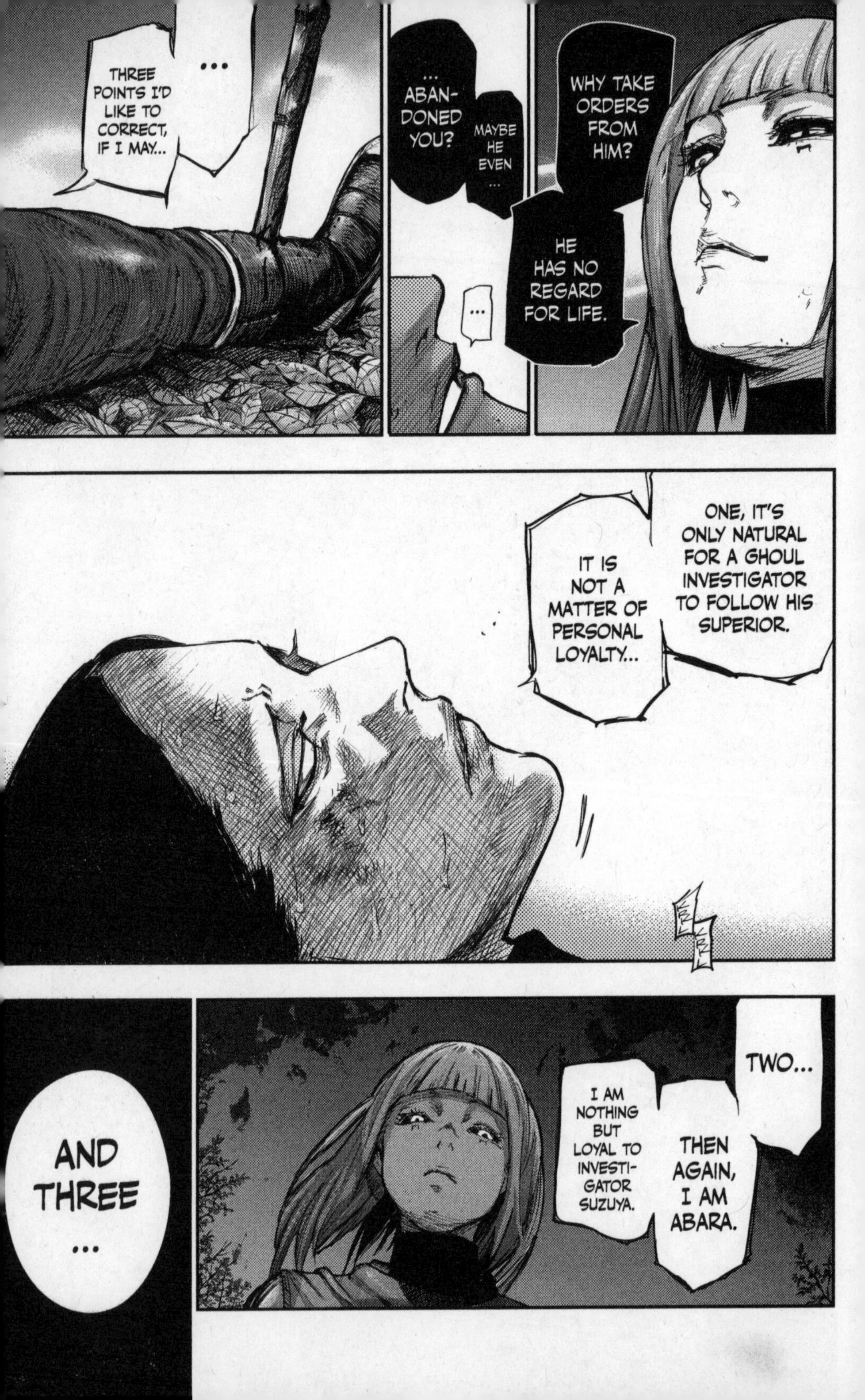
WHY TAKE ORDERS FROM HIM?
HE HAS NO REGARD FOR LIFE.
MAYBE HE EVEN ...
... ABAN-DONED YOU?
...
...
THREE POINTS I'D LIKE TO CORRECT, IF I MAY...
ONE, IT'S ONLY NATURAL FOR A GHOUL INVESTIGATOR TO FOLLOW HIS SUPERIOR.
IT IS NOT A MATTER OF PERSONAL LOYALTY...
TWO...
THEN AGAIN, I AM ABARA.
I AM NOTHING BUT LOYAL TO INVESTI-GATOR SUZUYA.
AND THREE ...

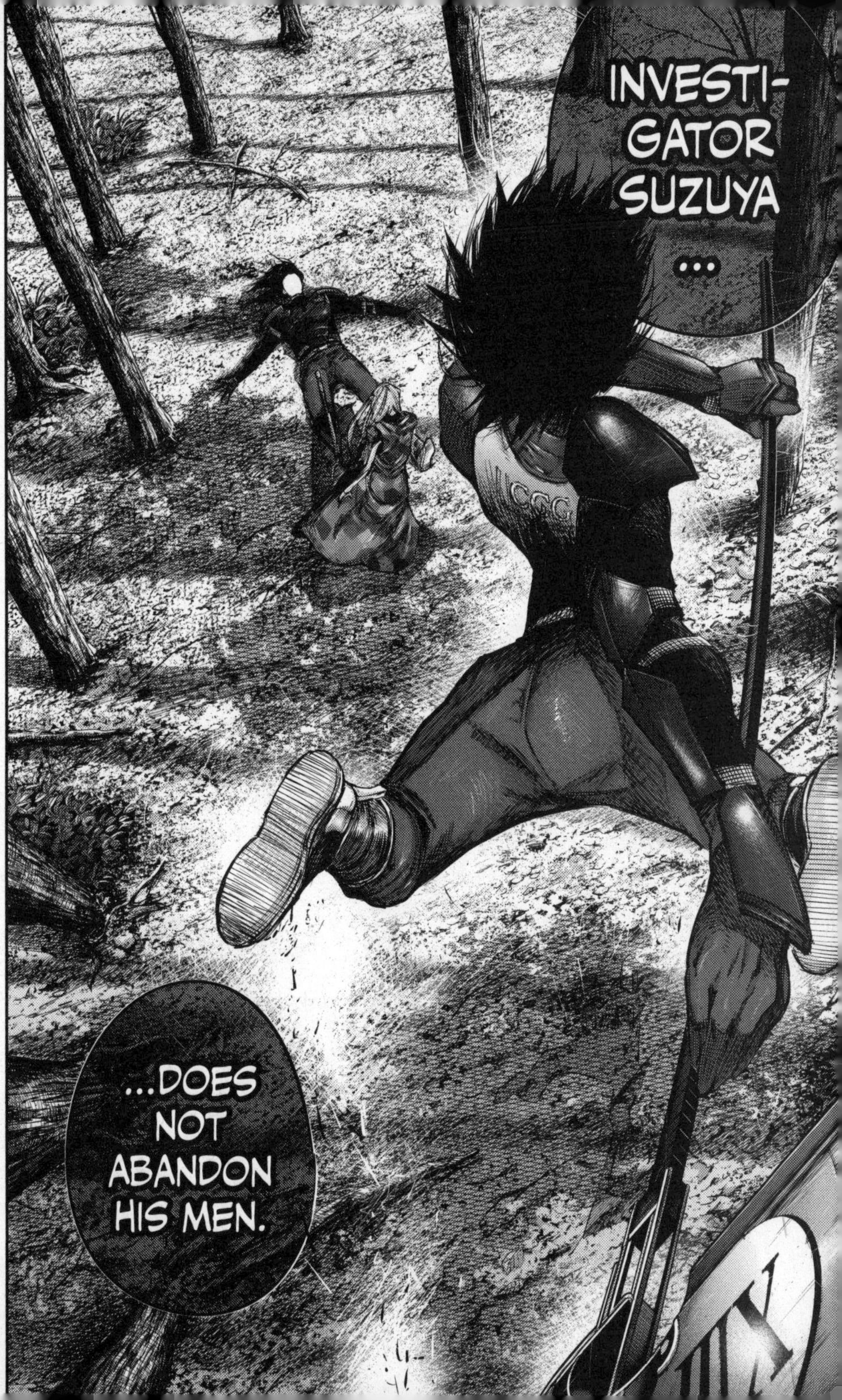
INVESTI-GATOR SUZUYA ...
...DOES NOT ABANDON HIS MEN.

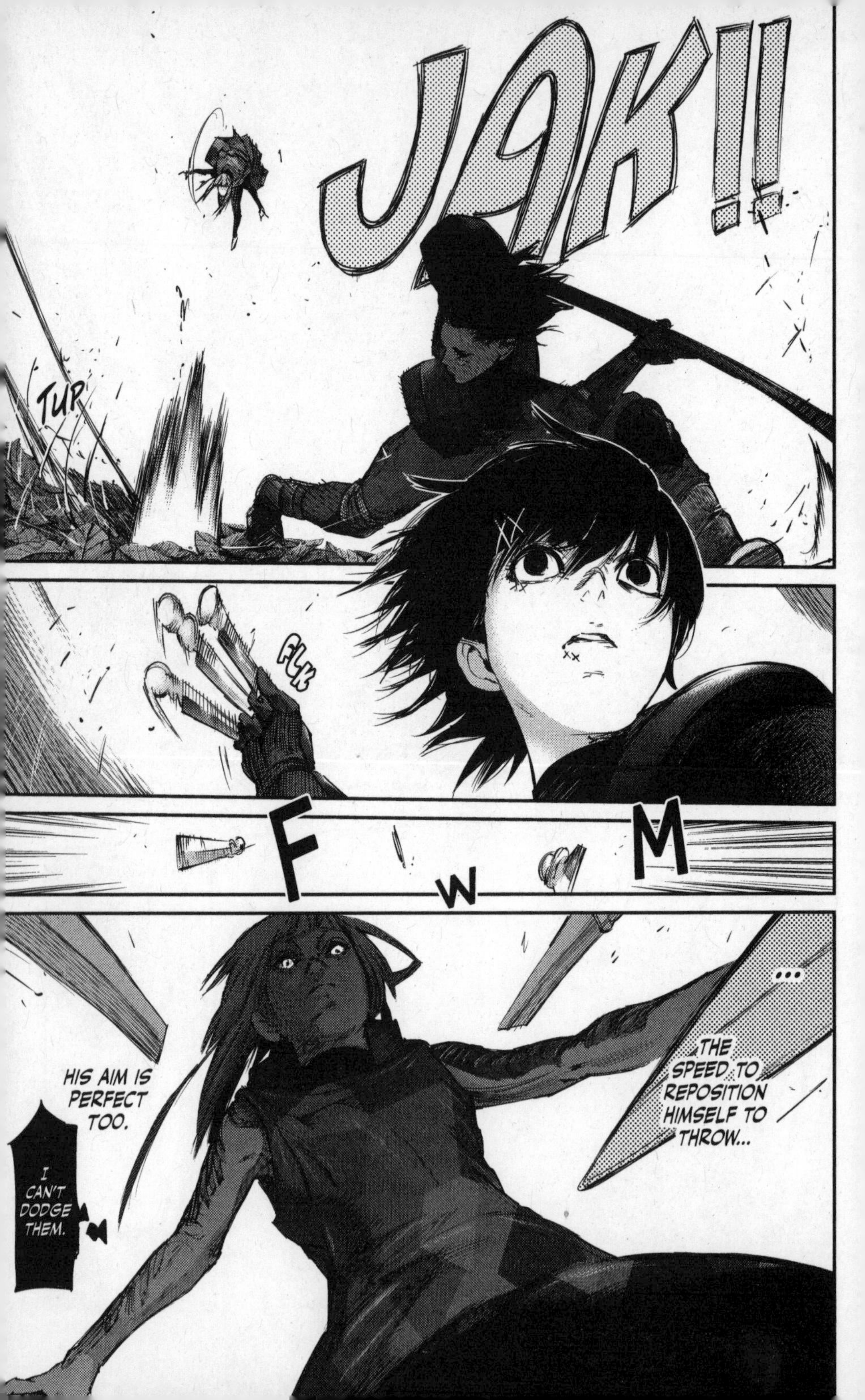
JAK!!
TUP
FLK
FWM
...
THE SPEED TO REPOSITION HIMSELF TO THROW...
HIS AIM IS PERFECT TOO.
I CAN'T DODGE THEM.

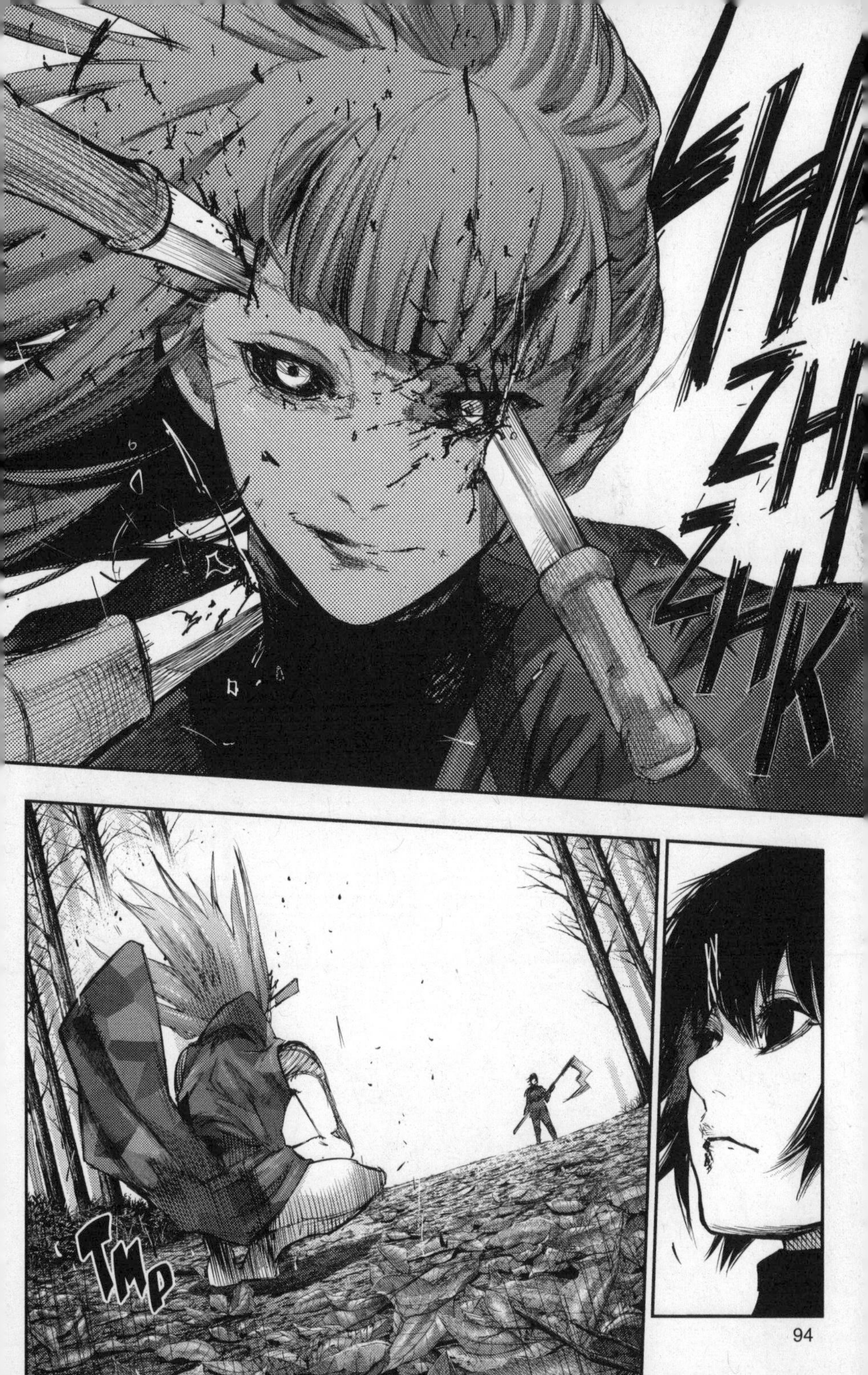
ZHK
TMP

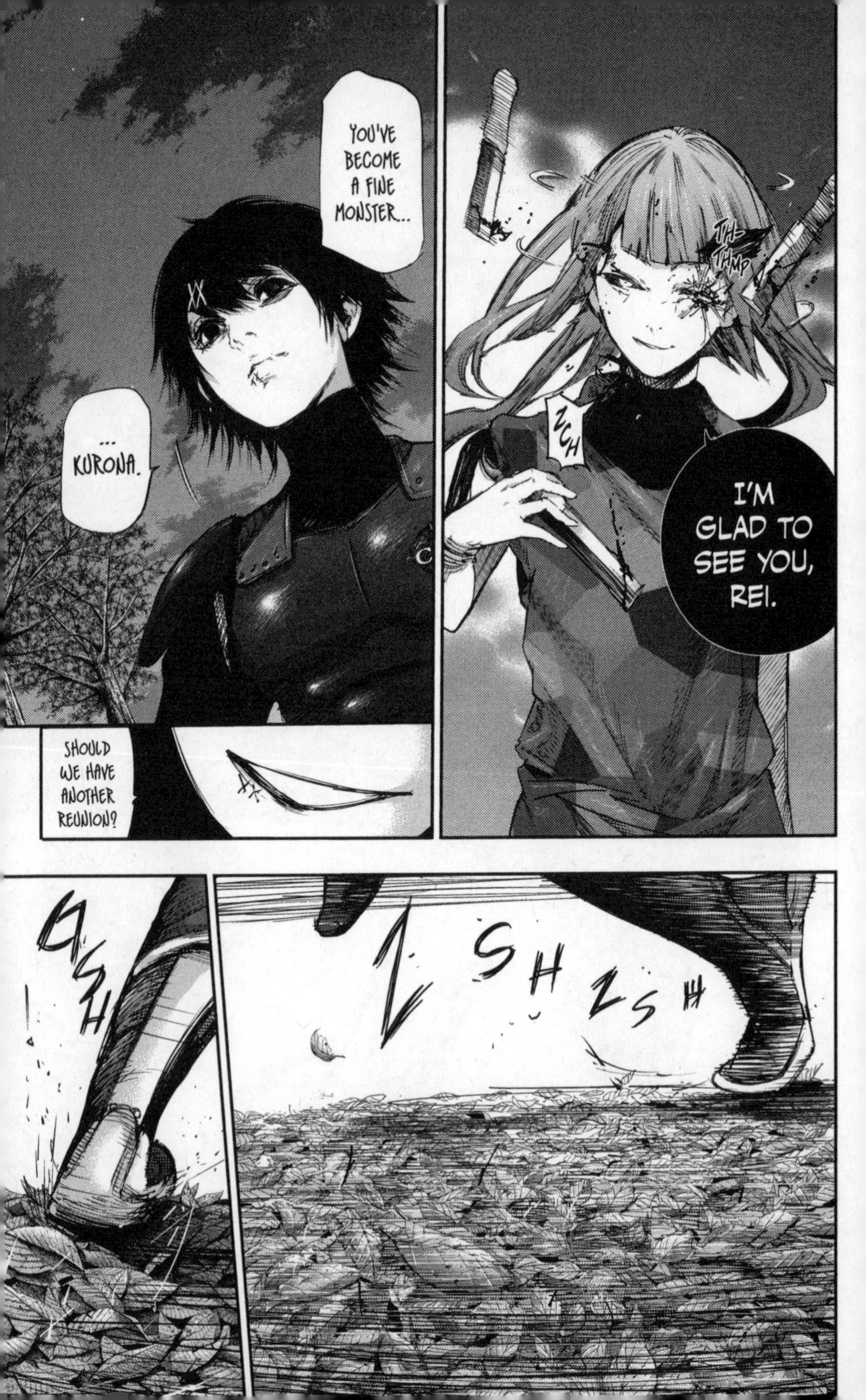
TH-THMP
ZCH
I'M GLAD TO SEE YOU, REI.
YOU'VE BECOME A FINE MONSTER...
... KURONA.
SHOULD WE HAVE ANOTHER REUNION?
SHZSH

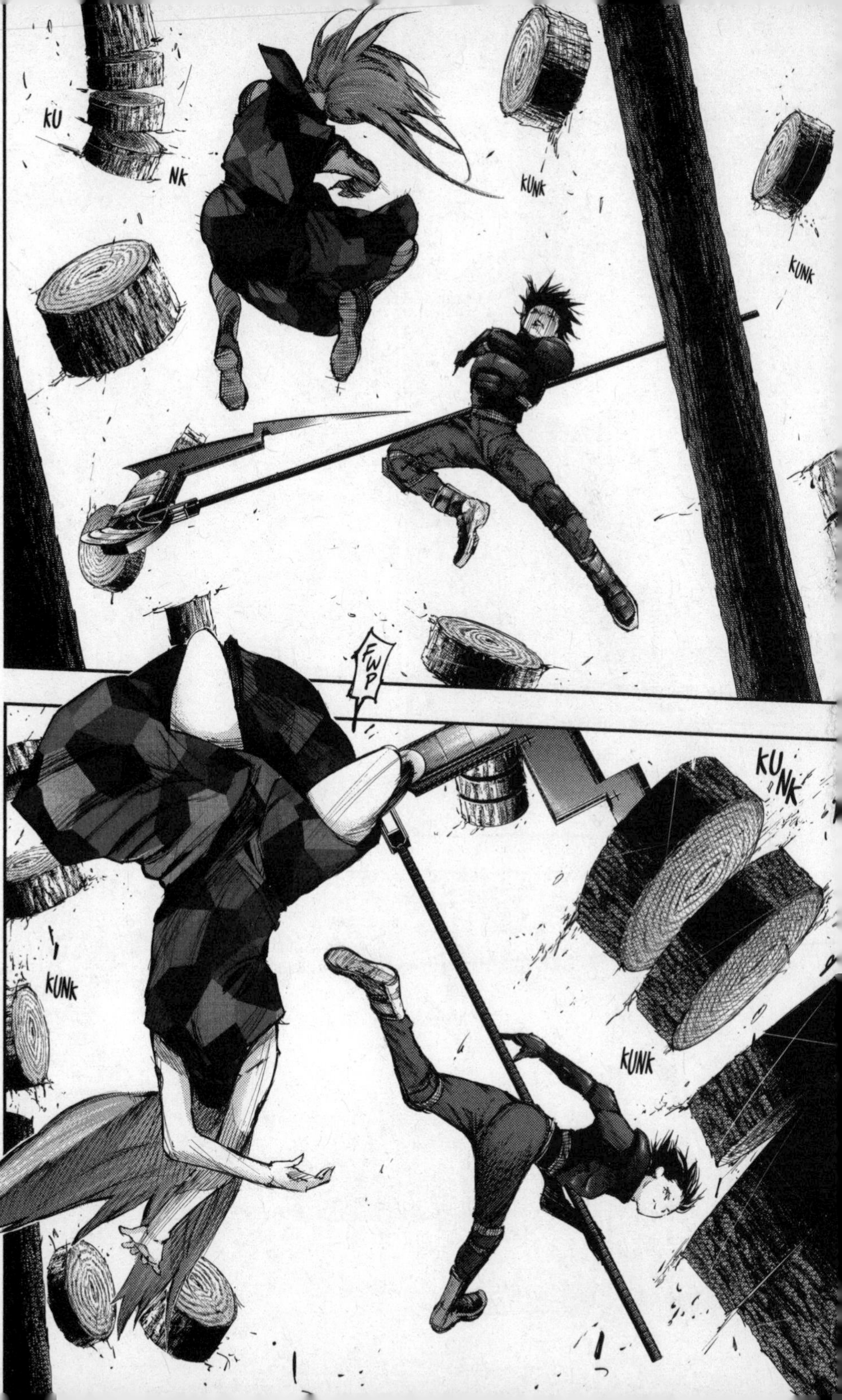
KUNK
KUNK
KU
NK
KUNK
KUNK
FWP
KUNK

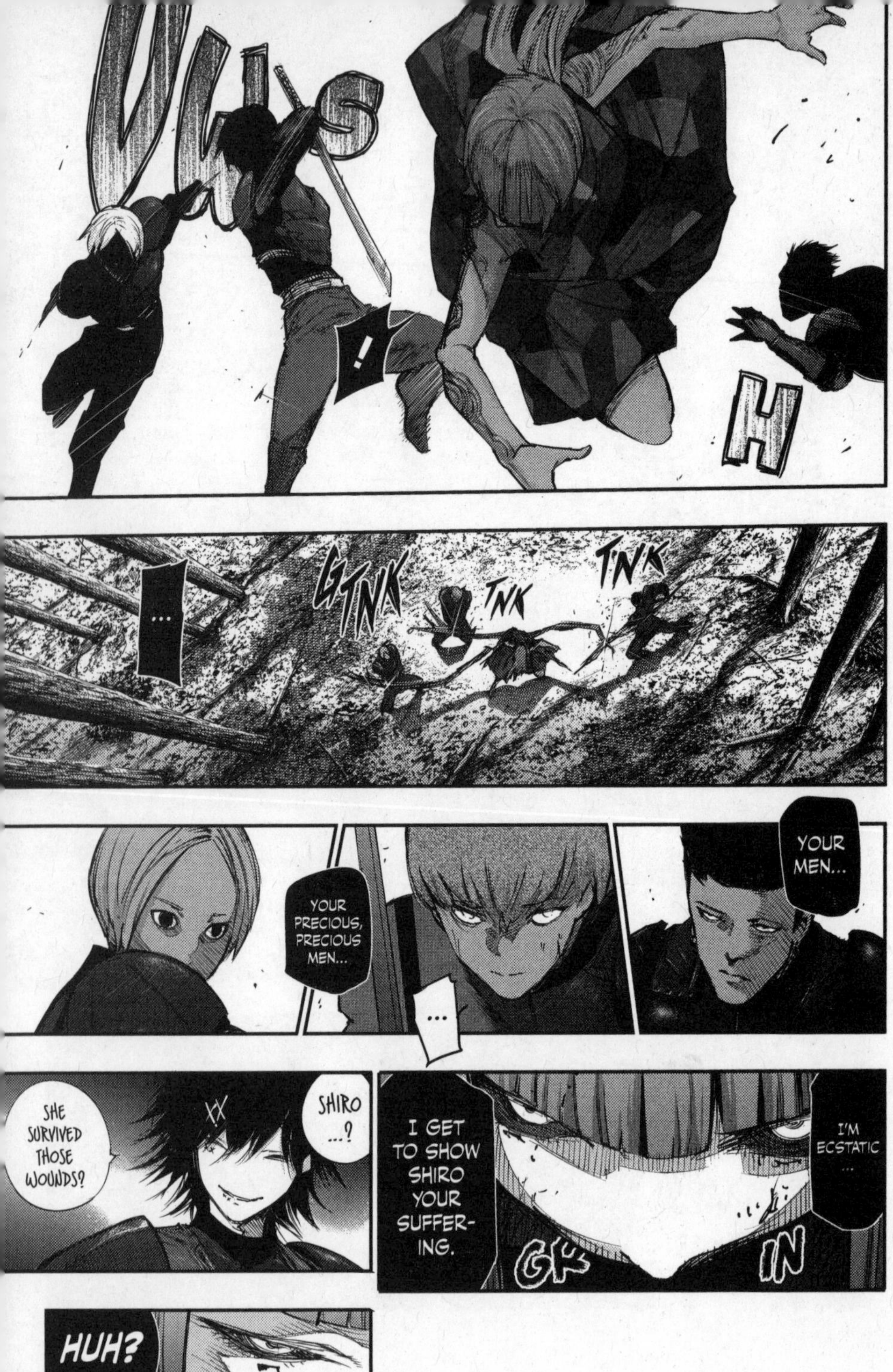

H
!
TNK
TNK
GTNK
...
YOUR MEN...
YOUR PRECIOUS, PRECIOUS MEN...
...
I'M ECSTATIC ...
I GET TO SHOW SHIRO YOUR SUFFER-ING.
GK
IN
SHIRO ...?
SHE SURVIVED THOSE WOUNDS?
HUH?

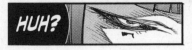

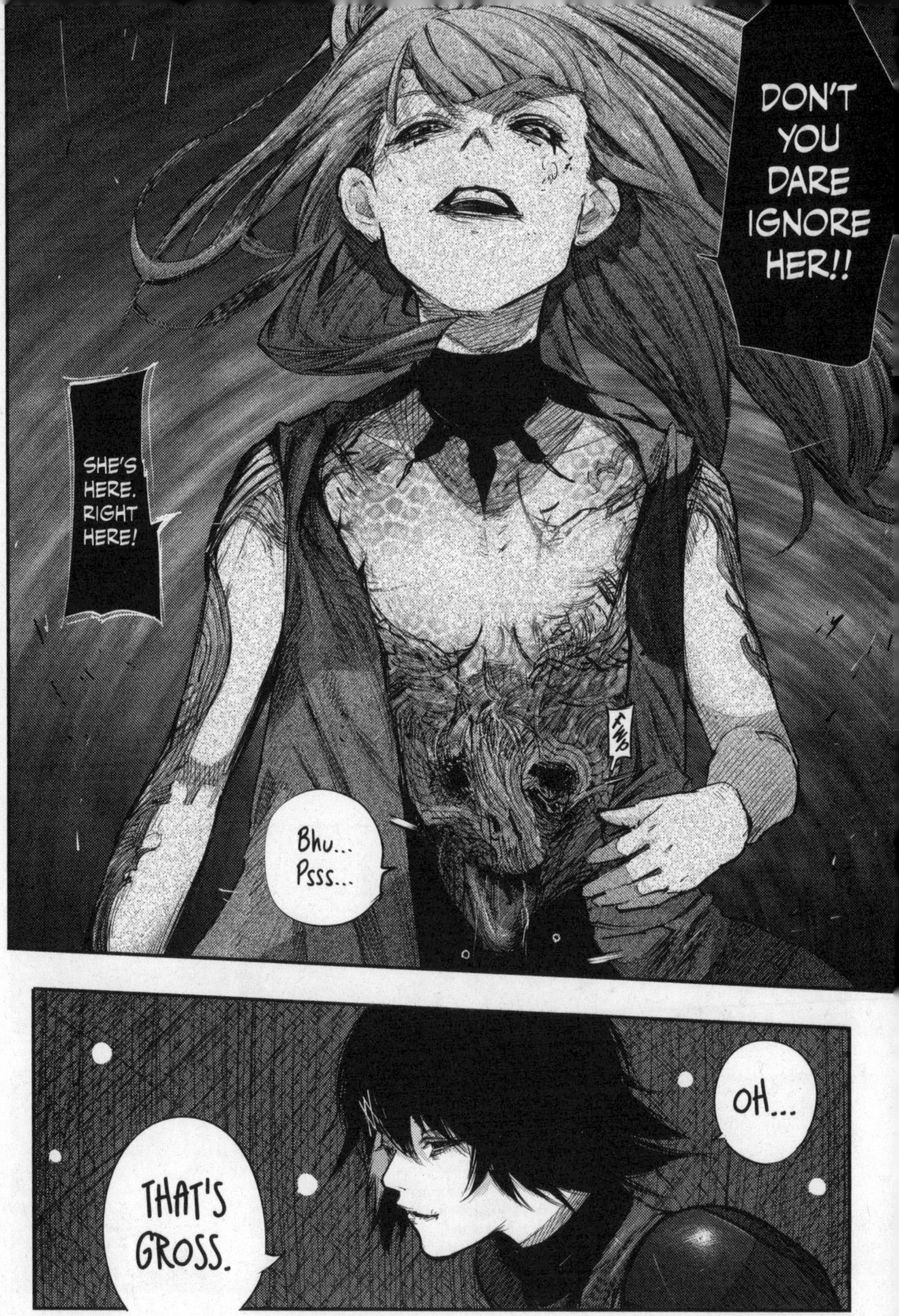
DON'T YOU DARE IGNORE HER!!
SHE'S HERE. RIGHT HERE!
FWP
Bhu... Psss...
OH...
THAT'S GROSS.

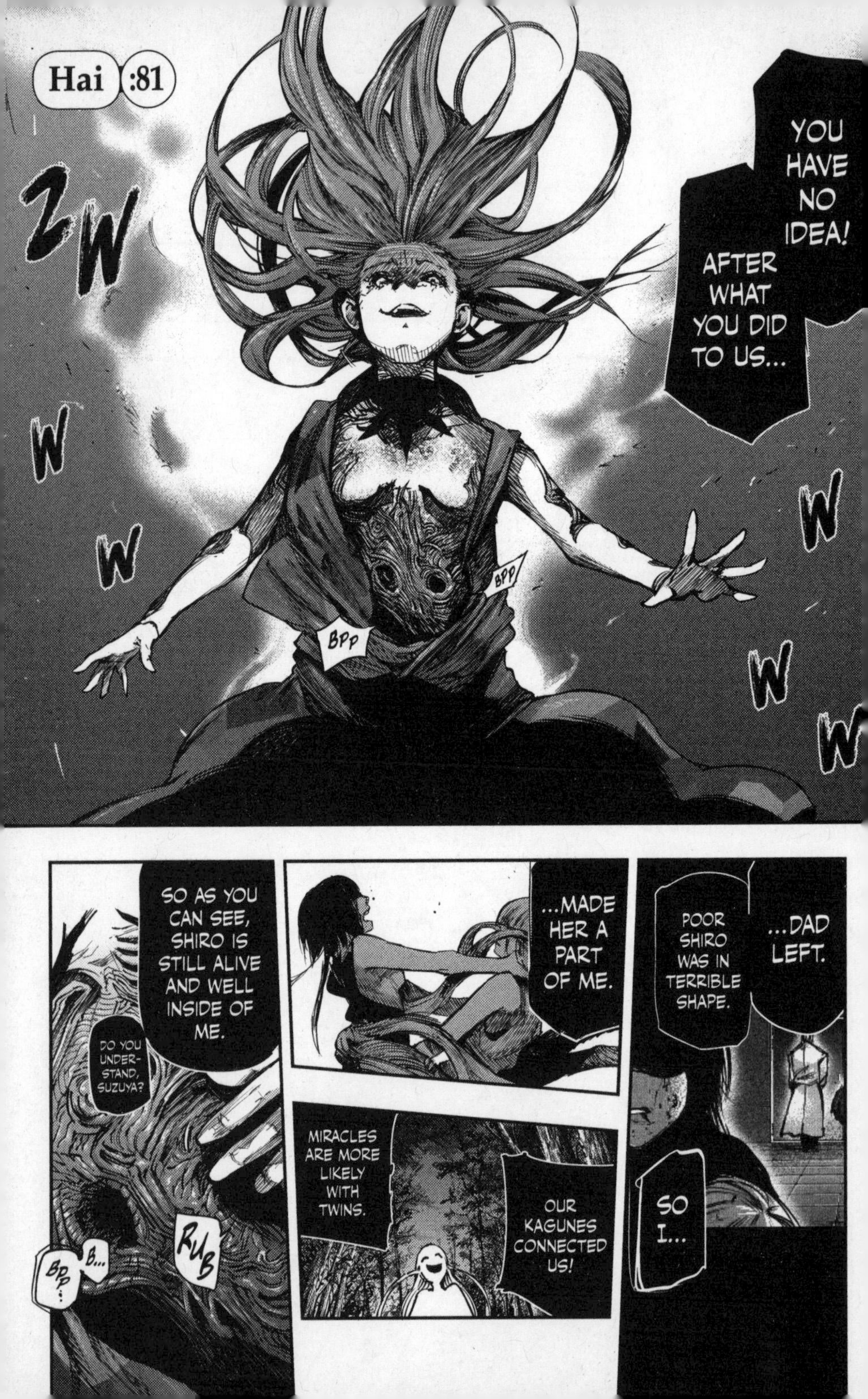

Hai :81
YOU HAVE NO IDEA!
AFTER WHAT YOU DID TO US...
ZWWWWWWW
BPP
BPP
...DAD LEFT.
POOR SHIRO WAS IN TERRIBLE SHAPE.
SO I...
...MADE HER A PART OF ME.
MIRACLES ARE MORE LIKELY WITH TWINS.
OUR KAGUNES CONNECTED US!
SO AS YOU CAN SEE, SHIRO IS STILL ALIVE AND WELL INSIDE OF ME.
DO YOU UNDER-STAND, SUZUYA?
RUB
B...
BPP...

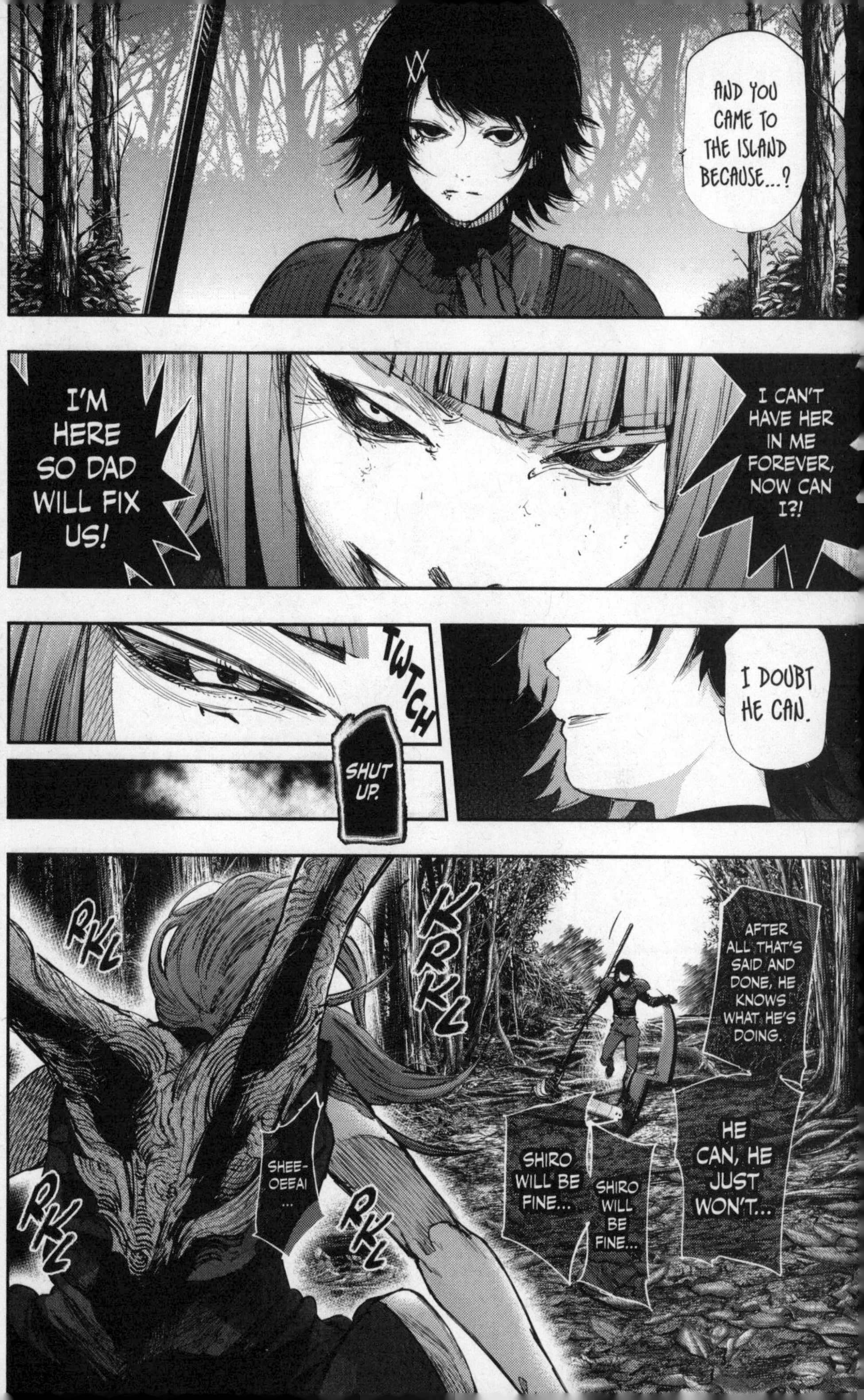
AND YOU CAME TO THE ISLAND BECAUSE...?
I CAN'T HAVE HER IN ME FOREVER, NOW CAN I?!
I'M HERE SO DAD WILL FIX US!
I DOUBT HE CAN.
TWTCH
SHUT UP.
AFTER ALL THAT'S SAID AND DONE, HE KNOWS WHAT HE'S DOING.
HE CAN, HE JUST WON'T...
KRKL
SHIRO WILL BE FINE...
SHIRO WILL BE FINE...
SHEE-OEEAI ...
RKL
RKL
RKL

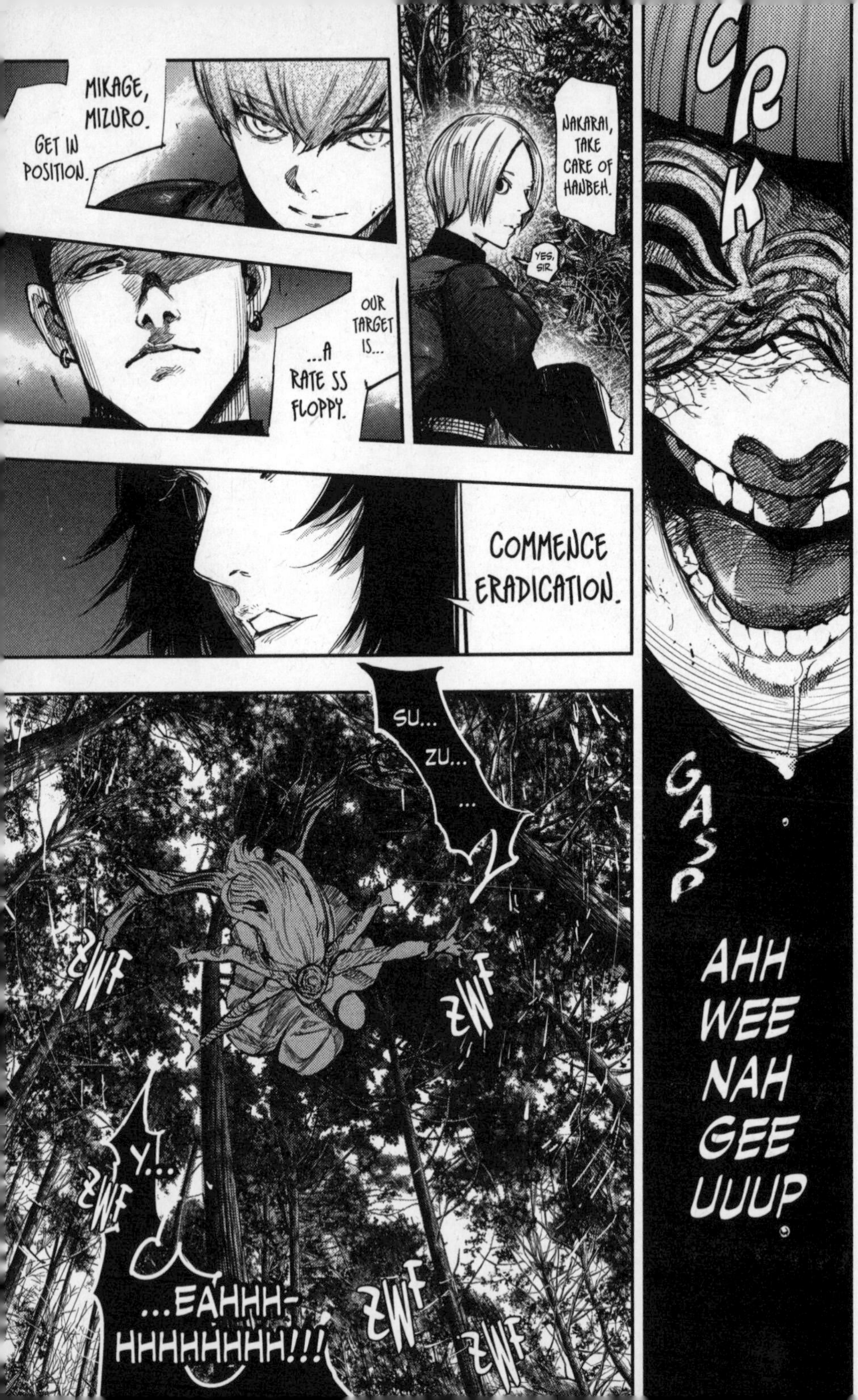
CRK
GASP
AHH WEE NAH GEE UUUP
NAKARAI, TAKE CARE OF HANBEH.
YES, SIR.
MIKAGE, MIZURO.
GET IN POSITION.
OUR TARGET IS...
...A RATE SS FLOPPY.
COMMENCE ERADICATION.
SU... ZU... ...
ZWF
ZWF
Y...
ZWF
...EAHHH-HHHHHHHH!!!
ZWF
ZWF

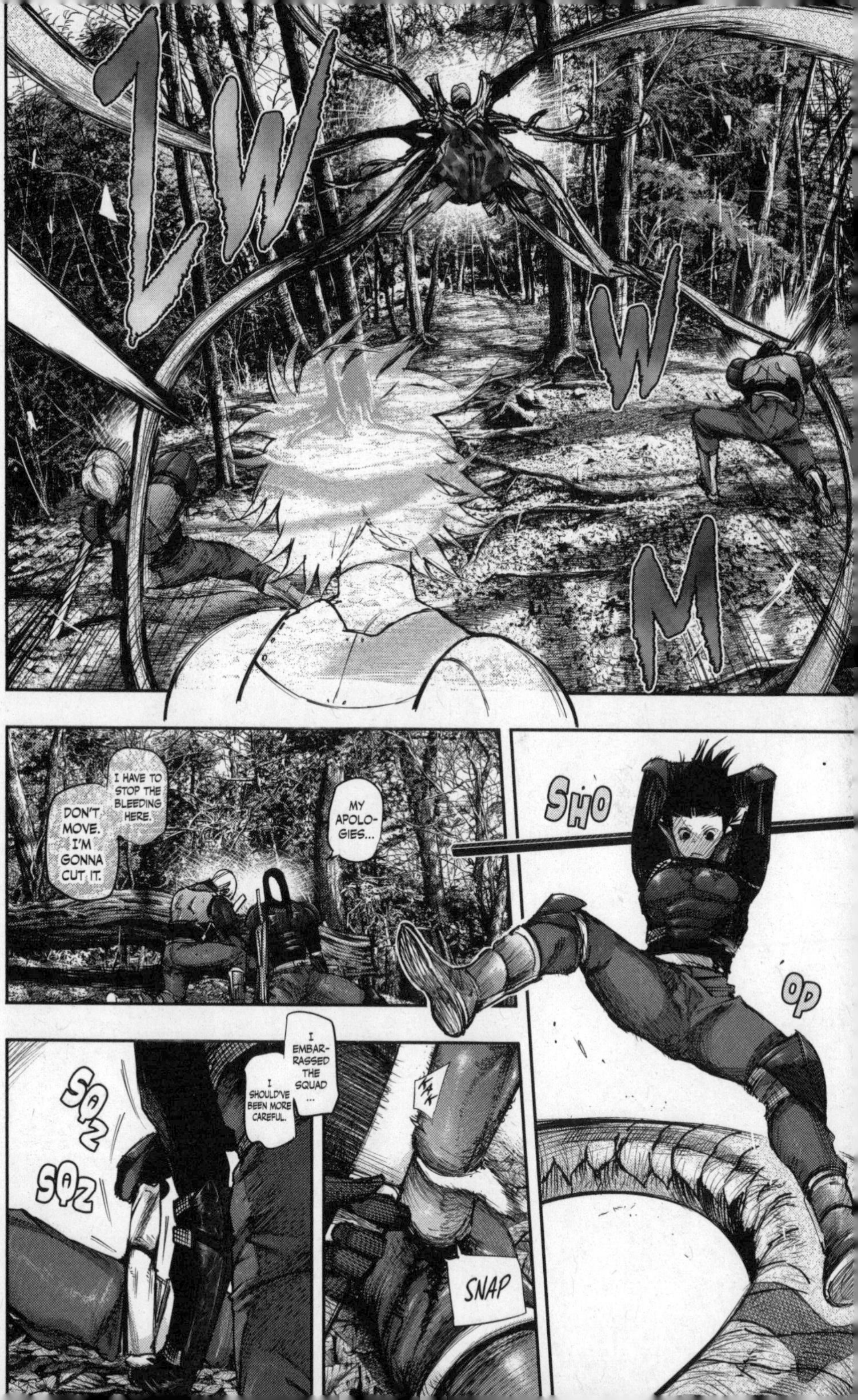
ZW
W
M
SHO
OP
MY APOLOGIES...
I HAVE TO STOP THE BLEEDING HERE.
DON'T MOVE. I'M GONNA CUT IT.
I EMBARRASSED THE SQUAD...
I SHOULD'VE BEEN MORE CAREFUL.
KAK
SNAP
SQZ
SQZ

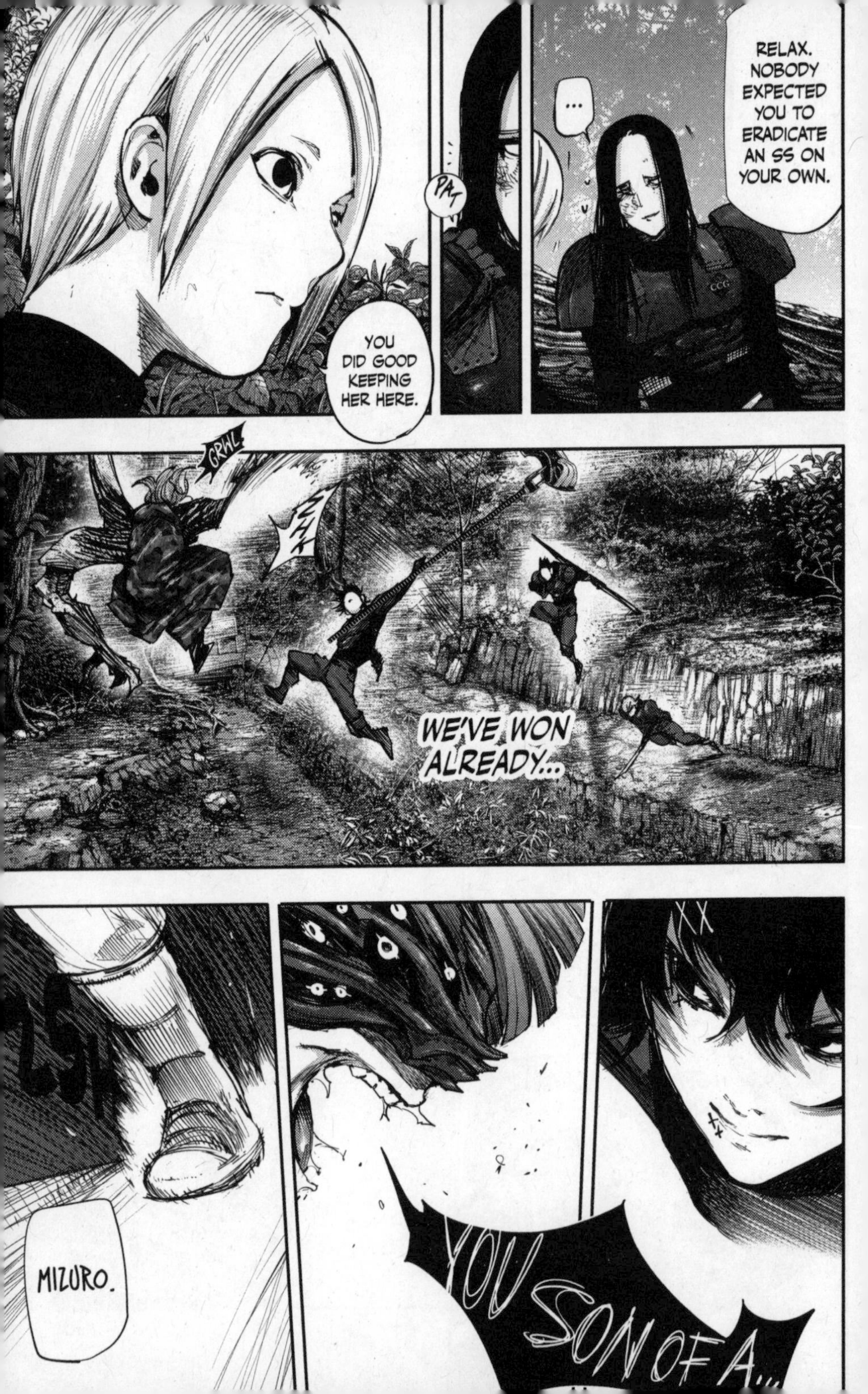
RELAX. NOBODY EXPECTED YOU TO ERADICATE AN SS ON YOUR OWN.
...
PAT
YOU DID GOOD KEEPING HER HERE.
GRWL
WE'VE WON ALREADY...
YOU SON OF A...
MIZURO.

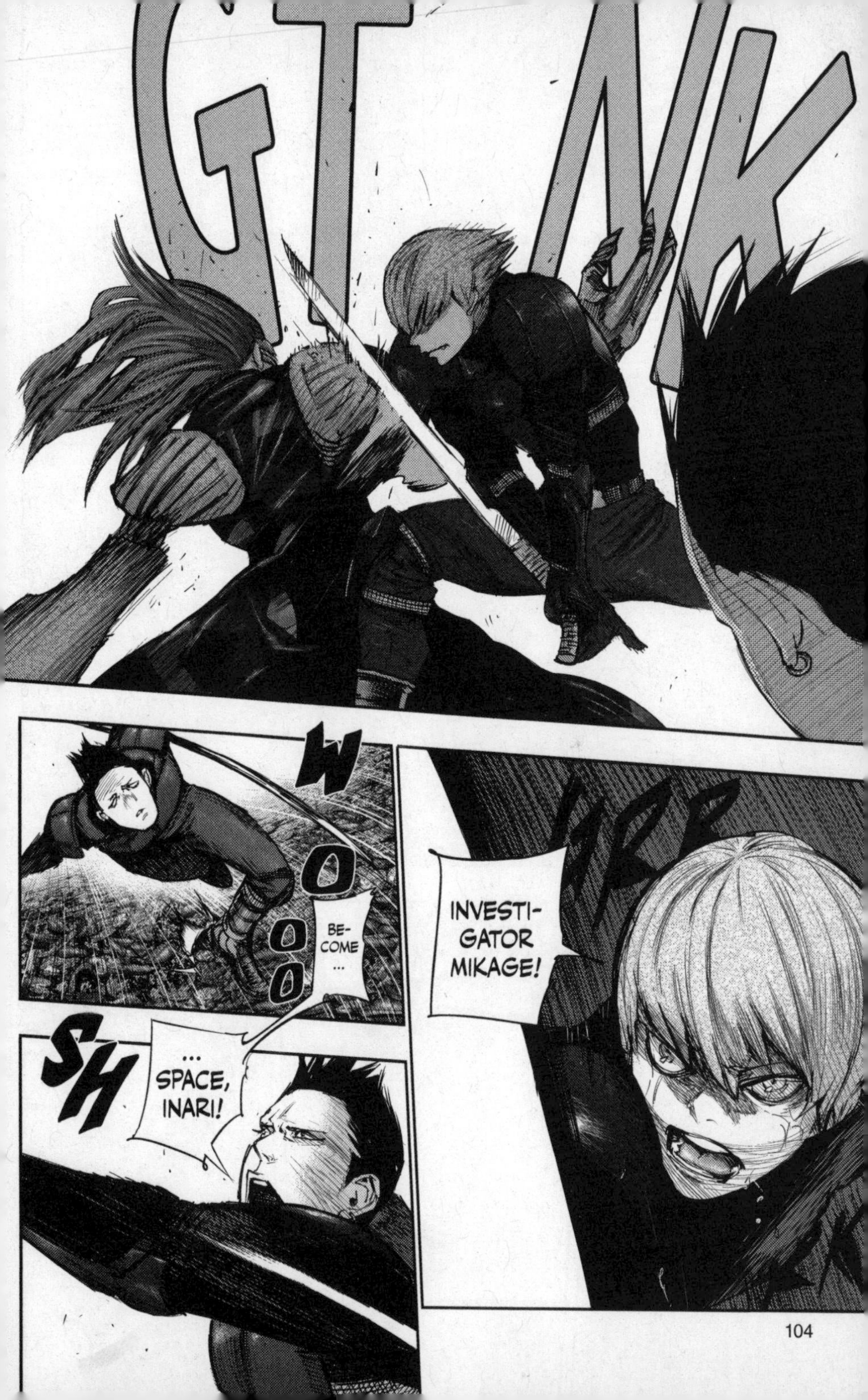
GTANK
INVESTI-GATOR MIKAGE!
WOOOO
BE-COME...
SH
...SPACE, INARI!

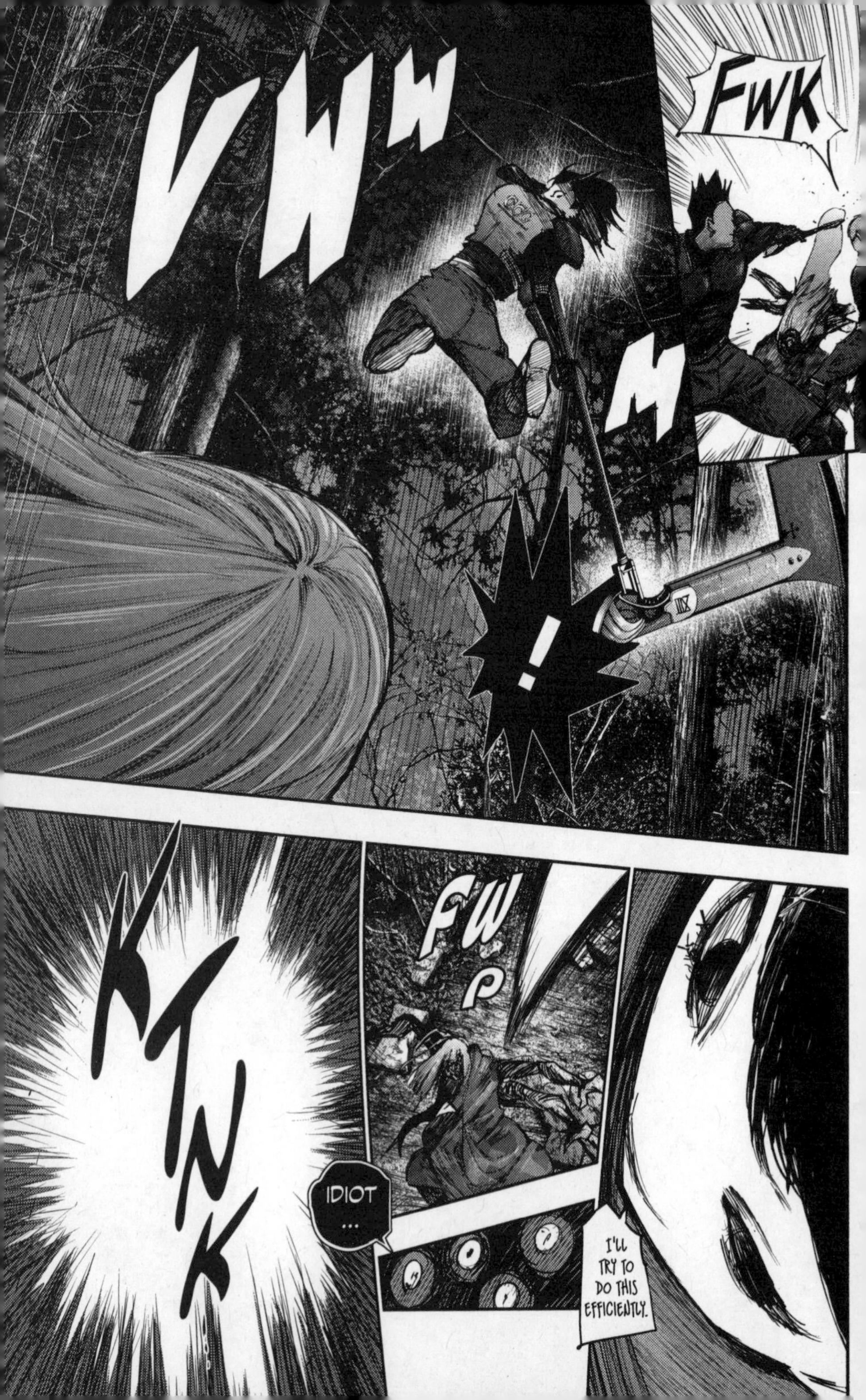
FWK
VWWM
!
I'LL TRY TO DO THIS EFFICIENTLY.
FWP
IDIOT ...
KLNK

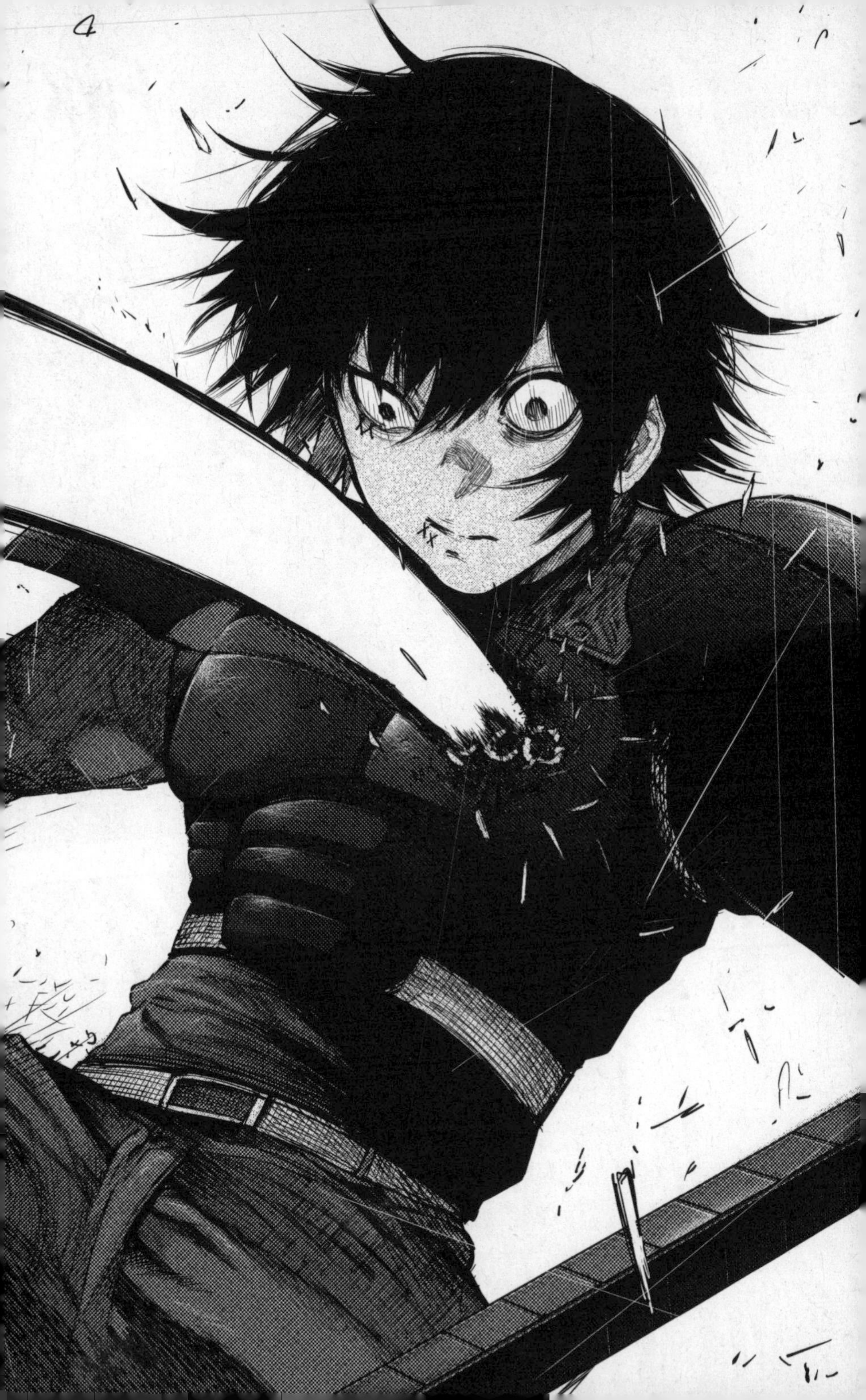

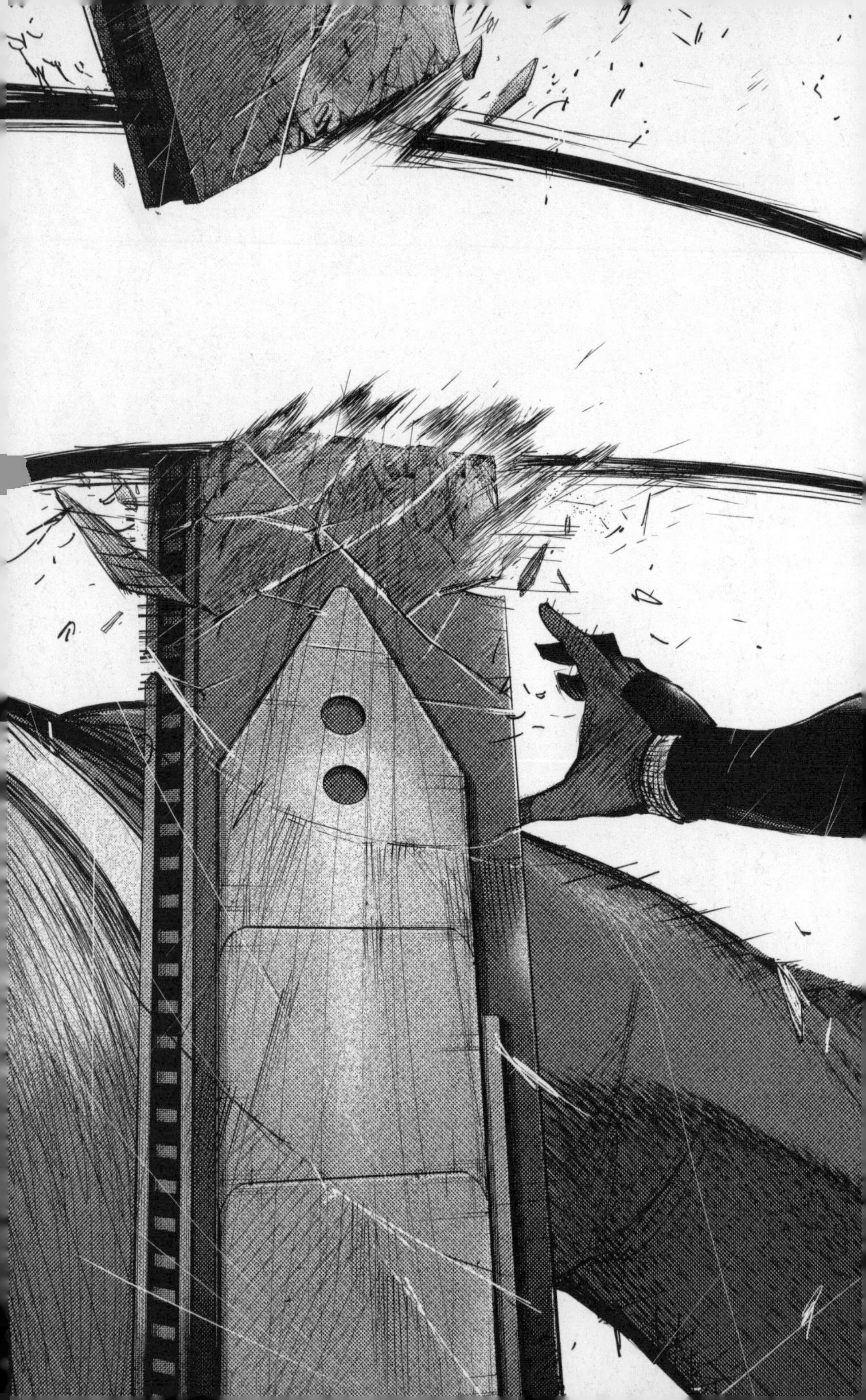

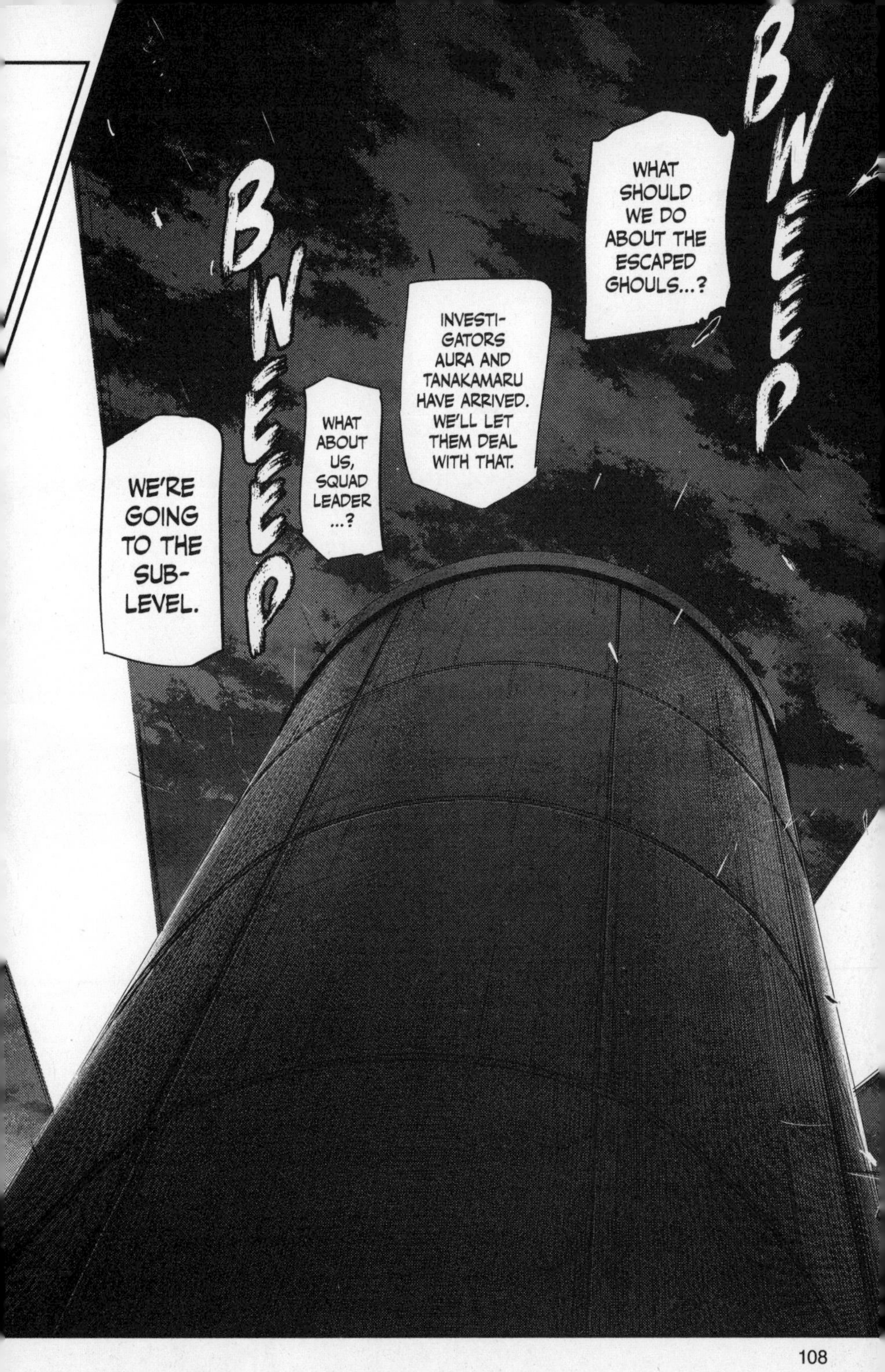
BWEEP
WHAT SHOULD WE DO ABOUT THE ESCAPED GHOULS...?
INVESTIGATORS AURA AND TANAKAMARU HAVE ARRIVED. WE'LL LET THEM DEAL WITH THAT.
WHAT ABOUT US, SQUAD LEADER...?
BWEEP
WE'RE GOING TO THE SUB-LEVEL.

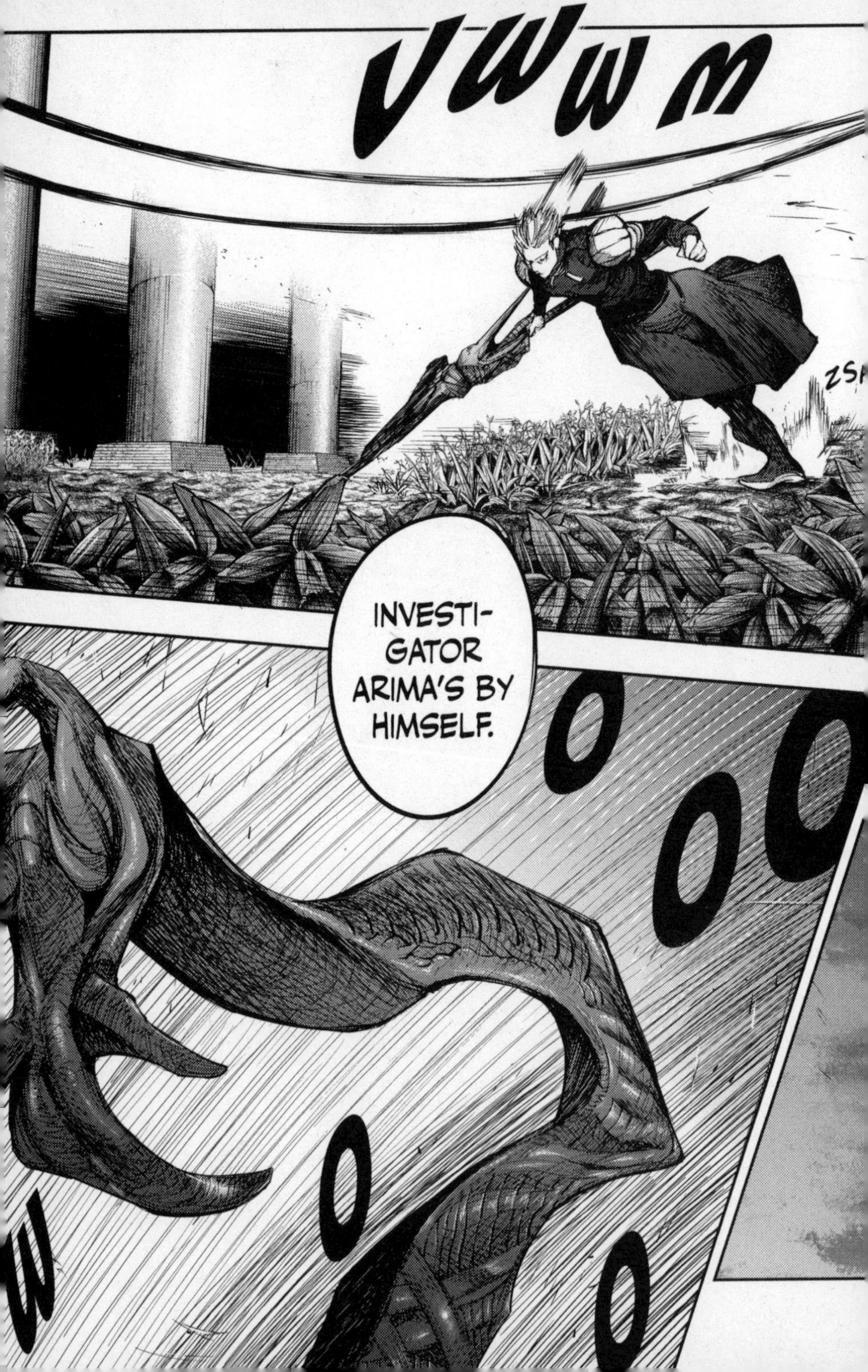
VWWM
ZS
INVESTI-GATOR ARIMA'S BY HIMSELF.

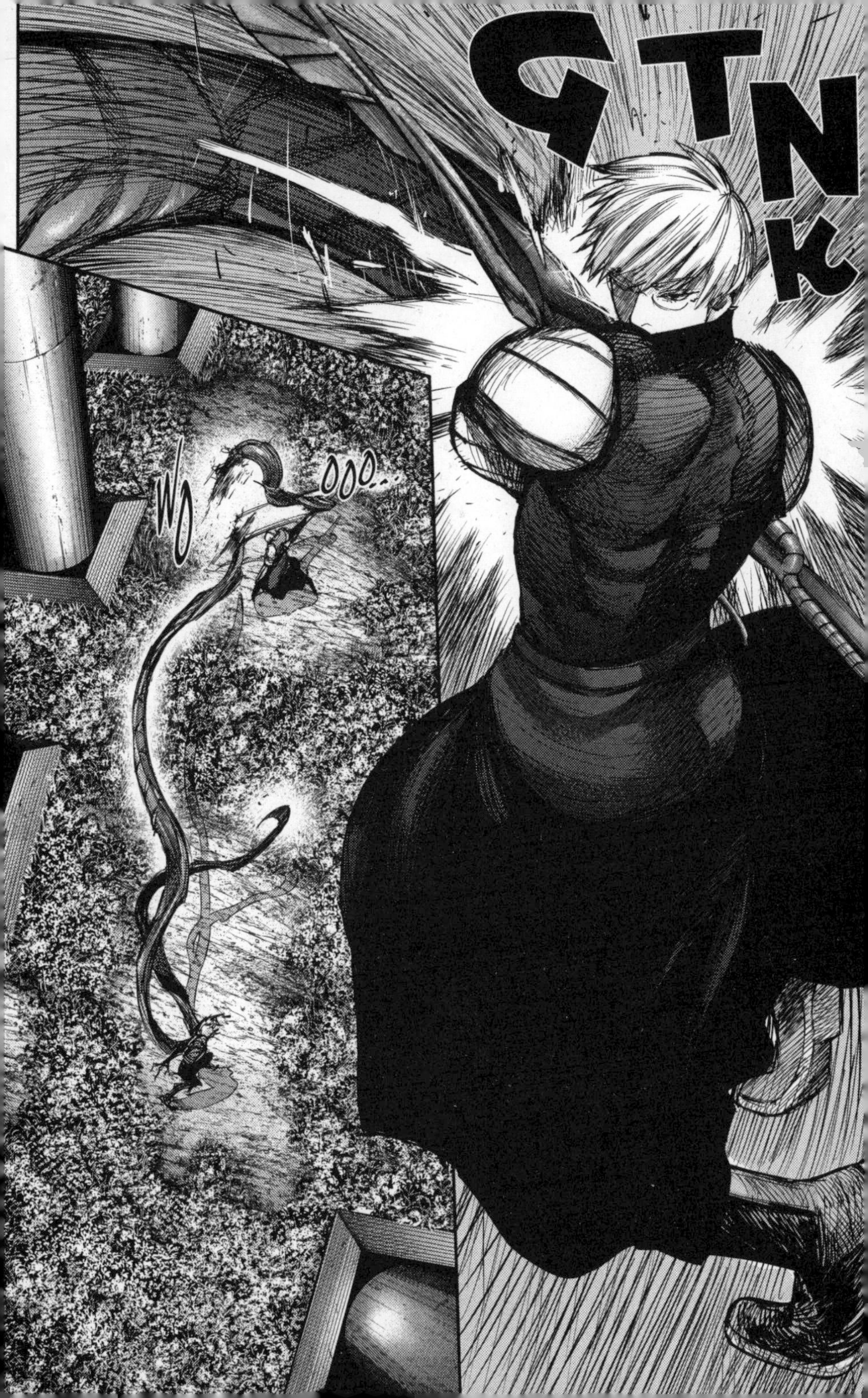
GTNK
WOOOO...

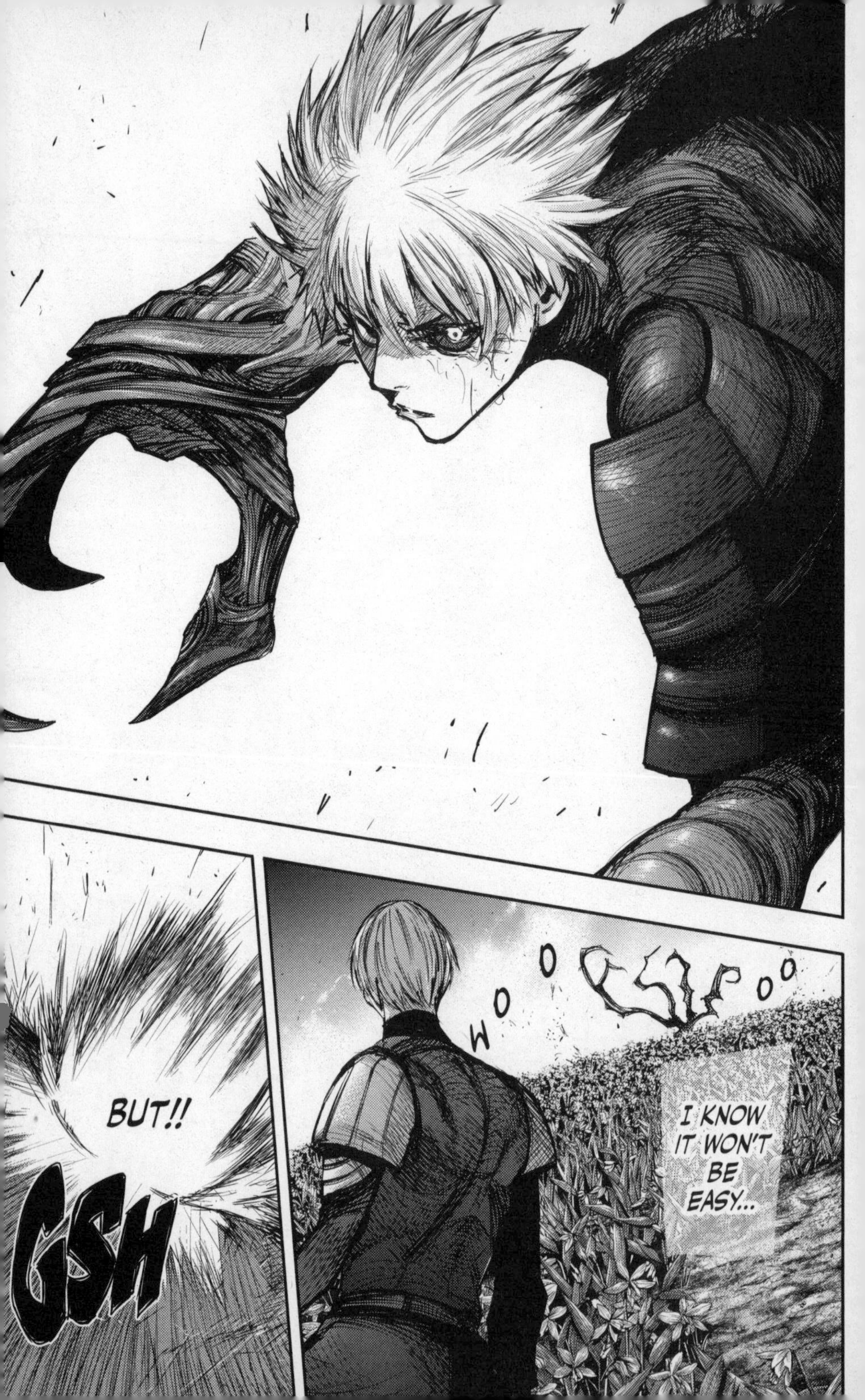
WOOSHOOO
I KNOW IT WON'T BE EASY...
BUT!!
GSH

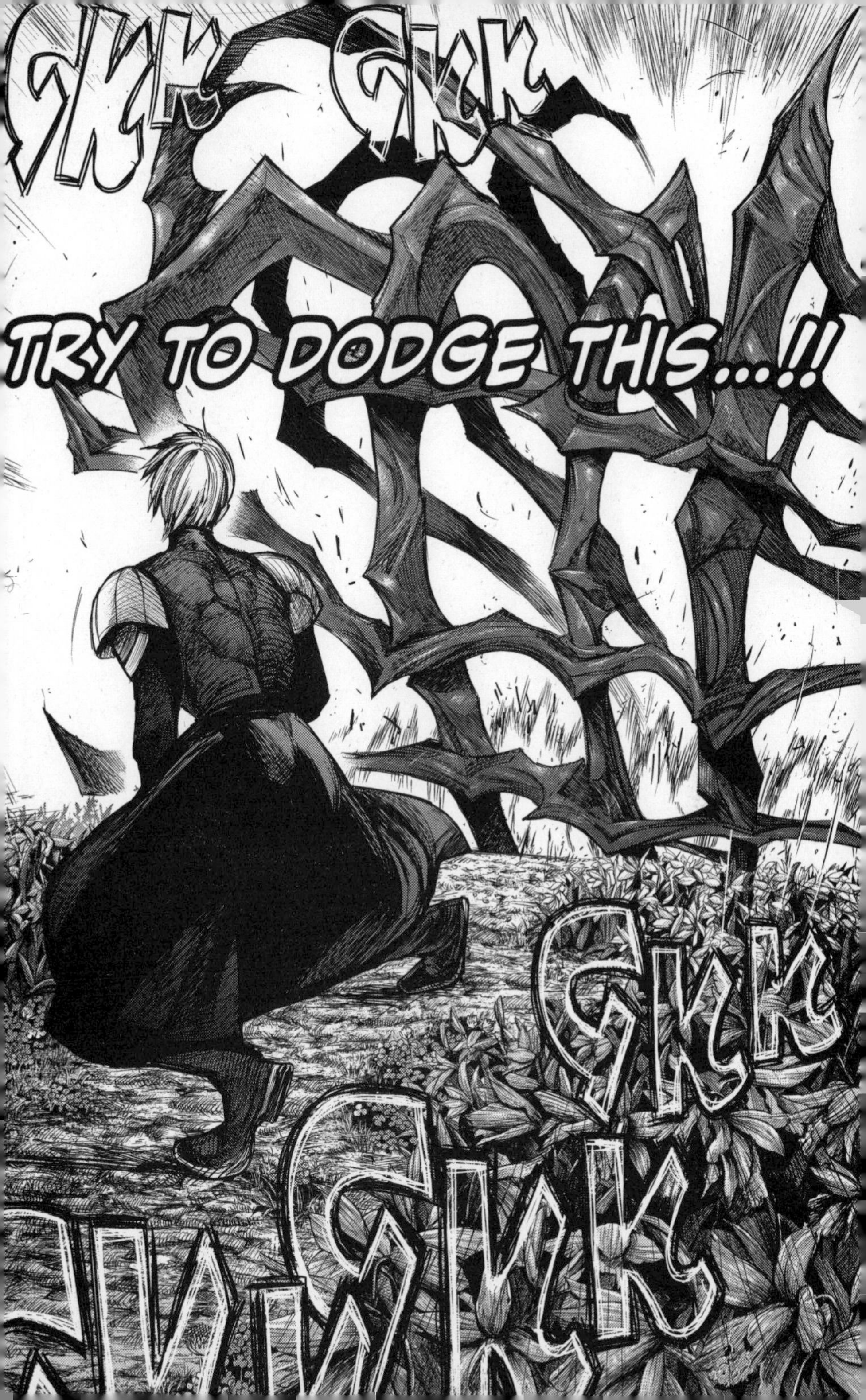
GKRK
GKRK
TRY TO DODGE THIS...!!
GKRK
GKRK

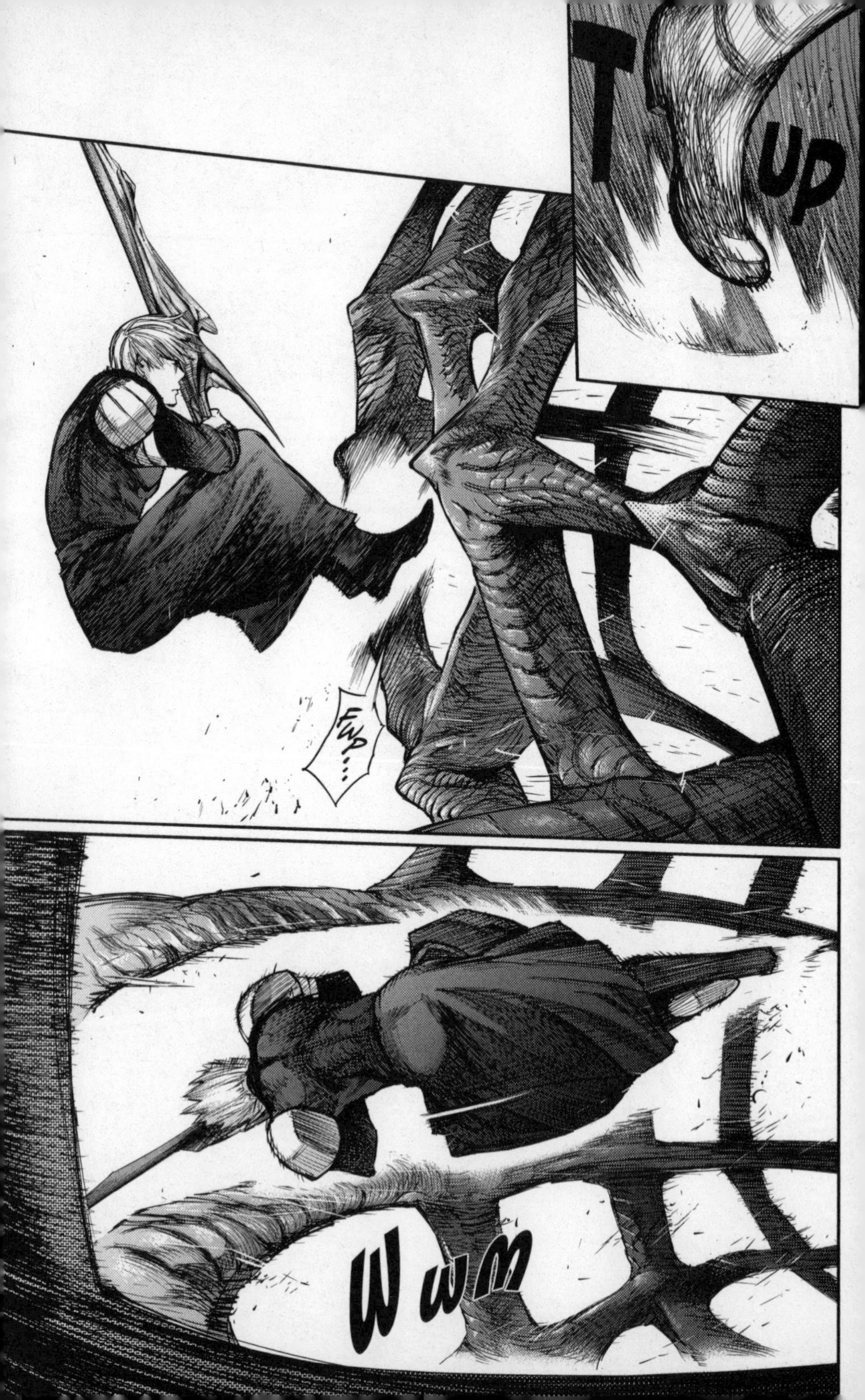
TUP
FWP...
WWM

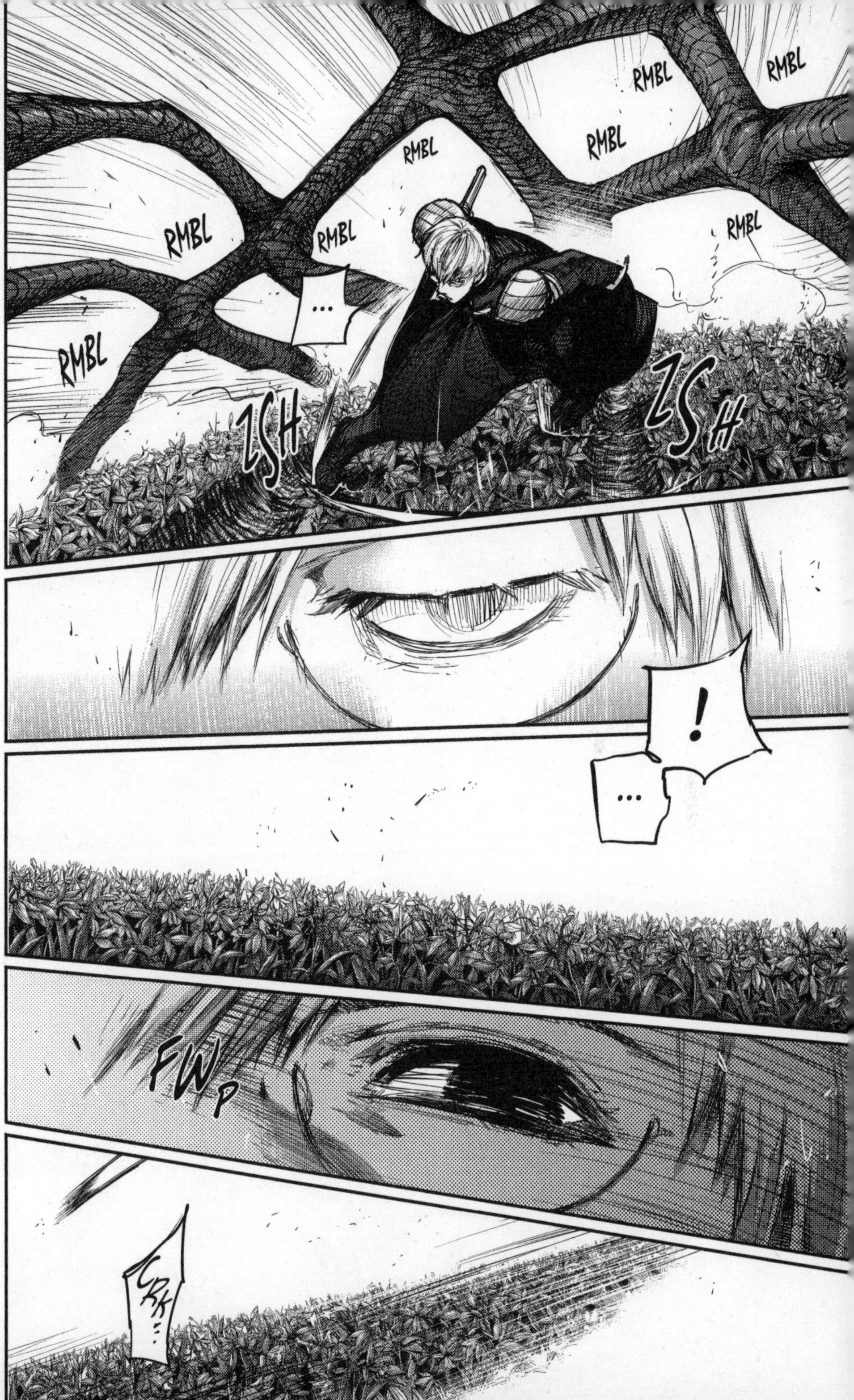
RMBL
RMBL
RMBL
RMBL
RMBL
RMBL
RMBL
...
RMBL
ZSH
ZSH
!
...
FWP
CRK...

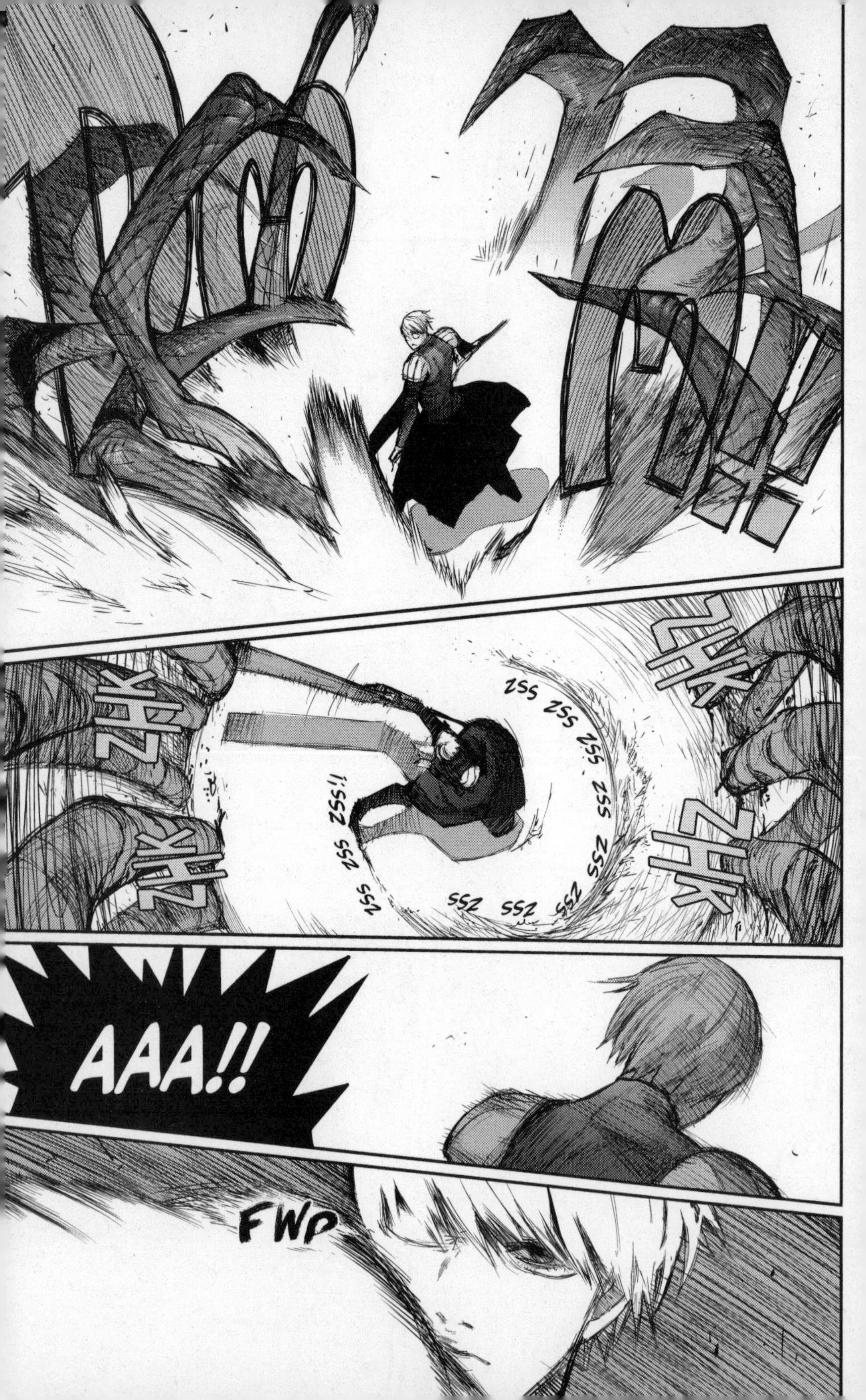
ZHK
ZHK
ZHK
ZHK
ZSS ZSS ZSS ZSS ZSS ZSS ZSS ZSS ZSS ZSS ZSSZ!!
AAA!!
FWP

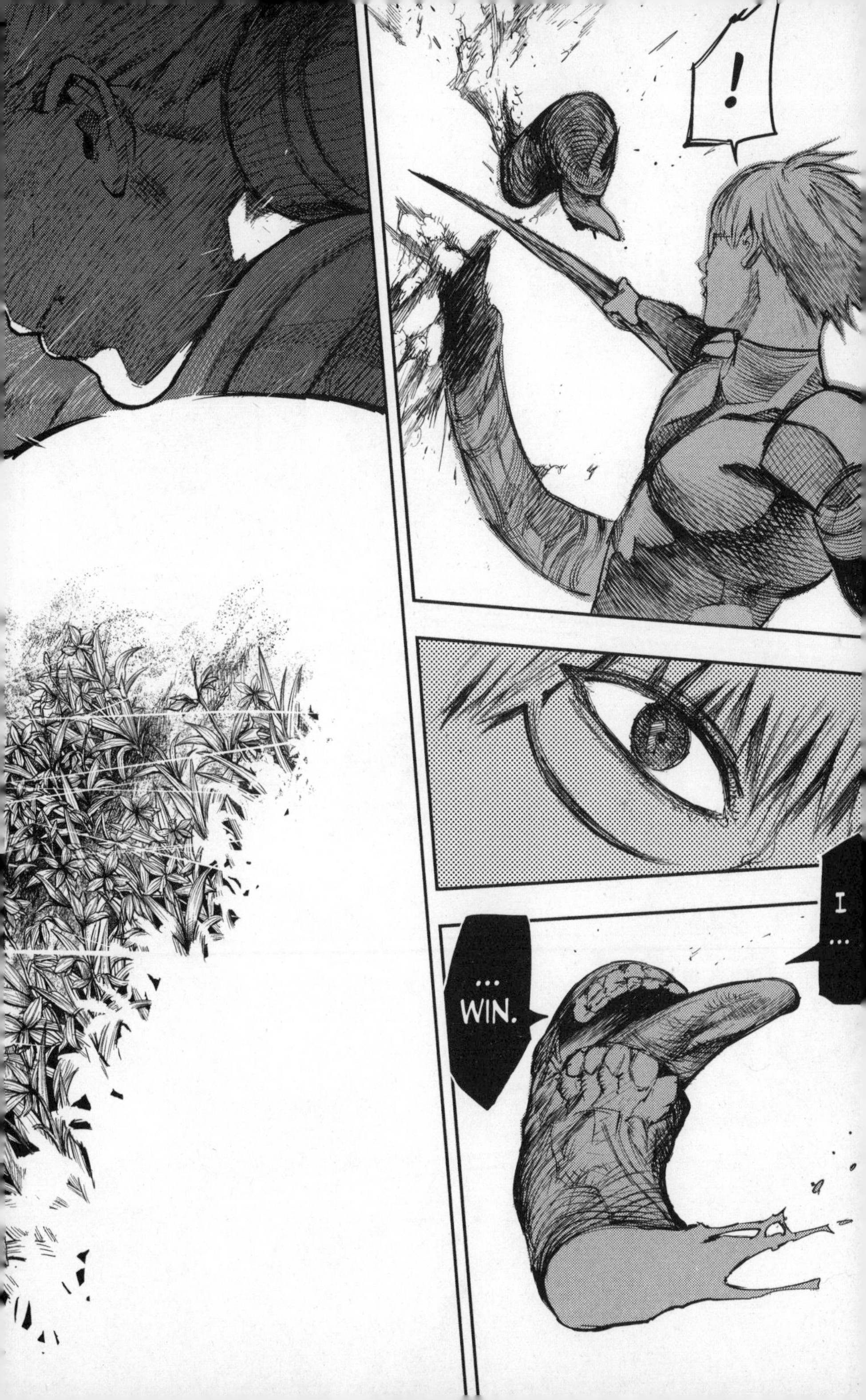
!
I...
...WIN.

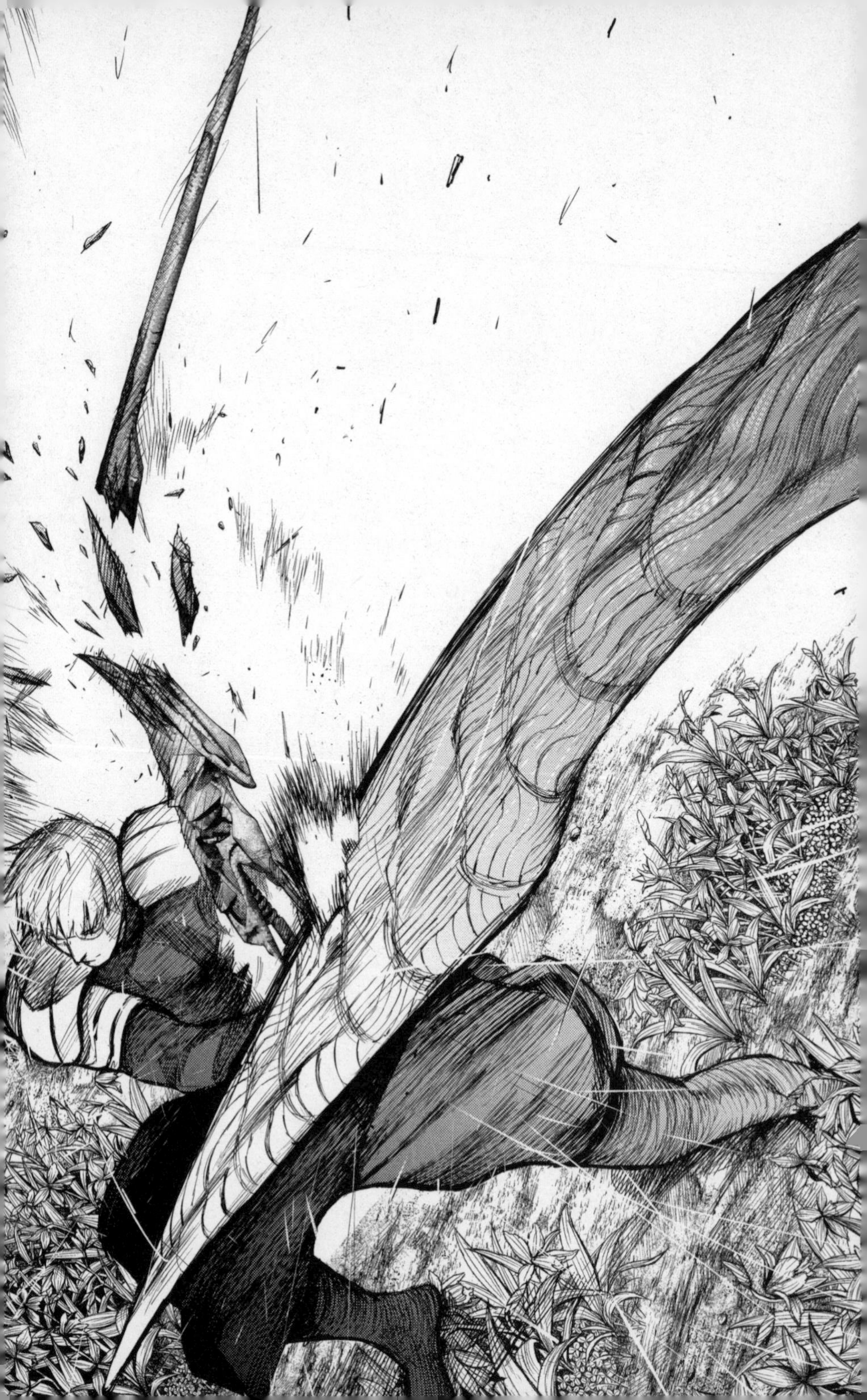

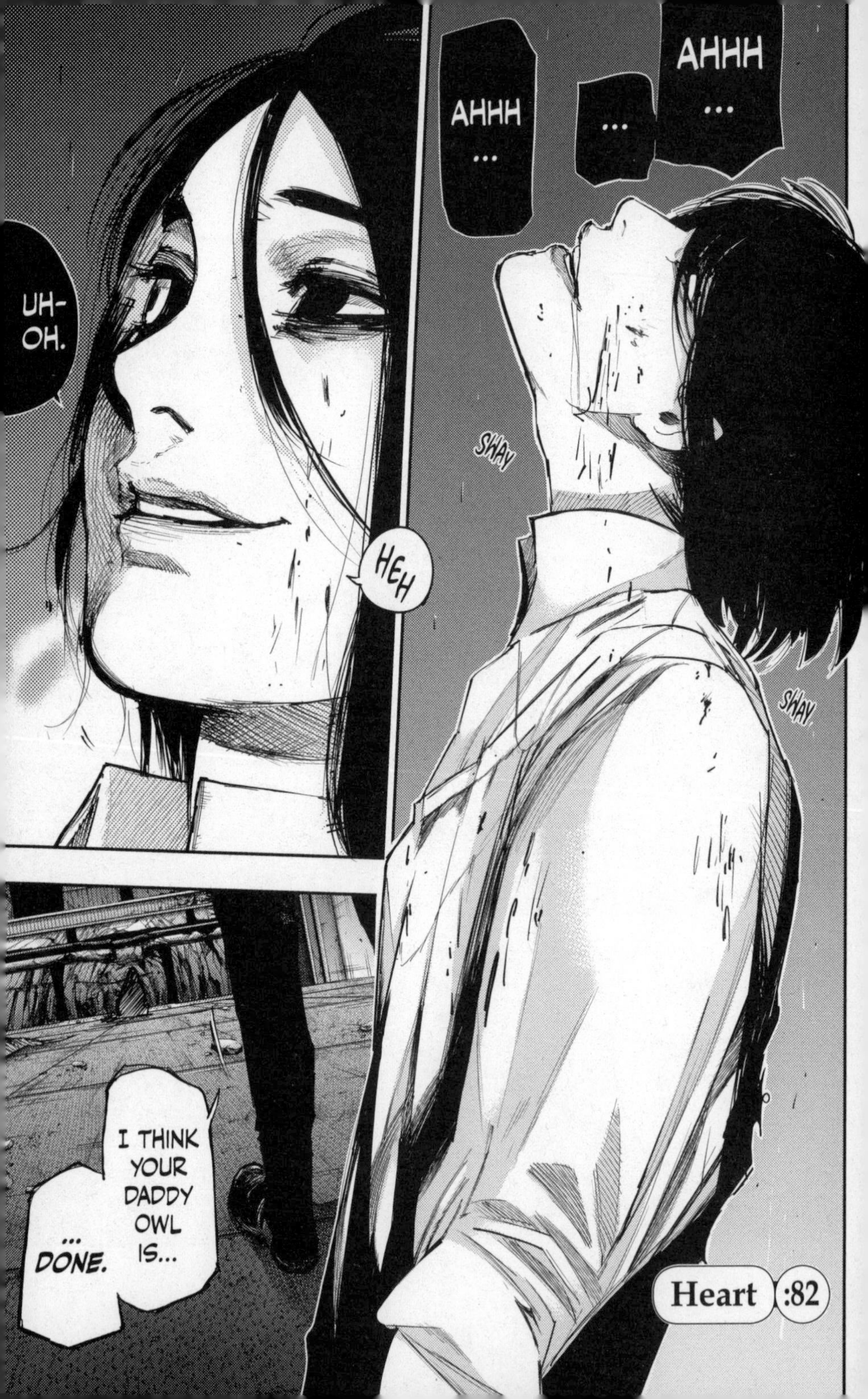
AHHH ...
...
AHHH ...
SWAY
SWAY
Heart :82
HEH
UH-OH.
I THINK YOUR DADDY OWL IS...
... DONE.

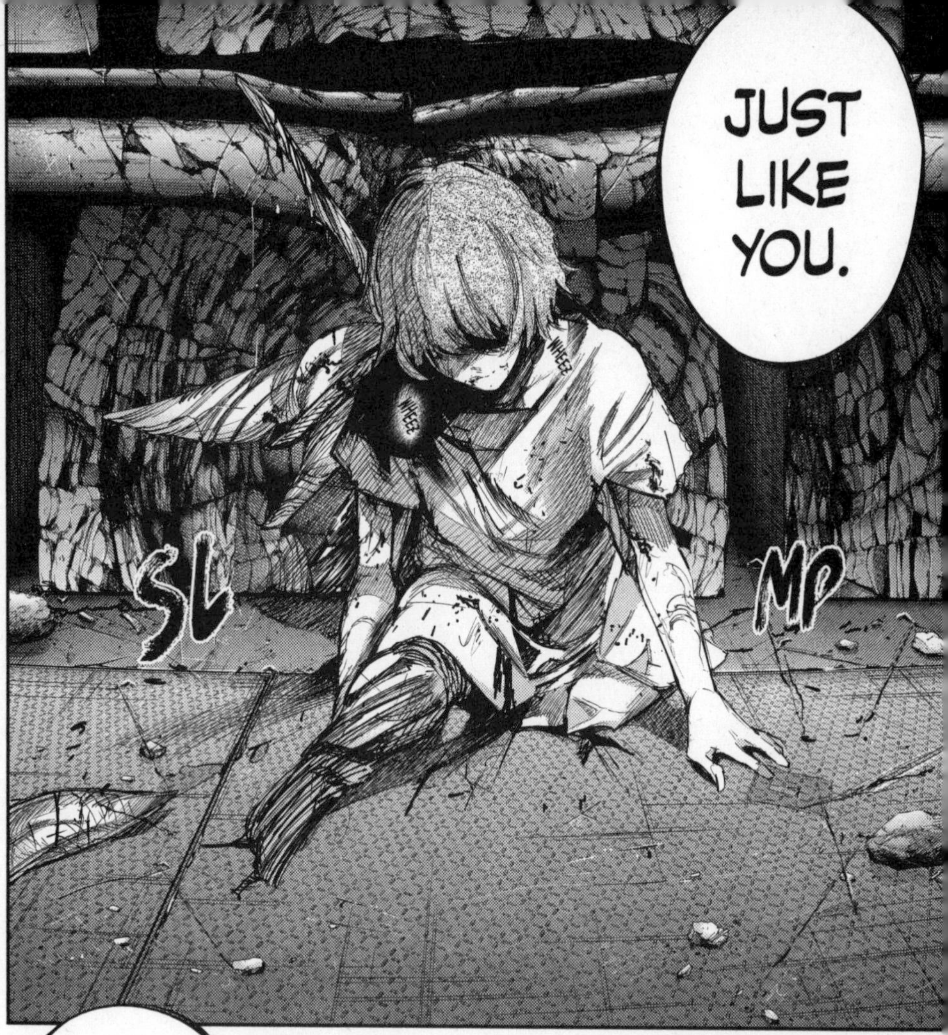
JUST LIKE YOU.
WHEEZ
WHEEZ
SL
MP

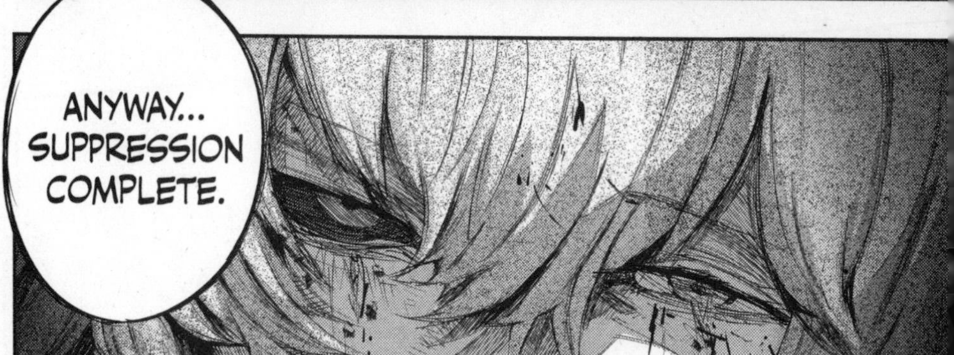
ANYWAY... SUPPRESSION COMPLETE.

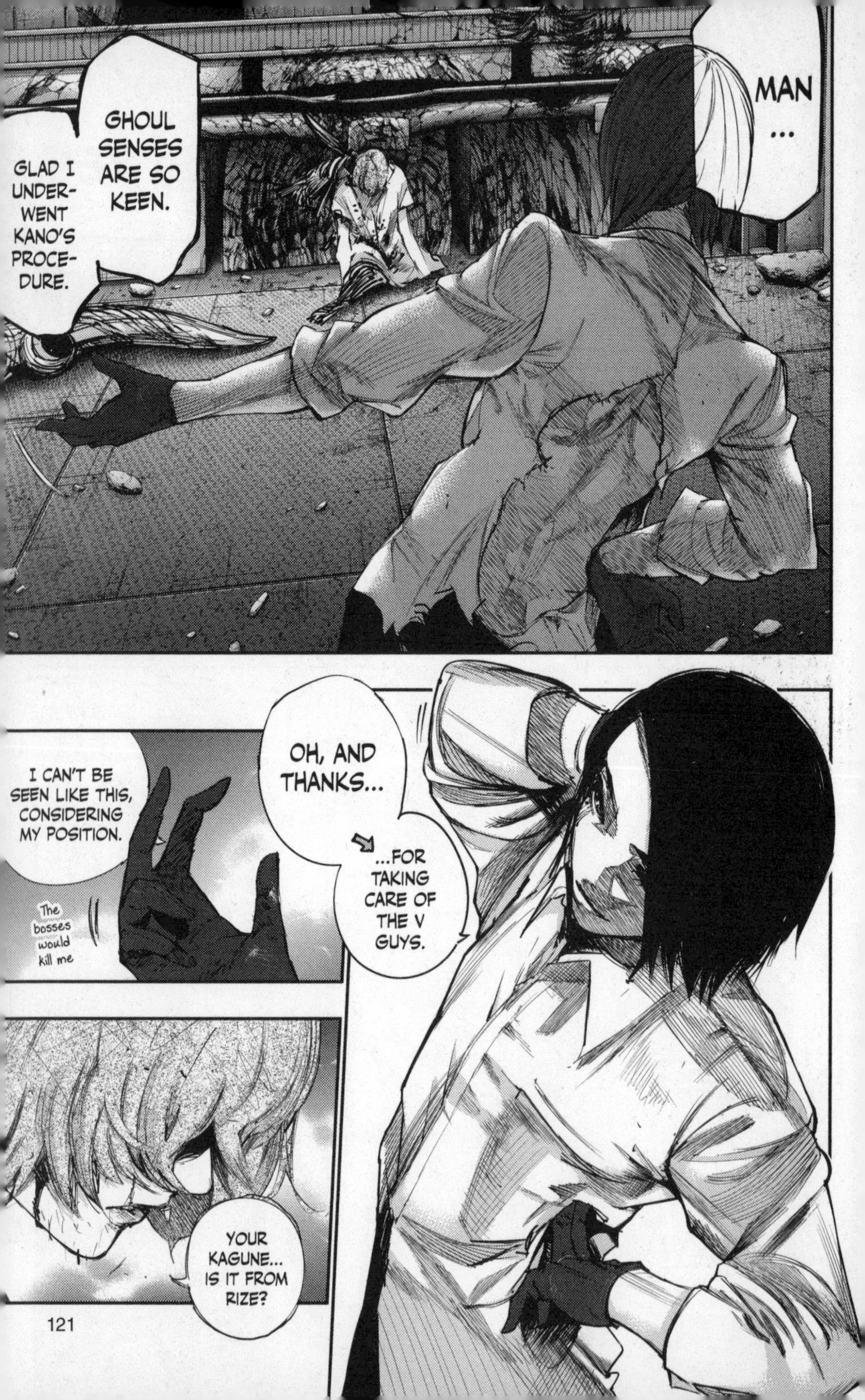
MAN...
GHOUL SENSES ARE SO KEEN.
GLAD I UNDERWENT KANO'S PROCEDURE.
OH, AND THANKS...
...FOR TAKING CARE OF THE V GUYS.
I CAN'T BE SEEN LIKE THIS, CONSIDERING MY POSITION.
The bosses would kill me
YOUR KAGUNE... IS IT FROM RIZE?

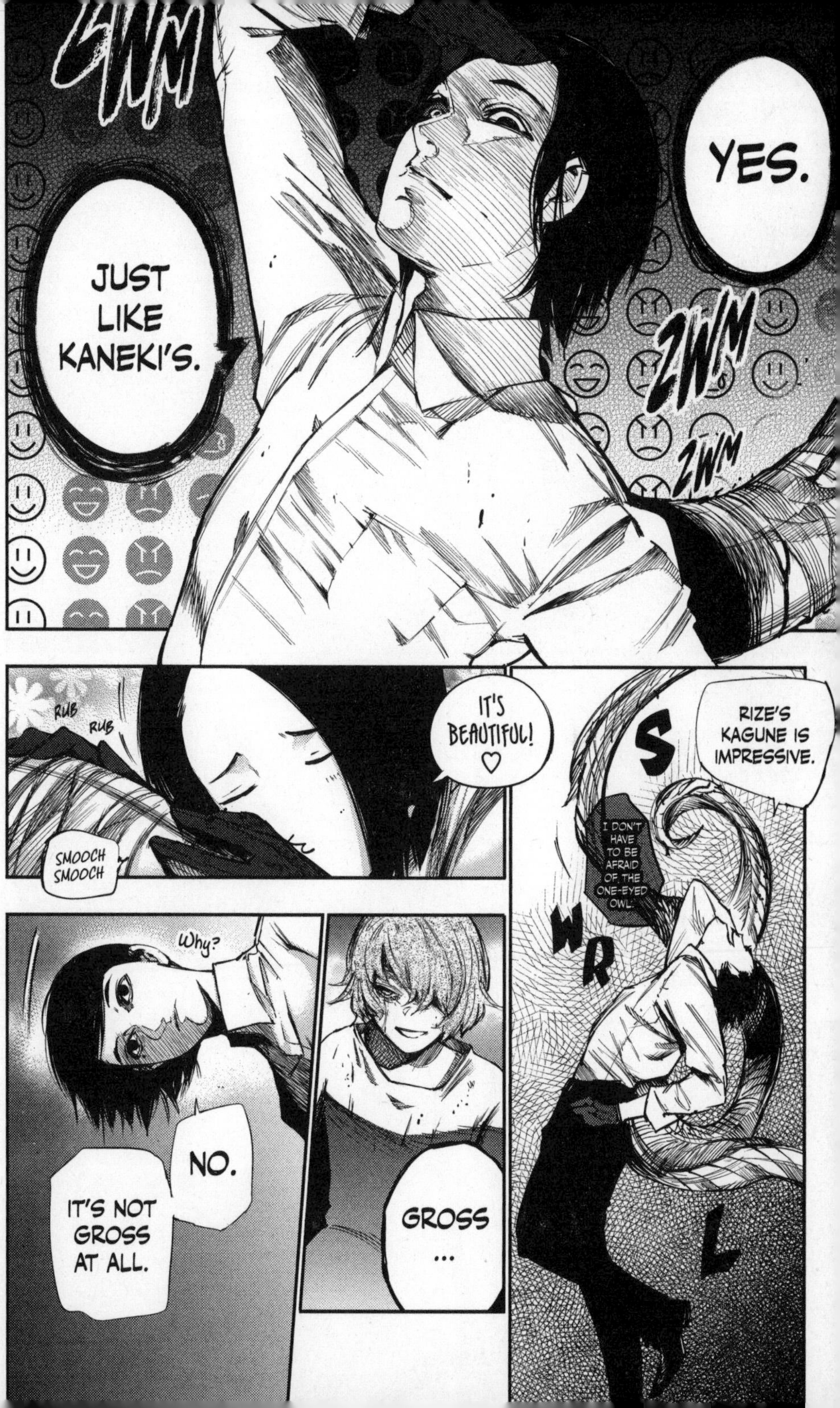
YES.
ZWM
ZWM
JUST LIKE KANEKI'S.
ZWM
RIZE'S KAGUNE IS IMPRESSIVE.
S
I DON'T HAVE TO BE AFRAID OF THE ONE-EYED OWL.
WR
L
IT'S BEAUTIFUL! ♡
RUB RUB
SMOOCH SMOOCH
GROSS ...
Why?
NO.
IT'S NOT GROSS AT ALL.

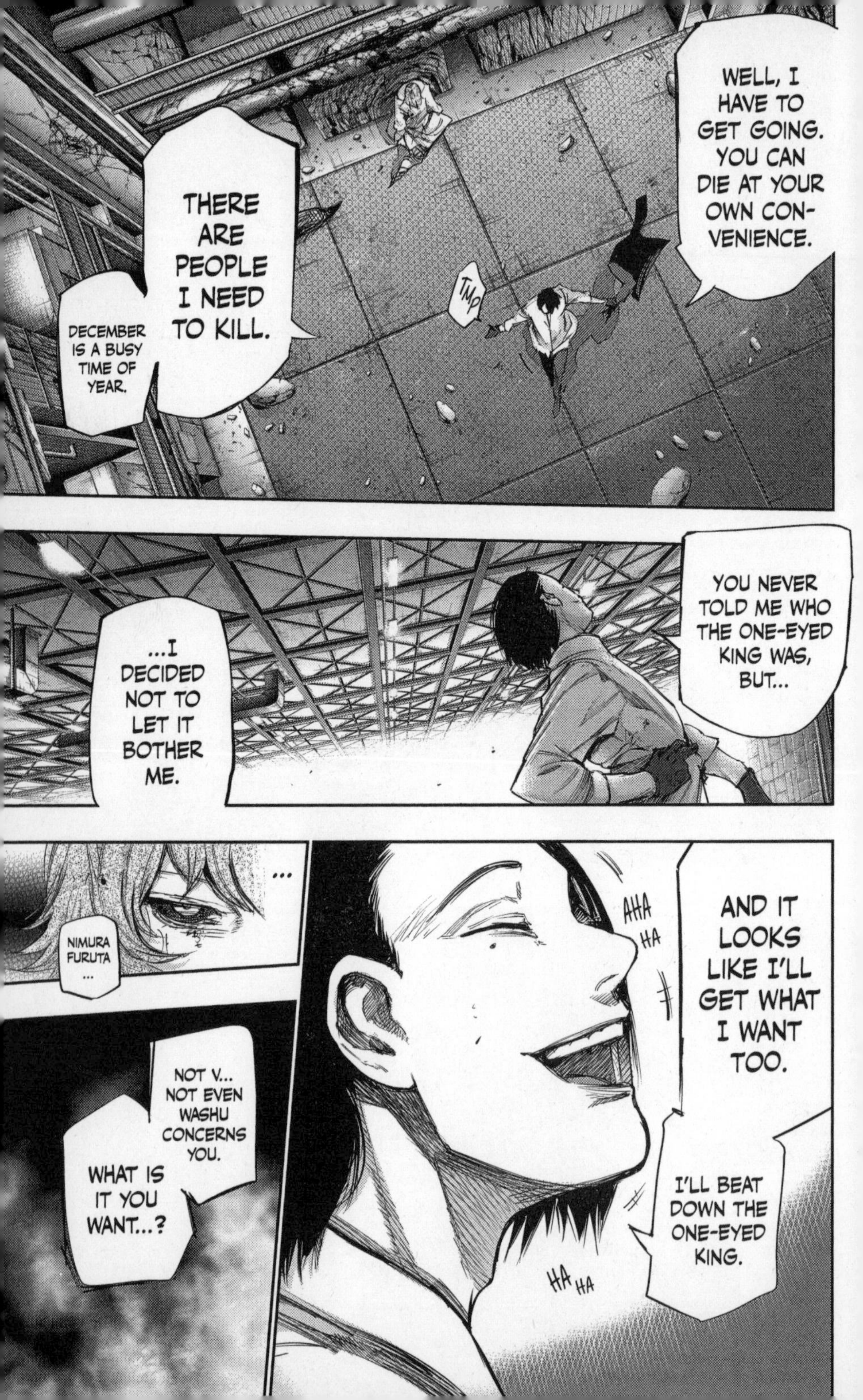
WELL, I HAVE TO GET GOING. YOU CAN DIE AT YOUR OWN CON-VENIENCE.
TMP
THERE ARE PEOPLE I NEED TO KILL.
DECEMBER IS A BUSY TIME OF YEAR.
YOU NEVER TOLD ME WHO THE ONE-EYED KING WAS, BUT...
...I DECIDED NOT TO LET IT BOTHER ME.
AND IT LOOKS LIKE I'LL GET WHAT I WANT TOO.
AHA HA
I'LL BEAT DOWN THE ONE-EYED KING.
HA HA
...
NIMURA FURUTA ...
NOT V... NOT EVEN WASHU CONCERNS YOU.
WHAT IS IT YOU WANT...?

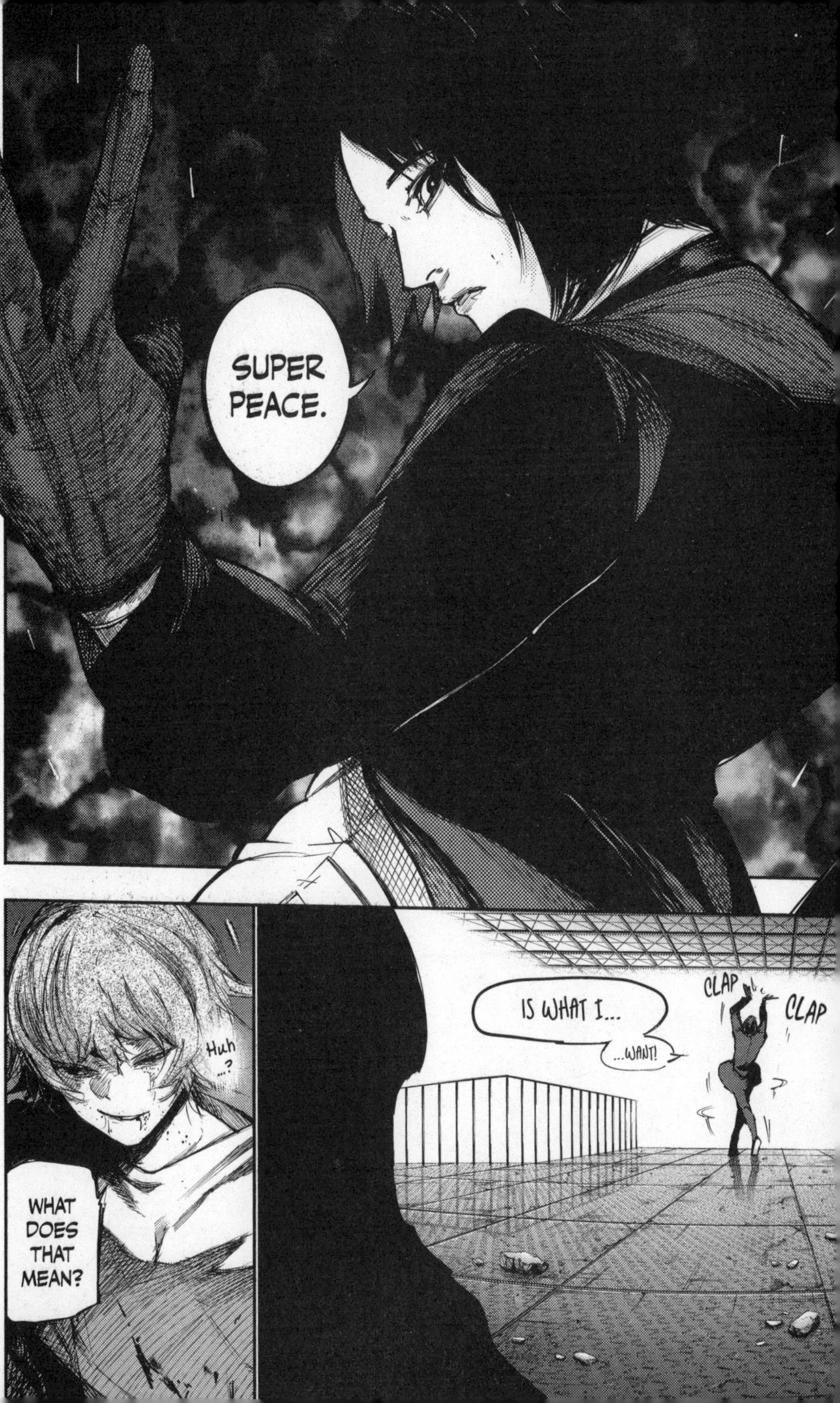
SUPER PEACE.
IS WHAT I...
...WANT!
CLAP
CLAP
Huh ...?
WHAT DOES THAT MEAN?

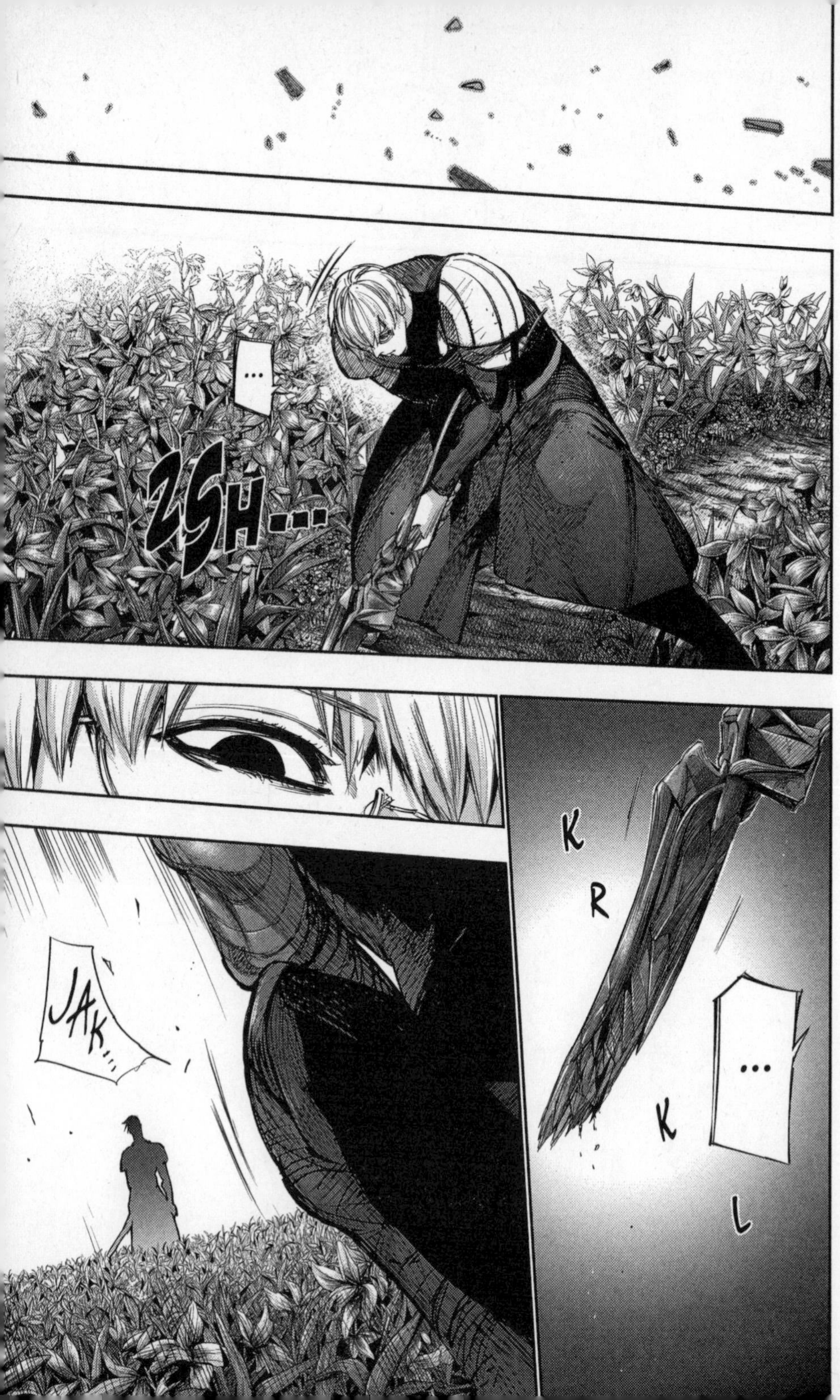
...
ZSH...
KRKL
...
JAK...

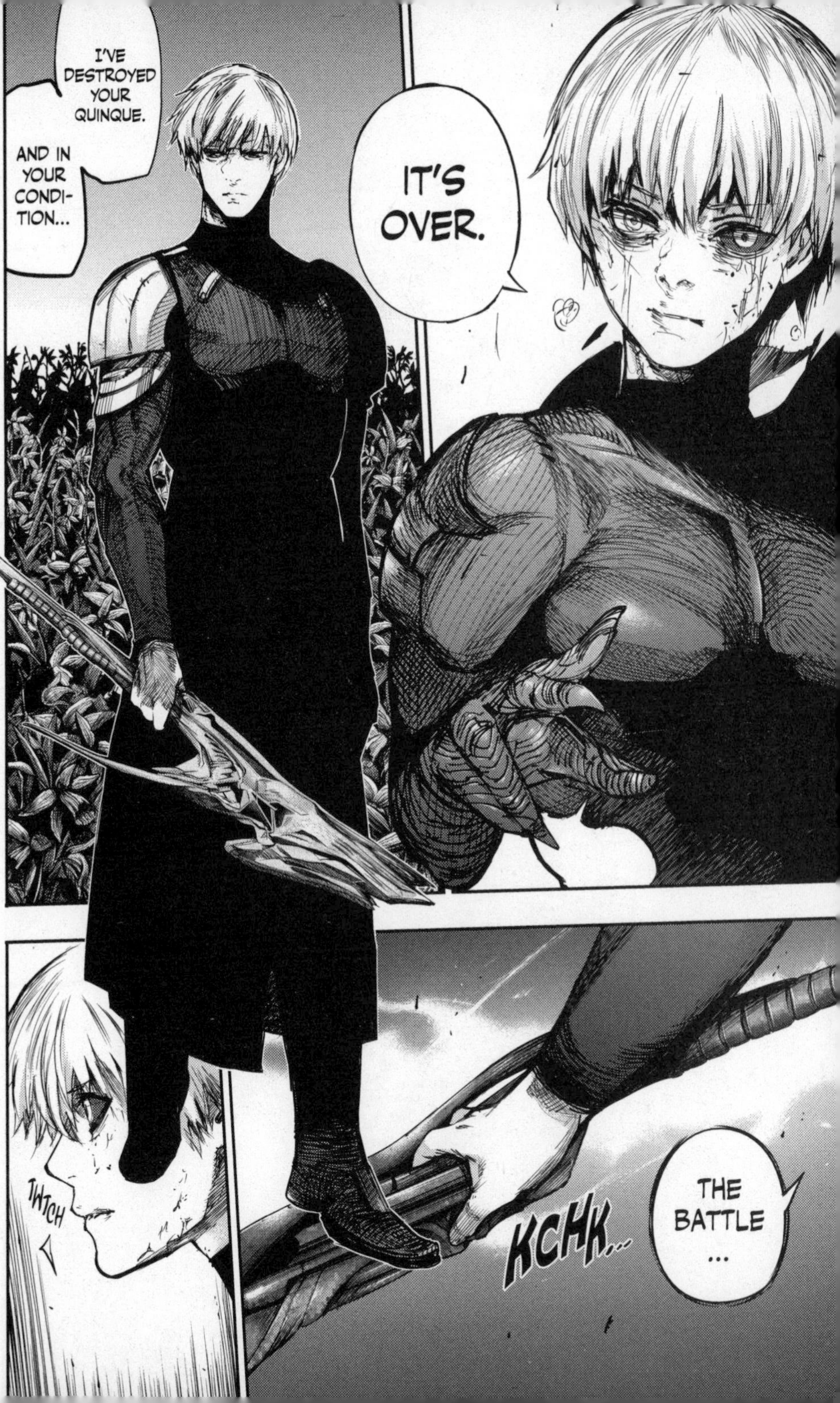
I'VE DESTROYED YOUR QUINQUE.
AND IN YOUR CONDITION...
IT'S OVER.
KCHK...
THE BATTLE ...
TWITCH

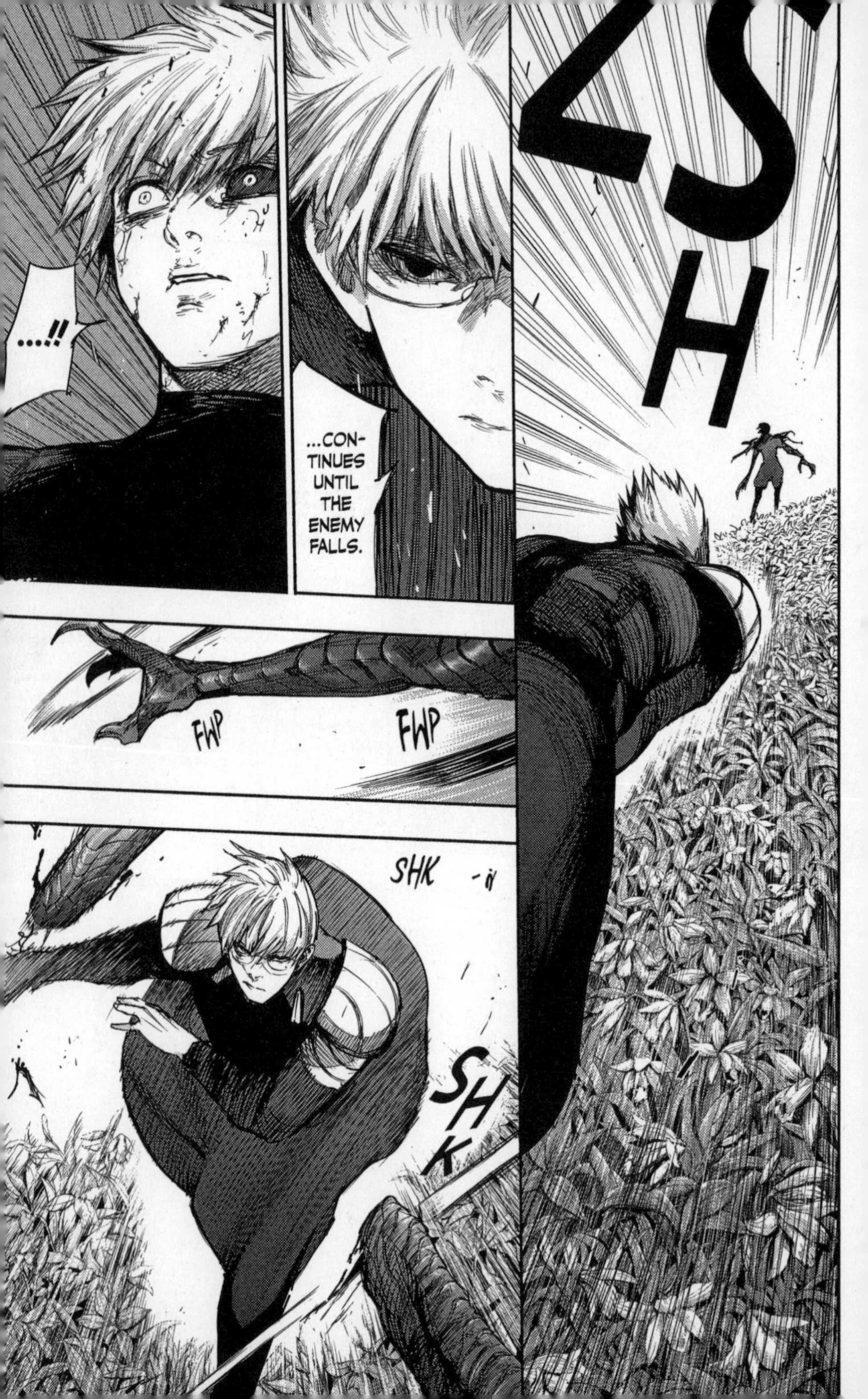
ZSH
...CONTINUES UNTIL THE ENEMY FALLS.
...!!
FWP
FWP
SHK
SHK

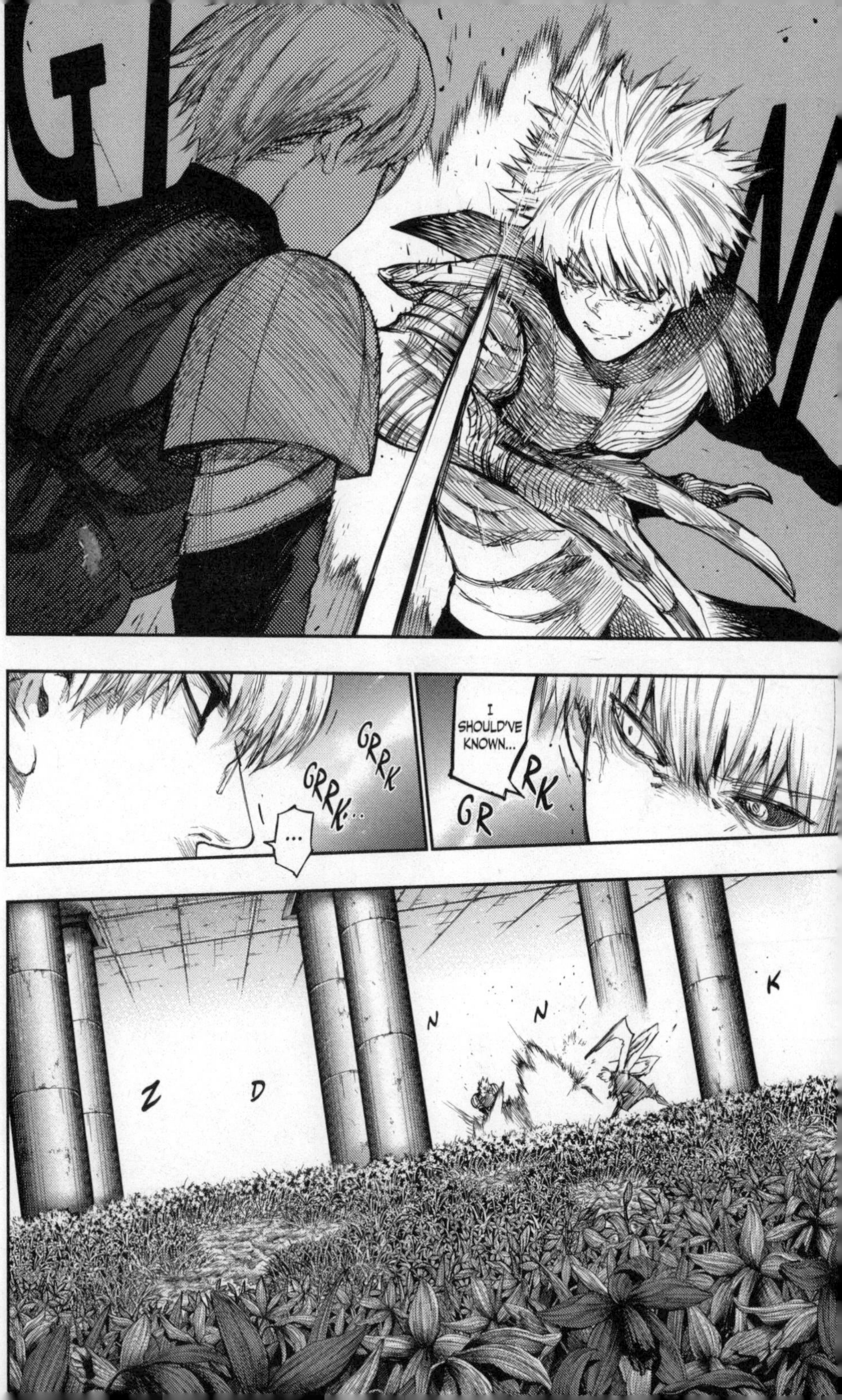
I SHOULD'VE KNOWN...
GR RK
GRRK
GRRK...
...
Z D N N K

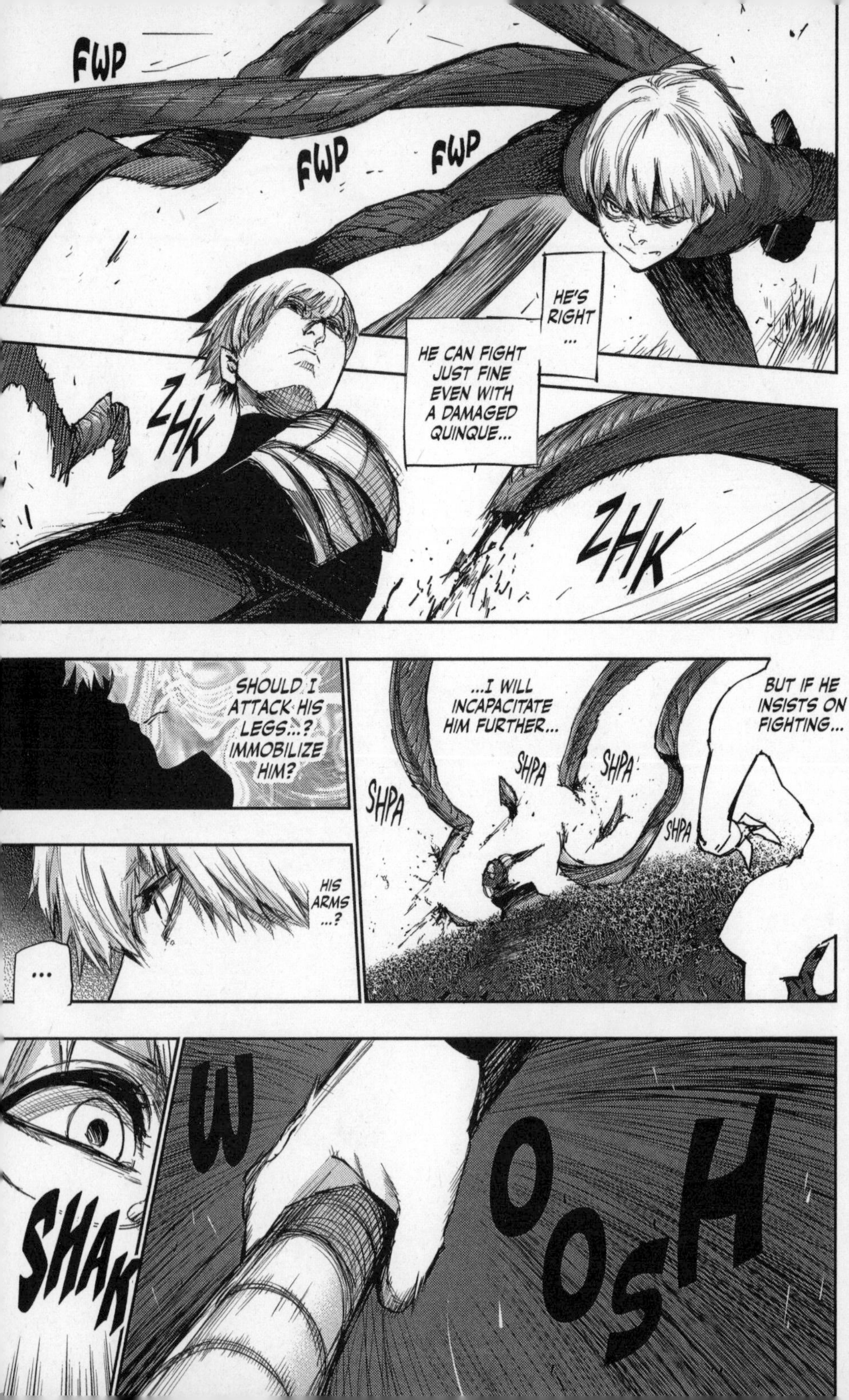
FWP
FWP
FWP
HE'S RIGHT ...
HE CAN FIGHT JUST FINE EVEN WITH A DAMAGED QUINQUE...
ZHK
ZHK
BUT IF HE INSISTS ON FIGHTING...
...I WILL INCAPACITATE HIM FURTHER...
SHPA
SHPA
SHPA
SHPA
SHOULD I ATTACK HIS LEGS...? IMMOBILIZE HIM?
HIS ARMS ...?
...
WOOSH
SHAK

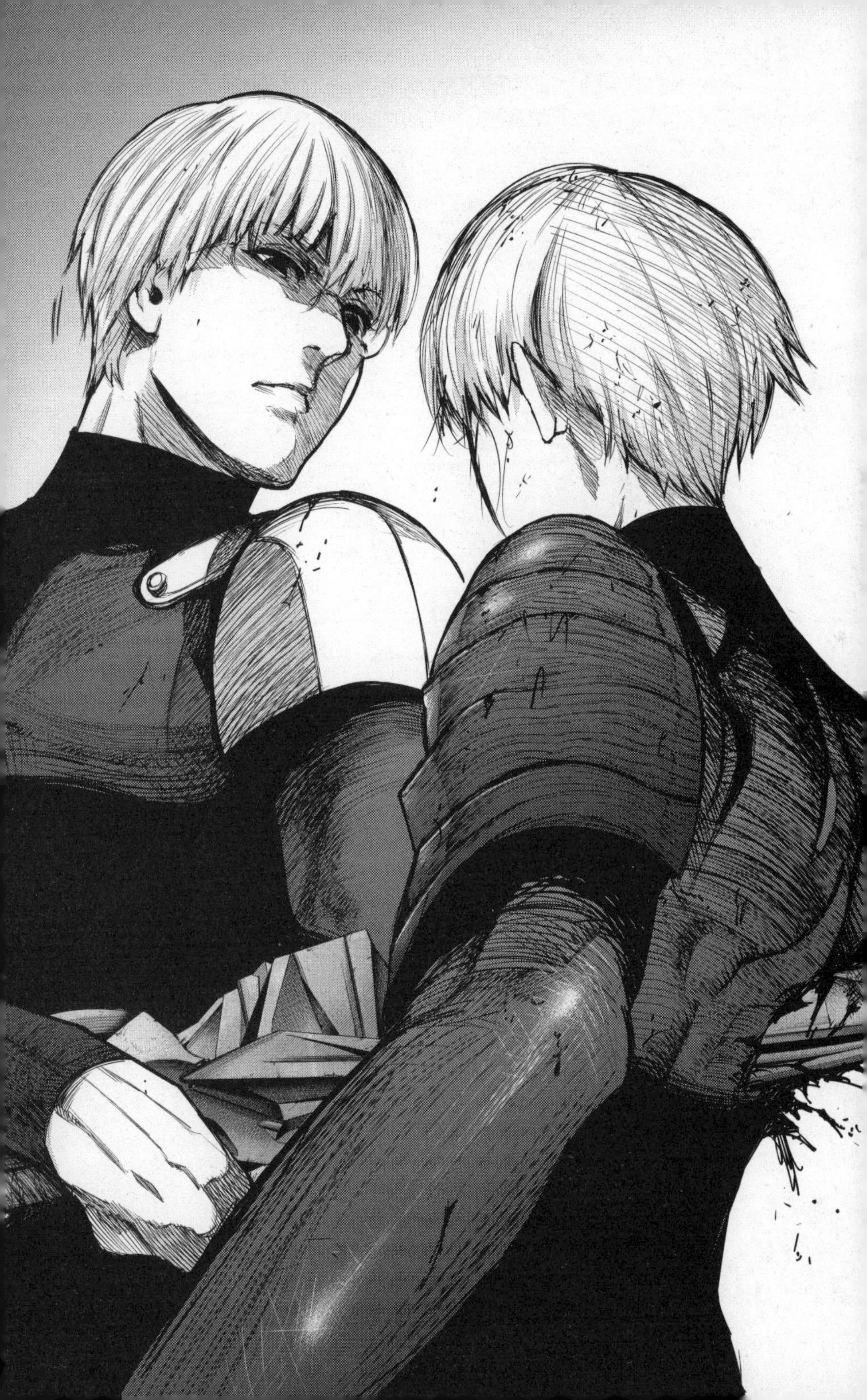

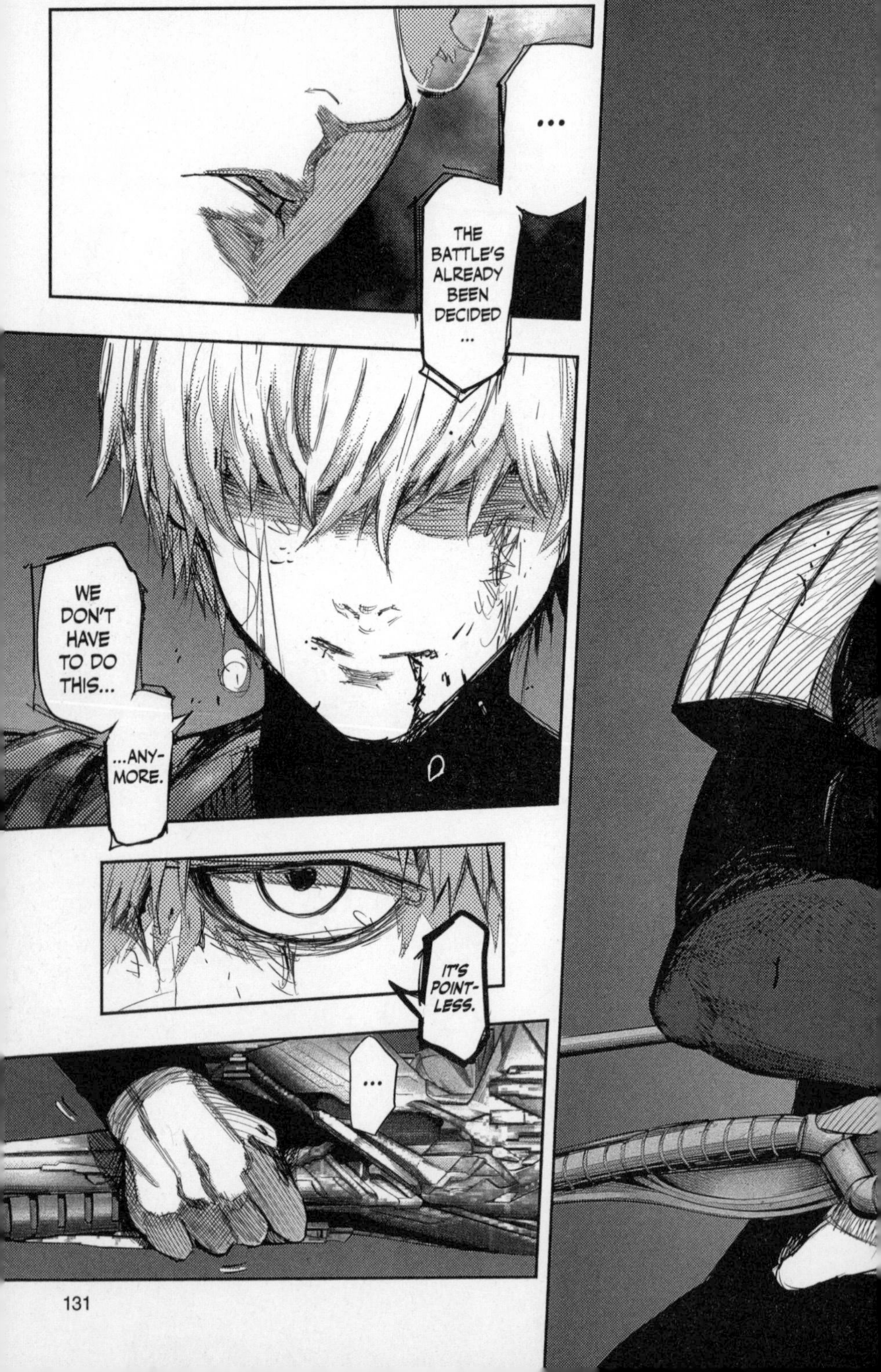
...
THE BATTLE'S ALREADY BEEN DECIDED...
WE DON'T HAVE TO DO THIS...
...ANYMORE.
IT'S POINTLESS.
...

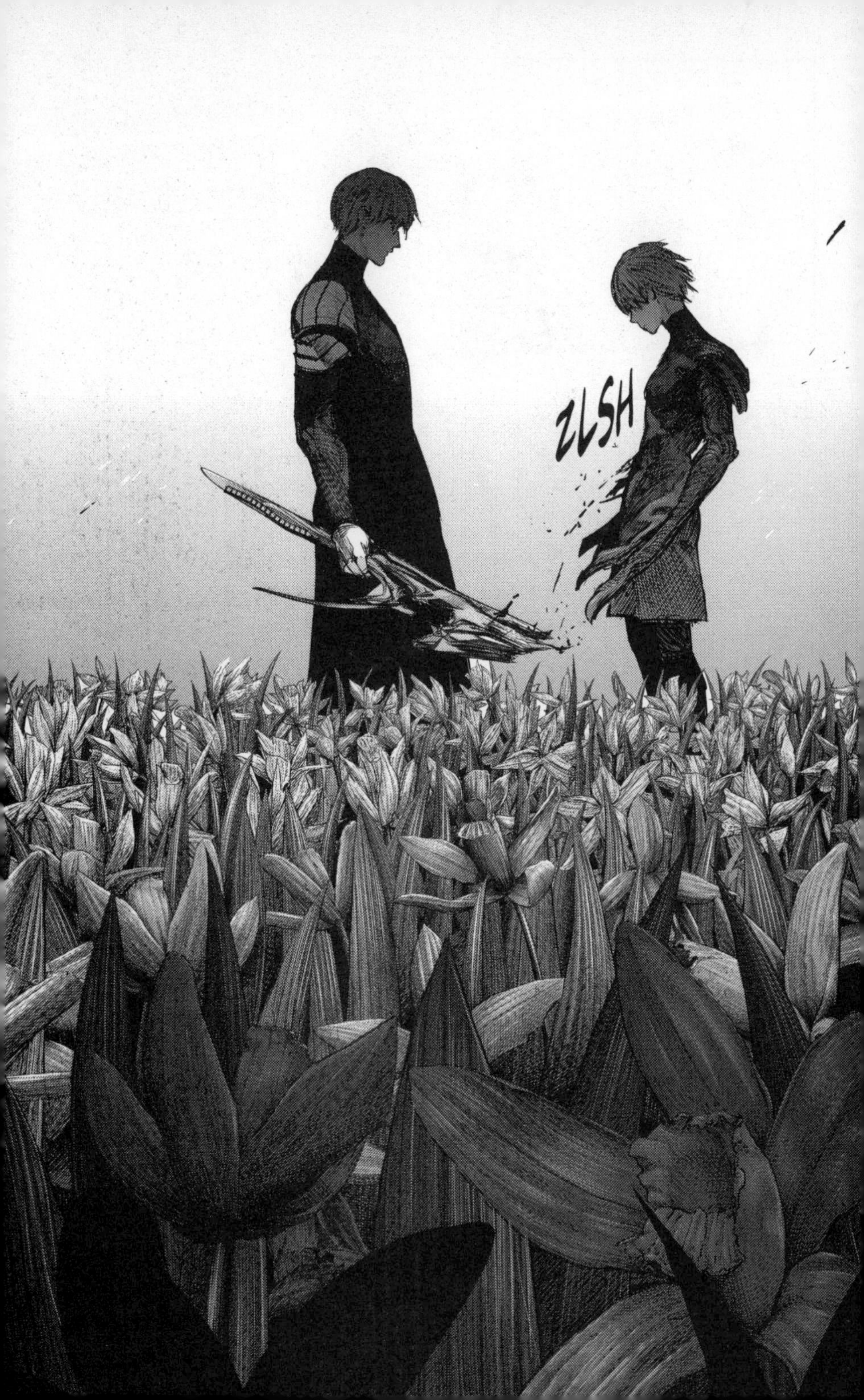
ZLSH

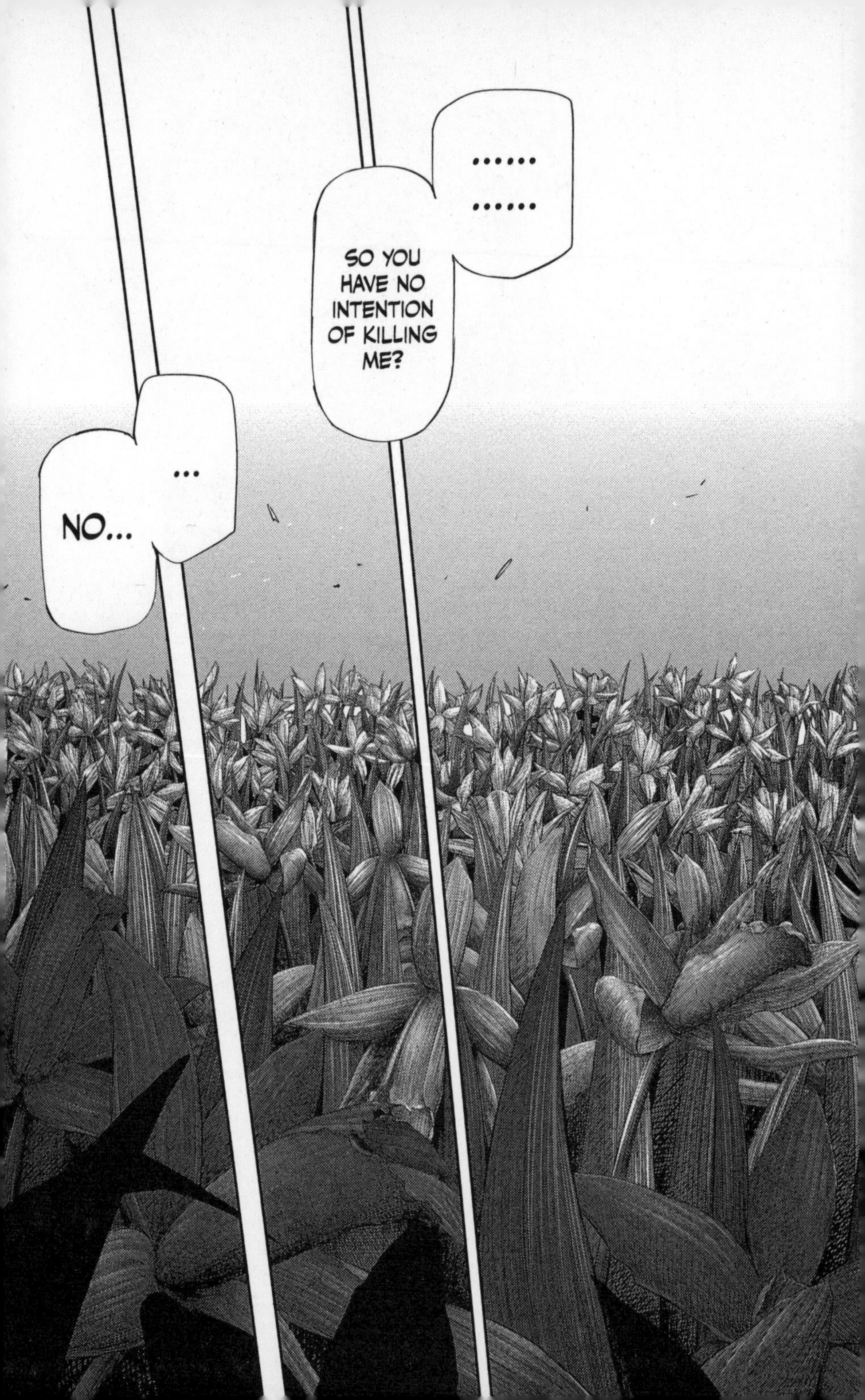

......
......
SO YOU HAVE NO INTENTION OF KILLING ME?
...
NO...

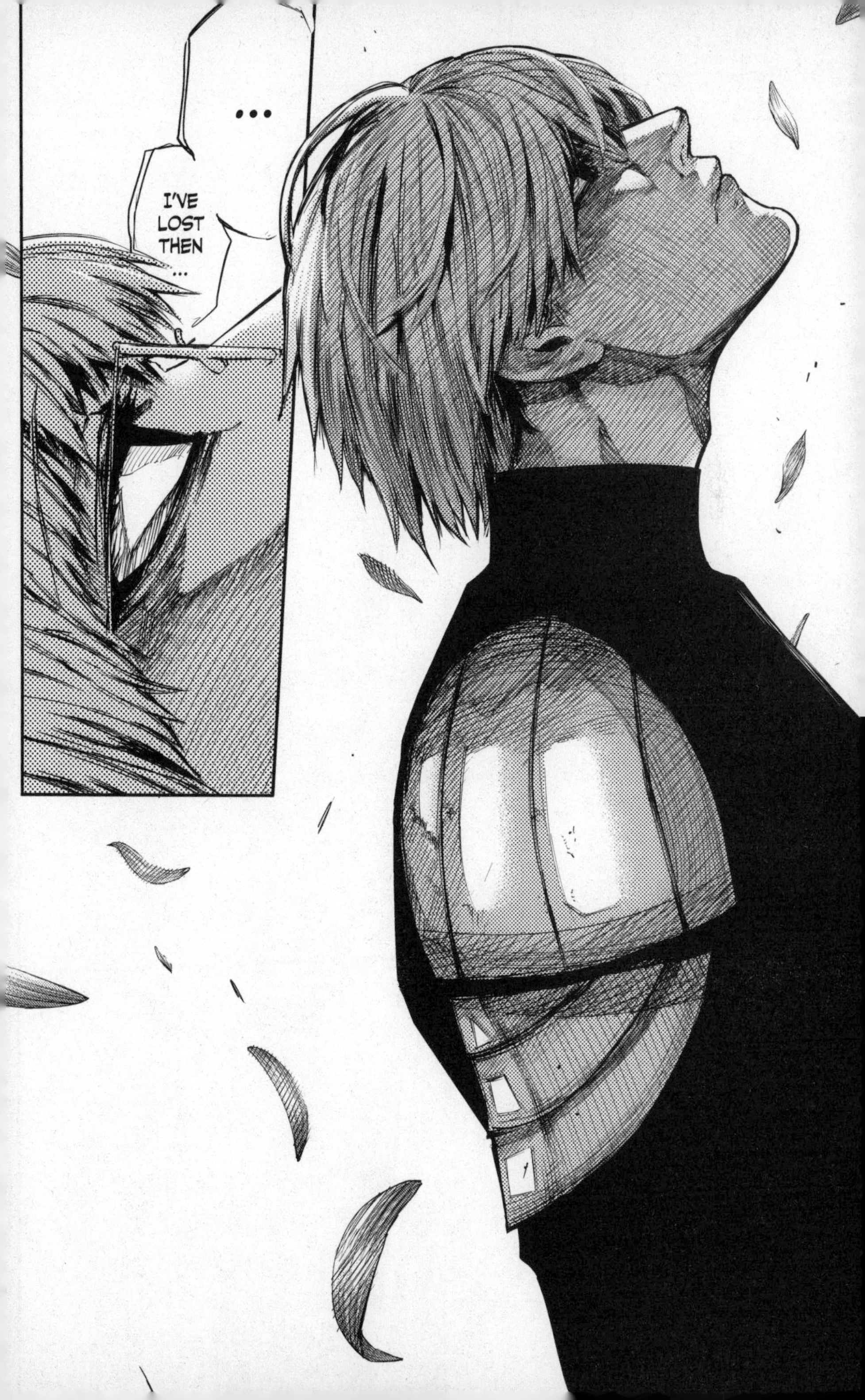
...
I'VE LOST THEN ...

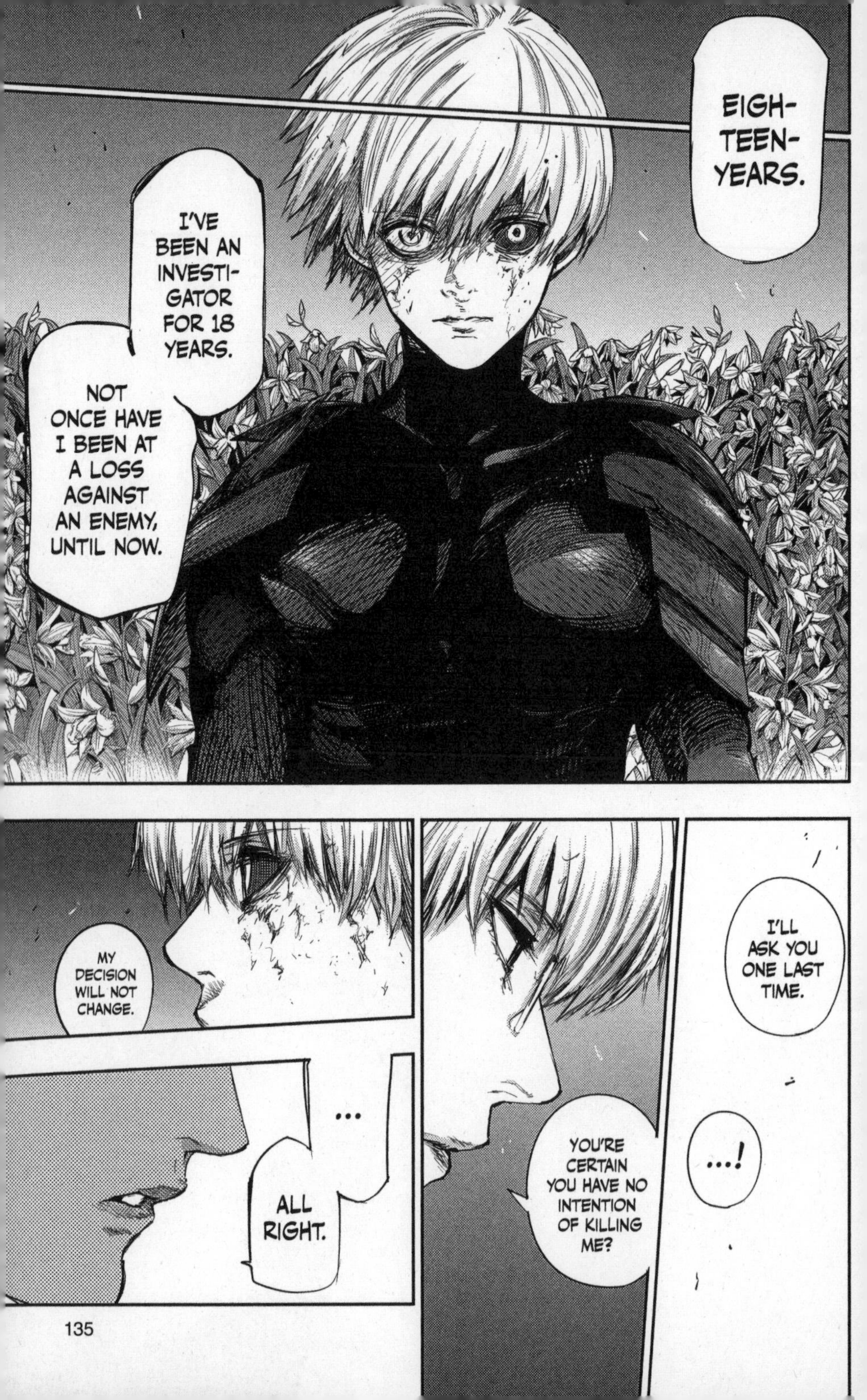
EIGH-TEEN-YEARS.
I'VE BEEN AN INVESTI-GATOR FOR 18 YEARS.
NOT ONCE HAVE I BEEN AT A LOSS AGAINST AN ENEMY, UNTIL NOW.
I'LL ASK YOU ONE LAST TIME.
...!
YOU'RE CERTAIN YOU HAVE NO INTENTION OF KILLING ME?
MY DECISION WILL NOT CHANGE.
...
ALL RIGHT.

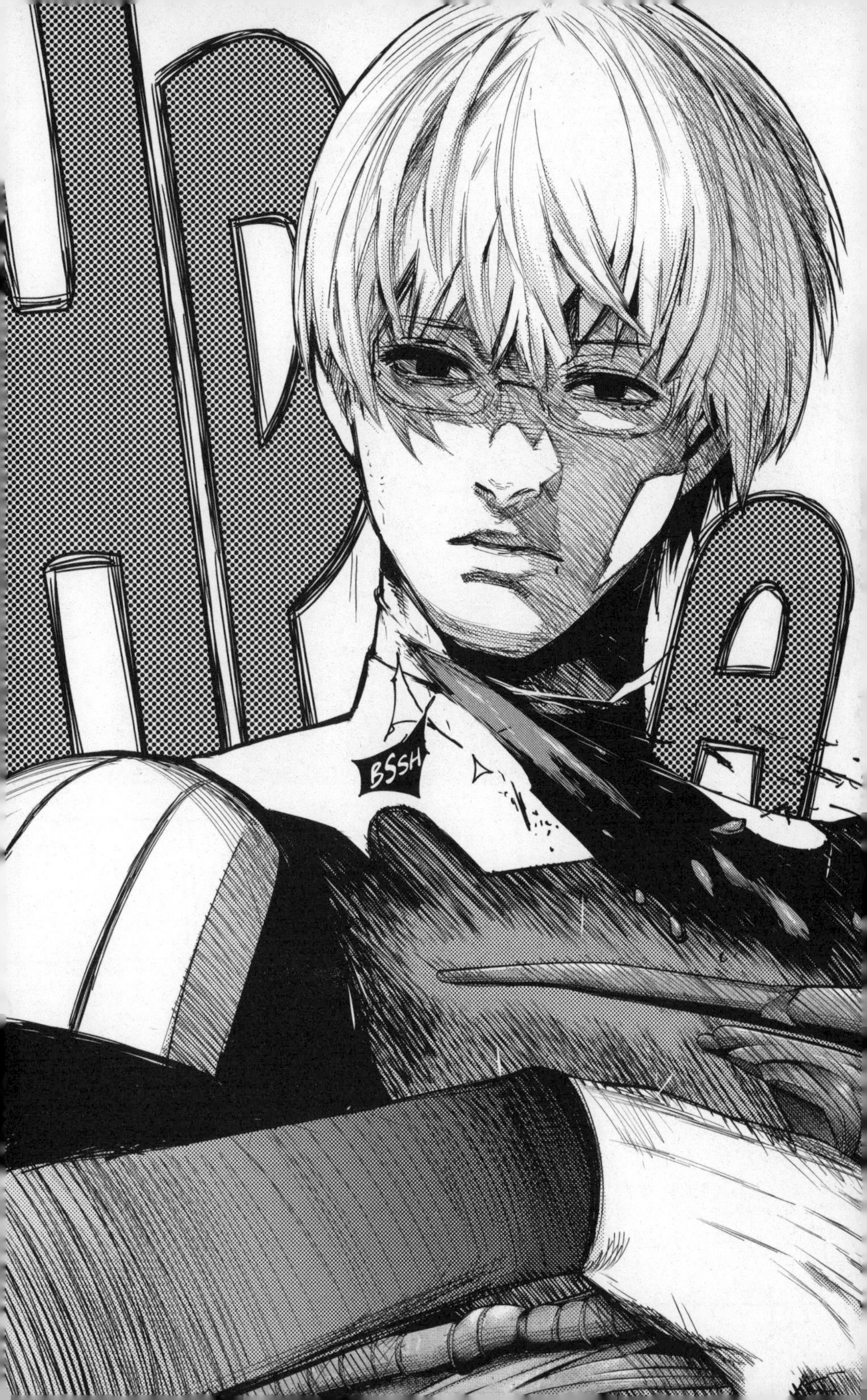
BSSH

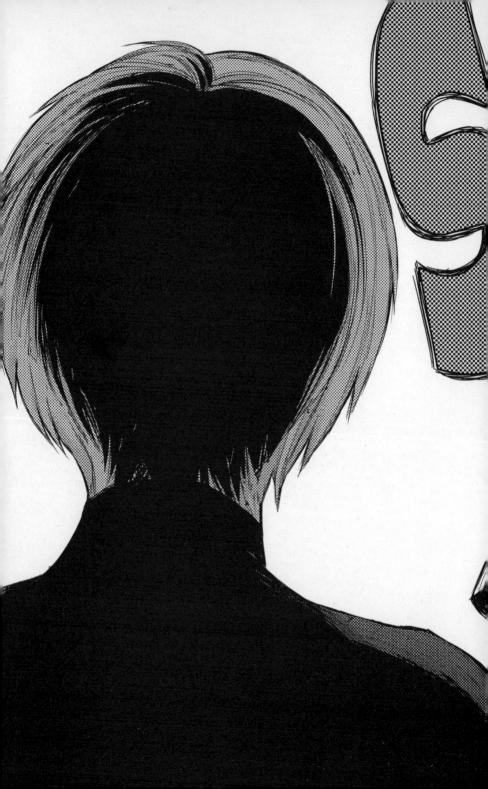

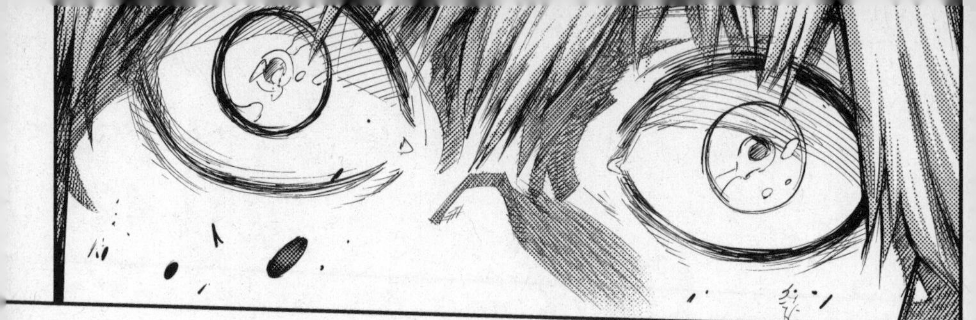

Heard the Sound of the Gate Closing :83

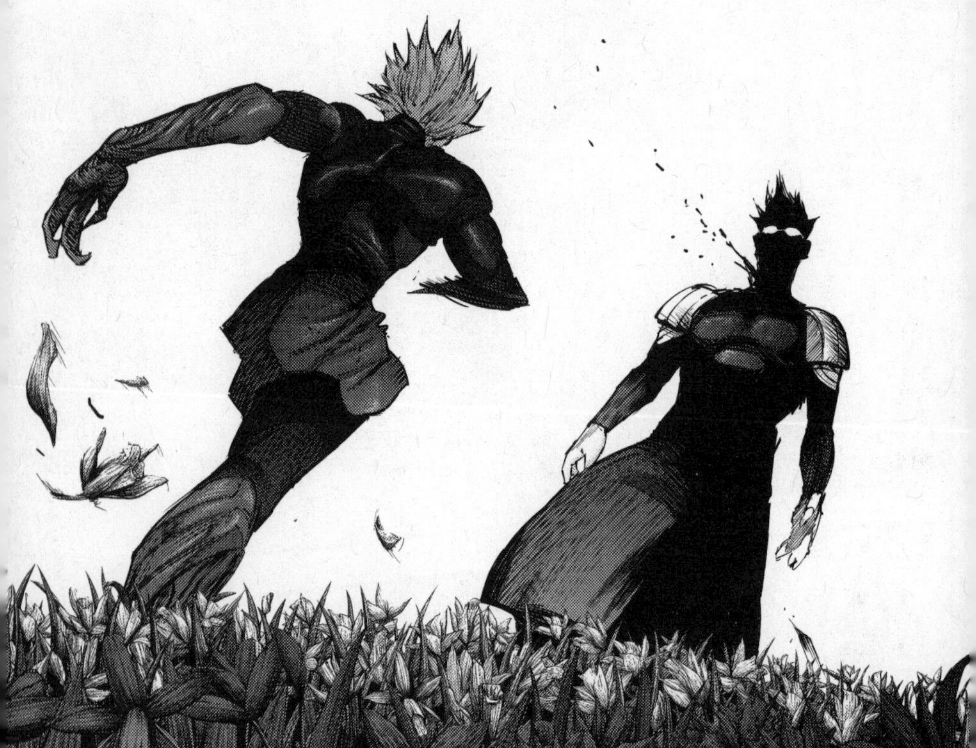

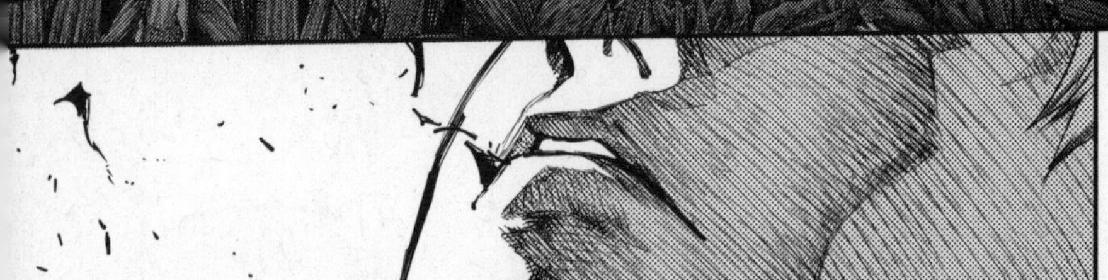

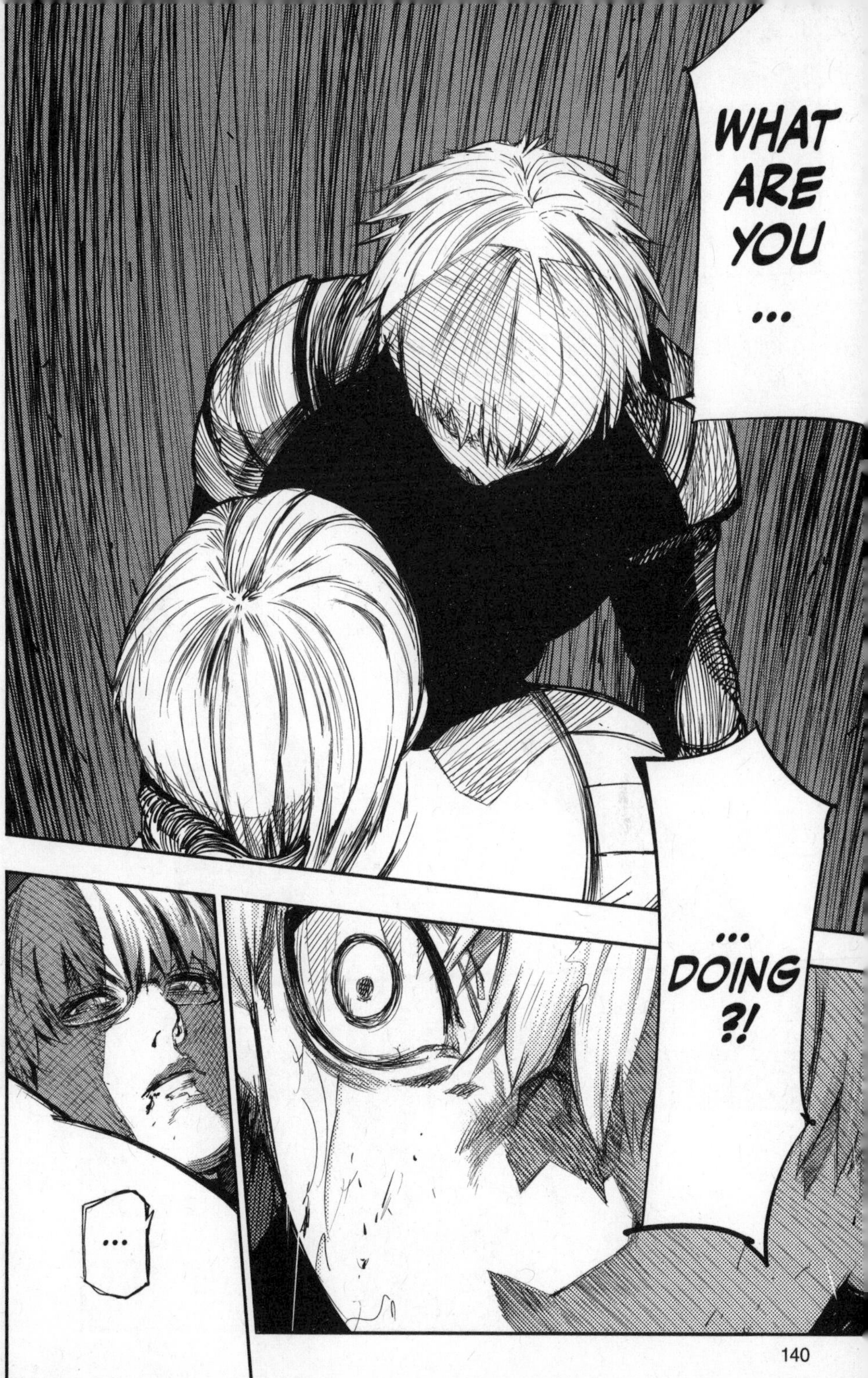
WHAT ARE YOU ...
... DOING ?!
...

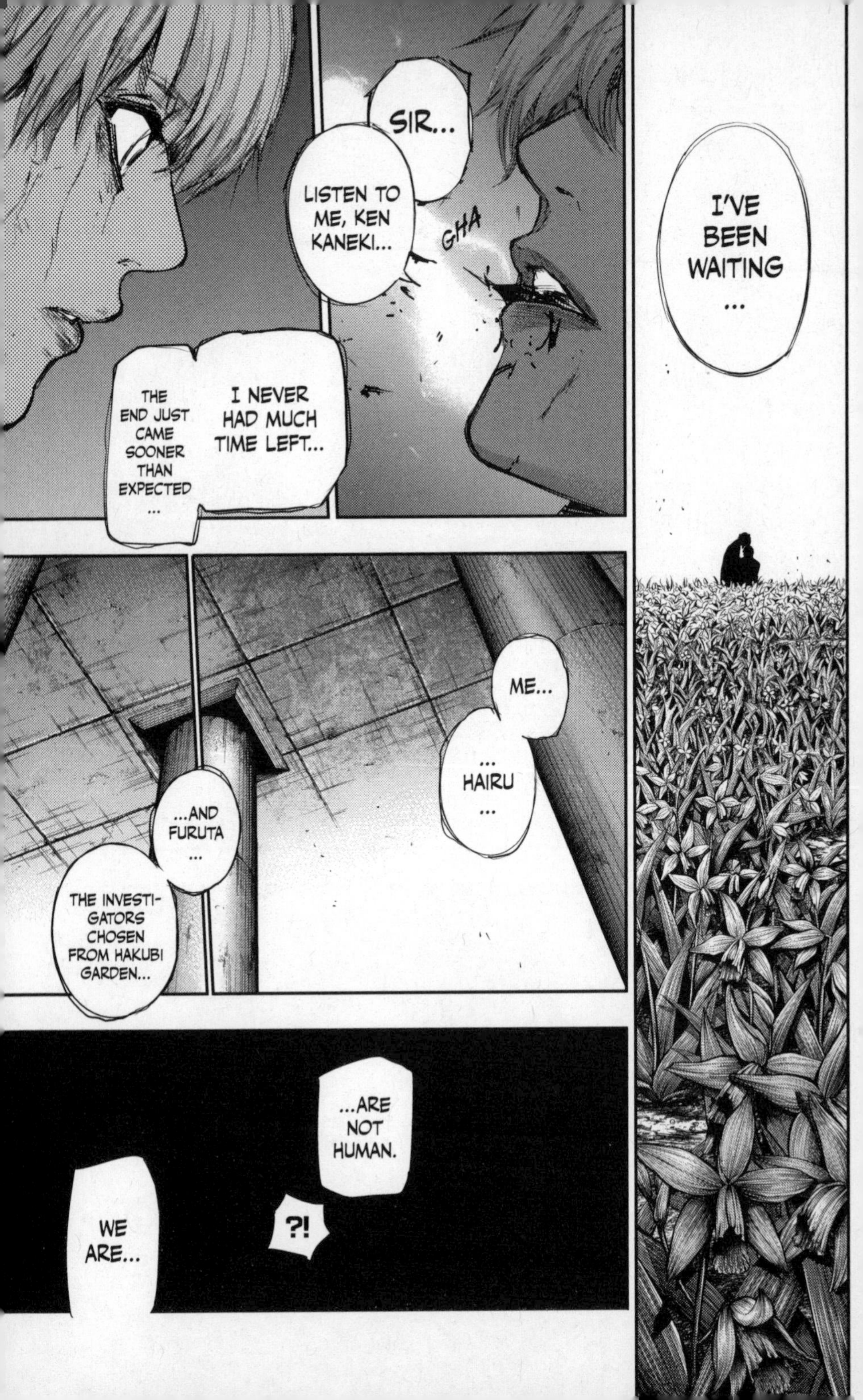
I'VE BEEN WAITING ...
SIR...
LISTEN TO ME, KEN KANEKI...
GHA
I NEVER HAD MUCH TIME LEFT...
THE END JUST CAME SOONER THAN EXPECTED ...
ME...
... HAIRU ...
...AND FURUTA ...
THE INVESTI- GATORS CHOSEN FROM HAKUBI GARDEN...
...ARE NOT HUMAN.
?!
WE ARE...

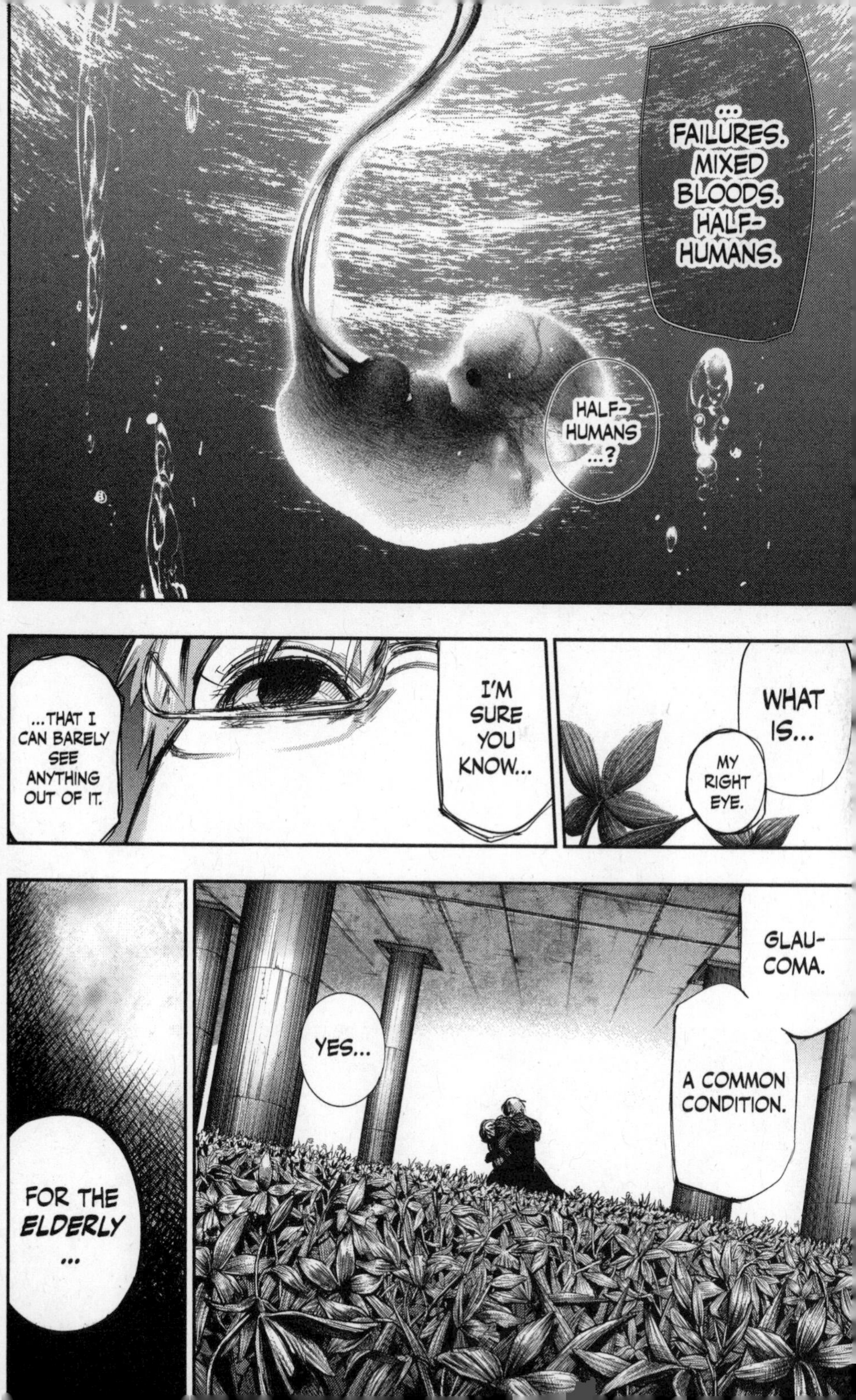
...FAILURES. MIXED BLOODS. HALF-HUMANS.
HALF-HUMANS ...?
WHAT IS...
MY RIGHT EYE.
I'M SURE YOU KNOW...
...THAT I CAN BARELY SEE ANYTHING OUT OF IT.
GLAU-COMA.
A COMMON CONDITION.
YES...
FOR THE *ELDERLY* ...

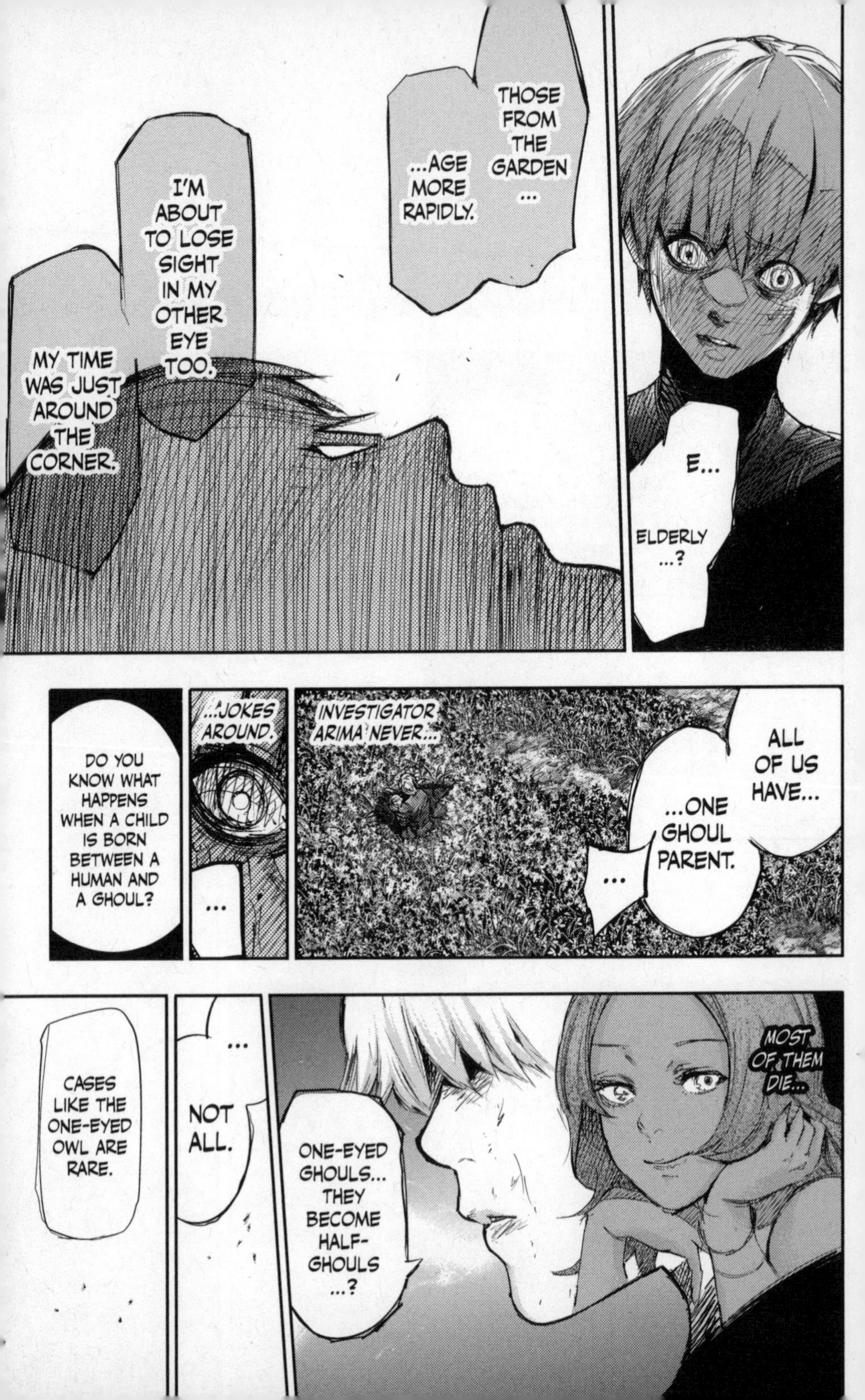
E...
ELDERLY ...?
THOSE FROM THE GARDEN ...
...AGE MORE RAPIDLY.
I'M ABOUT TO LOSE SIGHT IN MY OTHER EYE TOO.
MY TIME WAS JUST AROUND THE CORNER.
ALL OF US HAVE...
...ONE GHOUL PARENT.
...
INVESTIGATOR ARIMA NEVER...
...JOKES AROUND.
...
DO YOU KNOW WHAT HAPPENS WHEN A CHILD IS BORN BETWEEN A HUMAN AND A GHOUL?
MOST OF THEM DIE...
ONE-EYED GHOULS... THEY BECOME HALF-GHOULS ...?
...
NOT ALL.
CASES LIKE THE ONE-EYED OWL ARE RARE.

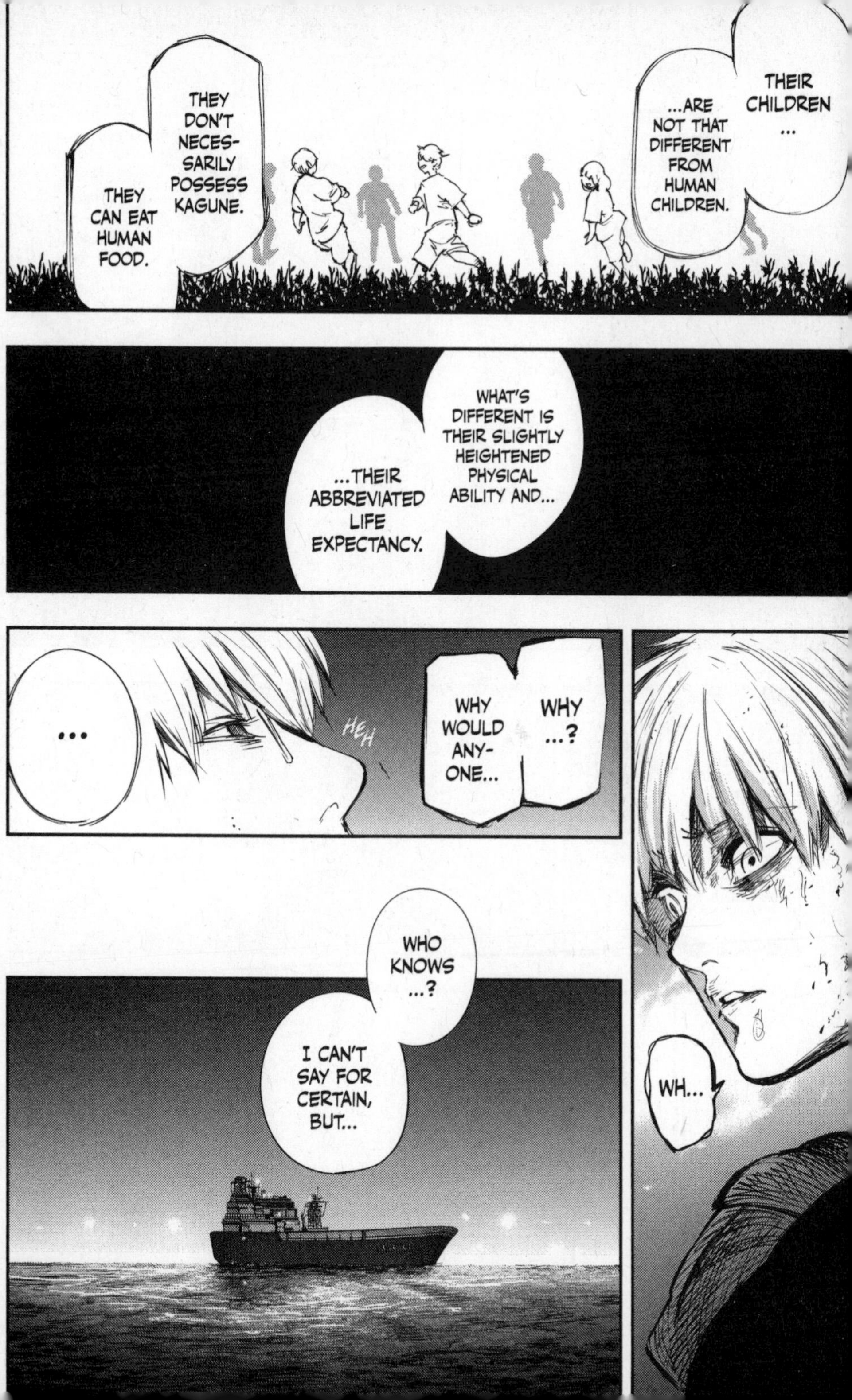
THEIR CHILDREN ...
...ARE NOT THAT DIFFERENT FROM HUMAN CHILDREN.
THEY DON'T NECES-SARILY POSSESS KAGUNE.
THEY CAN EAT HUMAN FOOD.
WHAT'S DIFFERENT IS THEIR SLIGHTLY HEIGHTENED PHYSICAL ABILITY AND...
...THEIR ABBREVIATED LIFE EXPECTANCY.
WH...
WHY ...?
WHY WOULD ANY-ONE...
HEH
...
WHO KNOWS ...?
I CAN'T SAY FOR CERTAIN, BUT...

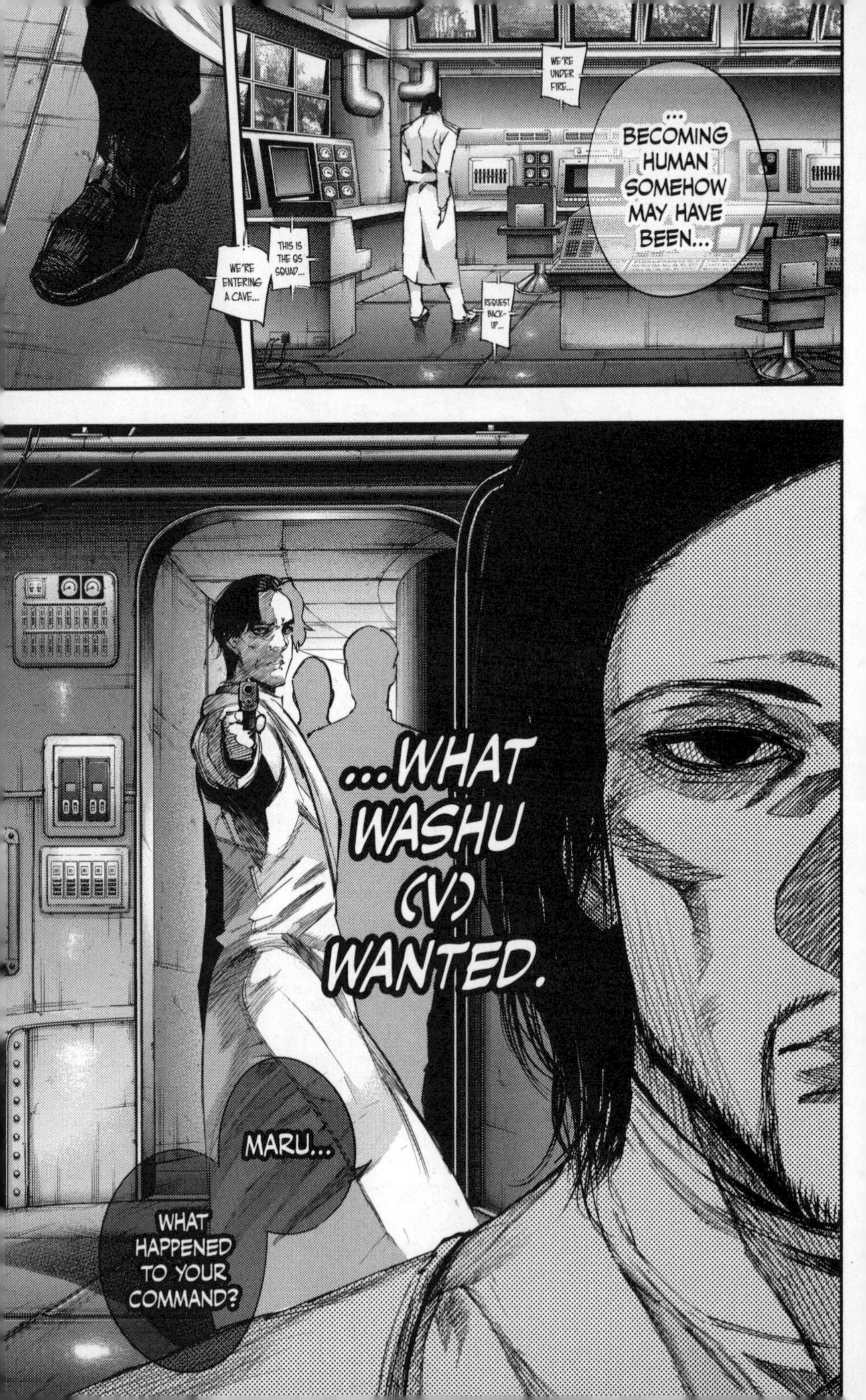
...BECOMING HUMAN SOMEHOW MAY HAVE BEEN...
WE'RE UNDER FIRE...
REQUEST BACK-UP...
THIS IS THE QS SQUAD...
WE'RE ENTERING A CAVE...
...WHAT WASHU (V) WANTED.
MARU...
WHAT HAPPENED TO YOUR COMMAND?

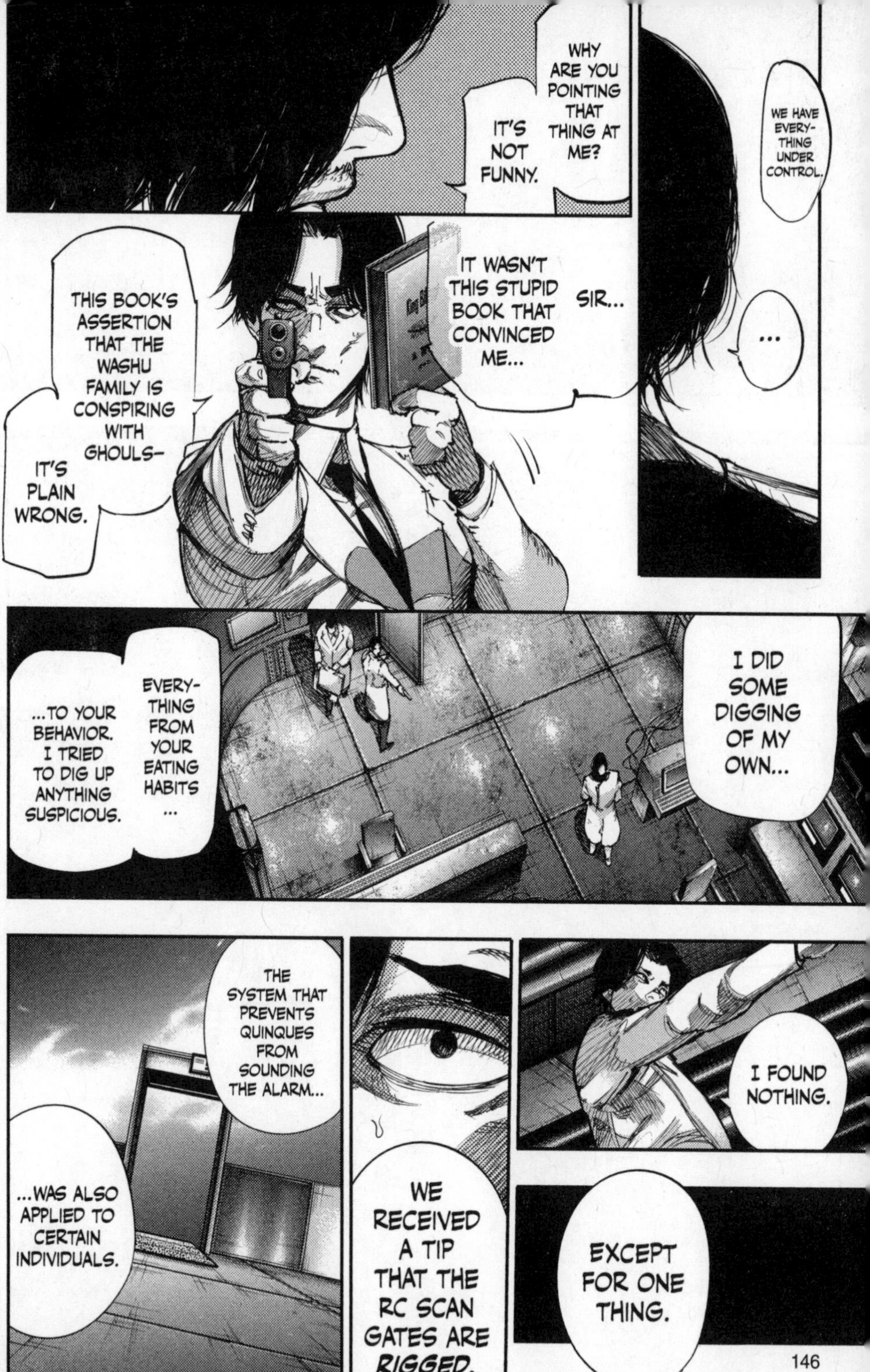
WE HAVE EVERYTHING UNDER CONTROL.
...
WHY ARE YOU POINTING THAT THING AT ME?
IT'S NOT FUNNY.
SIR...
IT WASN'T THIS STUPID BOOK THAT CONVINCED ME...
THIS BOOK'S ASSERTION THAT THE WASHU FAMILY IS CONSPIRING WITH GHOULS—
IT'S PLAIN WRONG.
I DID SOME DIGGING OF MY OWN...
EVERYTHING FROM YOUR EATING HABITS...
...TO YOUR BEHAVIOR. I TRIED TO DIG UP ANYTHING SUSPICIOUS.
I FOUND NOTHING.
EXCEPT FOR ONE THING.
WE RECEIVED A TIP THAT THE RC SCAN GATES ARE *RIGGED.*
THE SYSTEM THAT PREVENTS QUINQUES FROM SOUNDING THE ALARM...
...WAS ALSO APPLIED TO CERTAIN INDIVIDUALS.

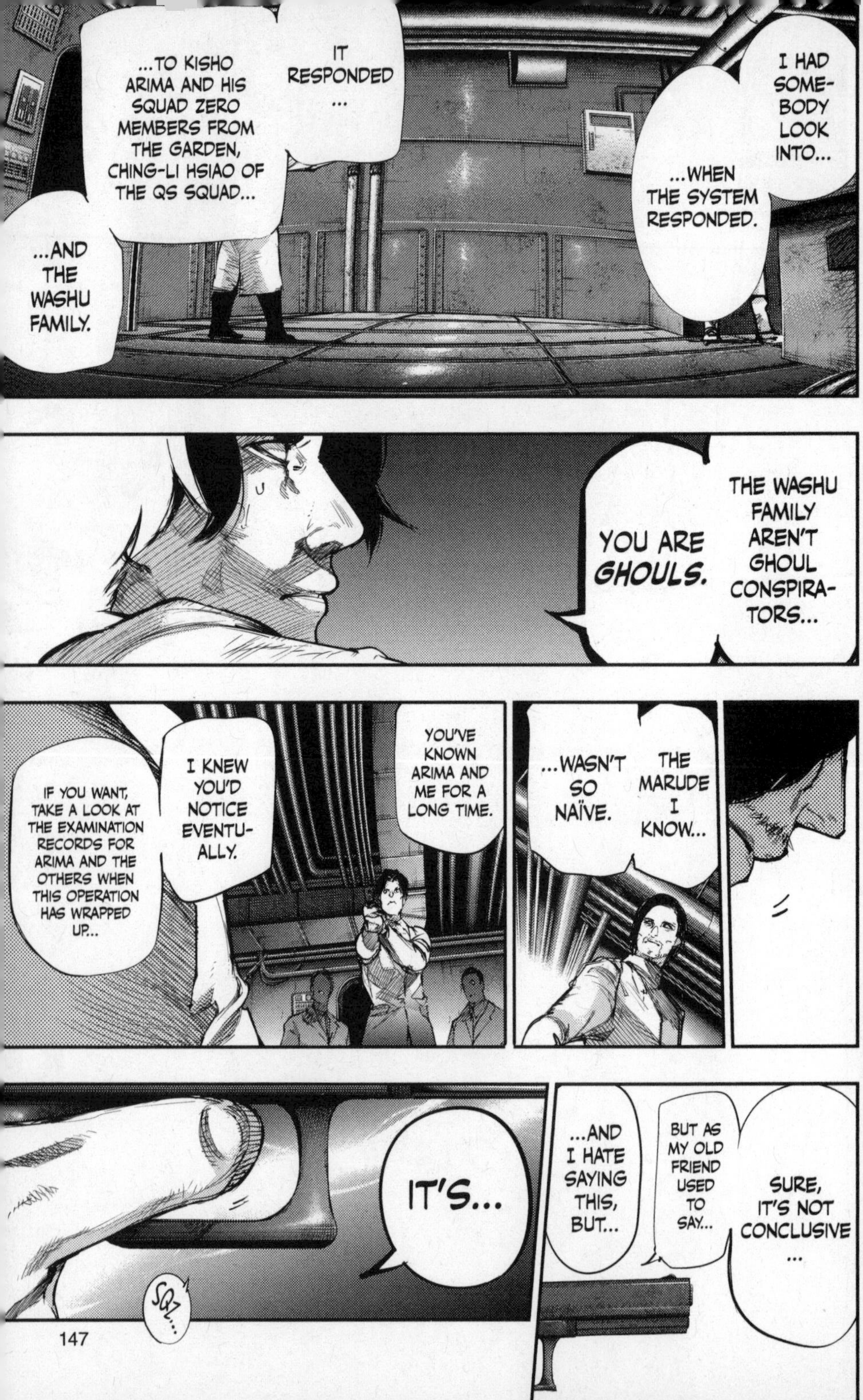
I HAD SOMEBODY LOOK INTO...
...WHEN THE SYSTEM RESPONDED.
IT RESPONDED...
...TO KISHO ARIMA AND HIS SQUAD ZERO MEMBERS FROM THE GARDEN, CHING-LI HSIAO OF THE QS SQUAD...
...AND THE WASHU FAMILY.
THE WASHU FAMILY AREN'T GHOUL CONSPIRATORS...
YOU ARE *GHOULS.*
THE MARUDE I KNOW...
...WASN'T SO NAÏVE.
YOU'VE KNOWN ARIMA AND ME FOR A LONG TIME.
I KNEW YOU'D NOTICE EVENTUALLY.
IF YOU WANT, TAKE A LOOK AT THE EXAMINATION RECORDS FOR ARIMA AND THE OTHERS WHEN THIS OPERATION HAS WRAPPED UP...
SURE, IT'S NOT CONCLUSIVE...
BUT AS MY OLD FRIEND USED TO SAY...
...AND I HATE SAYING THIS, BUT...
IT'S...
SQZ...

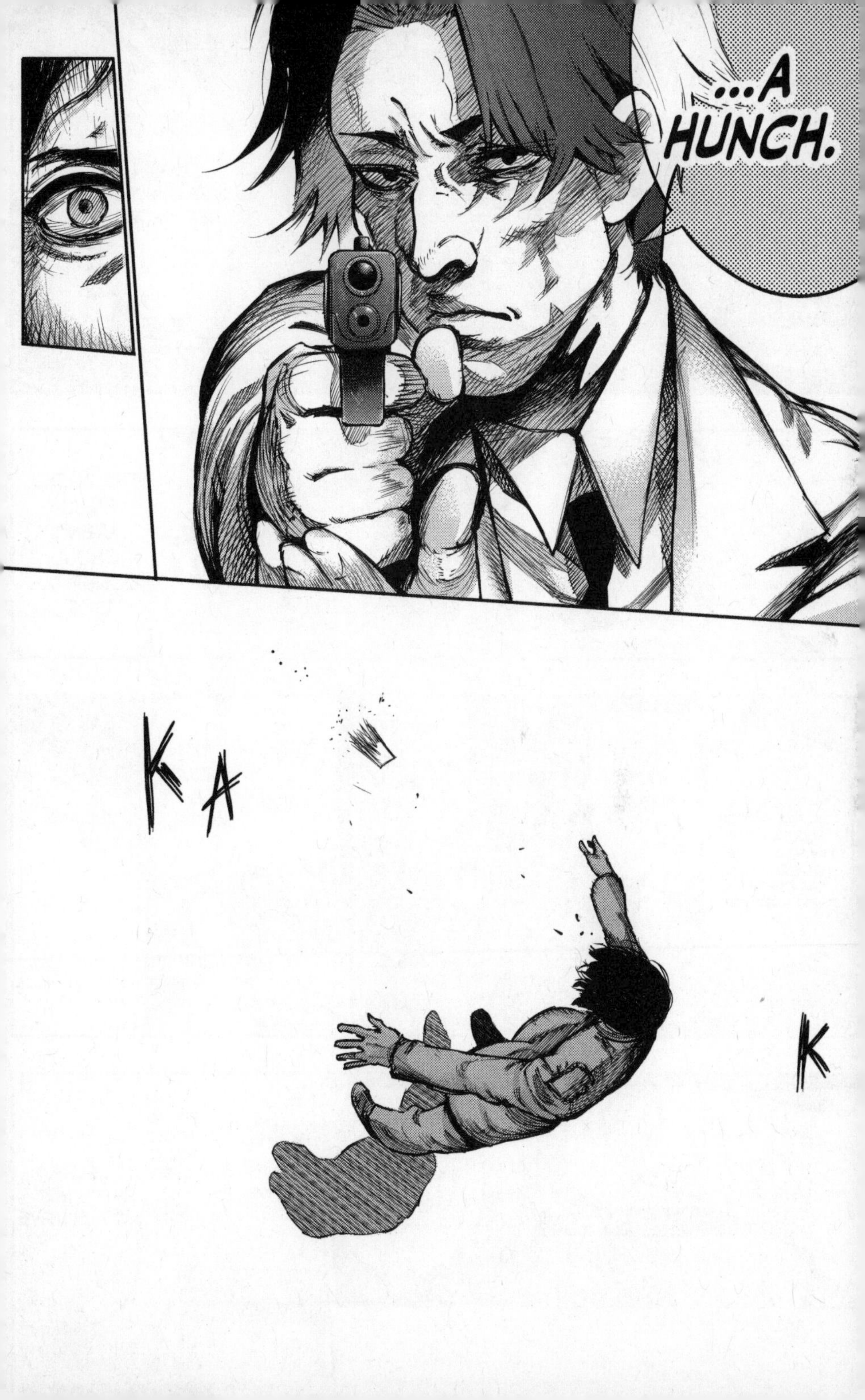
...A HUNCH.
KA
K

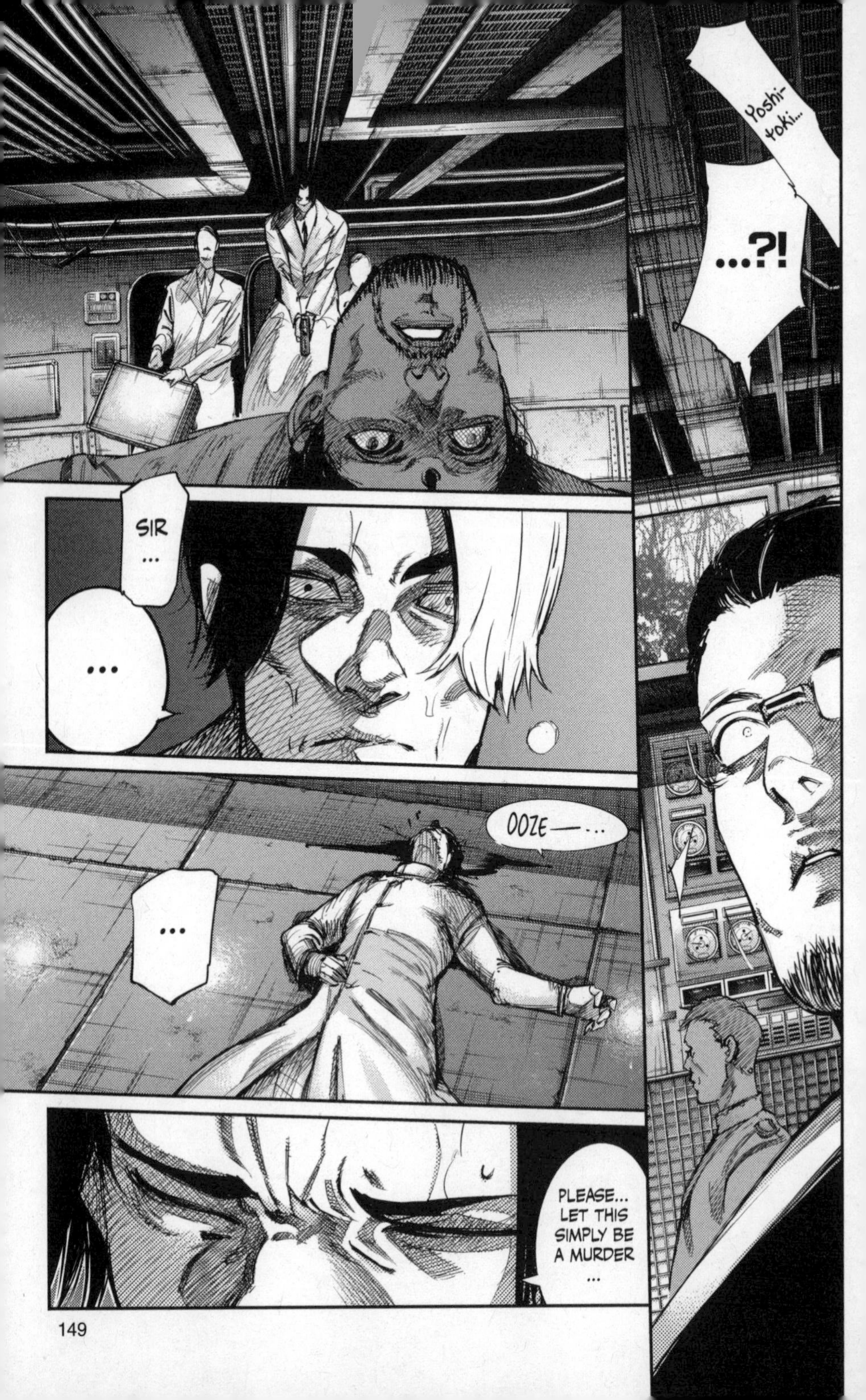
Yoshi-toki...
...?!
SIR...
...
OOZE—...
...
PLEASE... LET THIS SIMPLY BE A MURDER...

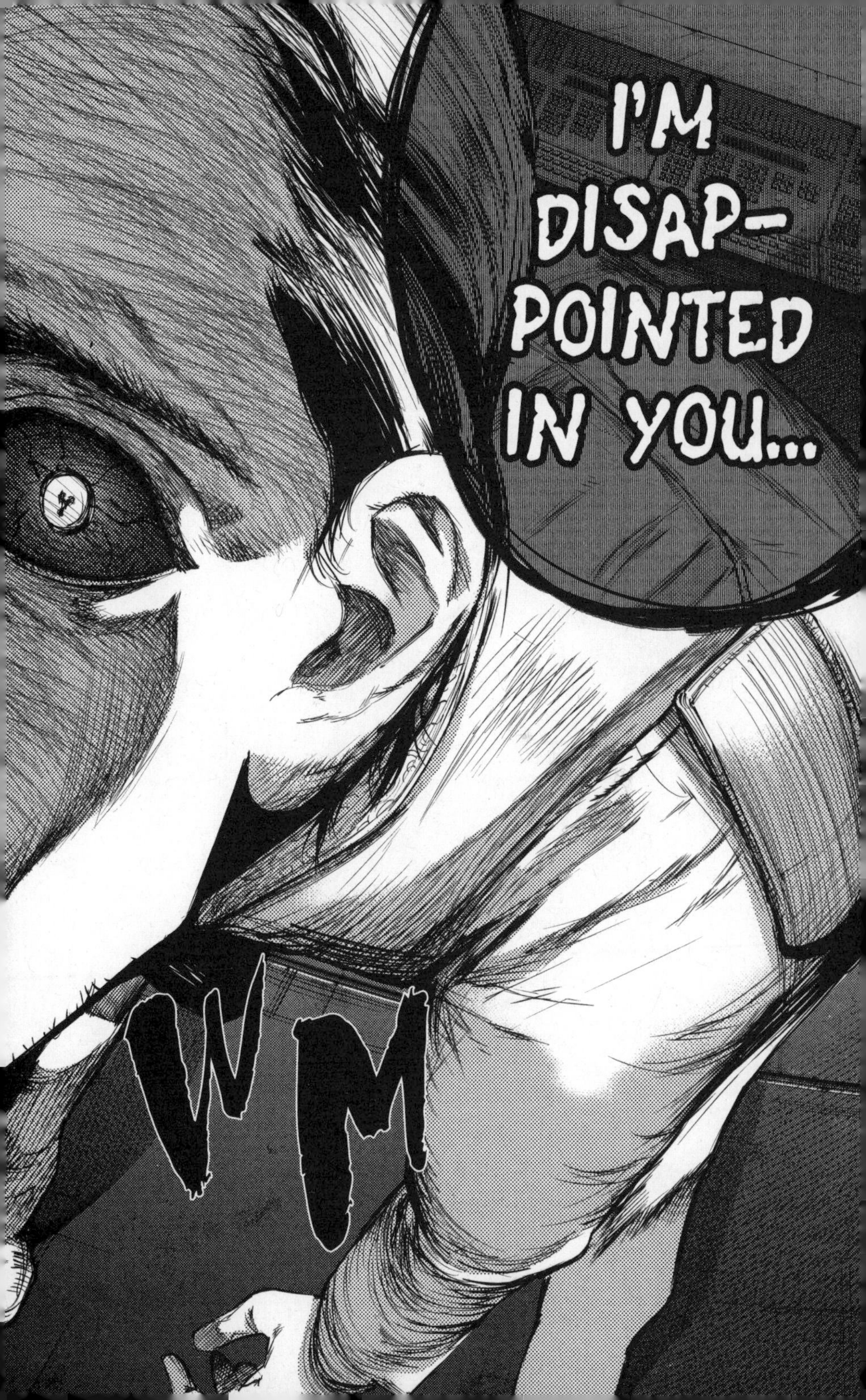
I'M DISAP-POINTED IN YOU...
WM

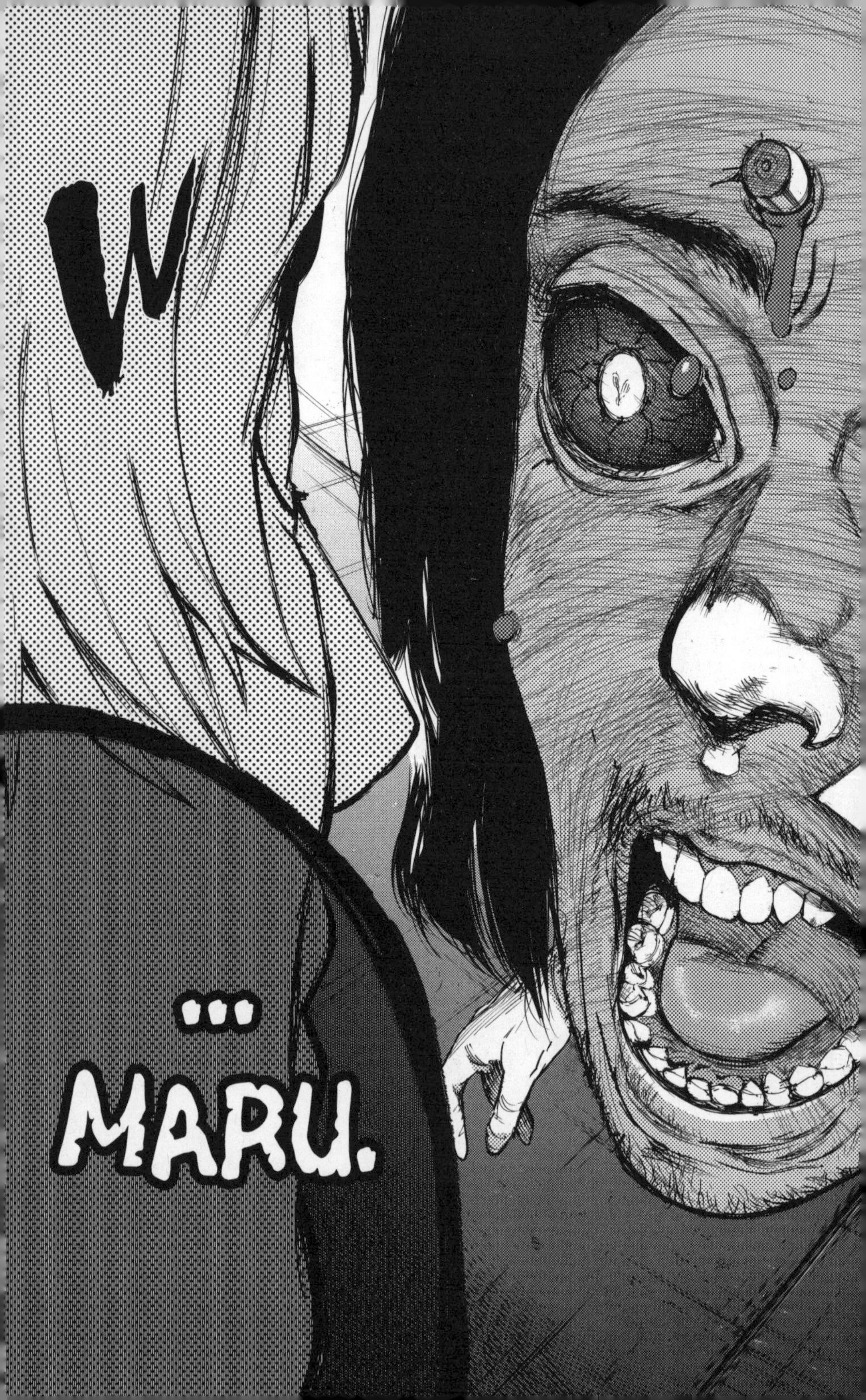
W
...
MARU.

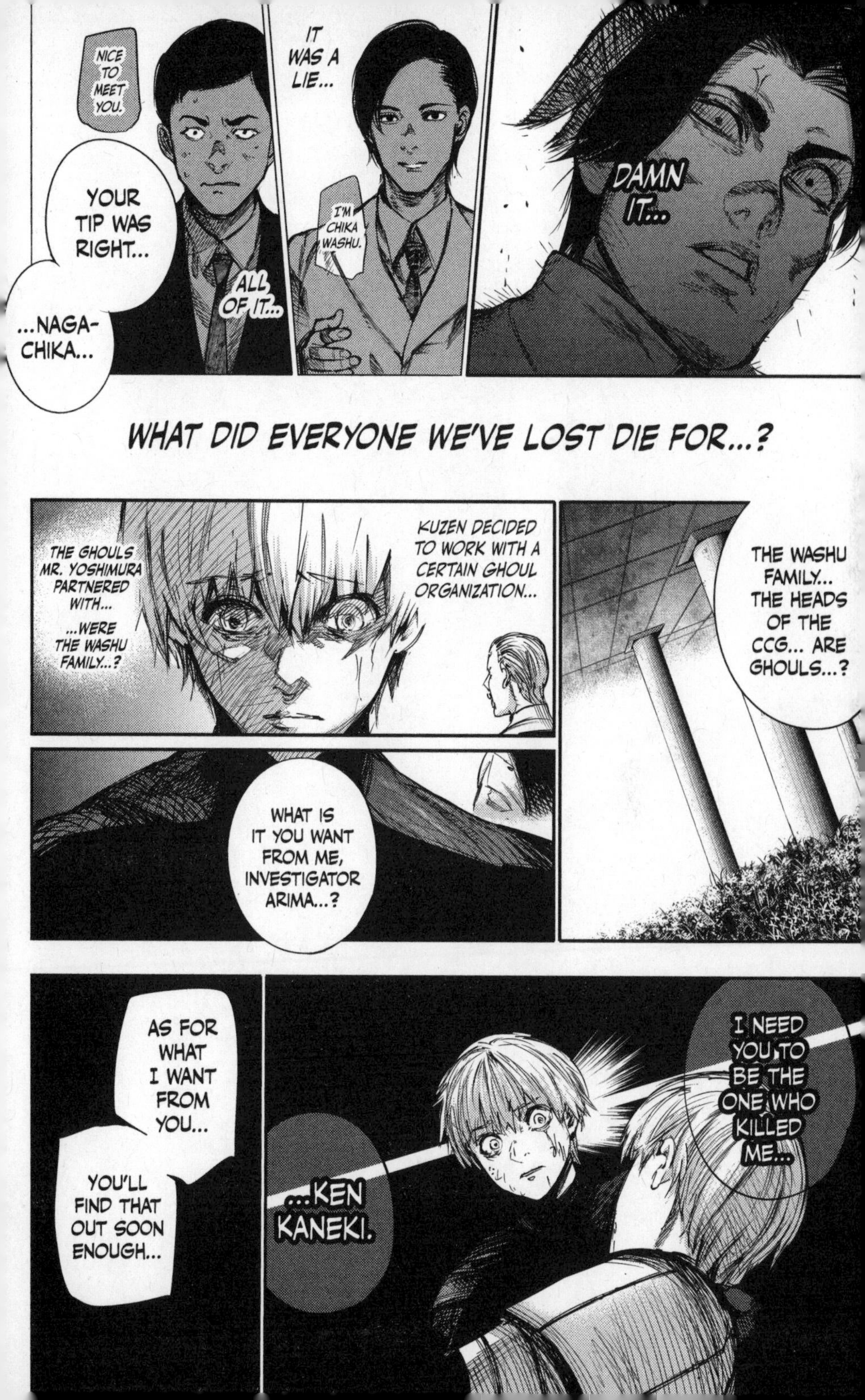
DAMN IT...
IT WAS A LIE...
I'M CHIKA WASHU.
NICE TO MEET YOU.
YOUR TIP WAS RIGHT...
ALL OF IT...
...NAGA-CHIKA...
WHAT DID EVERYONE WE'VE LOST DIE FOR...?
THE WASHU FAMILY... THE HEADS OF THE CCG... ARE GHOULS...?
KUZEN DECIDED TO WORK WITH A CERTAIN GHOUL ORGANIZATION...
THE GHOULS MR. YOSHIMURA PARTNERED WITH...
...WERE THE WASHU FAMILY...?
WHAT IS IT YOU WANT FROM ME, INVESTIGATOR ARIMA...?
I NEED YOU TO BE THE ONE WHO KILLED ME...
...KEN KANEKI.
AS FOR WHAT I WANT FROM YOU...
YOU'LL FIND THAT OUT SOON ENOUGH...

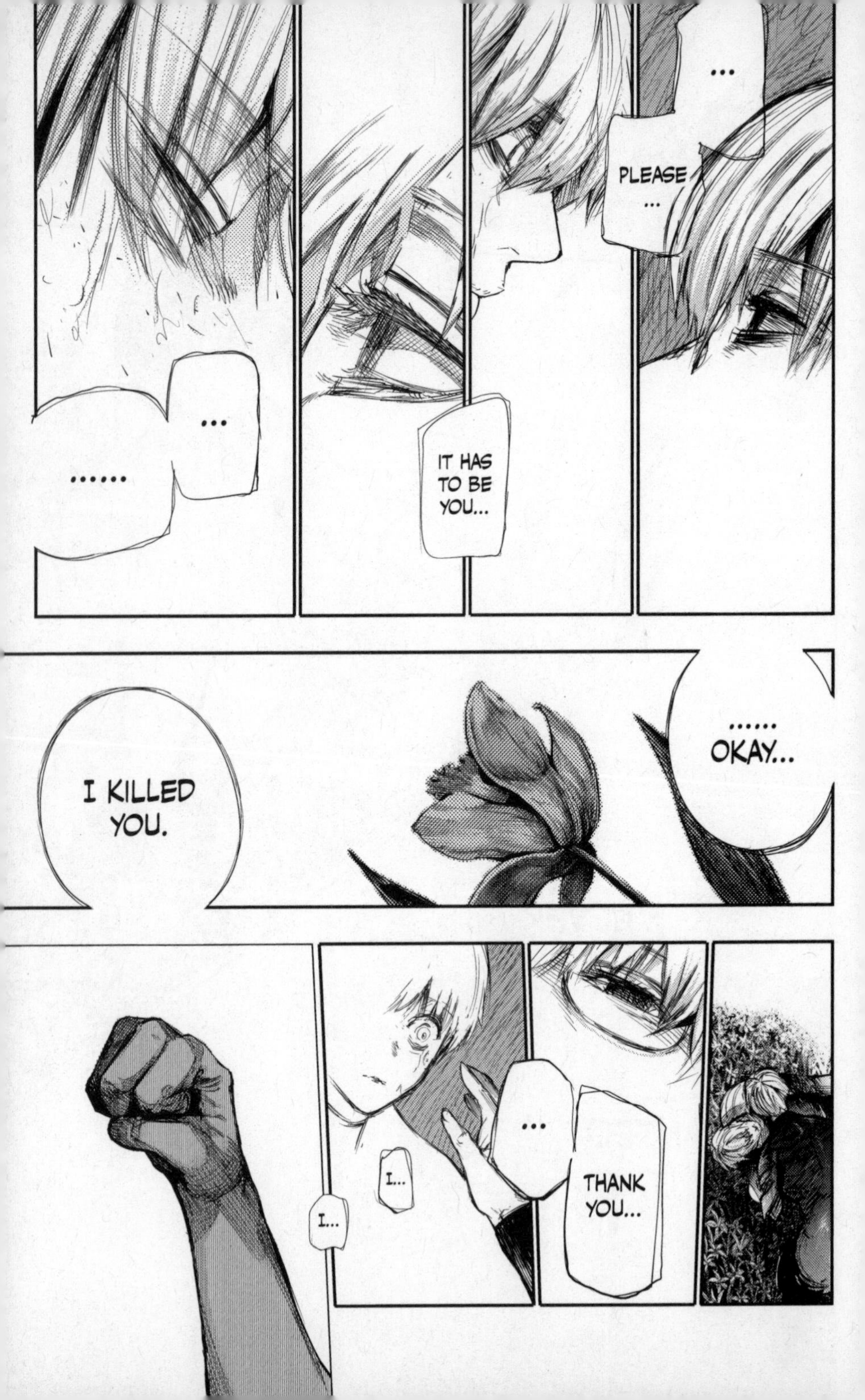
...
PLEASE ...
IT HAS TO BE YOU...
...
......
...... OKAY...
I KILLED YOU.
...
THANK YOU...
I...
I...

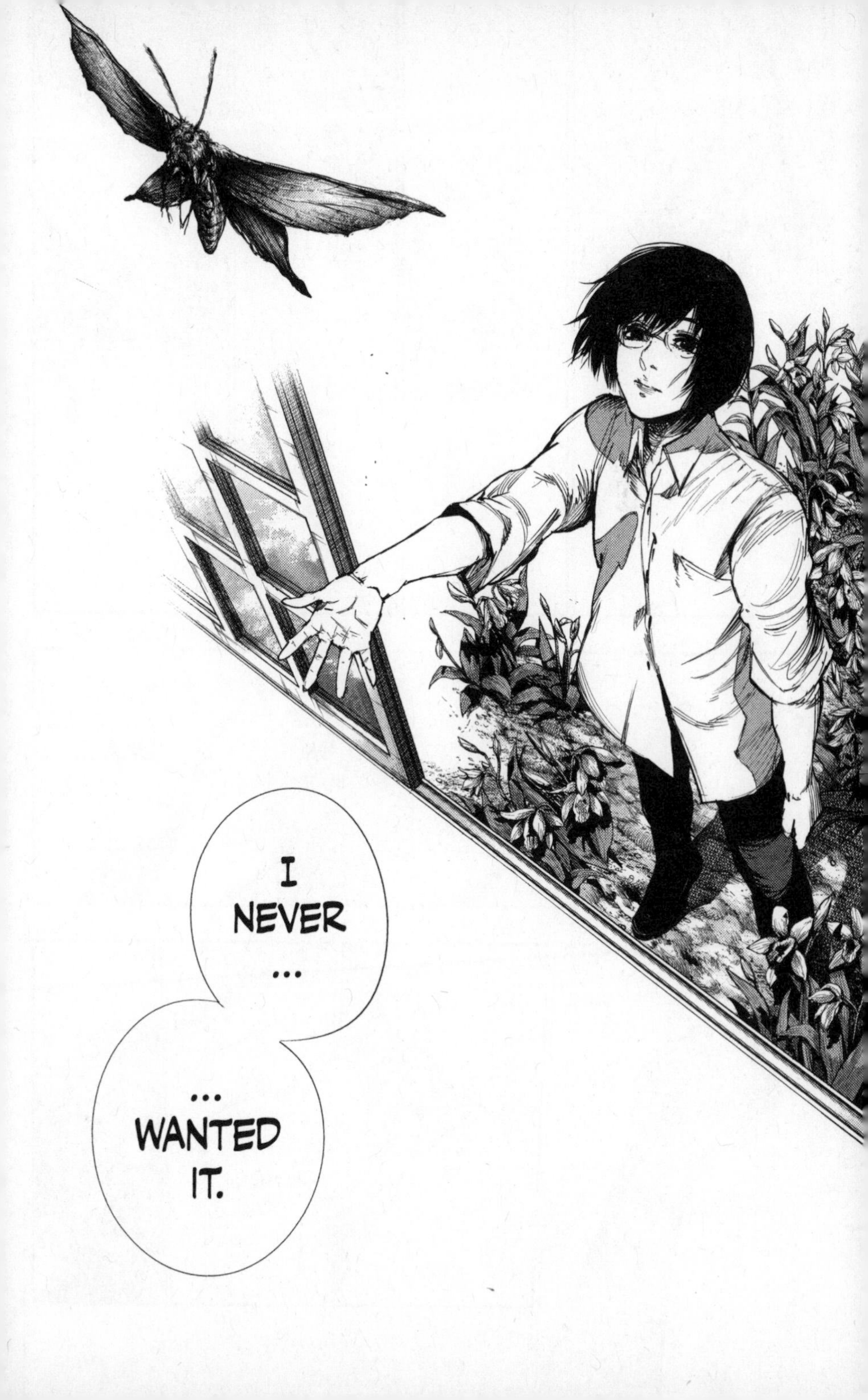
I NEVER ...
... WANTED IT.

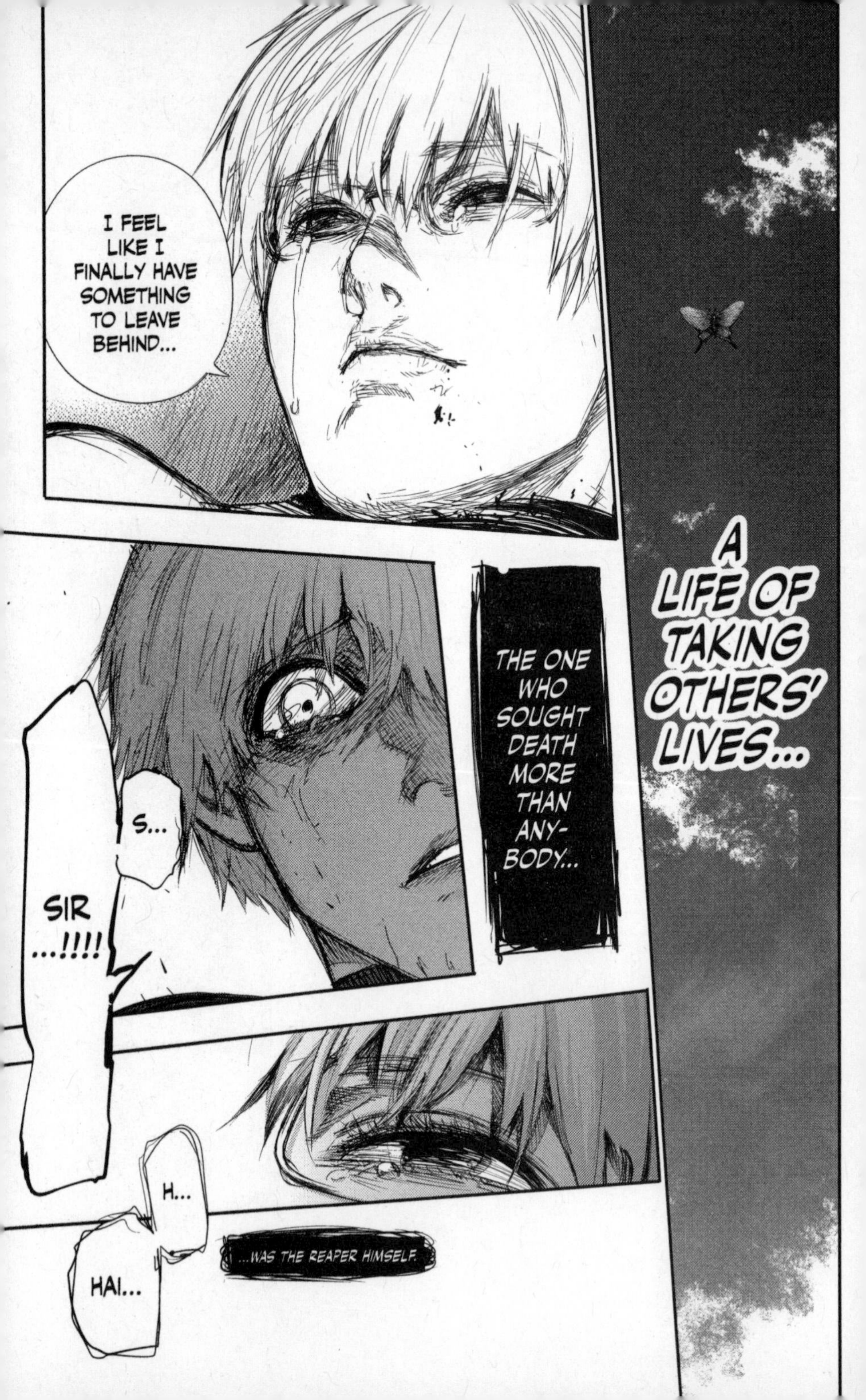
A LIFE OF TAKING OTHERS' LIVES...
I FEEL LIKE I FINALLY HAVE SOMETHING TO LEAVE BEHIND...
THE ONE WHO SOUGHT DEATH MORE THAN ANY-BODY...
S...
SIR ...!!!!
H...
...WAS THE REAPER HIMSELF.
HAI...

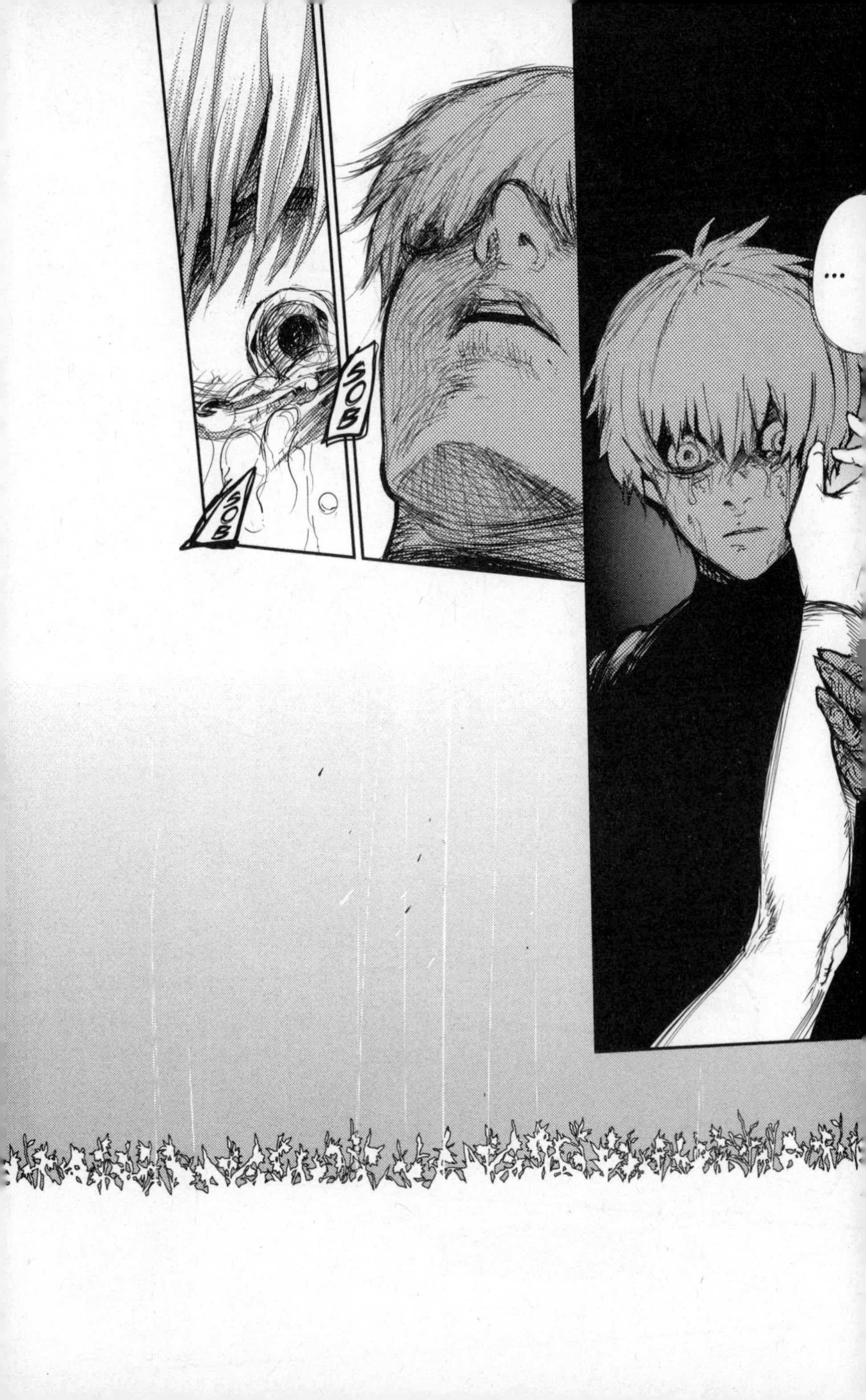
...
SOB
SOB

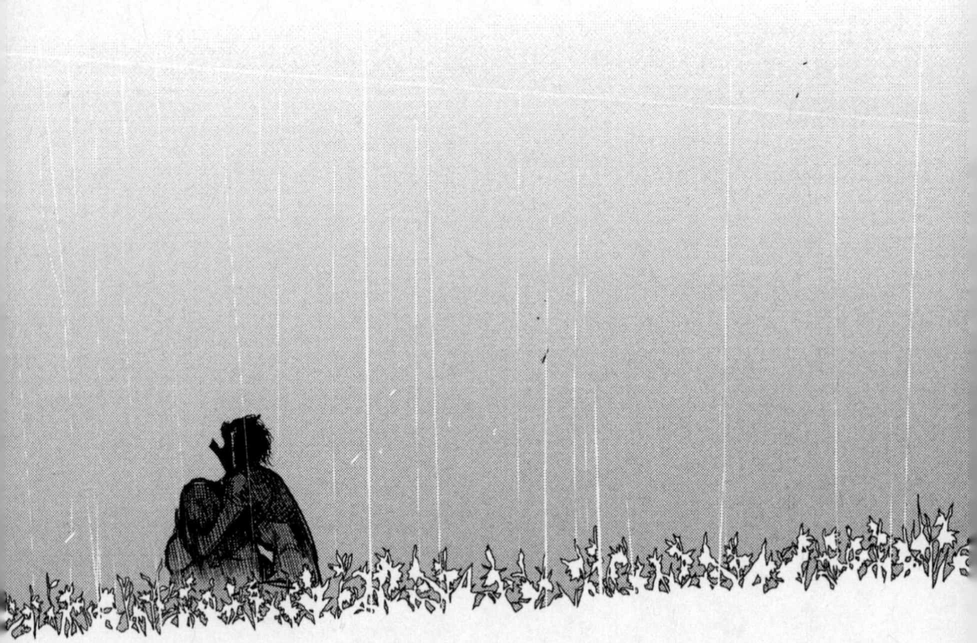

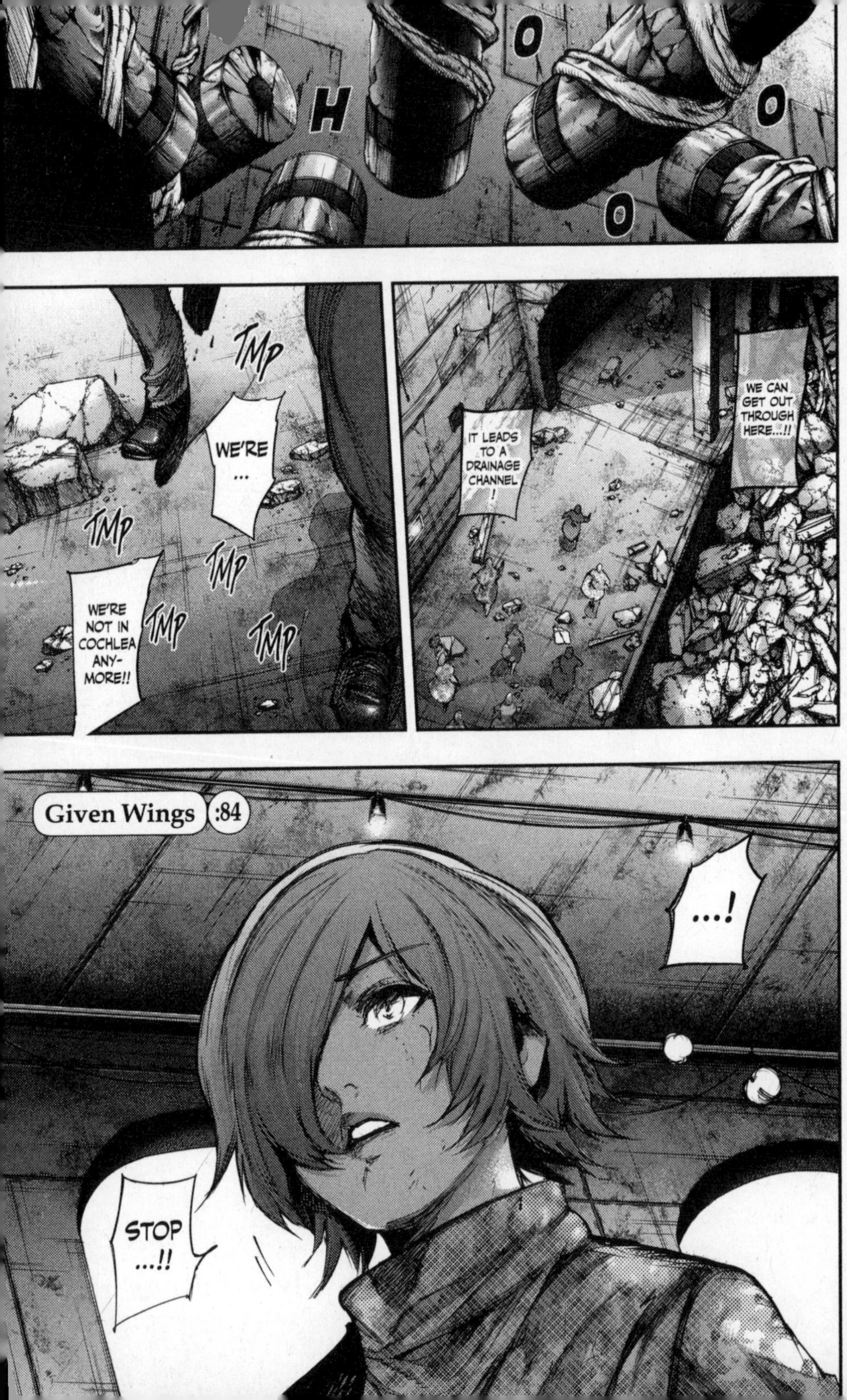
HOOOO
WE CAN GET OUT THROUGH HERE...!!
IT LEADS TO A DRAINAGE CHANNEL!
TMP
WE'RE...
TMP
TMP
WE'RE NOT IN COCHLEA ANYMORE!!
TMP
TMP
Given Wings :84
...!
STOP...!!

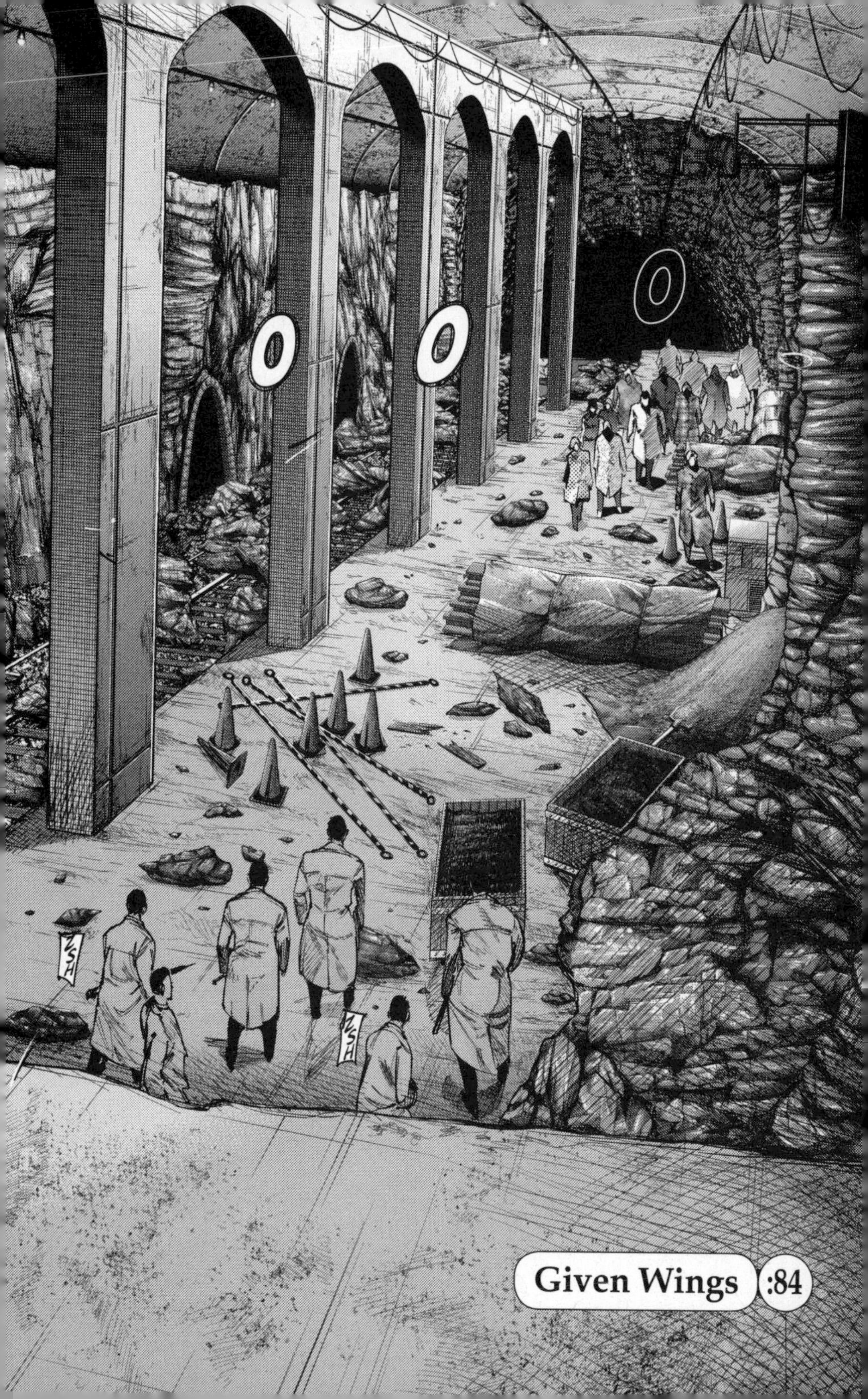
ZSH
ZSH
Given Wings :84

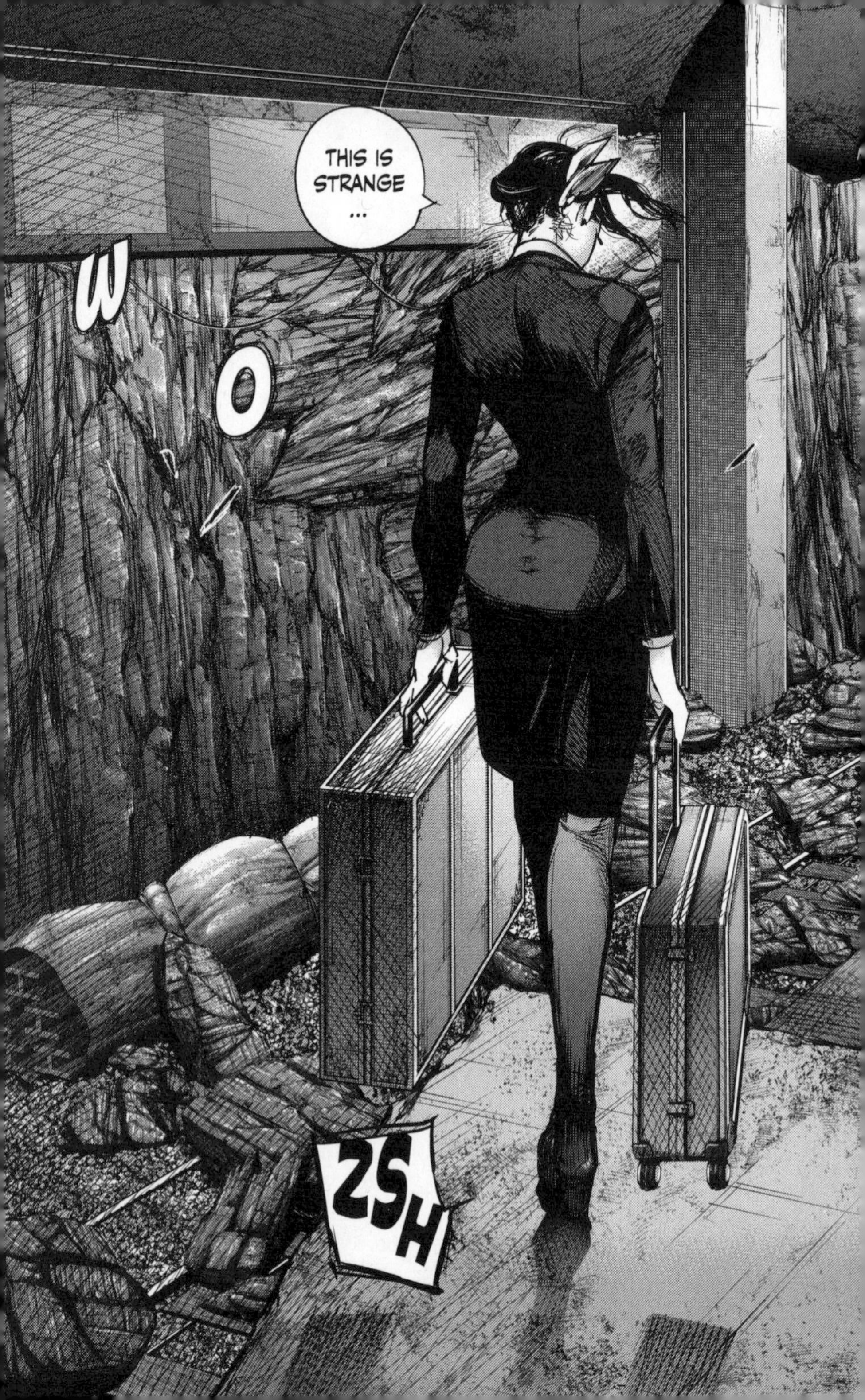

THIS IS STRANGE ...
WO
ZSH

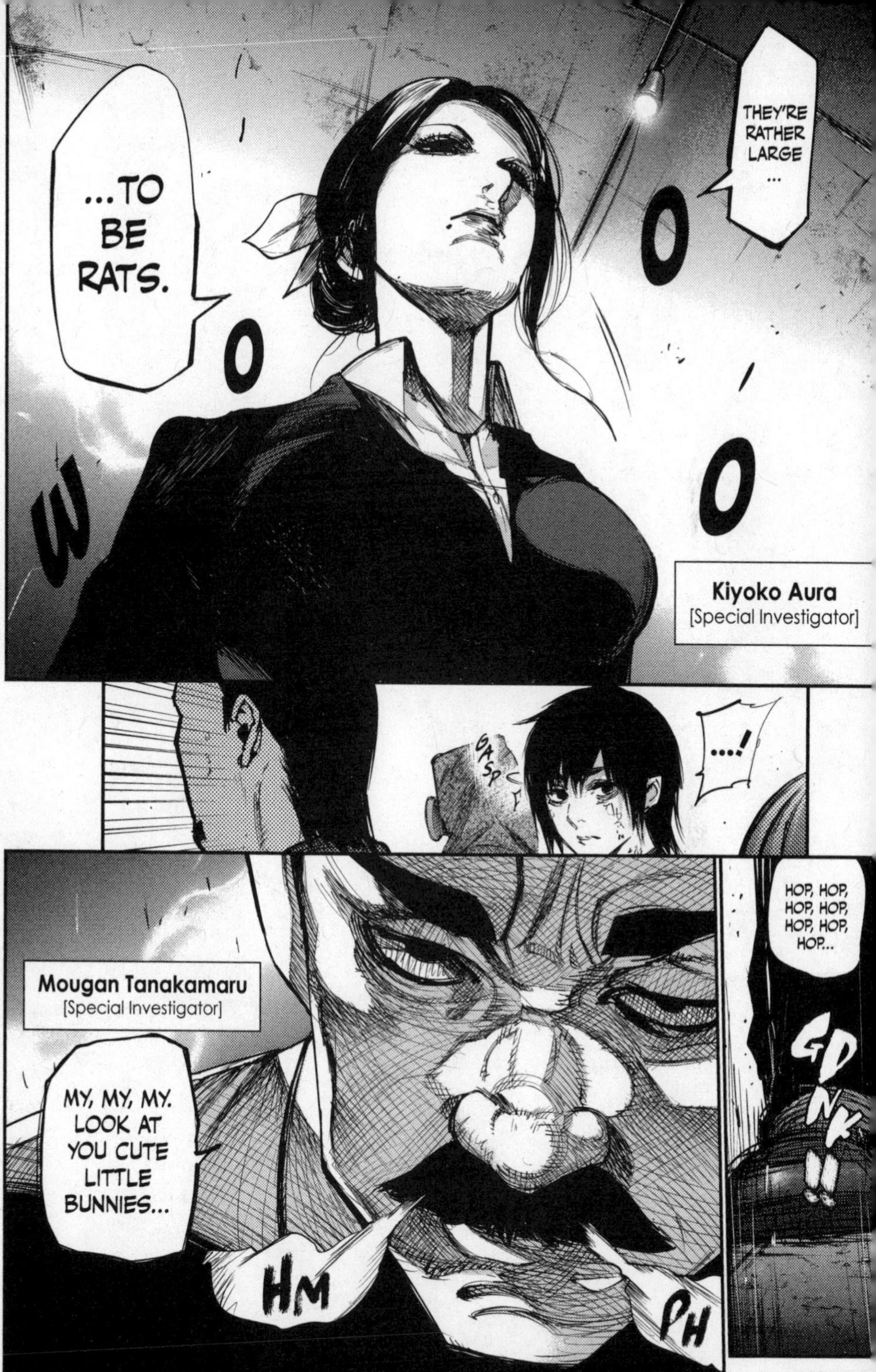
THEY'RE RATHER LARGE ...
...TO BE RATS.
WOOOO
Kiyoko Aura
[Special Investigator]
...!
GASP
HOP, HOP, HOP, HOP, HOP, HOP, HOP...
GDNK!!
Mougan Tanakamaru
[Special Investigator]
MY, MY, MY. LOOK AT YOU CUTE LITTLE BUNNIES...
HMPH

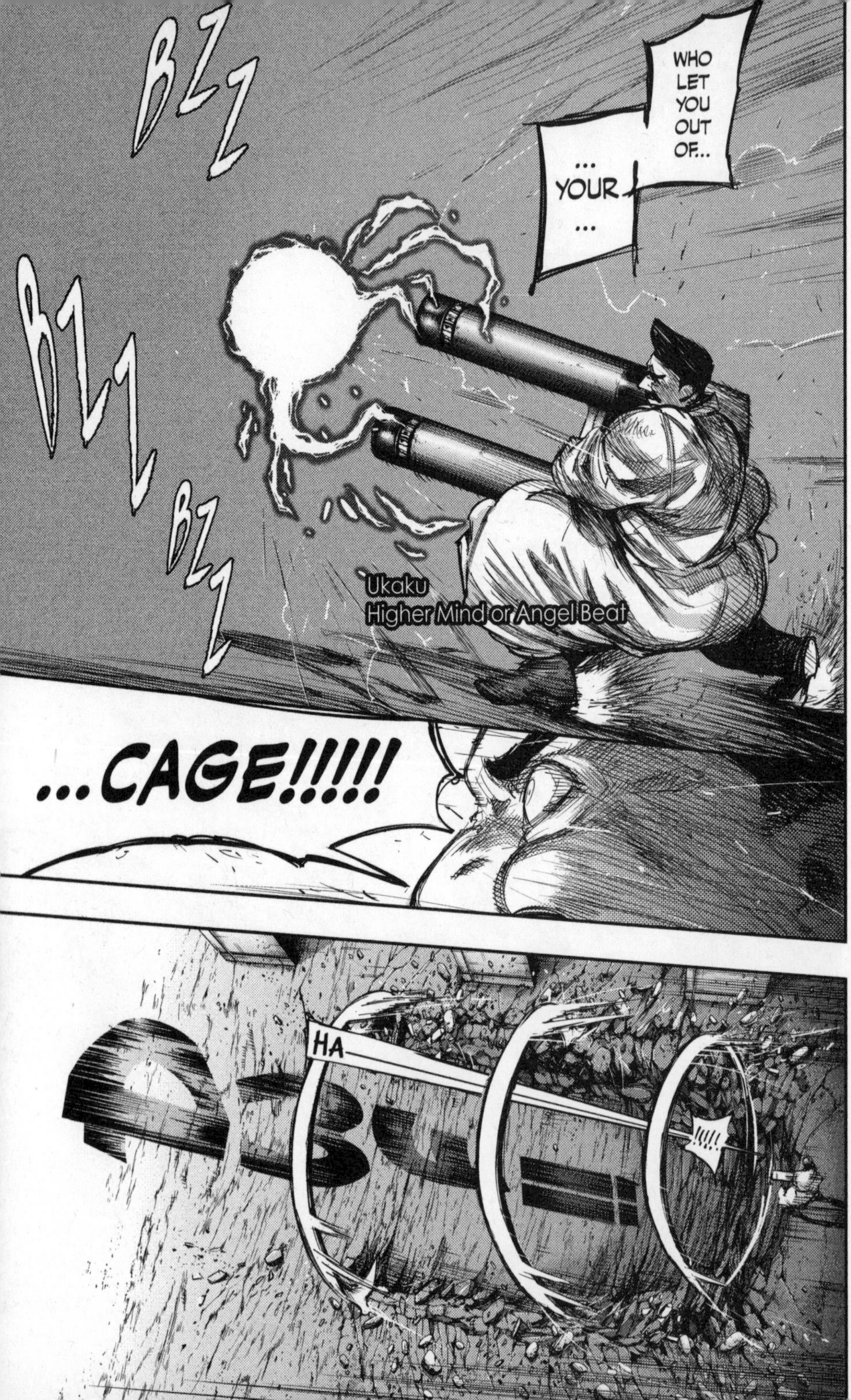
WHO LET YOU OUT OF...
... YOUR ...
BZZ
BZZ
BZZ
Ukaku
Higher Mind or Angel Beat
...CAGE!!!!!
HA
!!!!!

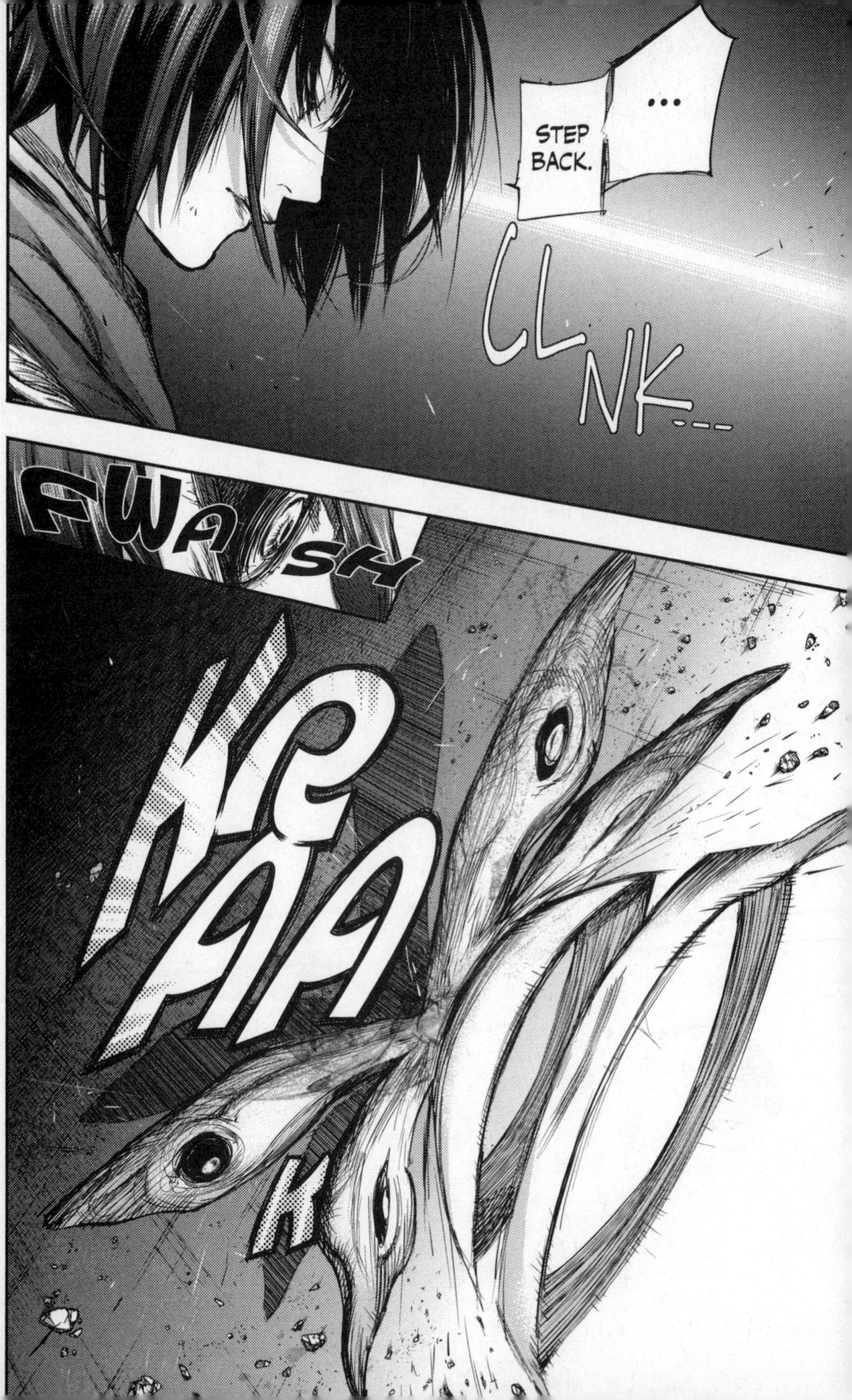
...
STEP BACK.
CL NK...
FWASH
KRAAA
K

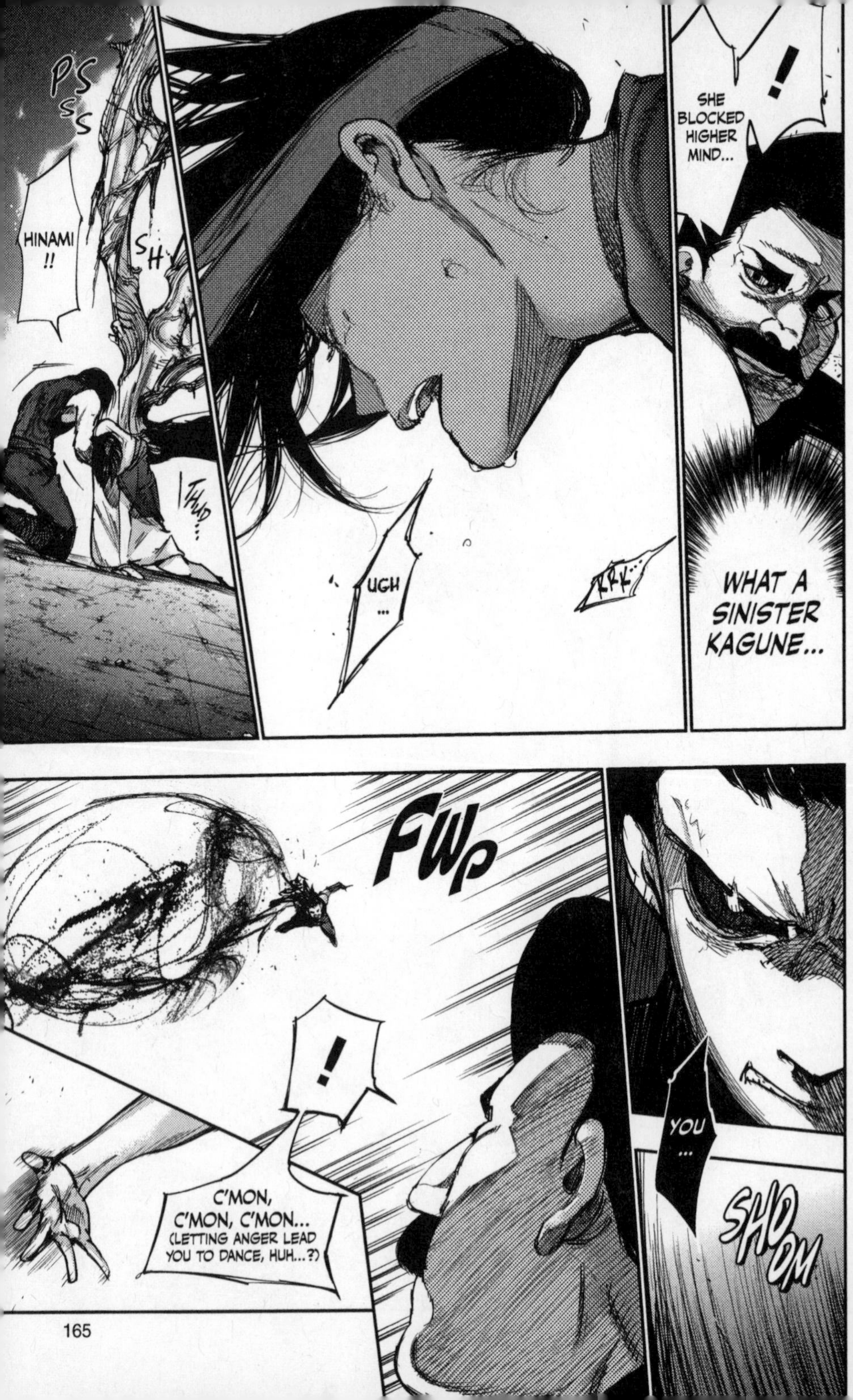
!
SHE BLOCKED HIGHER MIND...
WHAT A SINISTER KAGUNE...
KRK...
UGH...
PSSS
HINAMI!!
SH
THUD...
YOU...
SHOOM
FWP
!
C'MON, C'MON, C'MON... (LETTING ANGER LEAD YOU TO DANCE, HUH...?)

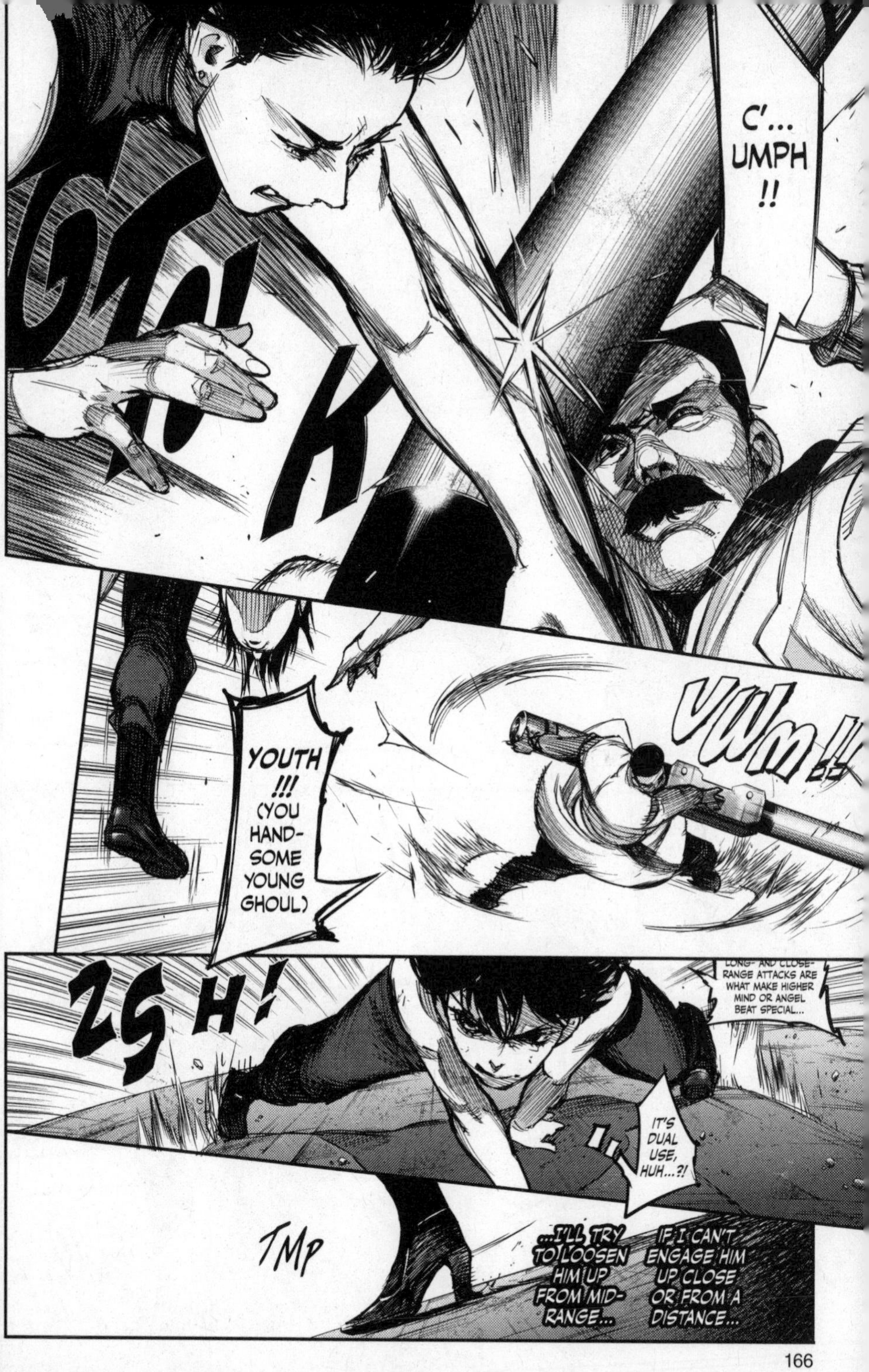
C'... UMPH !!
VWM!!
YOUTH !!! (YOU HANDSOME YOUNG GHOUL)
LONG- AND CLOSE-RANGE ATTACKS ARE WHAT MAKE HIGHER MIND OR ANGEL BEAT SPECIAL...
ZSH!
IT'S DUAL USE, HUH...?!
IF I CAN'T ENGAGE HIM UP CLOSE OR FROM A DISTANCE...
...I'LL TRY TO LOOSEN HIM UP FROM MID-RANGE...
TMP

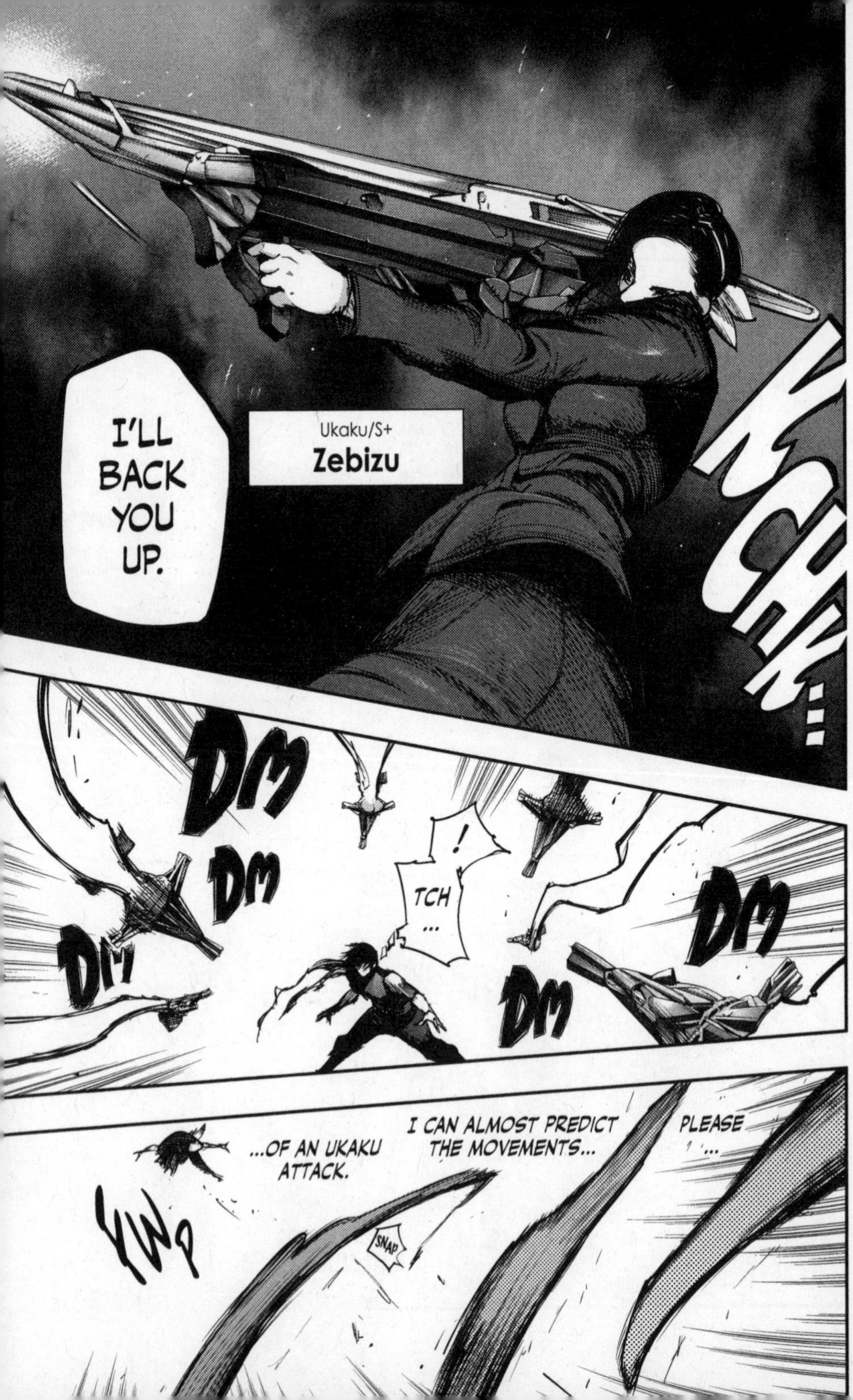
KCHK...
Ukaku/S+
Zebizu
I'LL BACK YOU UP.
DM
DM
DM
DM
DM
!
TCH ...
PLEASE ...
I CAN ALMOST PREDICT THE MOVEMENTS...
...OF AN UKAKU ATTACK.
SNAP

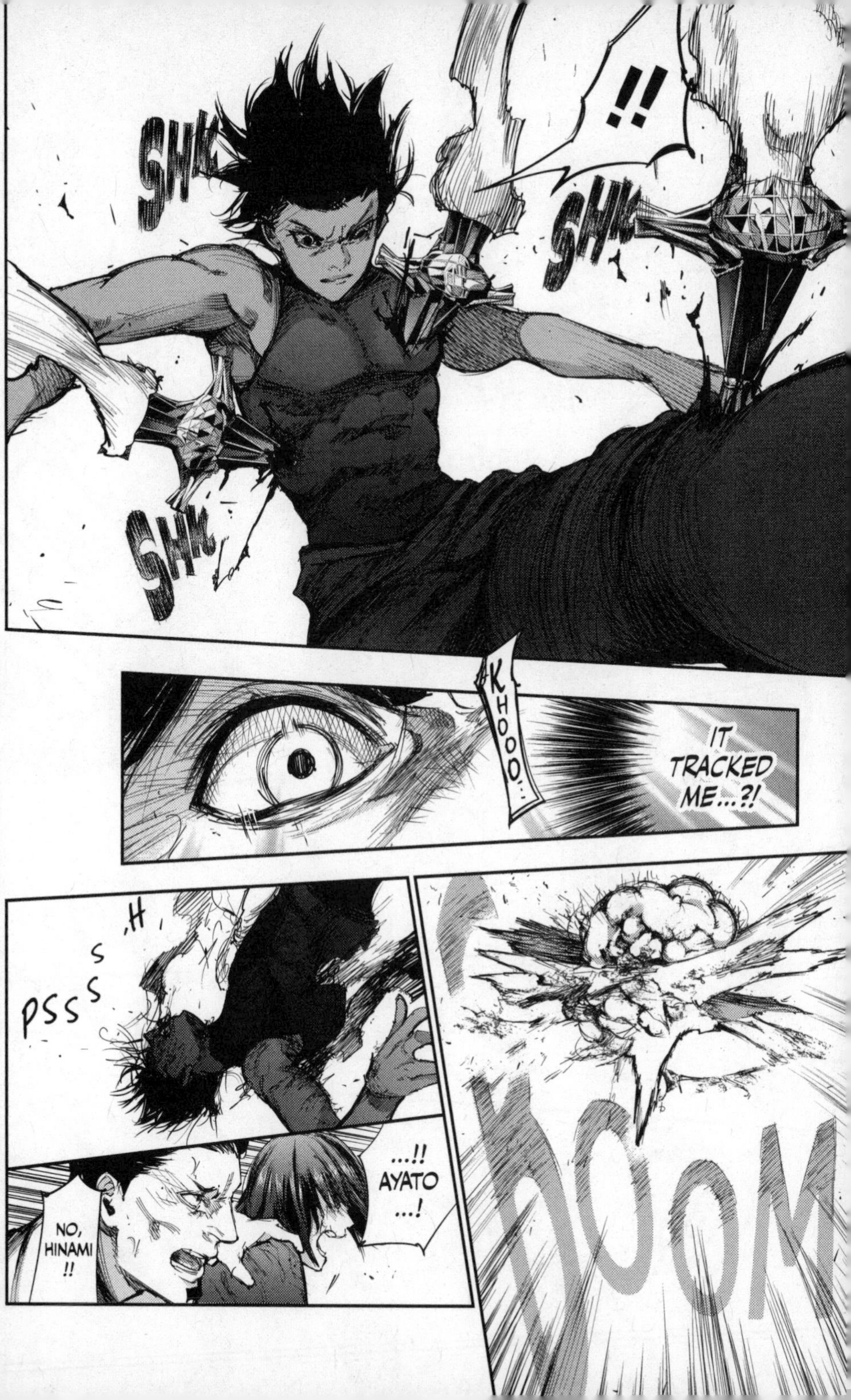

!!
SHK
SHK
SHK
KHOOO...
IT TRACKED ME...?!
BOOM
H
PSSS
...!! AYATO ...!
NO, HINAMI !!

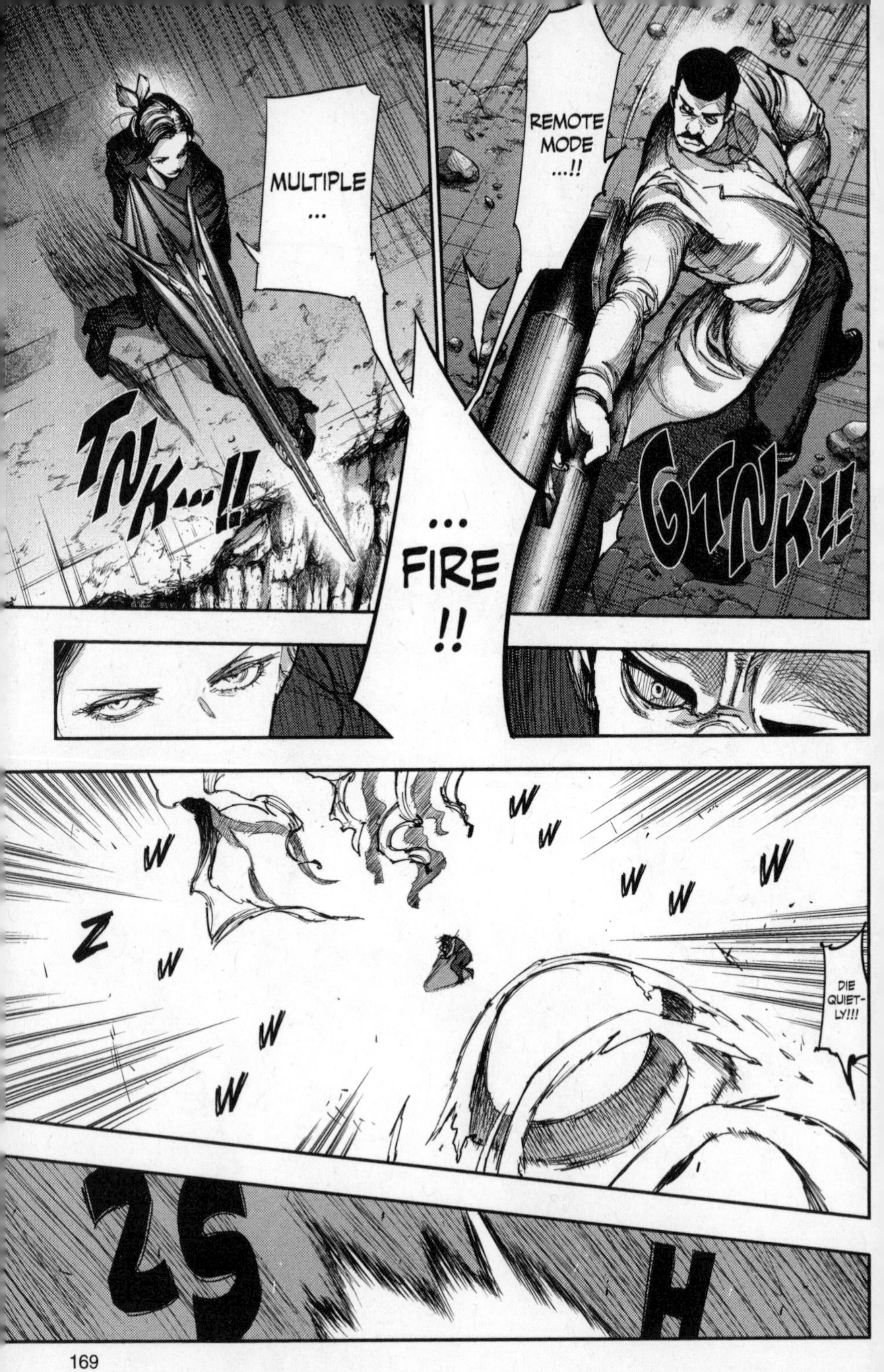
REMOTE MODE ...!!
GTINK!!
MULTIPLE ...
TNK...!!
... FIRE !!
DIE QUIET-LY!!!
ZWWWWWWWWWW
ZSH

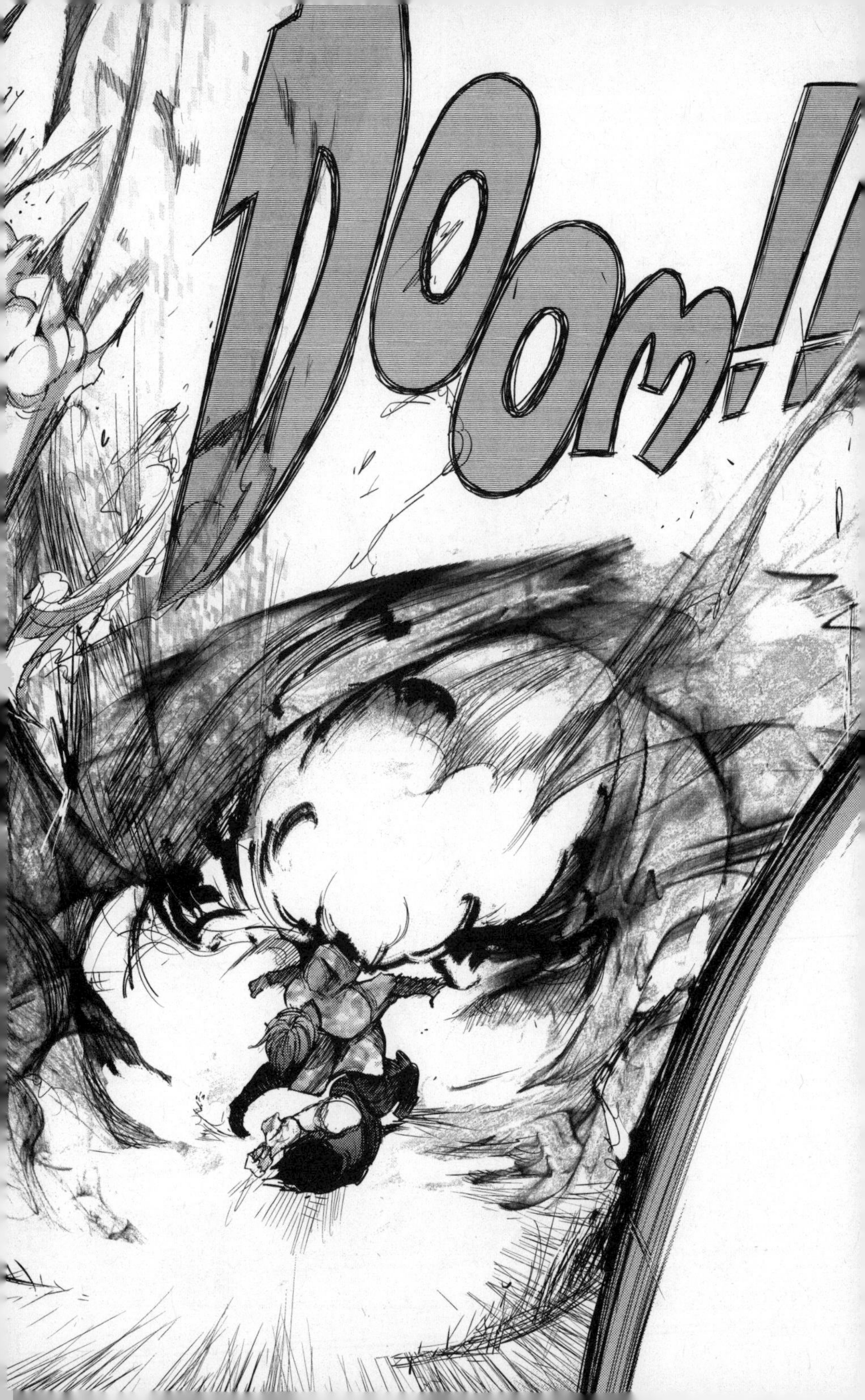
DOOM!!

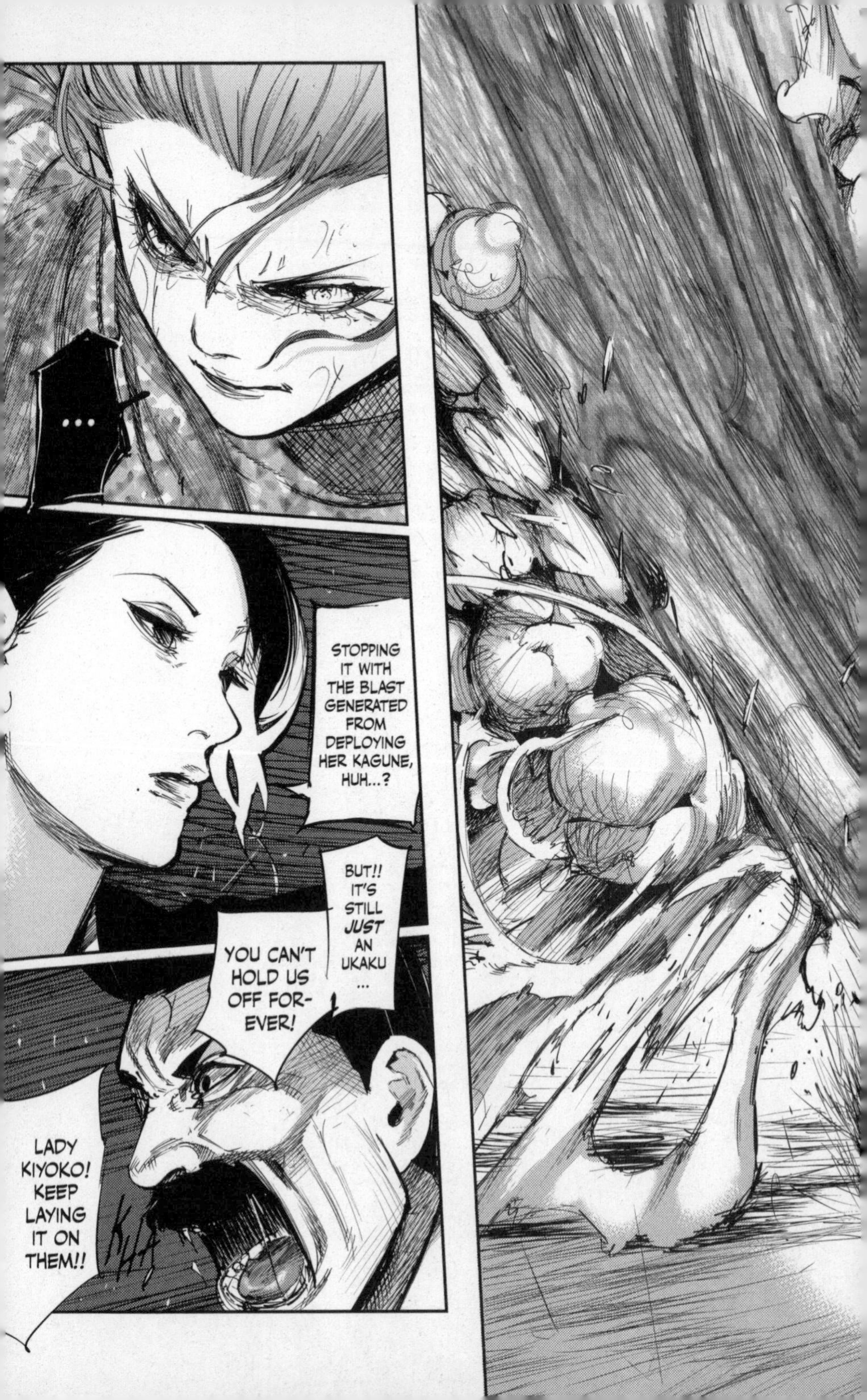
...
STOPPING IT WITH THE BLAST GENERATED FROM DEPLOYING HER KAGUNE, HUH...?
BUT!! IT'S STILL *JUST* AN UKAKU ...
YOU CAN'T HOLD US OFF FOR-EVER!
LADY KIYOKO! KEEP LAYING IT ON THEM!!

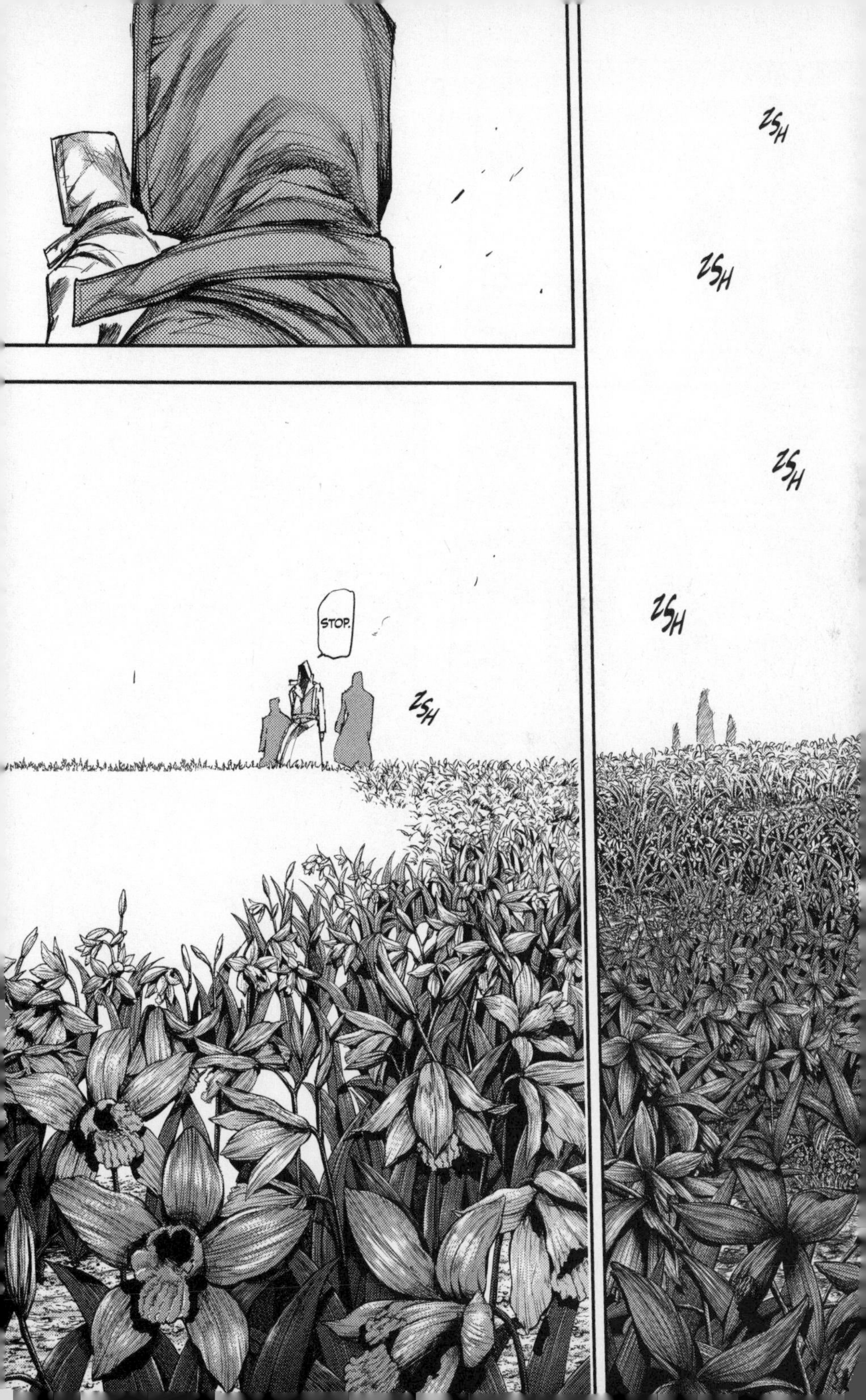
ZSH
ZSH
ZSH
ZSH
STOP.
ZSH

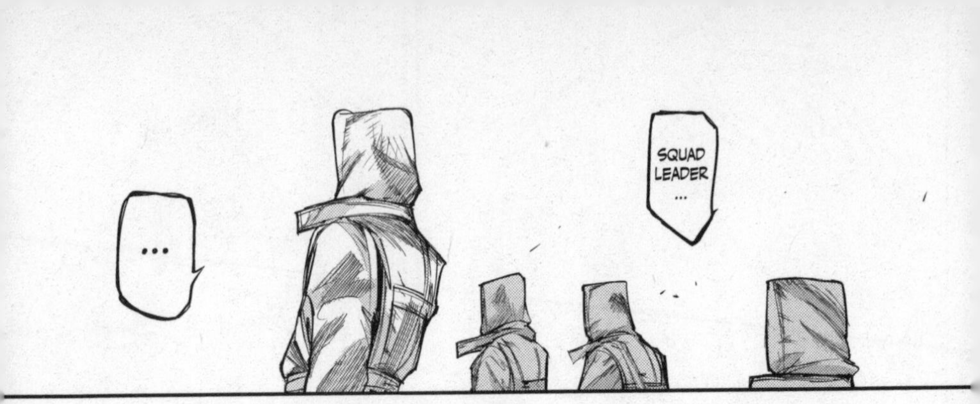
SQUAD LEADER ...
...
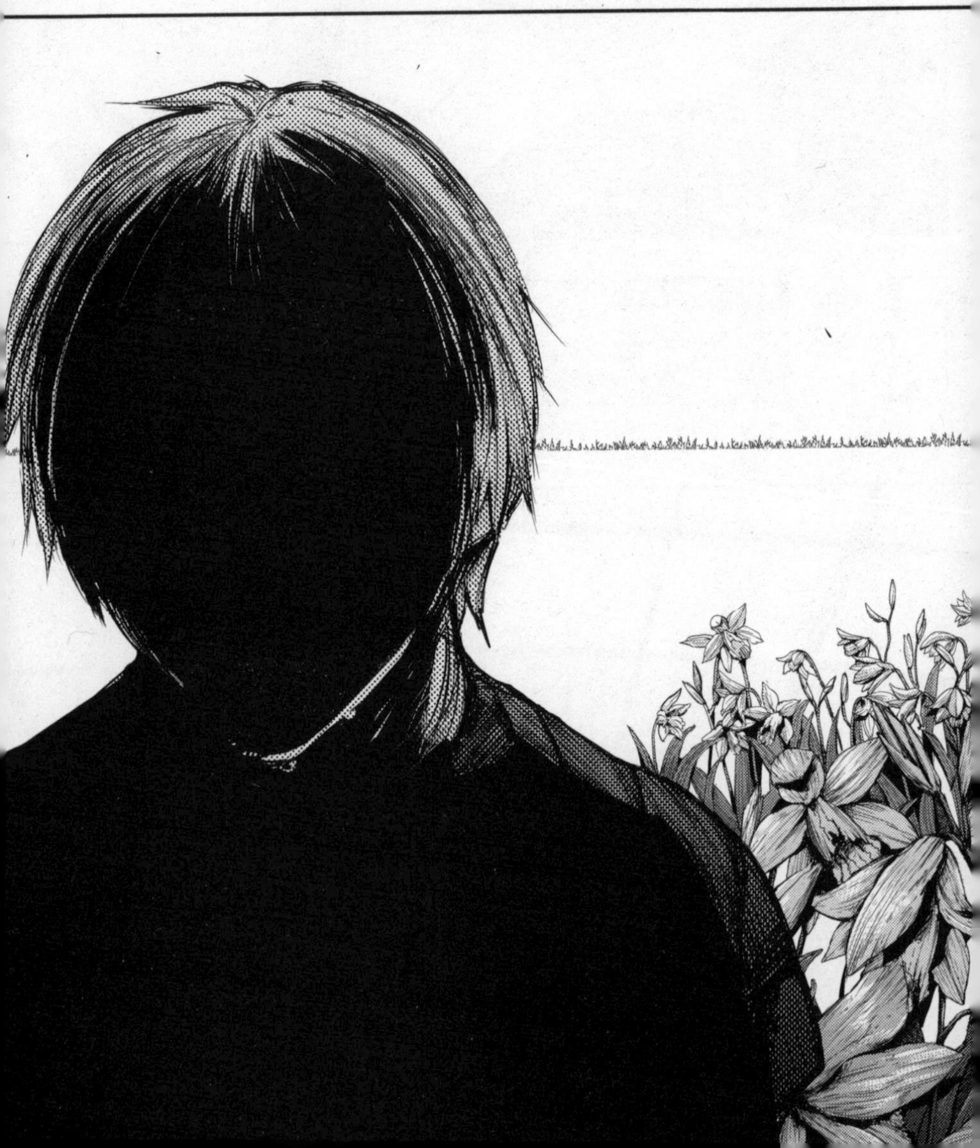

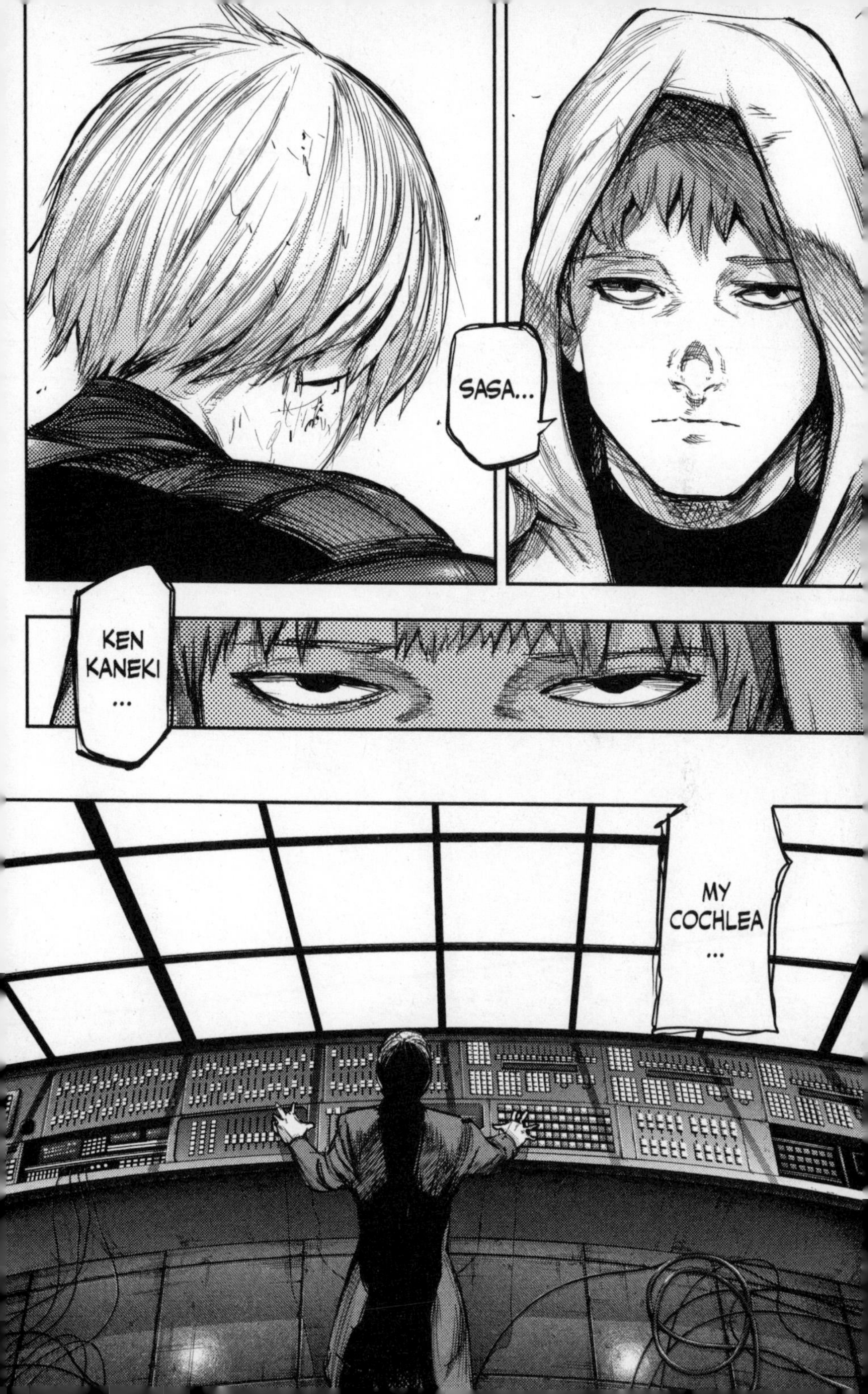
SASA...
KEN KANEKI ...
MY COCHLEA ...

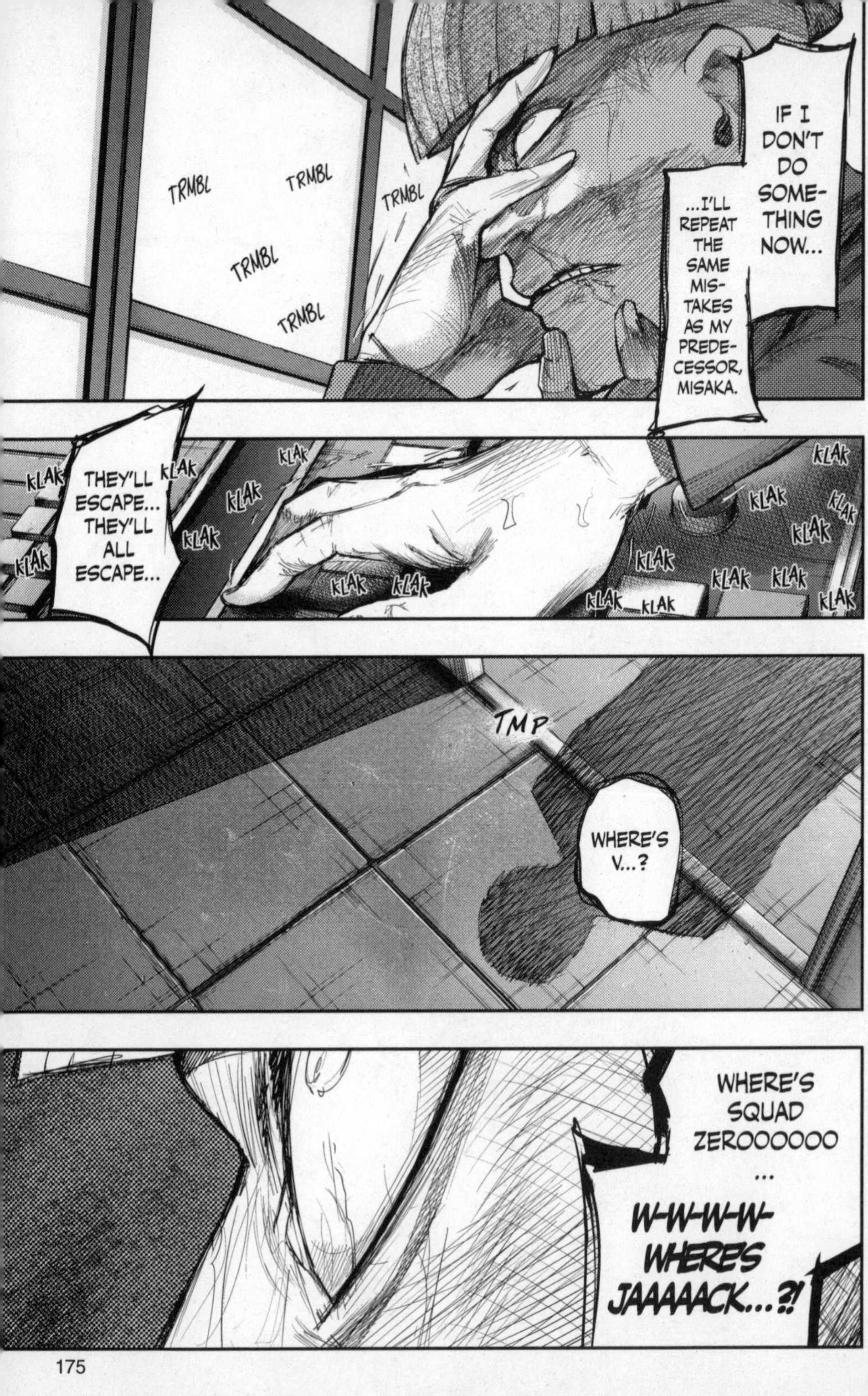
IF I DON'T DO SOME-THING NOW...
...I'LL REPEAT THE SAME MIS-TAKES AS MY PREDE-CESSOR, MISAKA.
TRMBL TRMBL TRMBL TRMBL TRMBL
KLAK KLAK KLAK KLAK KLAK KLAK KLAK KLAK
THEY'LL ESCAPE... THEY'LL ALL ESCAPE...
KLAK KLAK KLAK KLAK KLAK KLAK KLAK
TMP
WHERE'S V...?
WHERE'S SQUAD ZEROOOOOO ...
W-W-W-W-WHERE'S JAAAAACK...?!

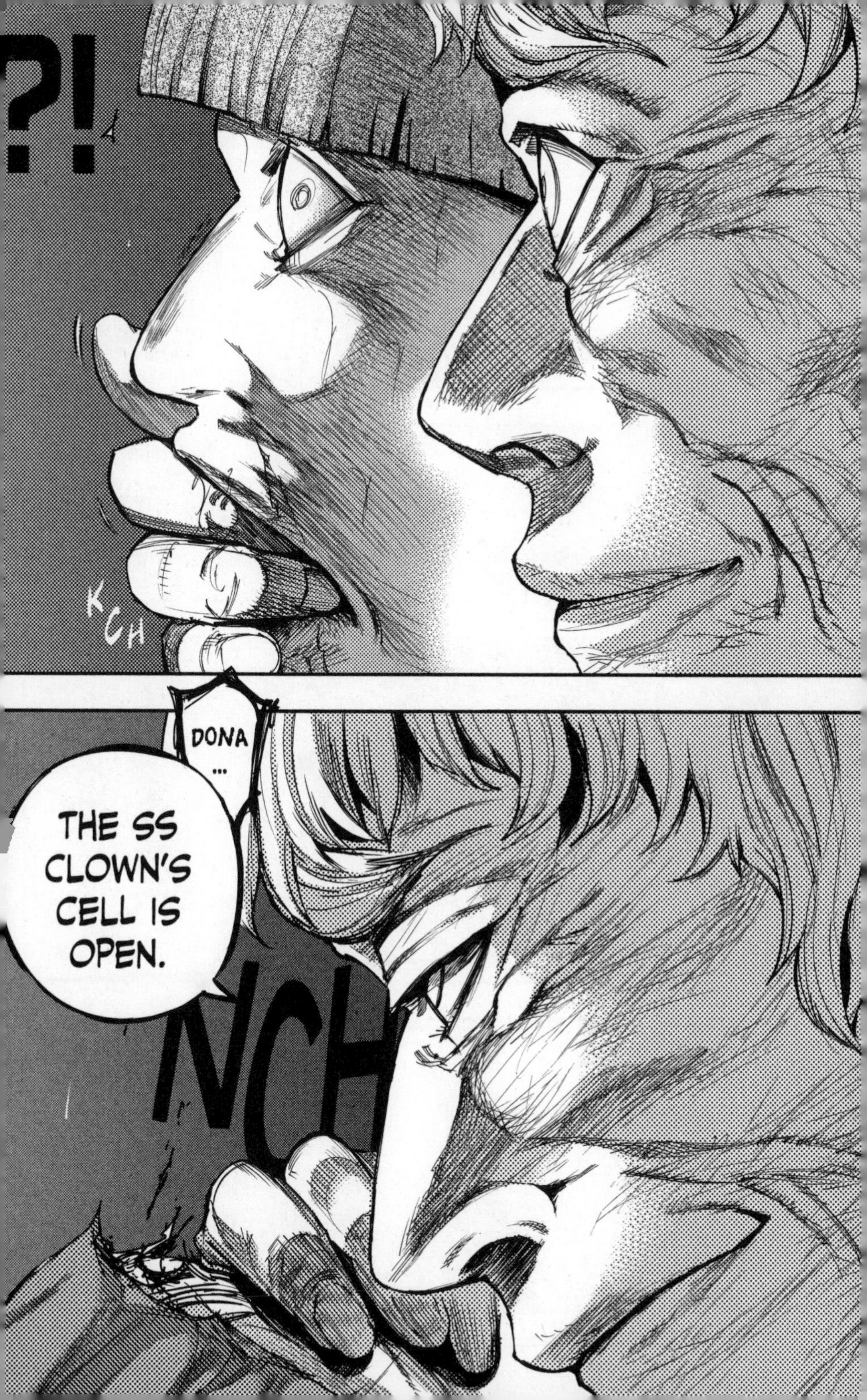
?!
KCH
DONA...
THE SS CLOWN'S CELL IS OPEN.
NCH

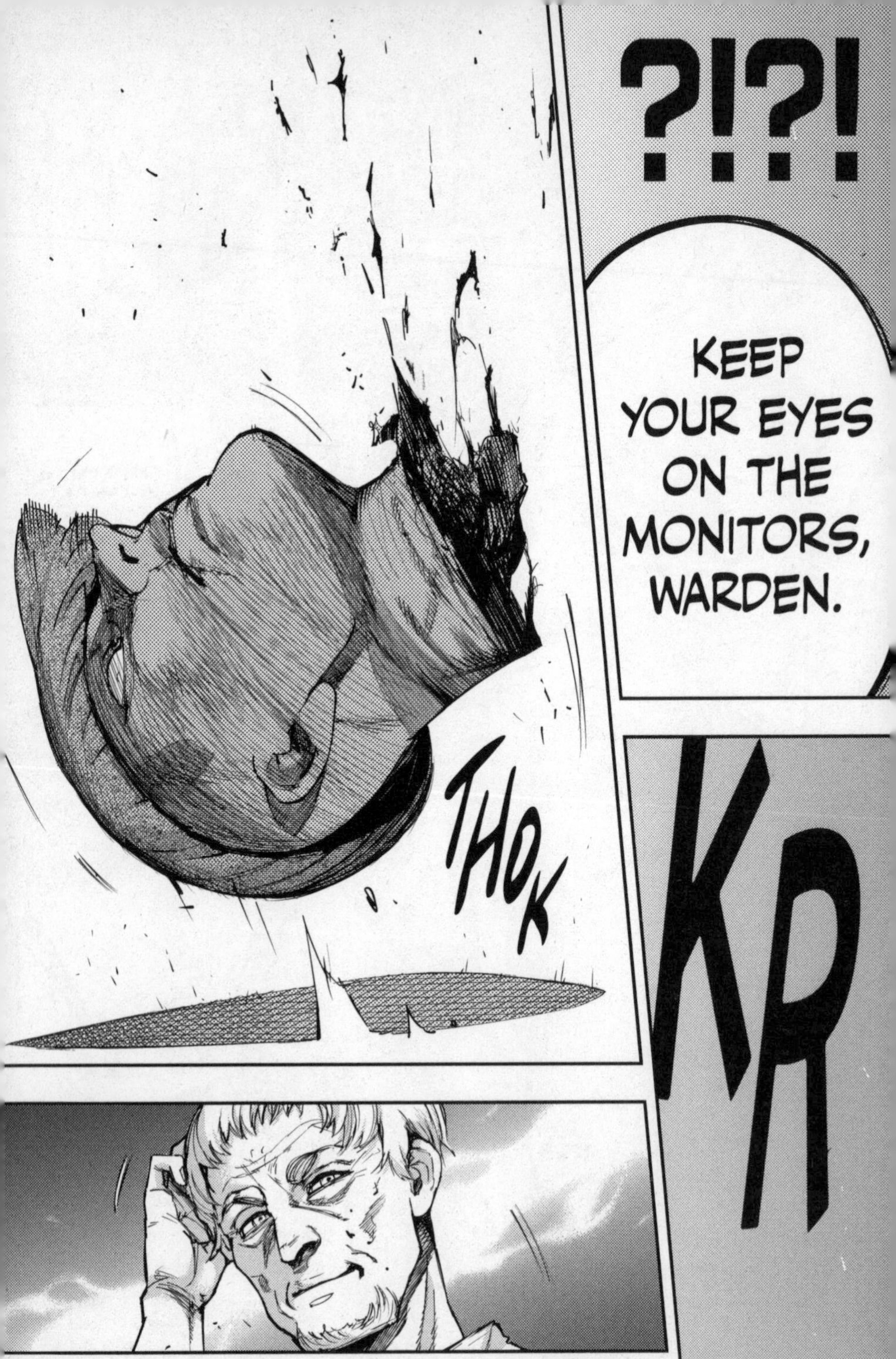
?!?!
KEEP YOUR EYES ON THE MONITORS, WARDEN.
KR
THOK

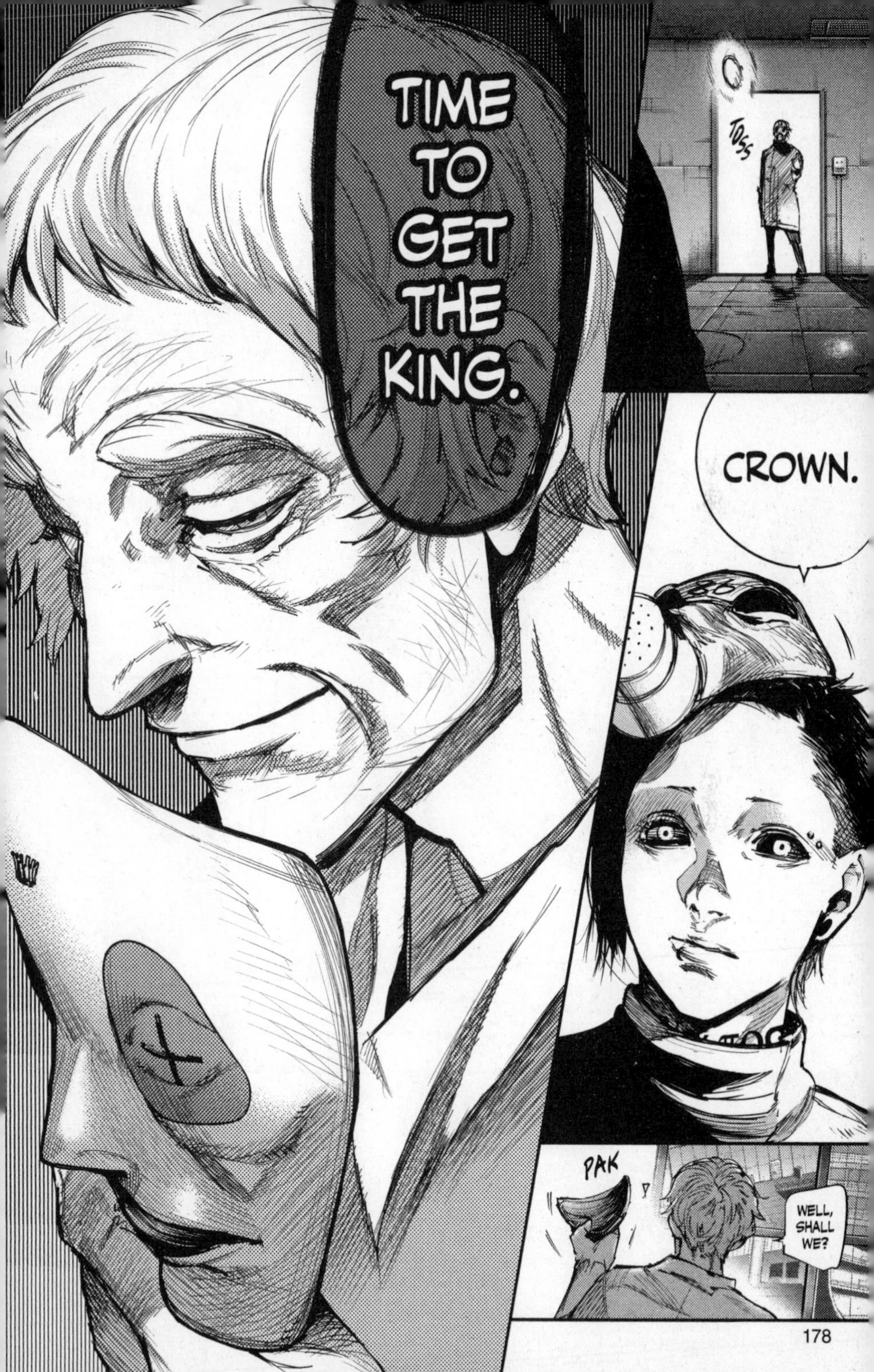
TOSS
TIME TO GET THE KING.
CROWN.
PAK
WELL, SHALL WE?

Tsukiyama at work ③

Delivery-man
WAREHOUSE B, TSUKIYAMA.
JA!
RATTL
RATTL
IT'S NOT A PROBLEM PHYSICALLY, BUT...
Hmm...
HAVING TO GO UP AND DOWN...
...ALL THOSE STAIRS WILL BE VERY INEFFICIENT...
DING
I KNOW!
SORRY FOR KEEPING MY SHOES ON!
NK
KLN
*Eighth floor
DO YOU KNOW WHAT'S MORE IMPORTANT THAN EFFICIENCY, HORI?!
THE LAW?
Fired again?
THAT'S RIGHT!!

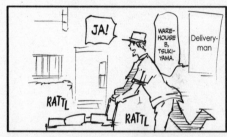

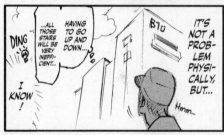

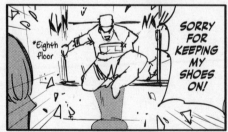

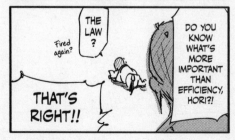

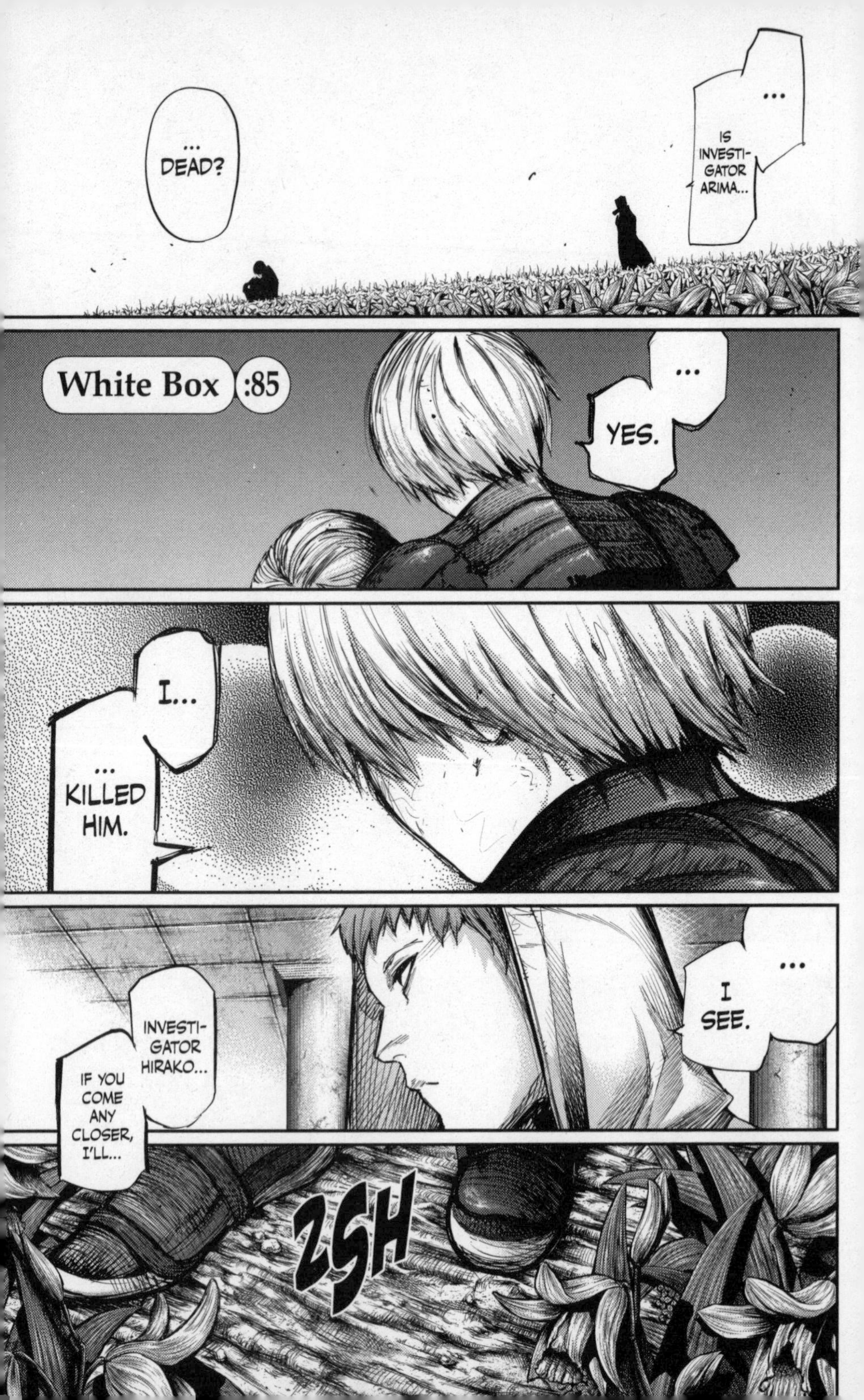
... IS INVESTIGATOR ARIMA...
... DEAD?
White Box :85
... YES.
I... ... KILLED HIM.
... I SEE.
INVESTIGATOR HIRAKO...
IF YOU COME ANY CLOSER, I'LL...
ZSH

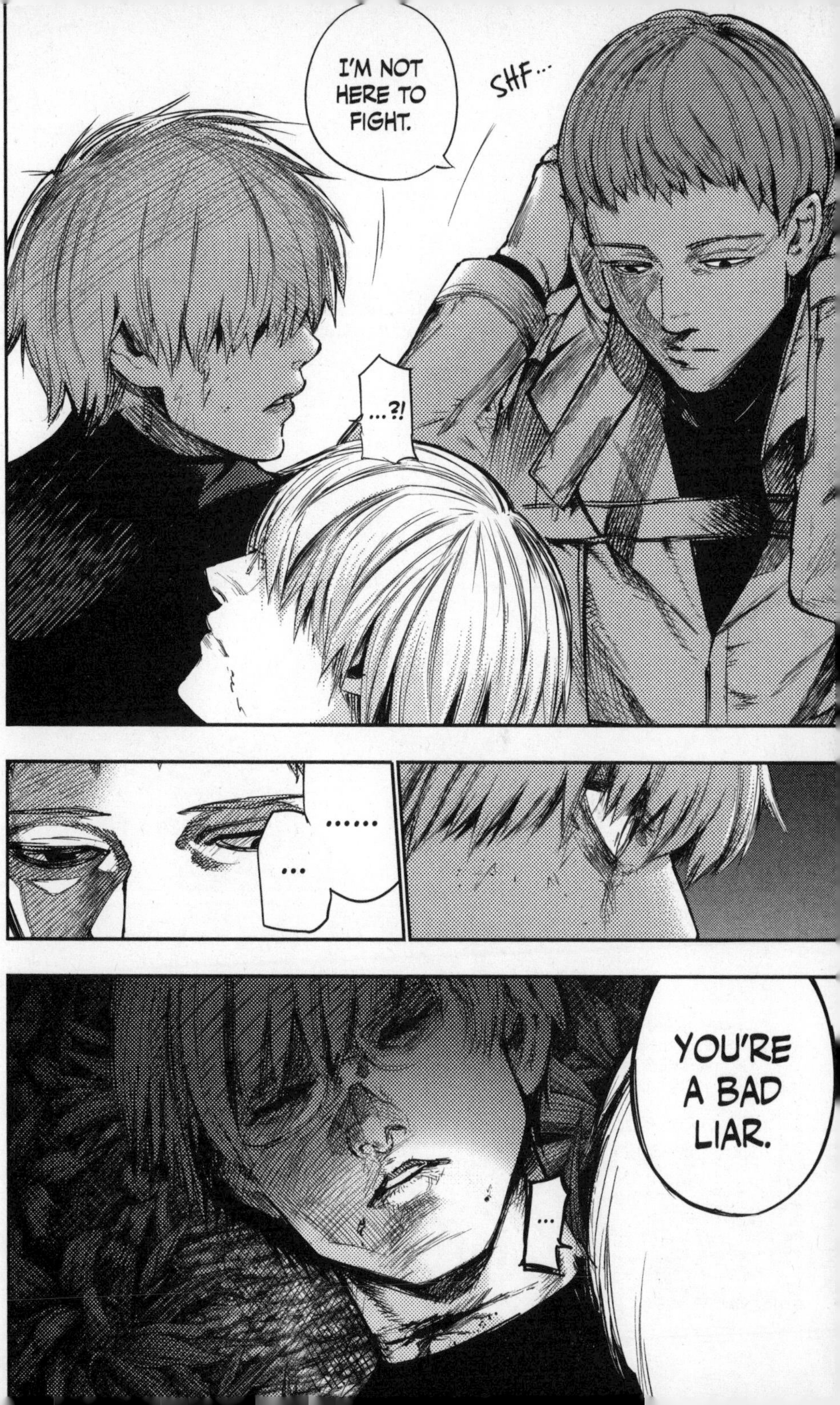
SHF...
I'M NOT HERE TO FIGHT.
...?!
......
...
YOU'RE A BAD LIAR.
...

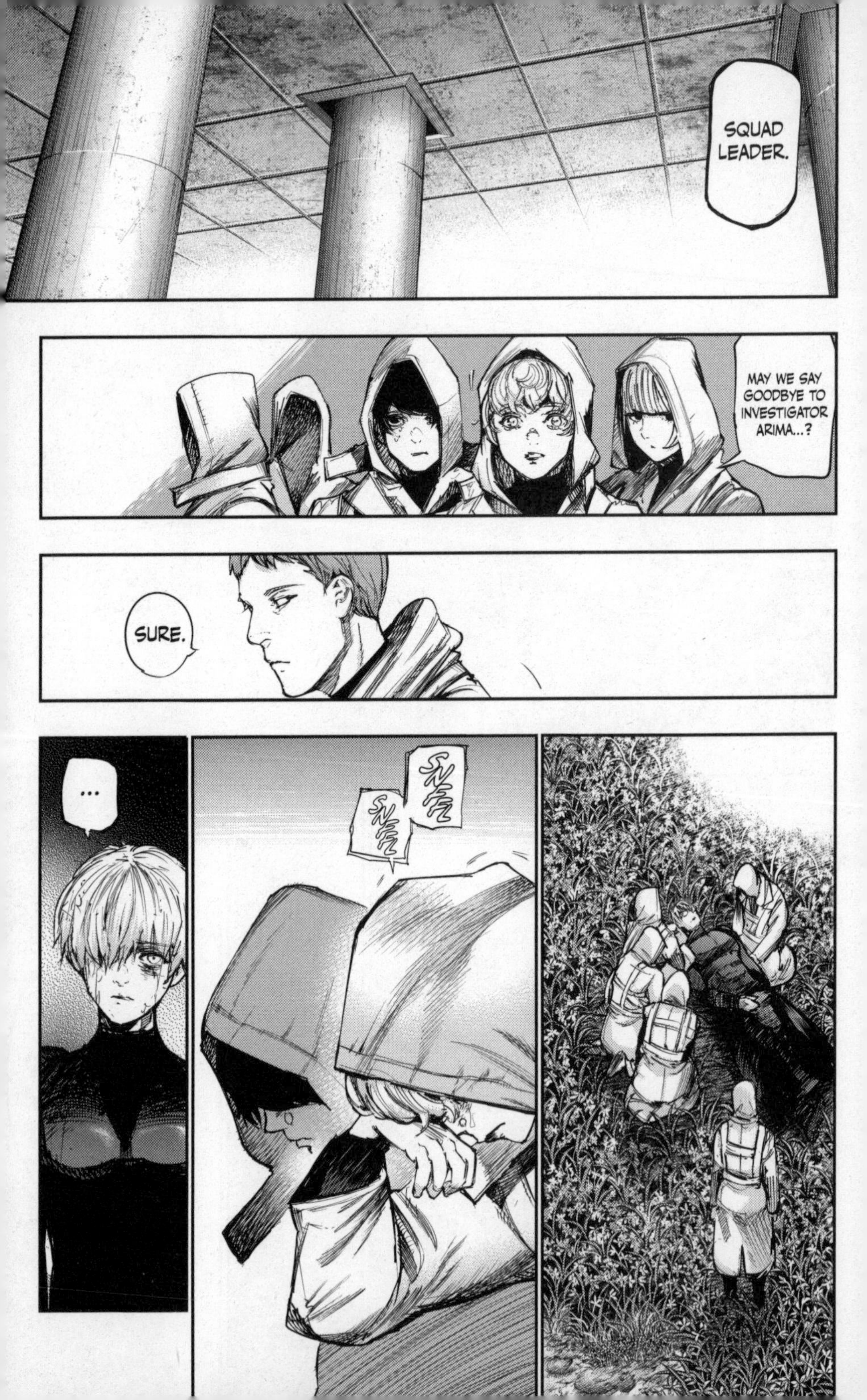
SQUAD LEADER.
MAY WE SAY GOODBYE TO INVESTIGATOR ARIMA...?
SURE.
SNFFL
SNFFL
...

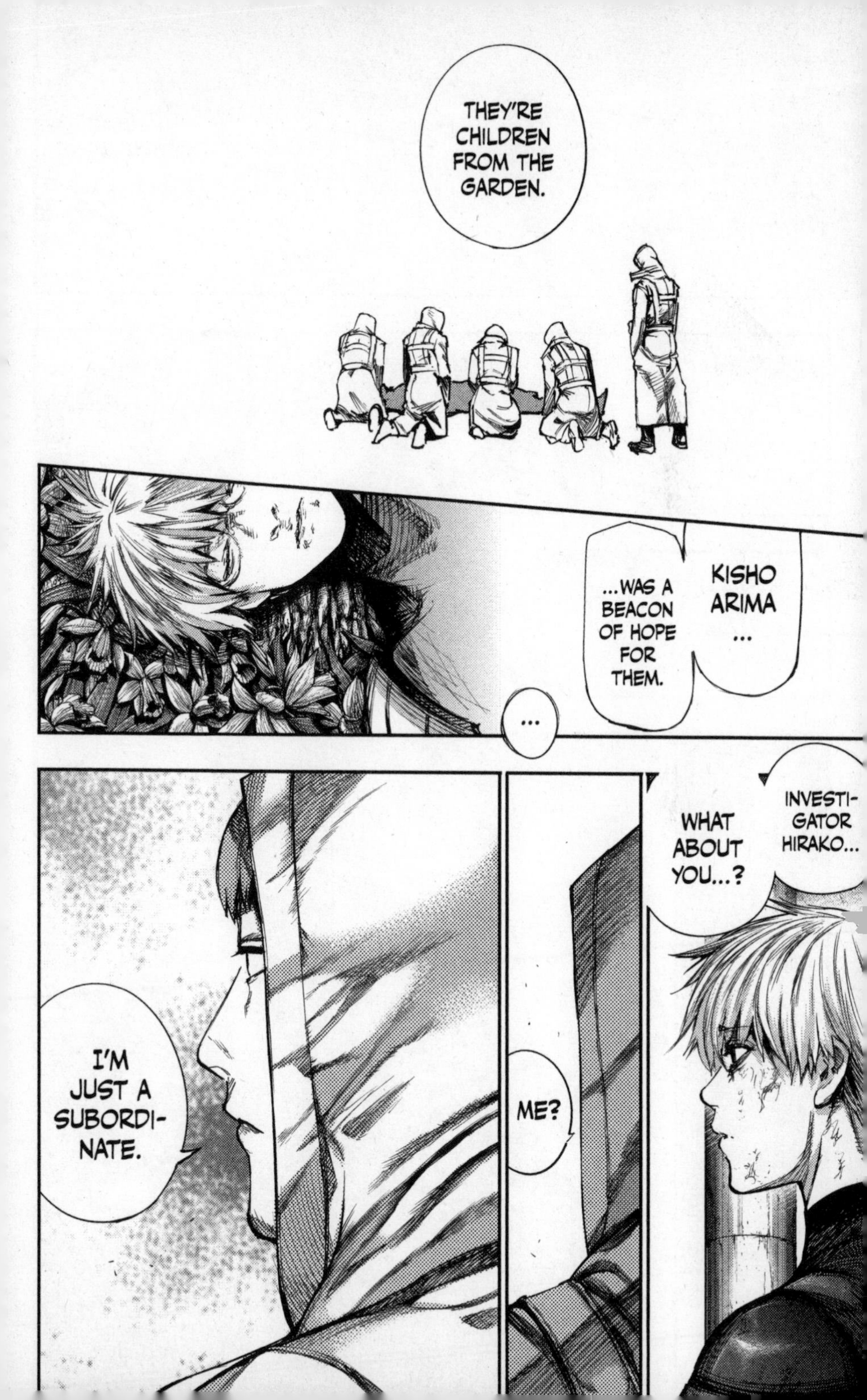
THEY'RE CHILDREN FROM THE GARDEN.
KISHO ARIMA...
...WAS A BEACON OF HOPE FOR THEM.
...
INVESTIGATOR HIRAKO...
WHAT ABOUT YOU...?
ME?
I'M JUST A SUBORDINATE.

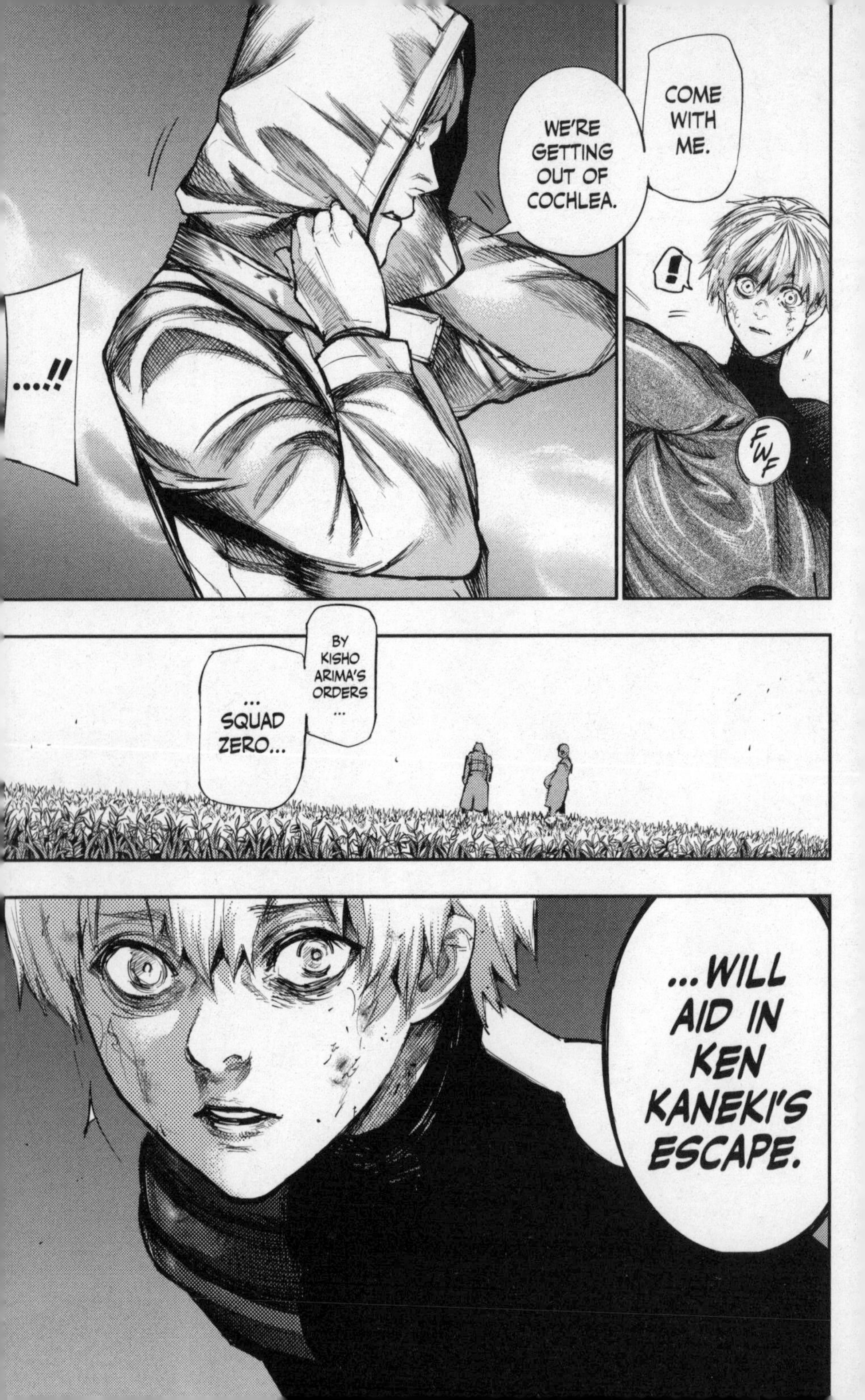

COME WITH ME.
WE'RE GETTING OUT OF COCHLEA.
!
FWF
...!!
BY KISHO ARIMA'S ORDERS ...
... SQUAD ZERO...
...WILL AID IN KEN KANEKI'S ESCAPE.

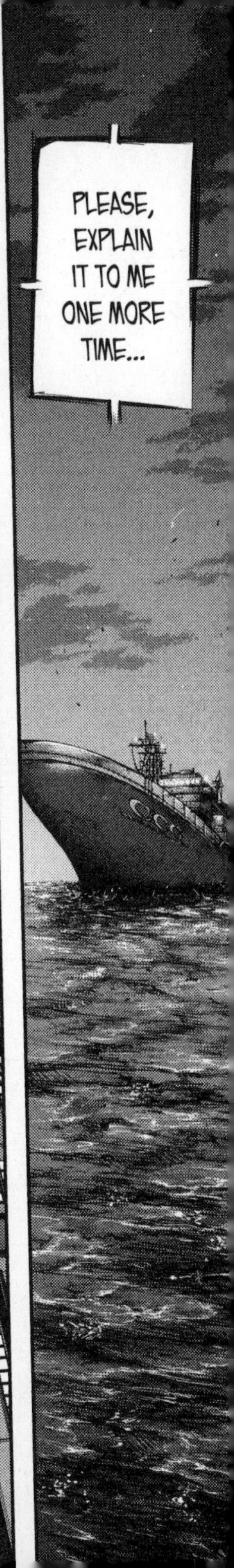
PLEASE, EXPLAIN IT TO ME ONE MORE TIME...
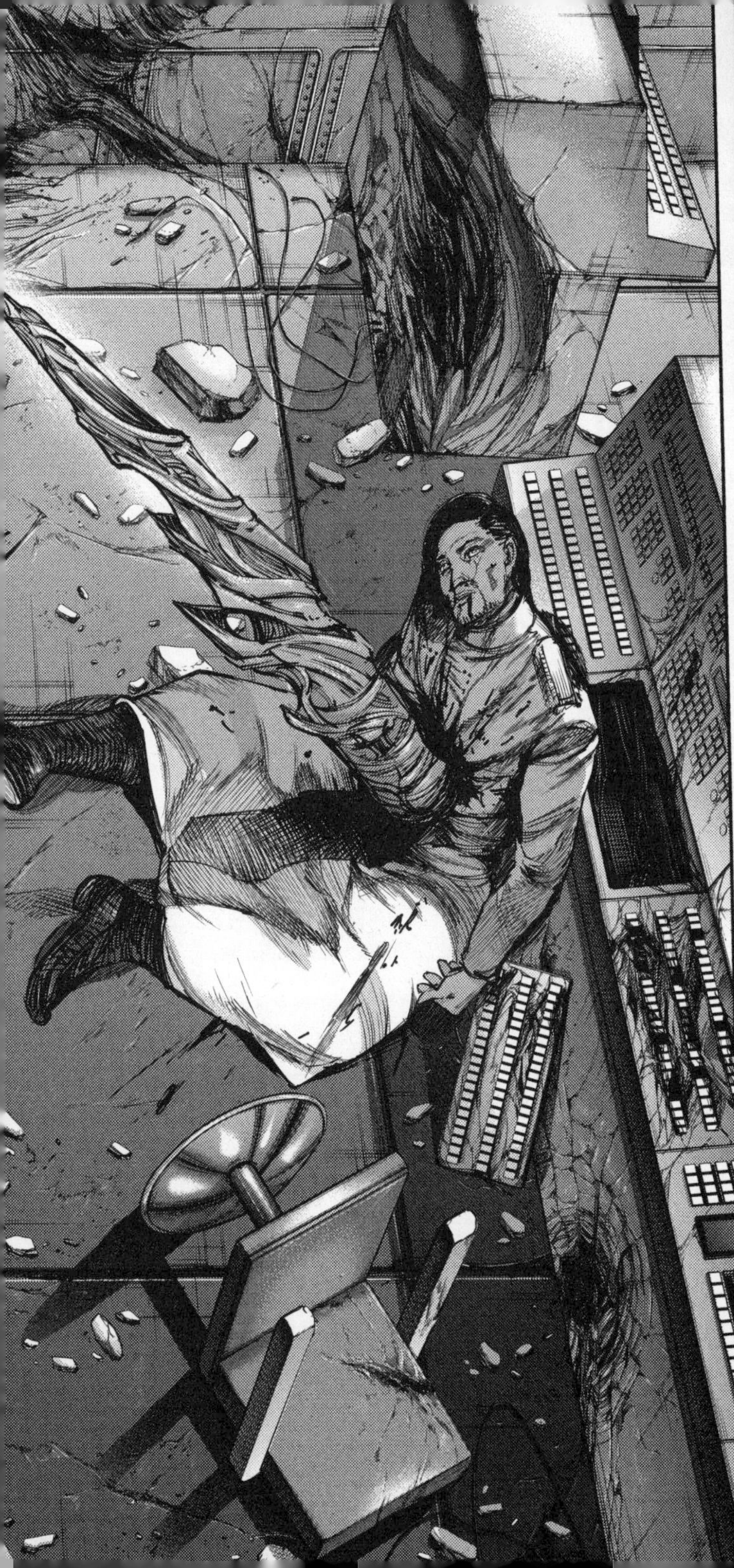

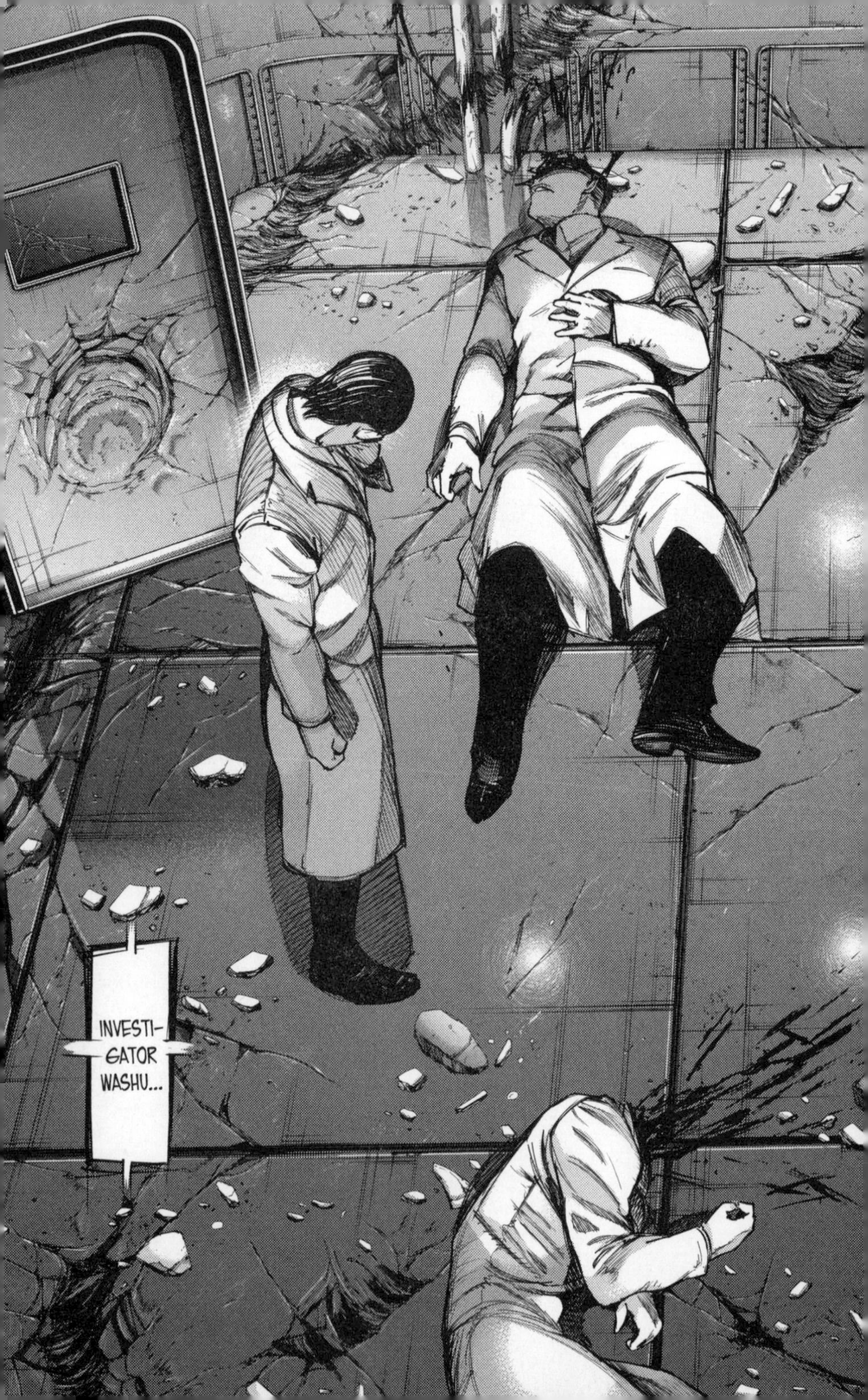
INVESTI-
GATOR
WASHU...

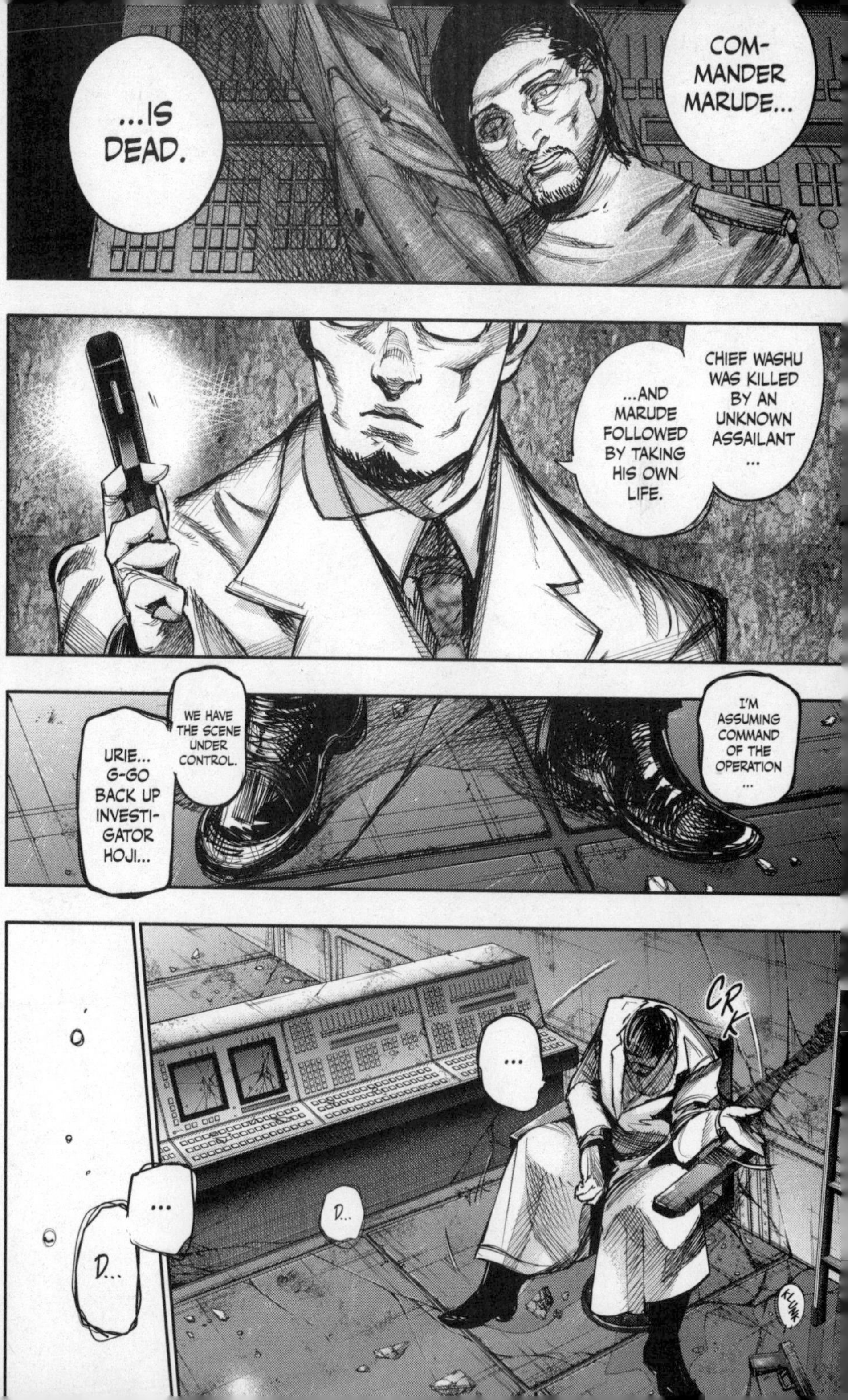
COM-MANDER MARUDE...
...IS DEAD.
CHIEF WASHU WAS KILLED BY AN UNKNOWN ASSAILANT ...
...AND MARUDE FOLLOWED BY TAKING HIS OWN LIFE.
I'M ASSUMING COMMAND OF THE OPERATION ...
WE HAVE THE SCENE UNDER CONTROL.
URIE... G-GO BACK UP INVESTI-GATOR HOJI...
CRK
...
KLUNK
D...
...
D...

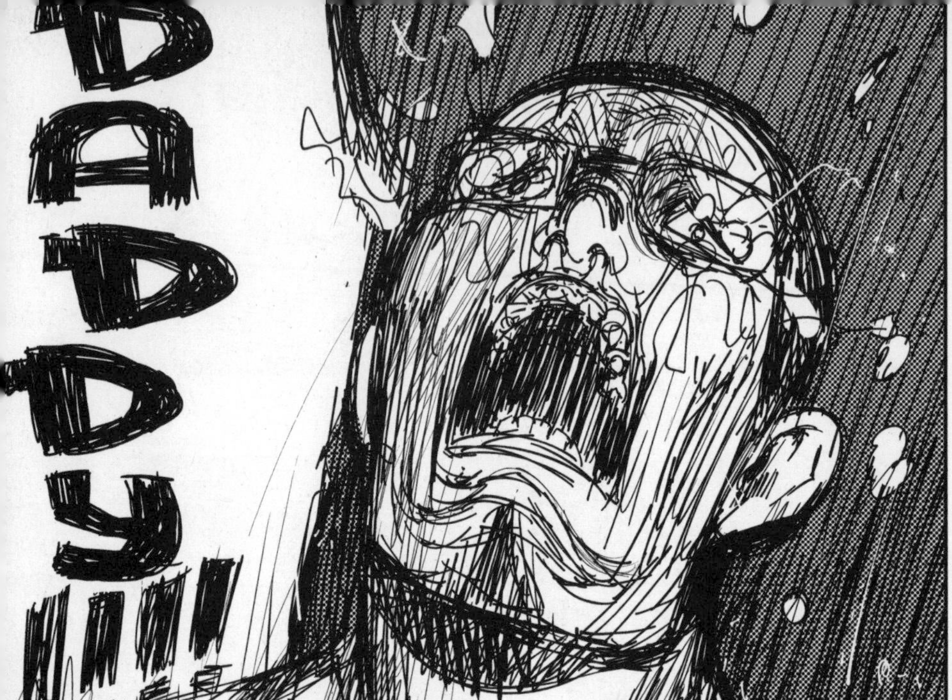
DADDY!!!!!

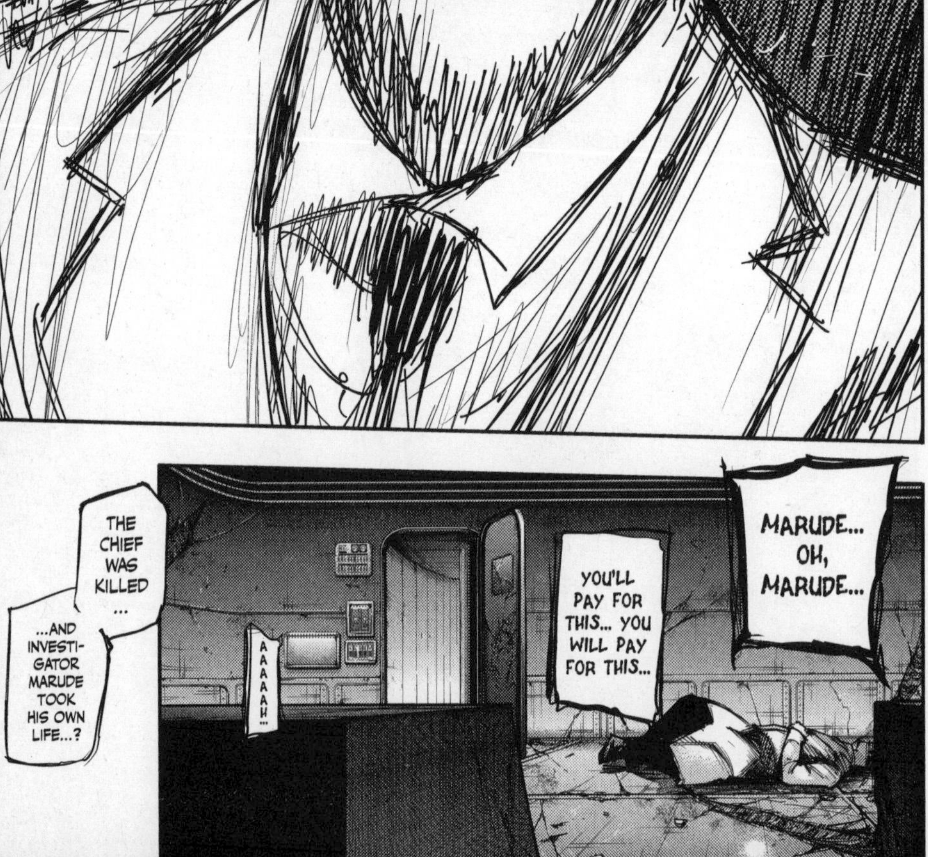
MARUDE... OH, MARUDE...
YOU'LL PAY FOR THIS... YOU WILL PAY FOR THIS...
AAAAAH...
THE CHIEF WAS KILLED...
...AND INVESTI-GATOR MARUDE TOOK HIS OWN LIFE...?

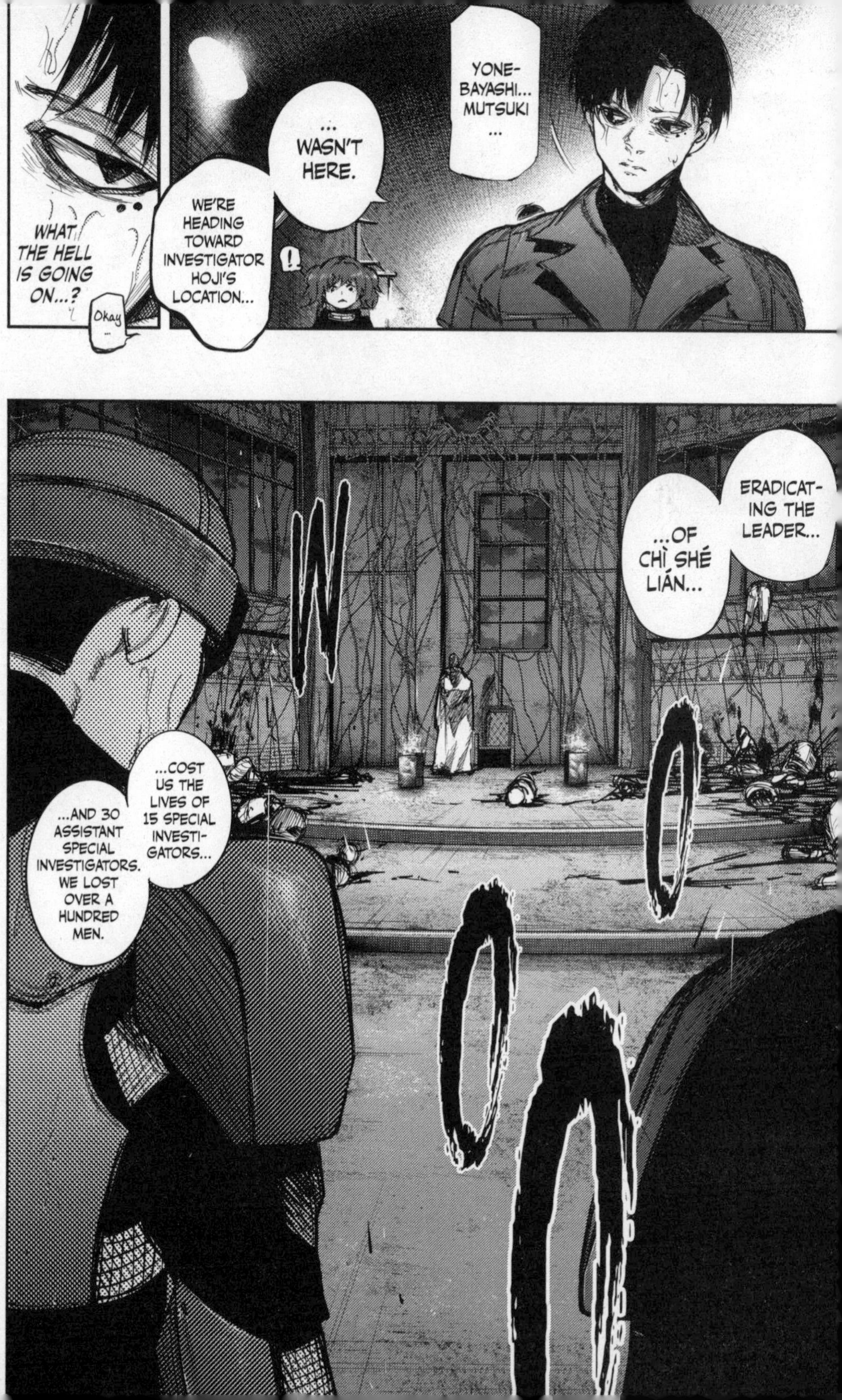
YONE-BAYASHI... MUTSUKI...
...WASN'T HERE.
WE'RE HEADING TOWARD INVESTIGATOR HOJI'S LOCATION...
!
WHAT THE HELL IS GOING ON...?
Okay...
ERADICATING THE LEADER...
...OF CHÌ SHÉ LIÁN...
...COST US THE LIVES OF 15 SPECIAL INVESTI-GATORS...
...AND 30 ASSISTANT SPECIAL INVESTIGATORS. WE LOST OVER A HUNDRED MEN.
WOOO

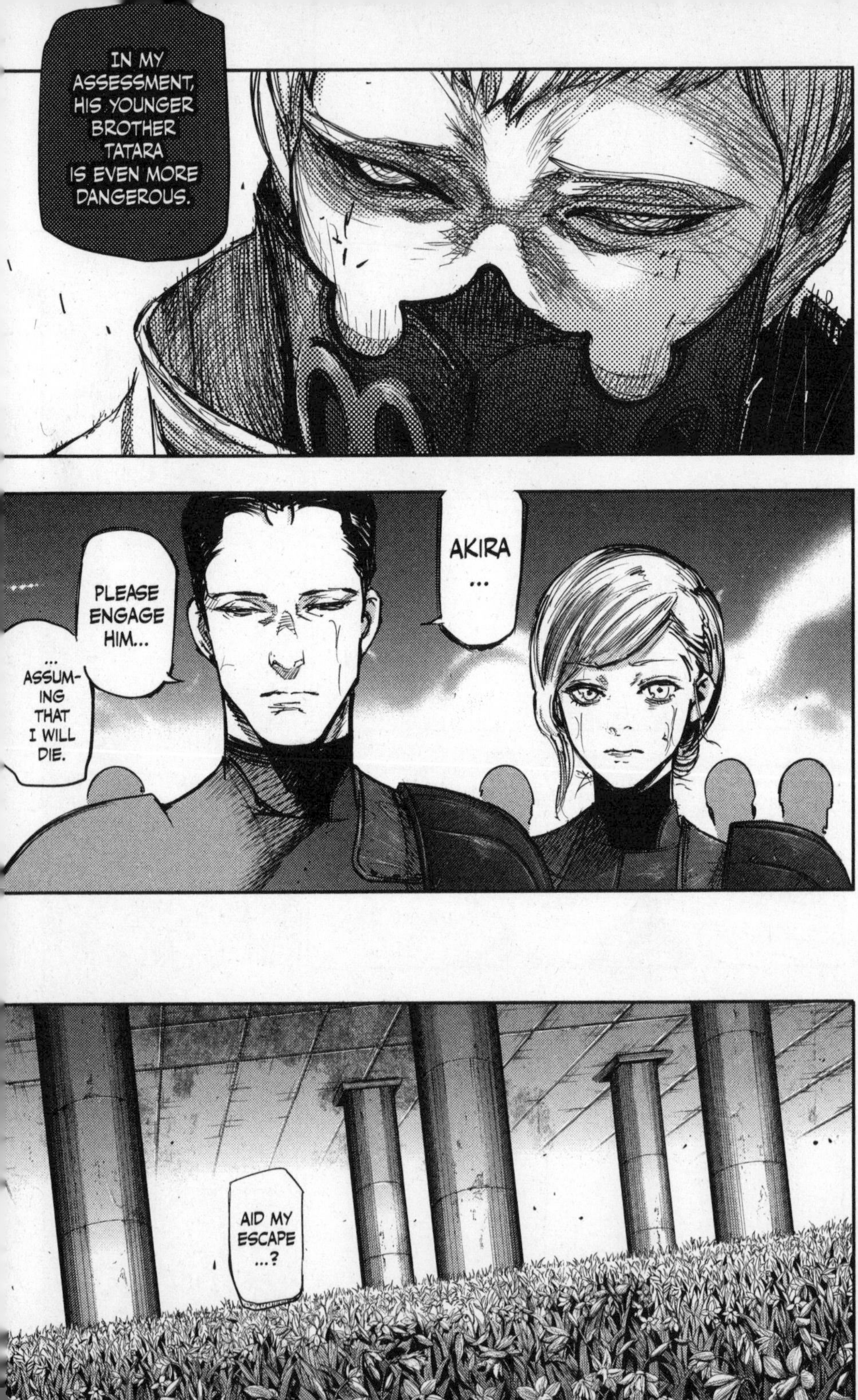
IN MY ASSESSMENT, HIS YOUNGER BROTHER TATARA IS EVEN MORE DANGEROUS.
AKIRA ...
PLEASE ENGAGE HIM...
... ASSUMING THAT I WILL DIE.
AID MY ESCAPE ...?

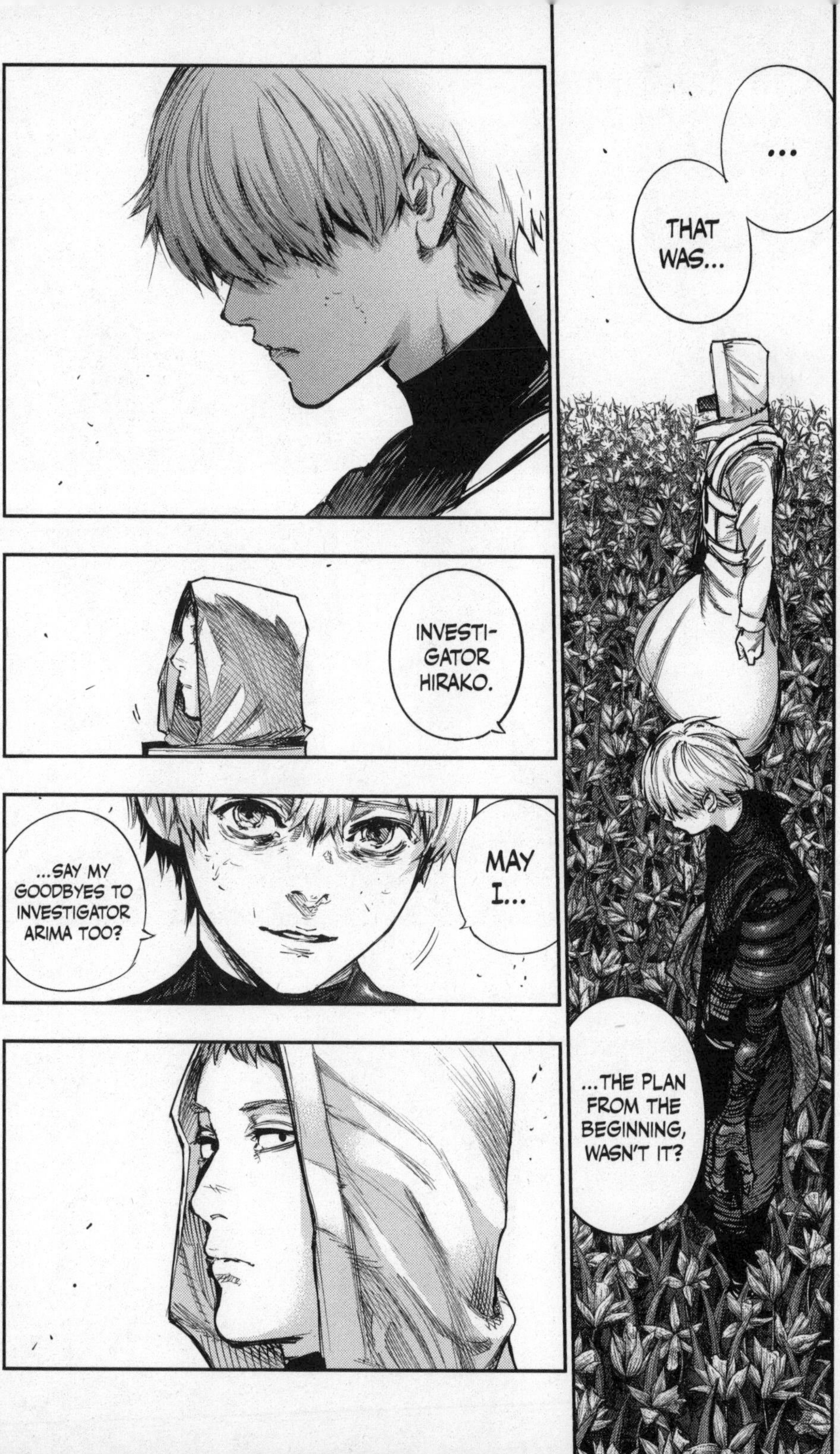
...
THAT WAS...
...THE PLAN FROM THE BEGINNING, WASN'T IT?
INVESTIGATOR HIRAKO.
MAY I...
...SAY MY GOODBYES TO INVESTIGATOR ARIMA TOO?

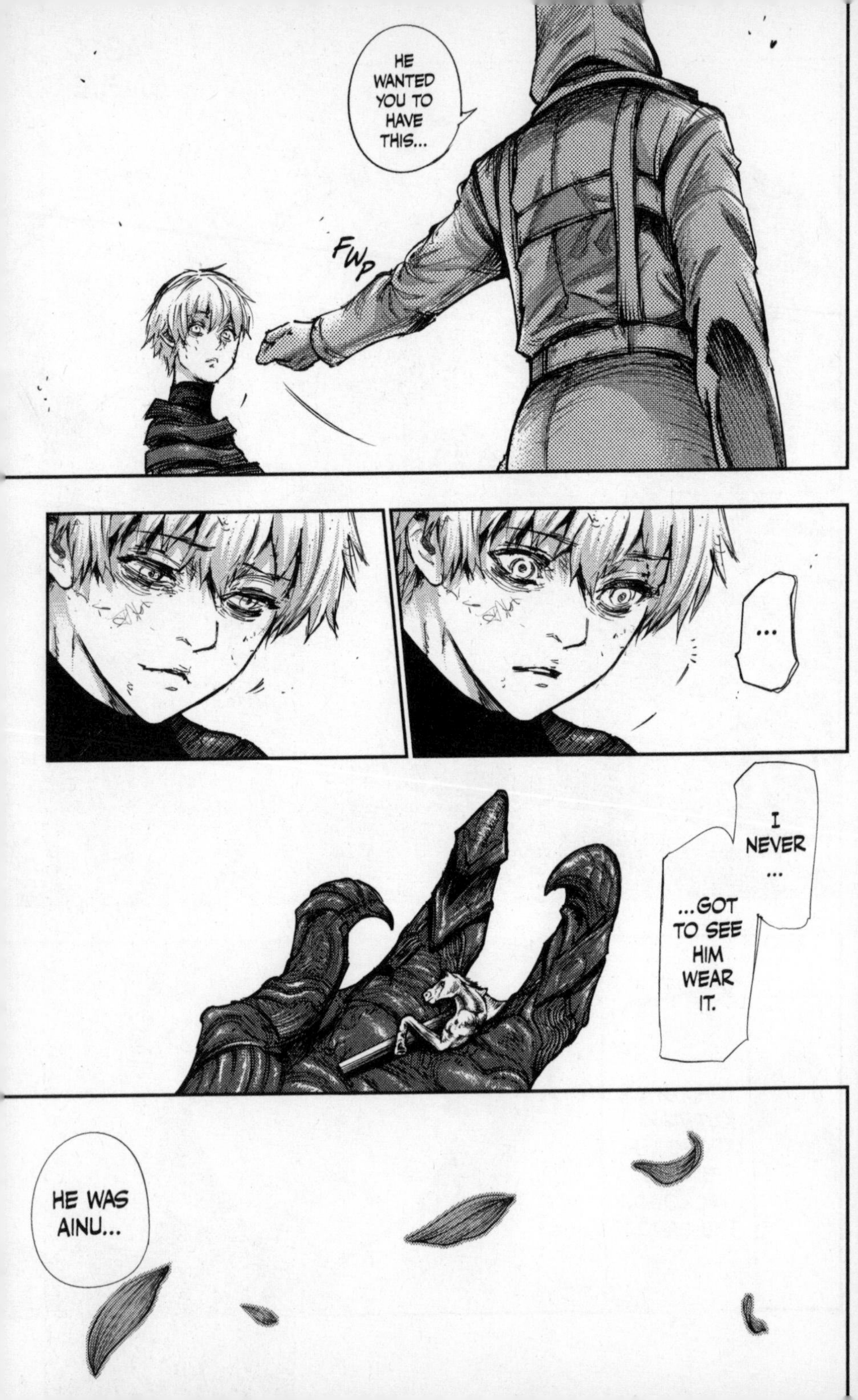
HE WANTED YOU TO HAVE THIS...
FWP
...
I NEVER ...
...GOT TO SEE HIM WEAR IT.
HE WAS AINU...

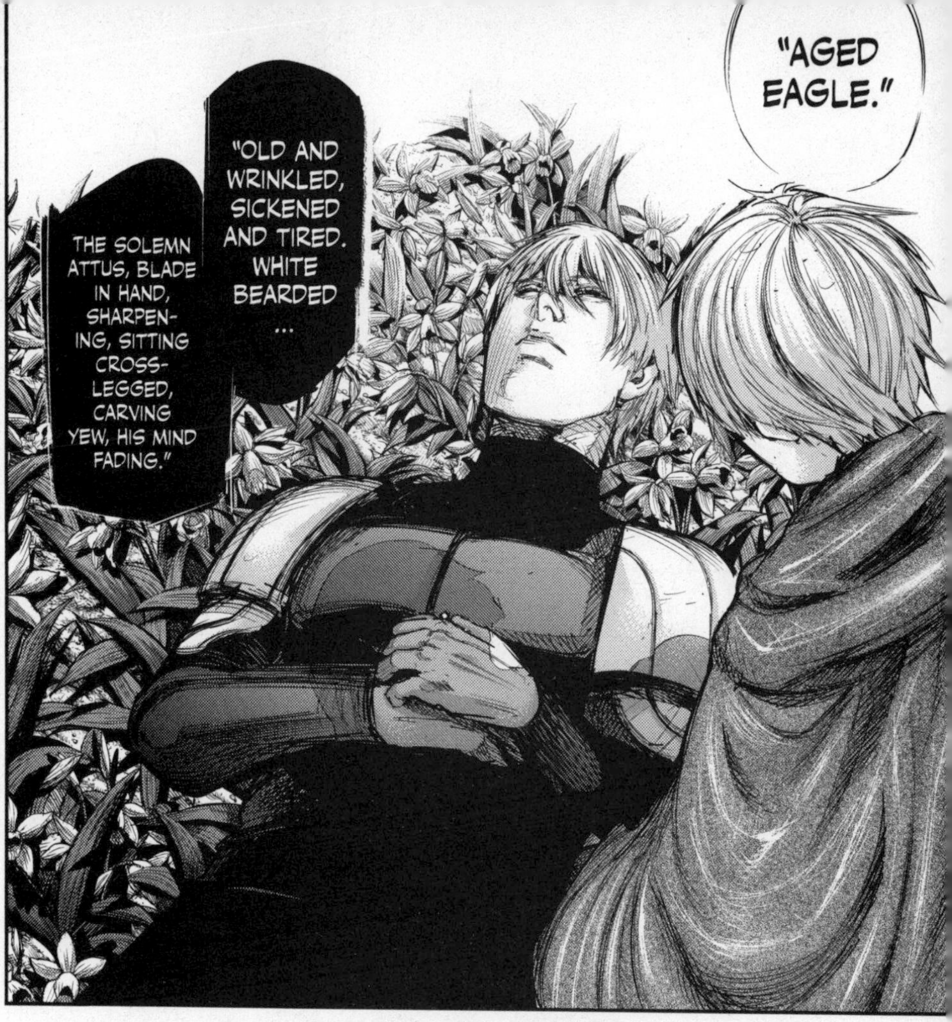
"AGED EAGLE."
"OLD AND WRINKLED, SICKENED AND TIRED. WHITE BEARDED ...
THE SOLEMN ATTUS, BLADE IN HAND, SHARPEN-ING, SITTING CROSS-LEGGED, CARVING YEW, HIS MIND FADING."
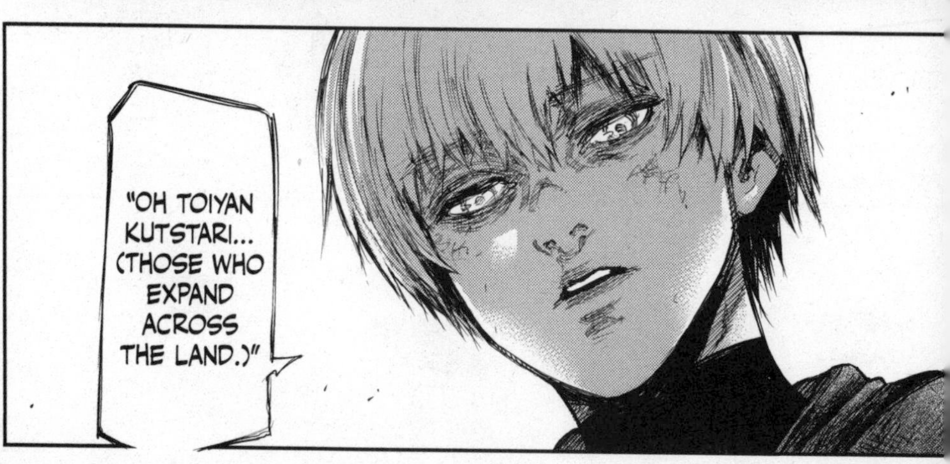
"OH TOIYAN KUTSTARI... (THOSE WHO EXPAND ACROSS THE LAND.)"

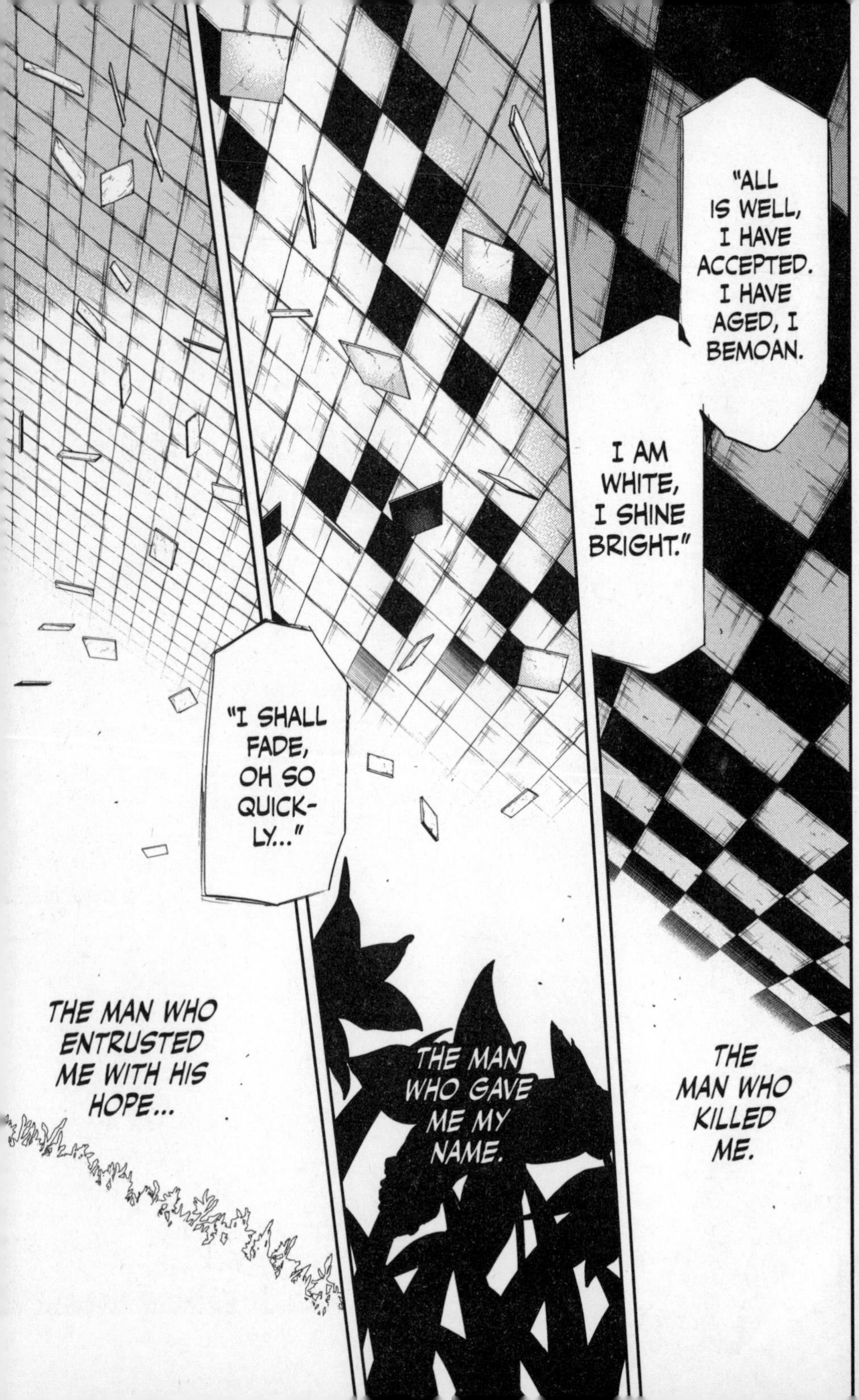
"ALL IS WELL, I HAVE ACCEPTED. I HAVE AGED, I BEMOAN.
I AM WHITE, I SHINE BRIGHT."
THE MAN WHO KILLED ME.
"I SHALL FADE, OH SO QUICKLY..."
THE MAN WHO GAVE ME MY NAME.
THE MAN WHO ENTRUSTED ME WITH HIS HOPE...

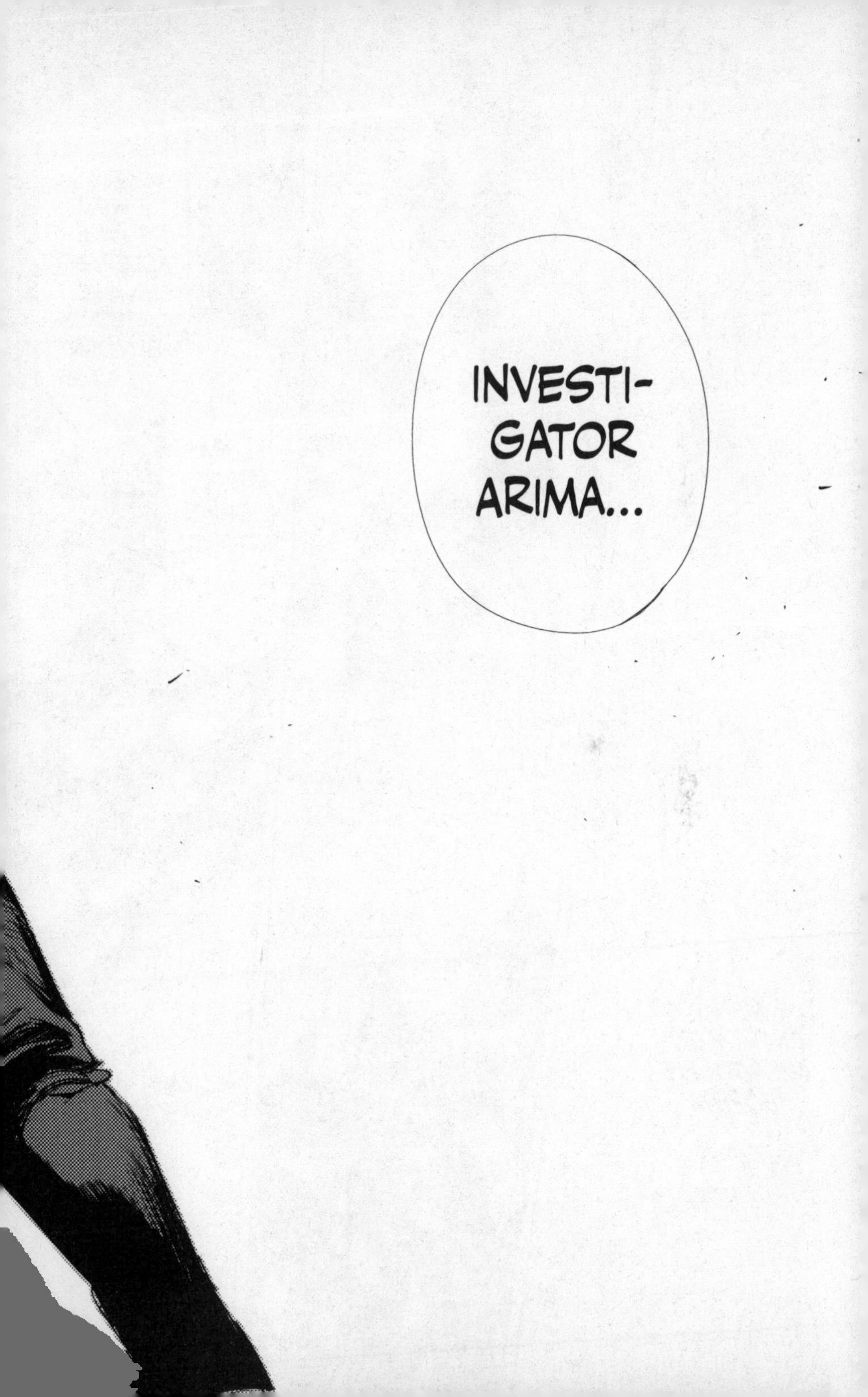
INVESTI-GATOR ARIMA...

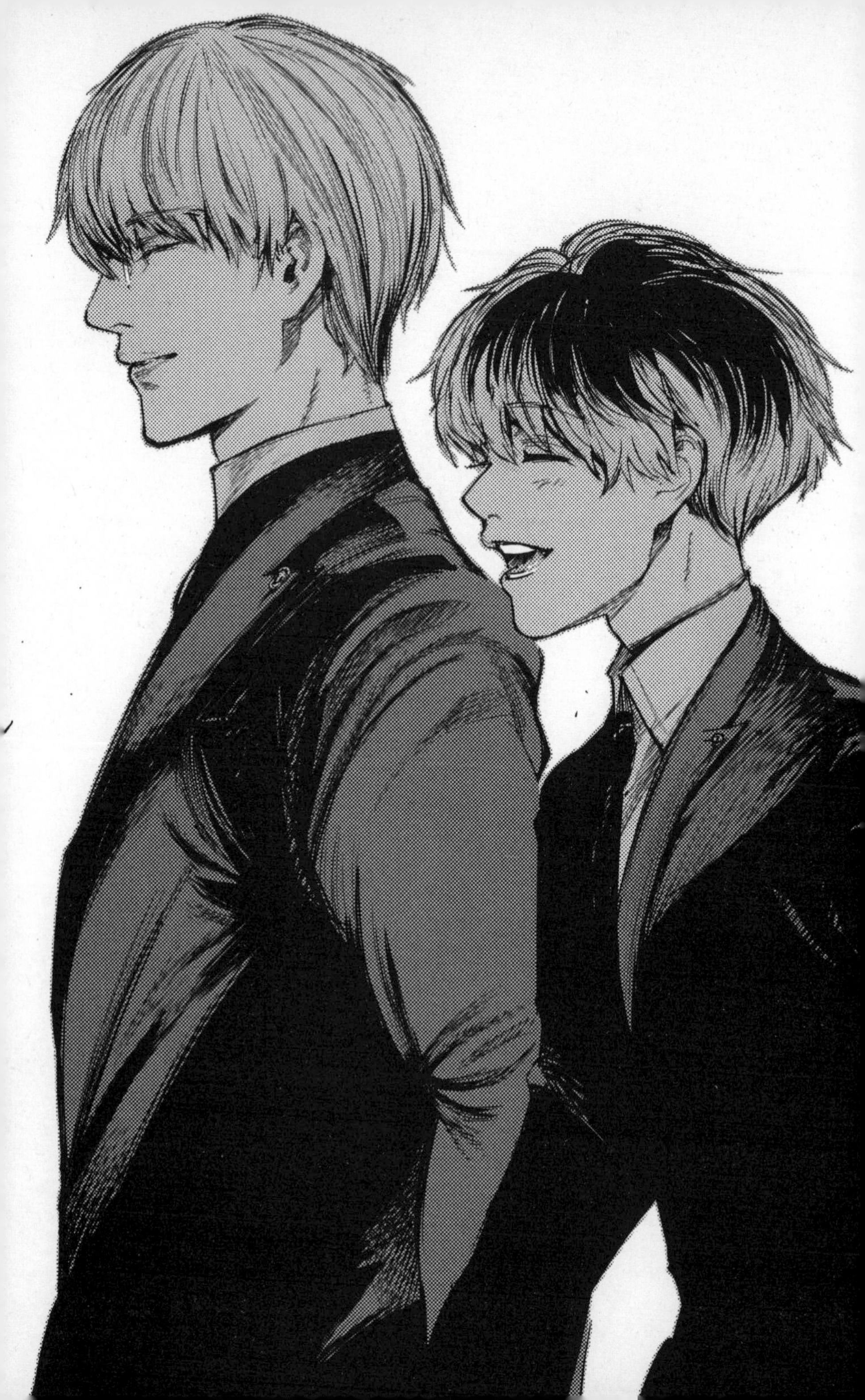

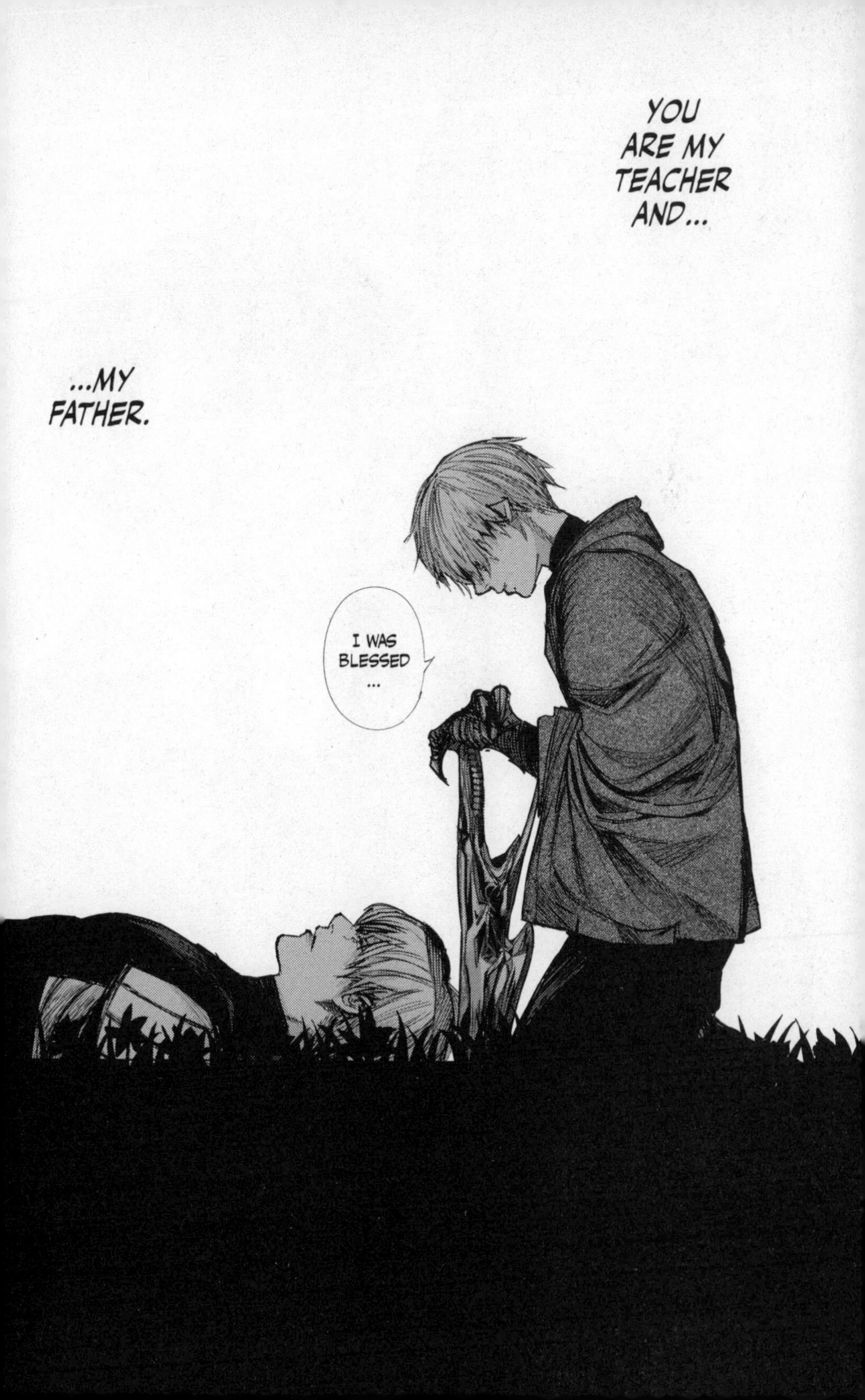
YOU ARE MY TEACHER AND...
...MY FATHER.
I WAS BLESSED ...

Tsukiyama at work ④

Très bien.
French Teacher
TGHE BIYON.
Non.
Très bien.
TGHE BE YAWN.
Noooo!!
Très Bien!!
UNTIL OUR WORD BALLOONS ARE SPELLED THE SAME!!
Très Bien!!
TGHE BE YAWN.
THAT'S HOW YOU'RE MEASURING SUCCESS?

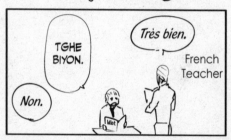

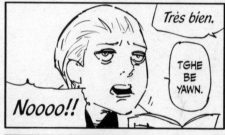

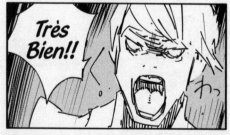

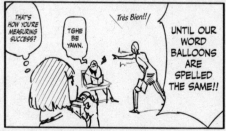

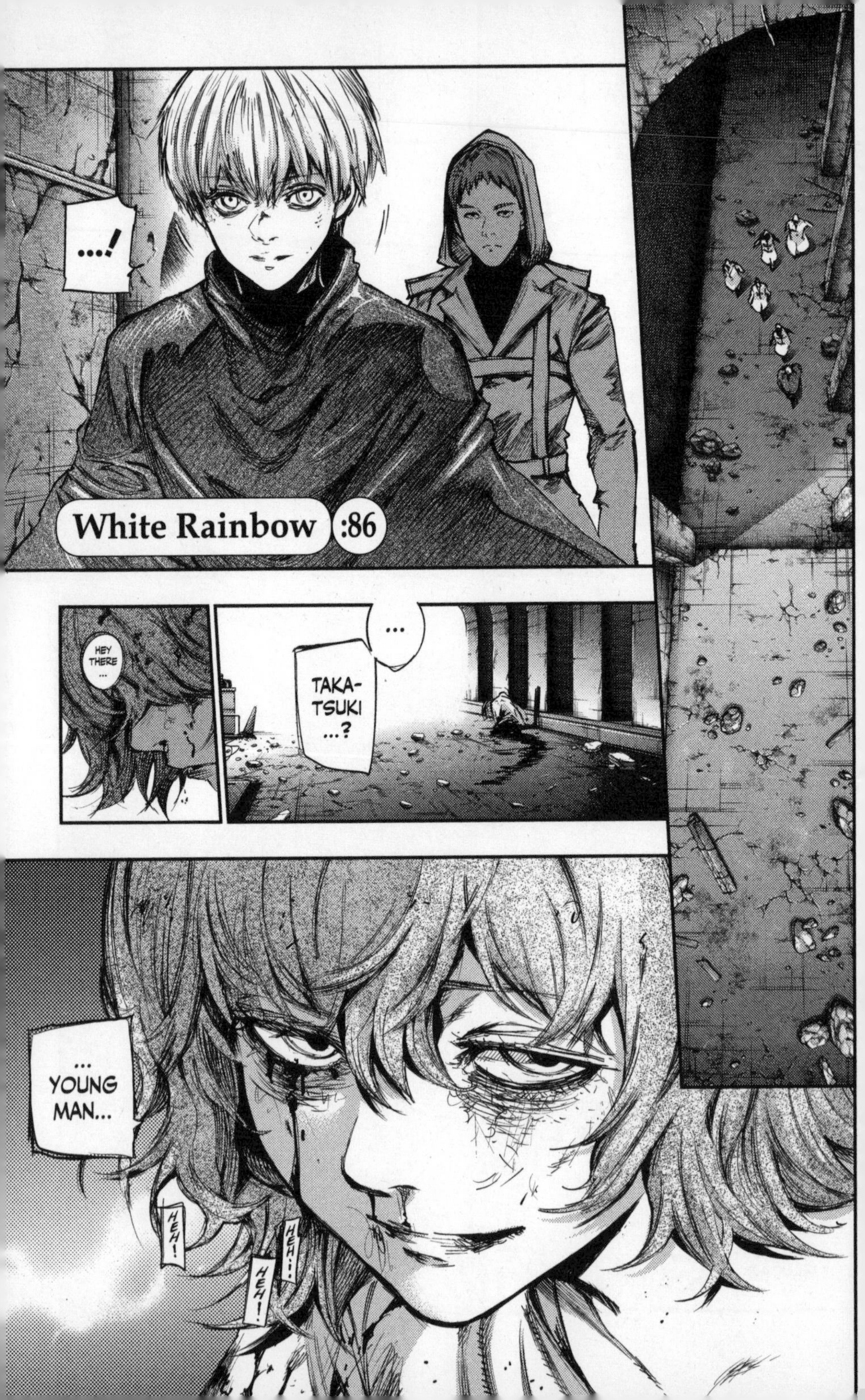
...!
White Rainbow :86
...
TAKA-TSUKI ...?
HEY THERE ...
... YOUNG MAN...
HEH!
HEH!
HEH!

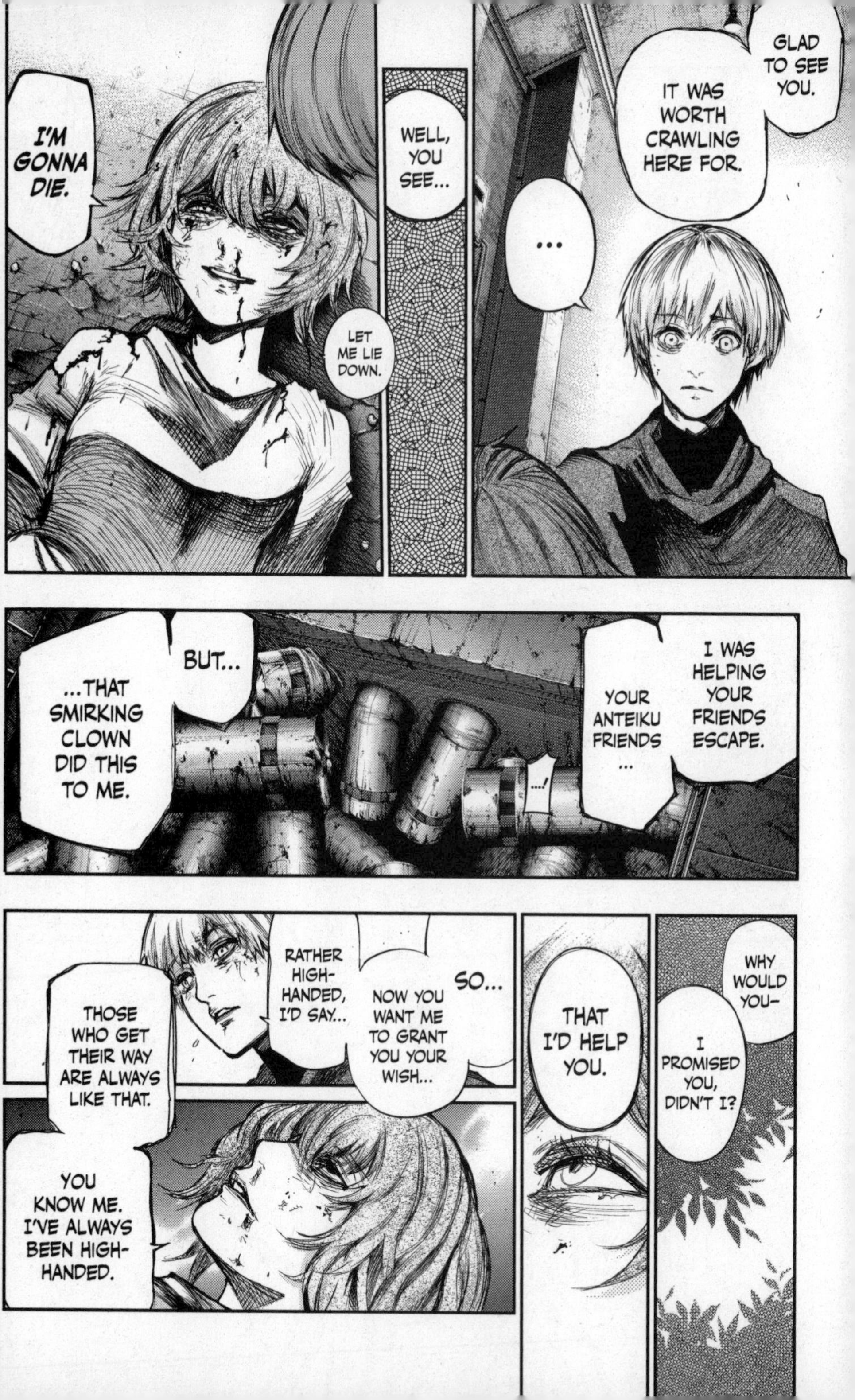
GLAD TO SEE YOU.
IT WAS WORTH CRAWLING HERE FOR.
...
WELL, YOU SEE...
I'M GONNA DIE.
LET ME LIE DOWN.
I WAS HELPING YOUR FRIENDS ESCAPE.
YOUR ANTEIKU FRIENDS ...
...!
BUT...
...THAT SMIRKING CLOWN DID THIS TO ME.
WHY WOULD YOU-
I PROMISED YOU, DIDN'T I?
THAT I'D HELP YOU.
SO...
NOW YOU WANT ME TO GRANT YOU YOUR WISH...
RATHER HIGH-HANDED, I'D SAY...
THOSE WHO GET THEIR WAY ARE ALWAYS LIKE THAT.
YOU KNOW ME. I'VE ALWAYS BEEN HIGH-HANDED.

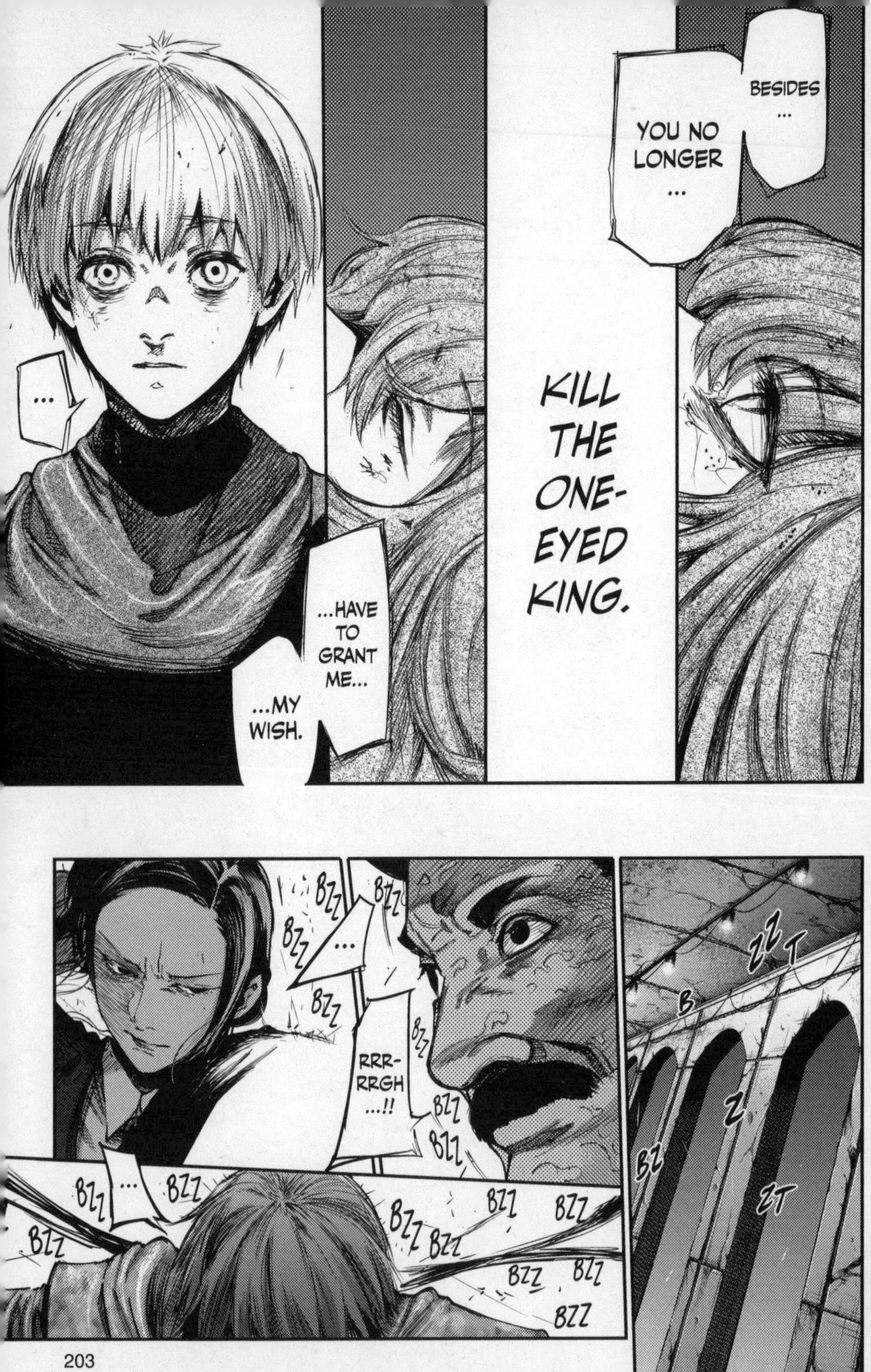
BESIDES ...
YOU NO LONGER ...
KILL THE ONE-EYED KING.
...HAVE TO GRANT ME...
...MY WISH.
...
B ZZZT
BZ Z ZT
BZZ
...
BZZ
RRR-RRGH ...!!
BZZ
BZZ
BZZ
BZZ
BZZ
...
BZZ
BZZ
BZZ
BZZ
BZZ
BZZ
BZZ
BZZ
BZZ
BZZ

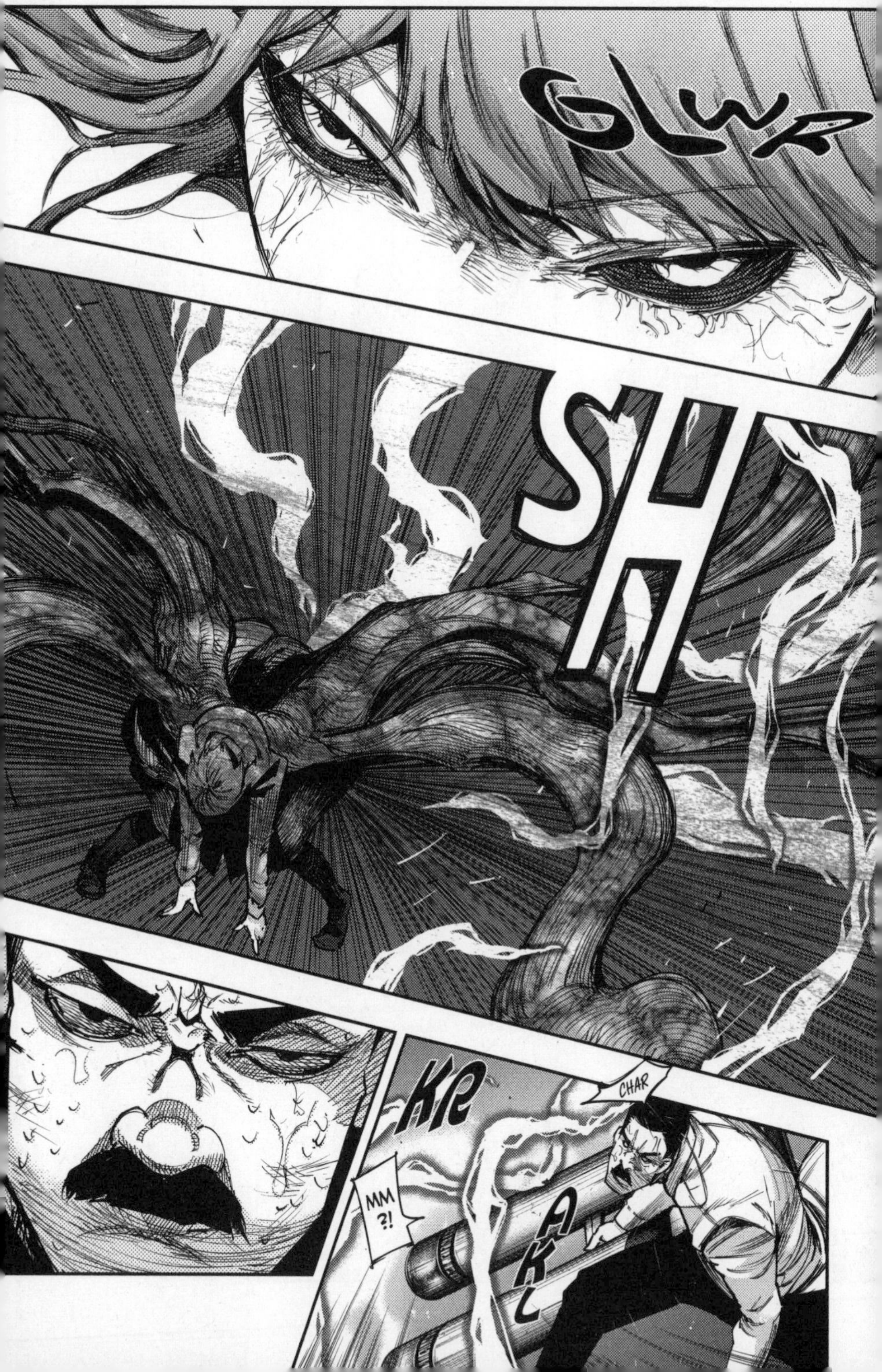
GLWR
SH
H
CHAR
KRE
AKL
MM ?!

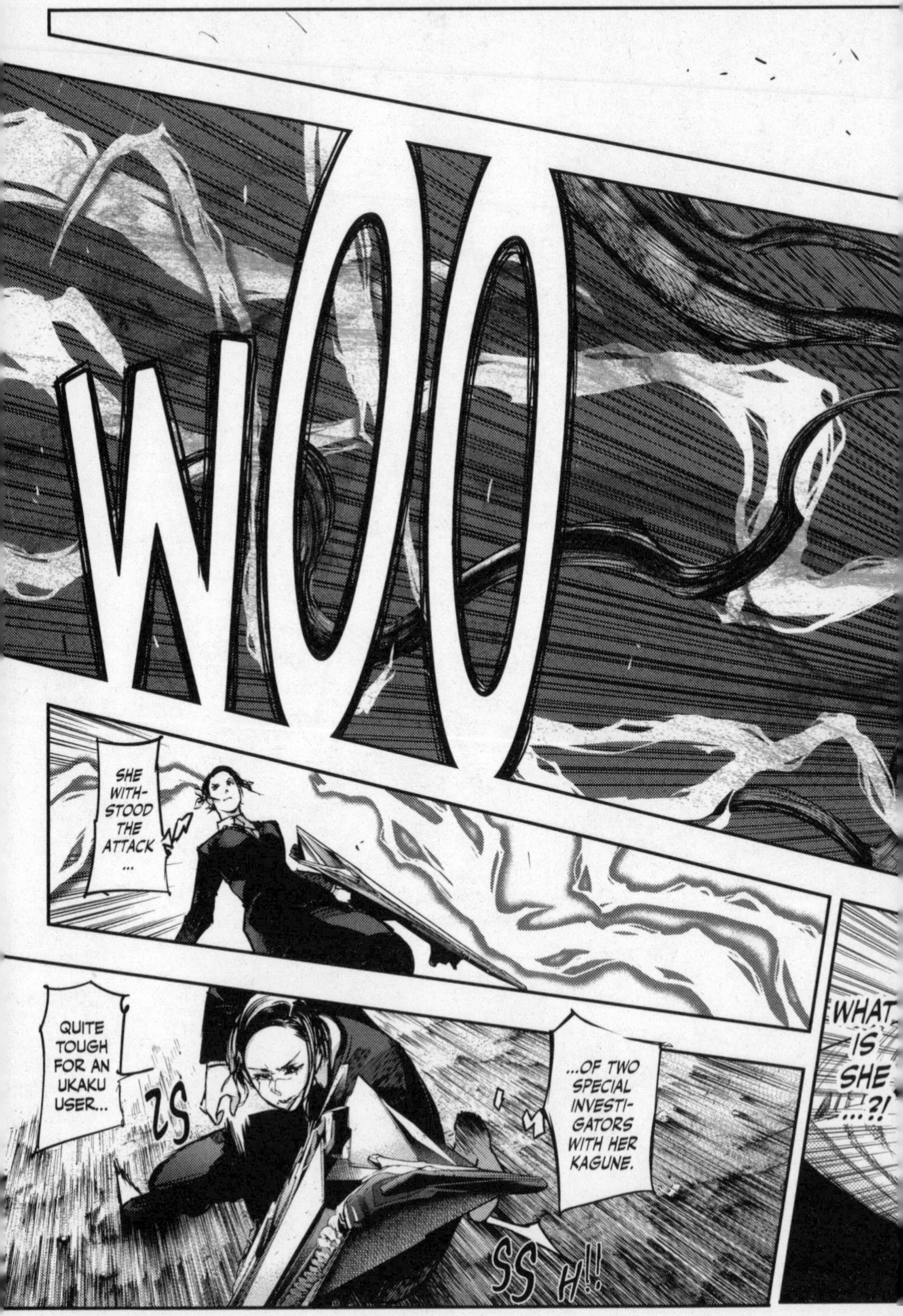
WOOO
WHAT IS SHE...?!
SHE WITH-STOOD THE ATTACK ...
...OF TWO SPECIAL INVESTI-GATORS WITH HER KAGUNE.
QUITE TOUGH FOR AN UKAKU USER...
SS
SSH!!

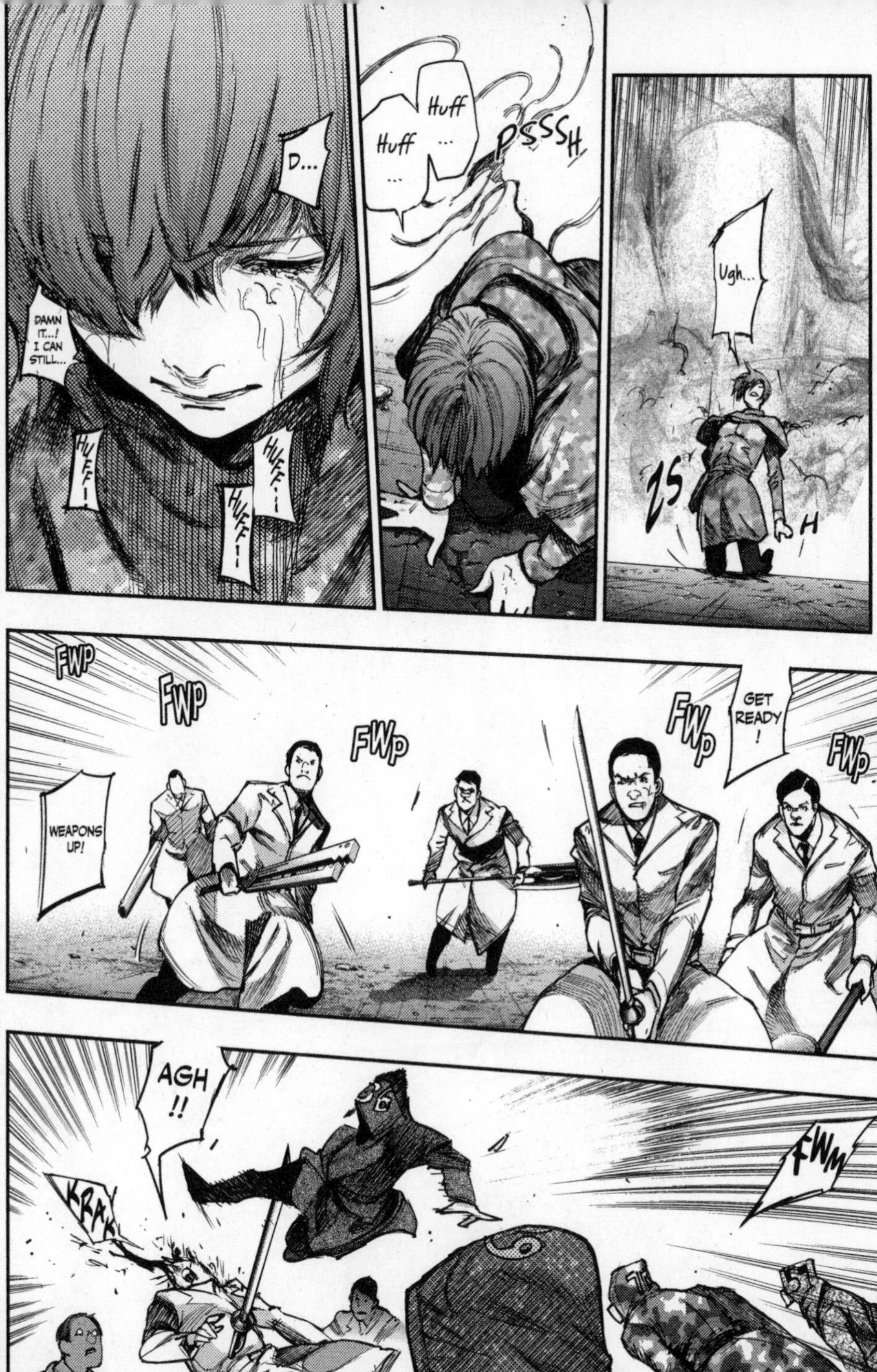
Ugh...
ZSH
Huff
Huff
...
...
PSSSH
D...
DAMN IT...! I CAN STILL...
HUFF!
HUFF!
HUFF!
FWp
GET READY!
FWp
FWp
FWp
FWp
WEAPONS UP!
FWM
AGH!!
KRAK

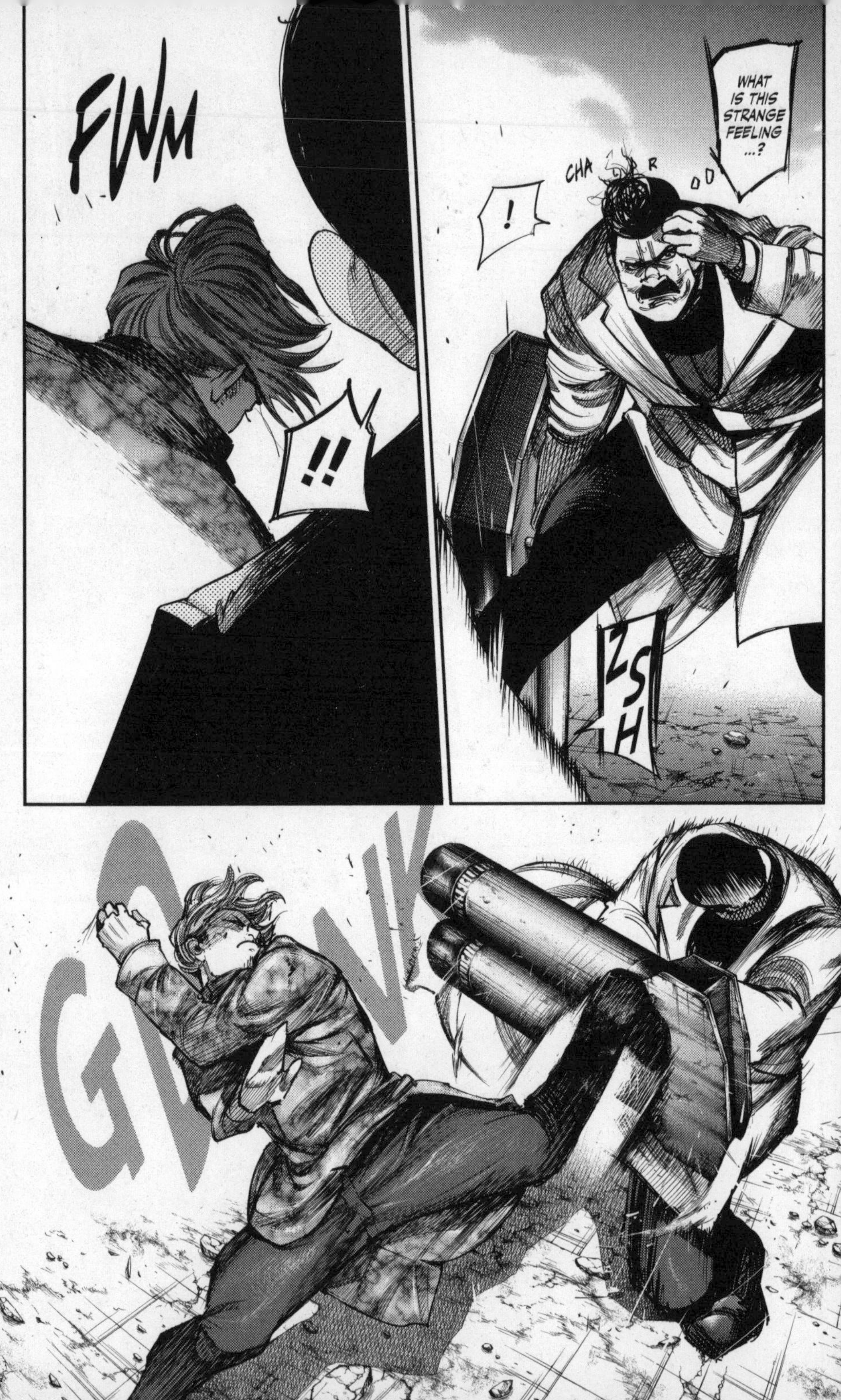
WHAT IS THIS STRANGE FEELING ...?
!
ZSH
FWM
!!

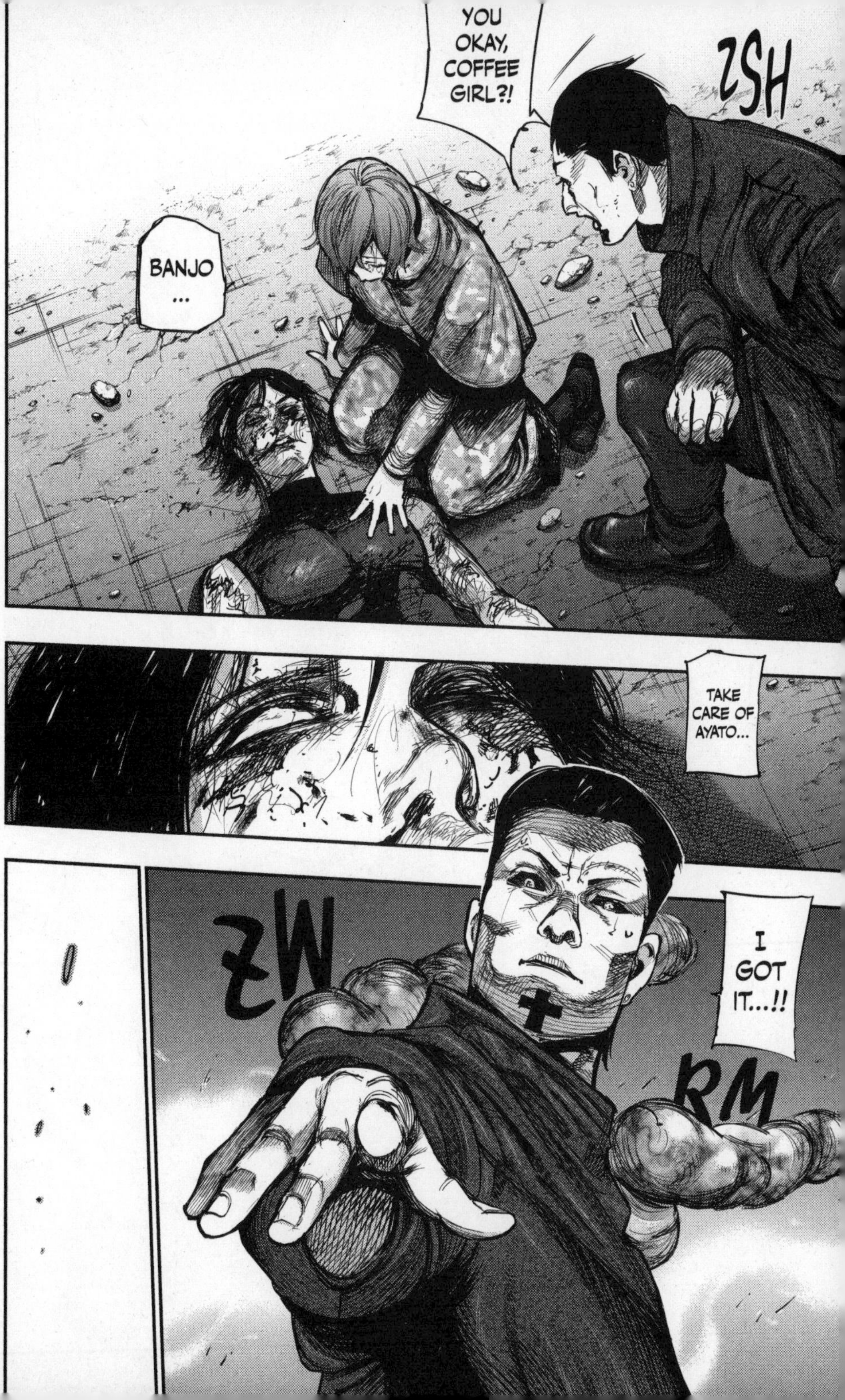
ZSH
YOU OKAY, COFFEE GIRL?!
BANJO ...
TAKE CARE OF AYATO...
I GOT IT...!!
ZW
RM

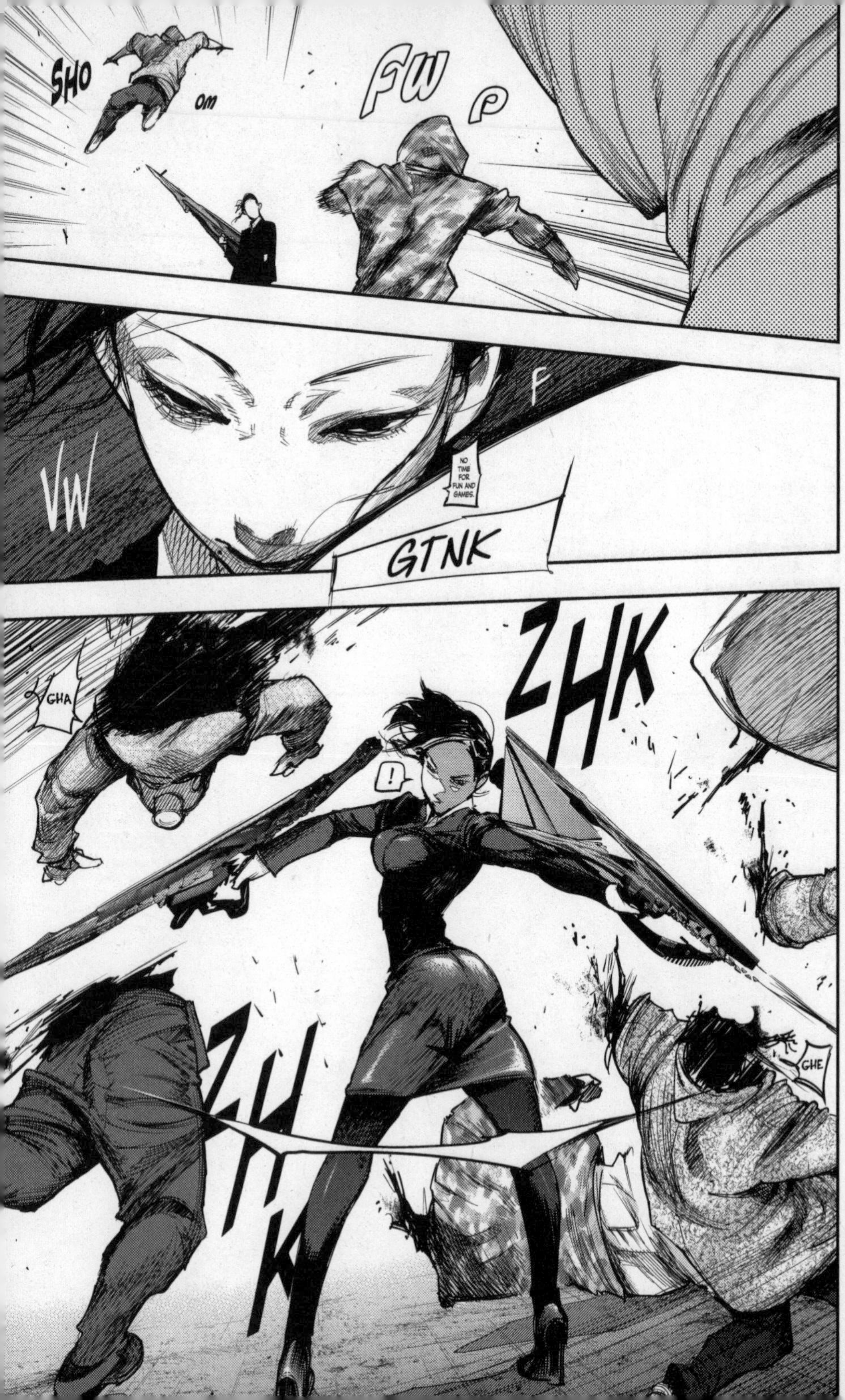
FWP
SHOom
F
NO TIME FOR FUN AND GAMES.
GTNK
VW
ZHK
!
GHE
GHA
ZHK

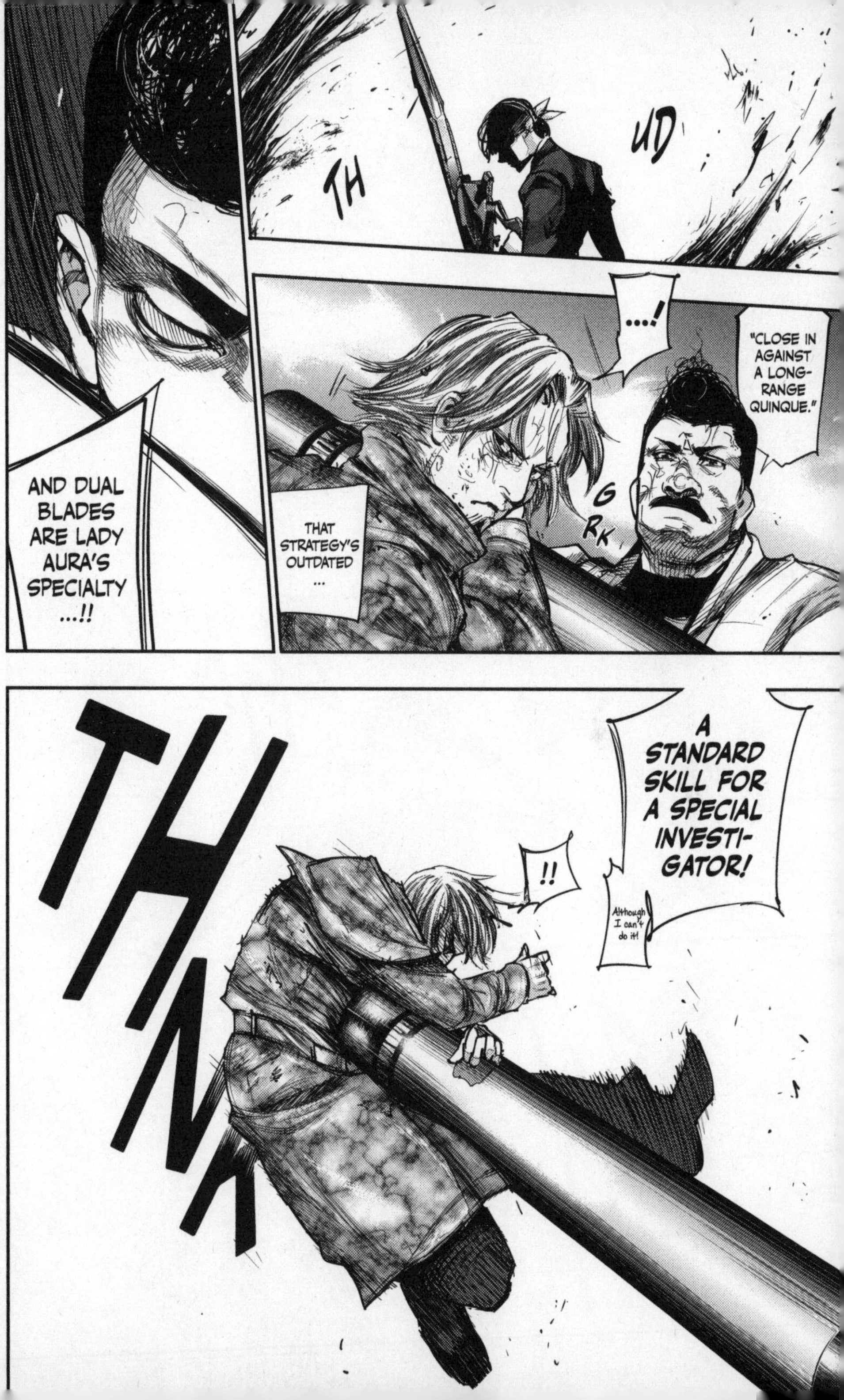
THUD
...!
"CLOSE IN AGAINST A LONG-RANGE QUINQUE."
GRK
THAT STRATEGY'S OUTDATED...
AND DUAL BLADES ARE LADY AURA'S SPECIALTY...!!
A STANDARD SKILL FOR A SPECIAL INVESTIGATOR!
Although I can't do it!
!!
THNK

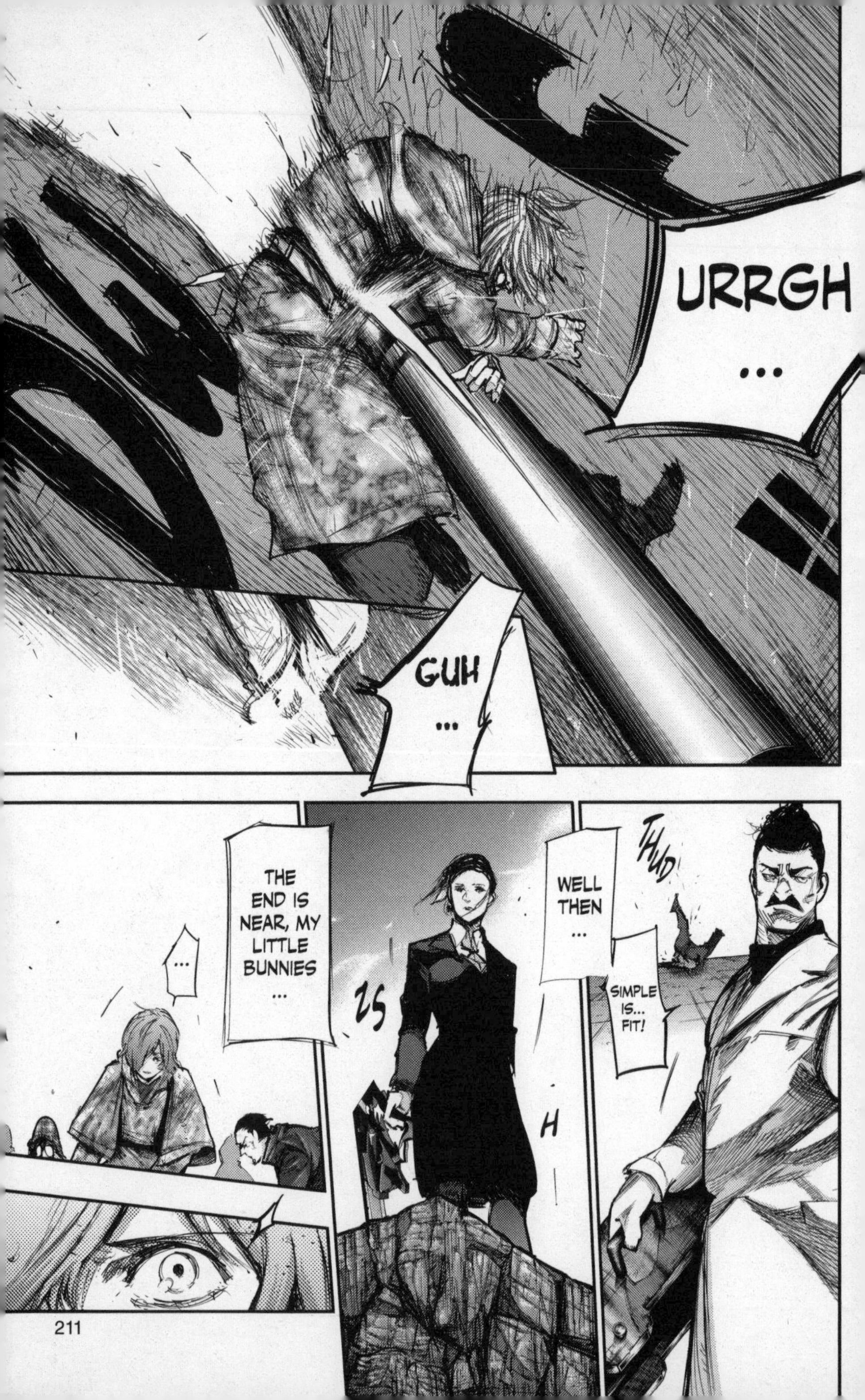
URRGH ...
GUH ...
THUD
WELL THEN ...
SIMPLE IS... FIT!
ZS
H
THE END IS NEAR, MY LITTLE BUNNIES ...
...

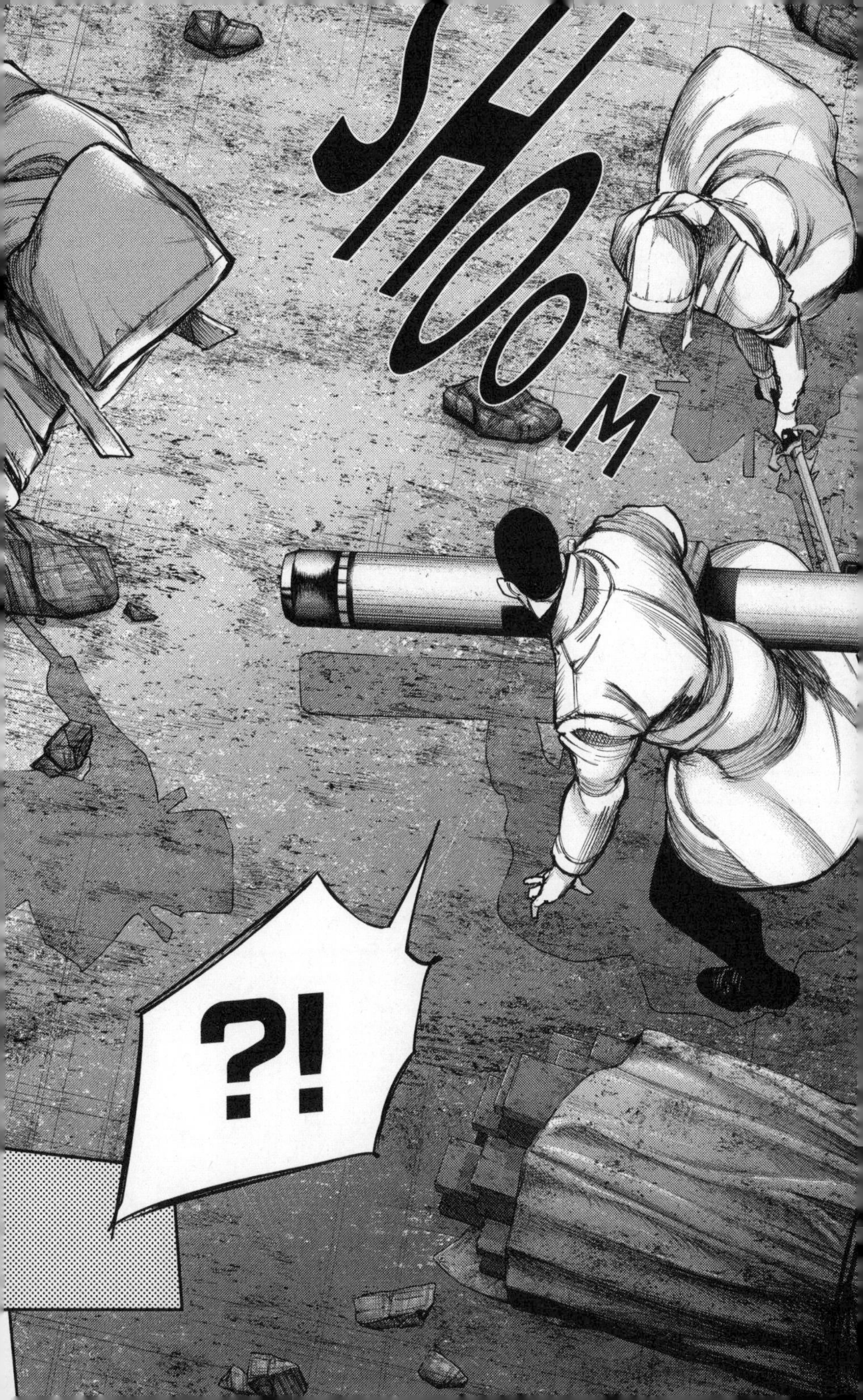
SHOOOM
?!

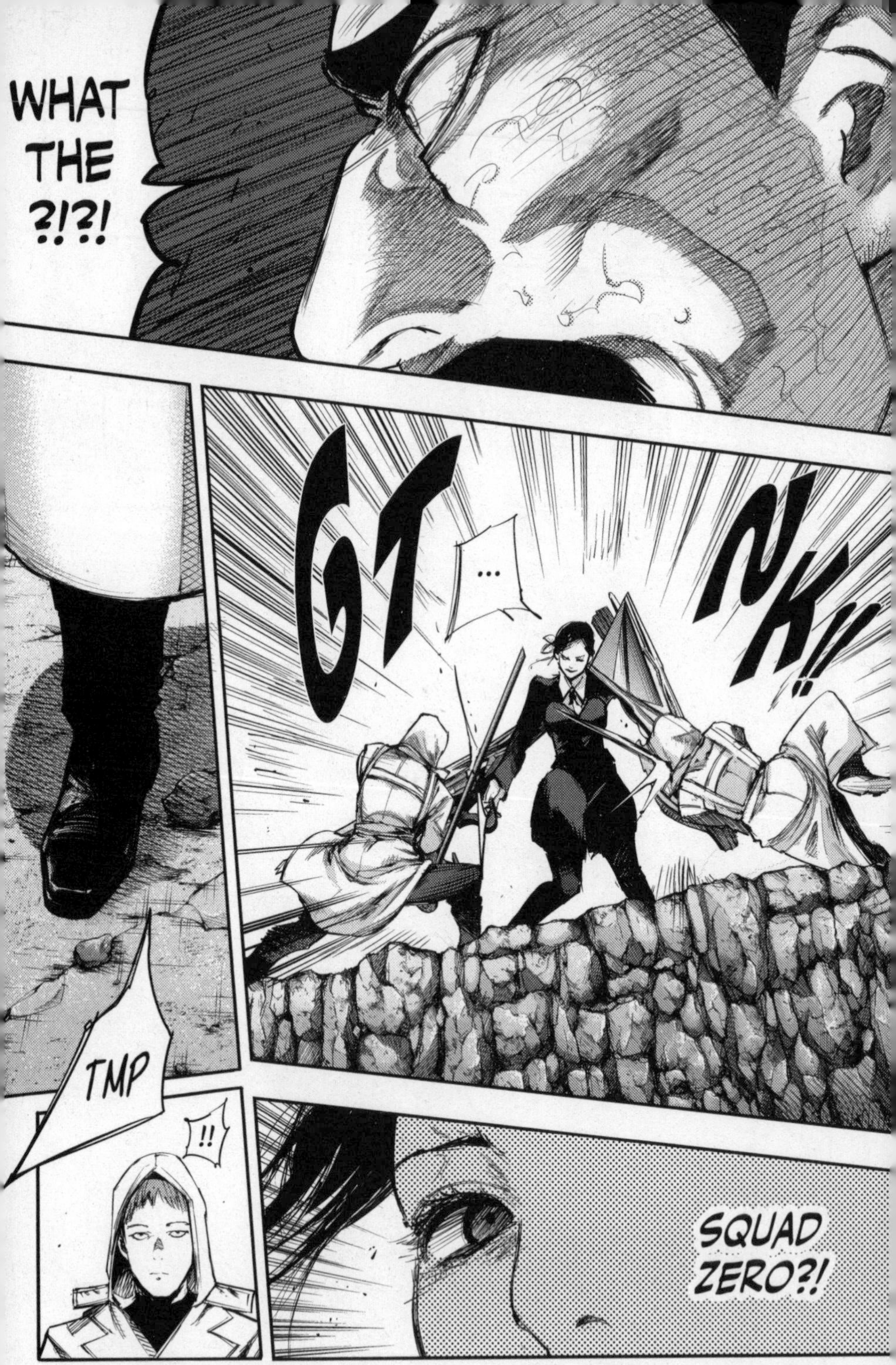
WHAT THE ?!?!
GT
NK!!
...
TMP
SQUAD ZERO?!
!!

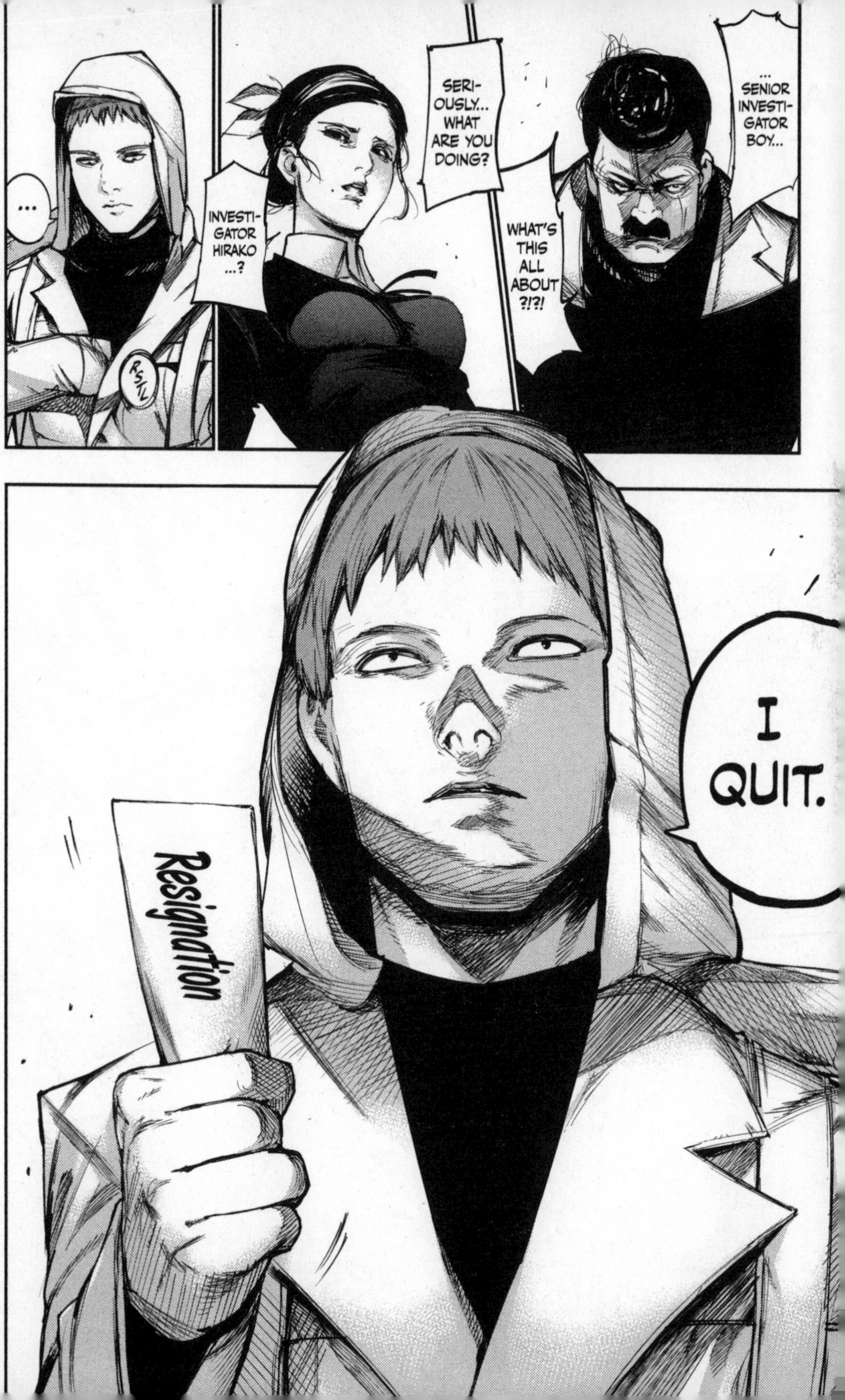
... SENIOR INVESTIGATOR BOY...
WHAT'S THIS ALL ABOUT?!?!
SERIOUSLY... WHAT ARE YOU DOING?
INVESTIGATOR HIRAKO ...?
...
I QUIT.
Resignation

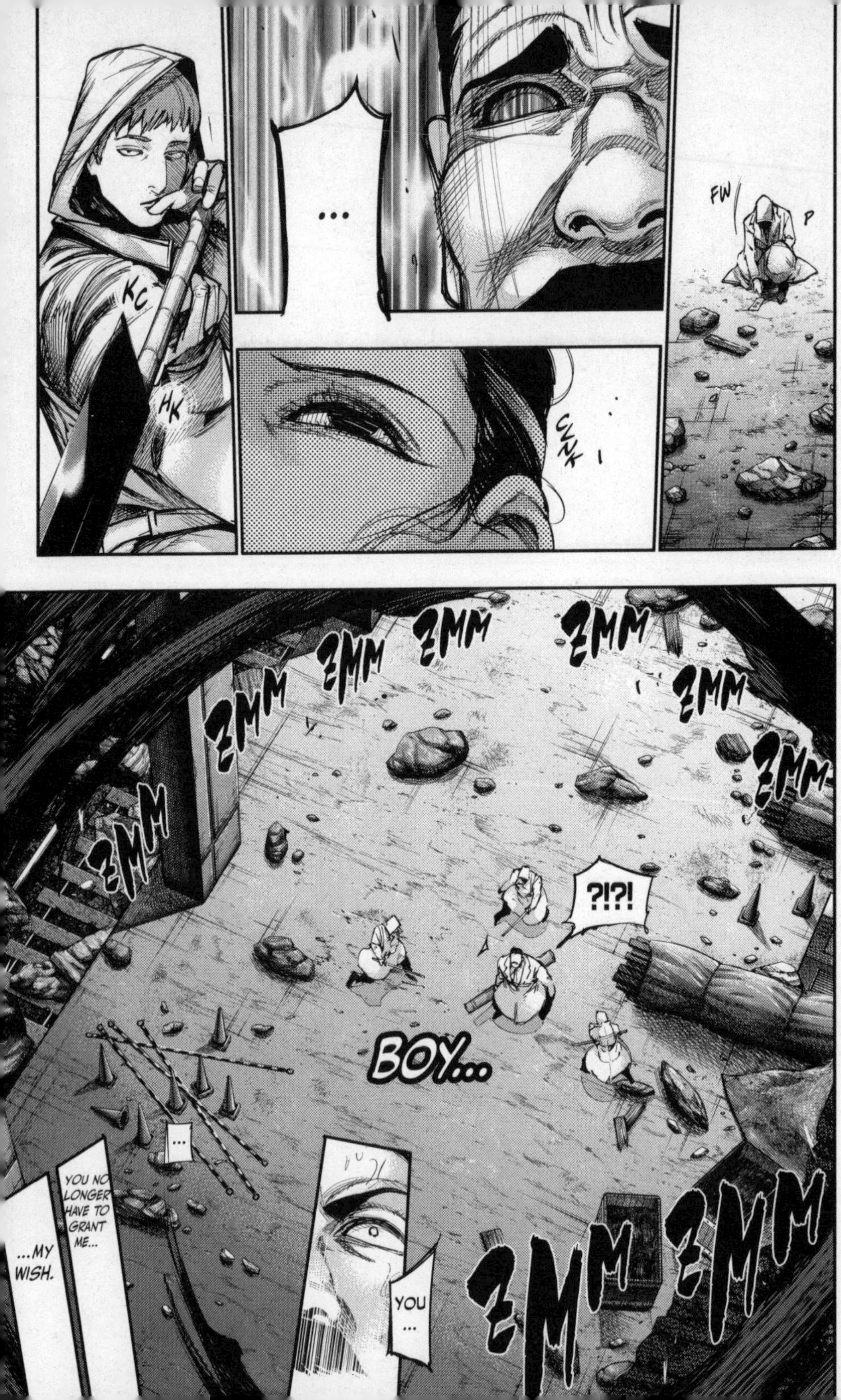
FW
P
...
CLNK
KC
HK
ZMM ZMM ZMM ZMM ZMM ZMM ZMM ZMM
?!?!
BOY...
ZMM ZMM
YOU ...
...
YOU NO LONGER HAVE TO GRANT ME...
...MY WISH.

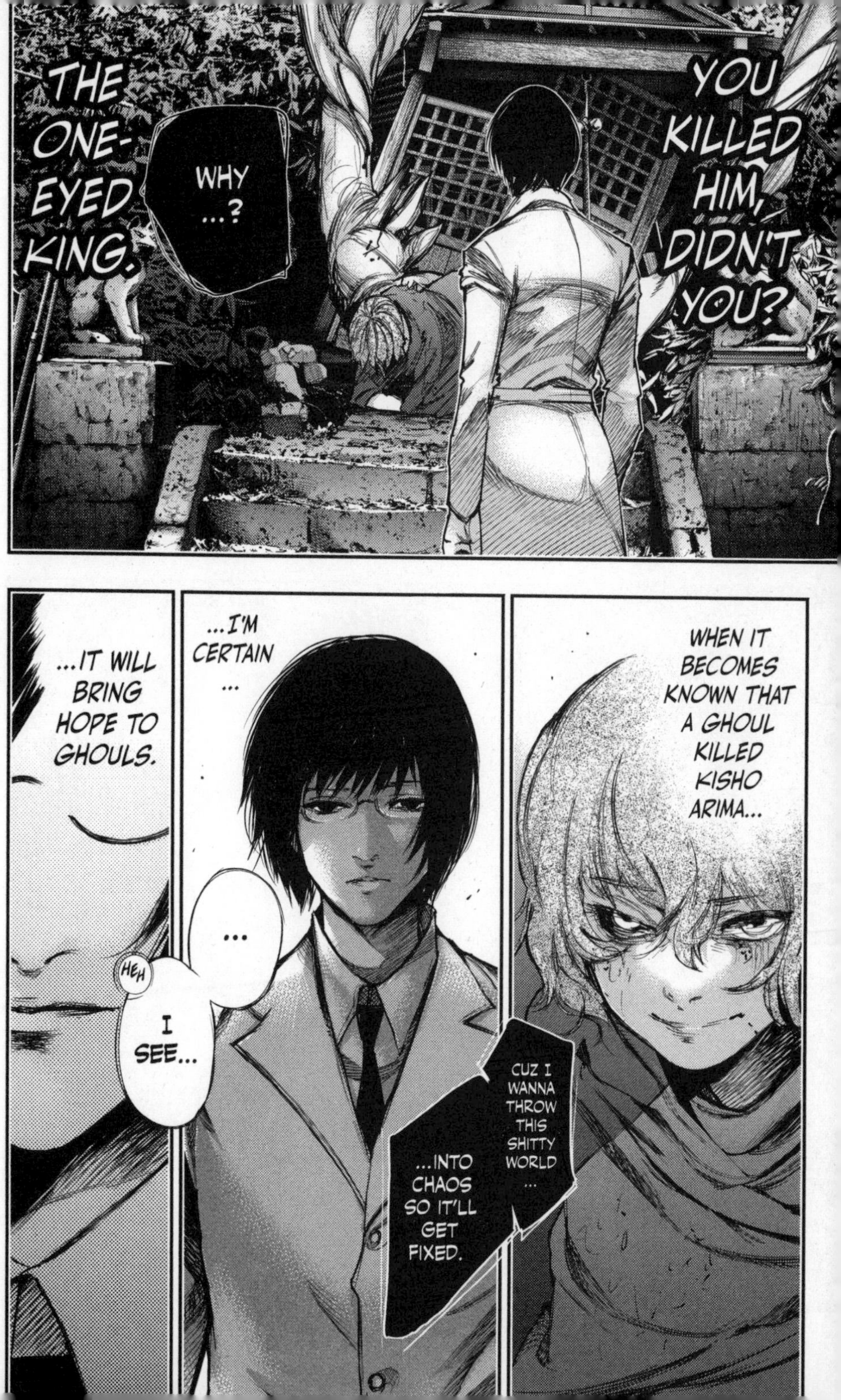
YOU KILLED HIM, DIDN'T YOU?
WHY ...?
THE ONE-EYED KING.
WHEN IT BECOMES KNOWN THAT A GHOUL KILLED KISHO ARIMA...
CUZ I WANNA THROW THIS SHITTY WORLD ...
...INTO CHAOS SO IT'LL GET FIXED.
...I'M CERTAIN ...
...
HEH
I SEE...
...IT WILL BRING HOPE TO GHOULS.

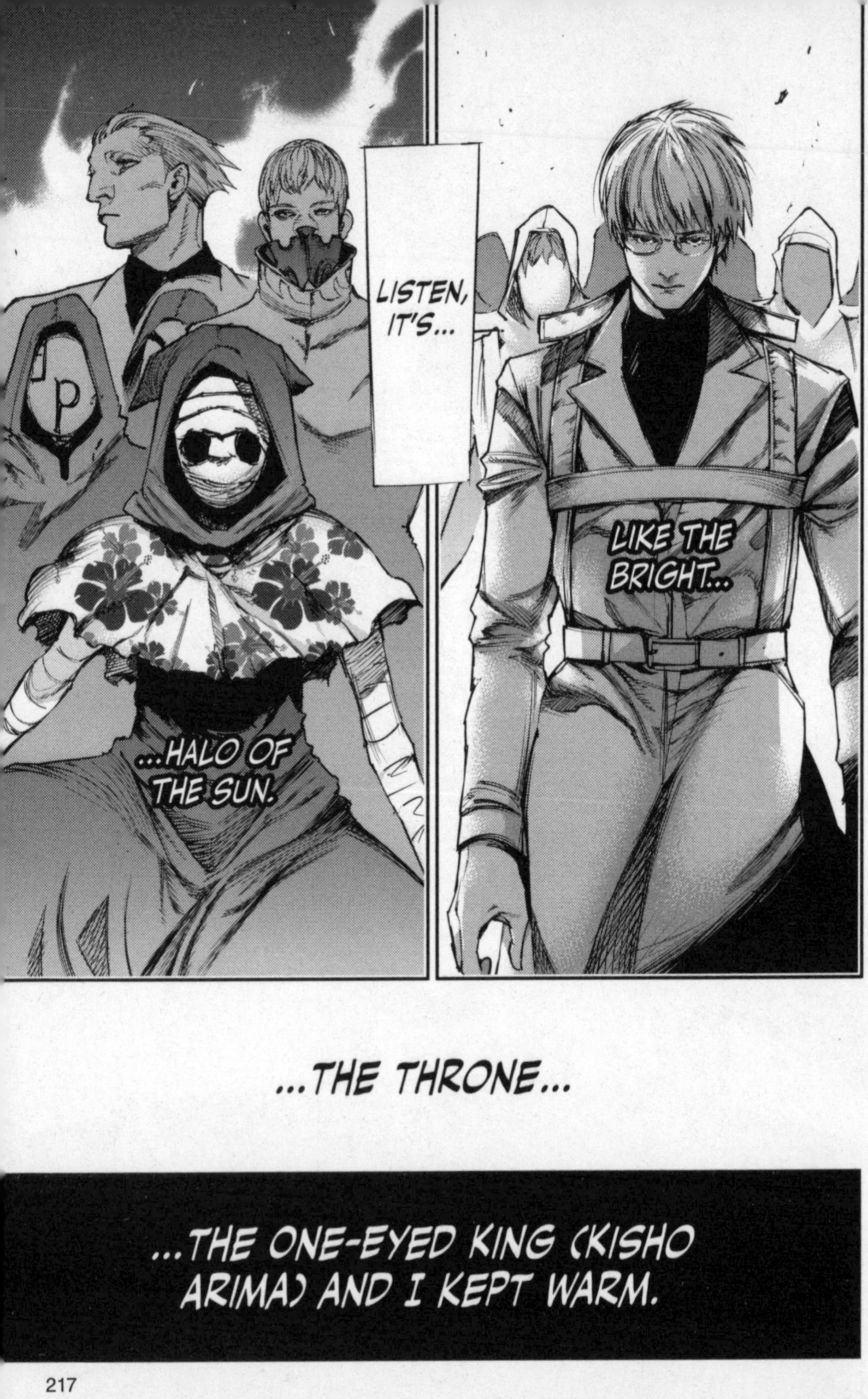
LISTEN, IT'S...
LIKE THE BRIGHT...
...HALO OF THE SUN.

...THE THRONE...

...THE ONE-EYED KING (KISHO ARIMA) AND I KEPT WARM.

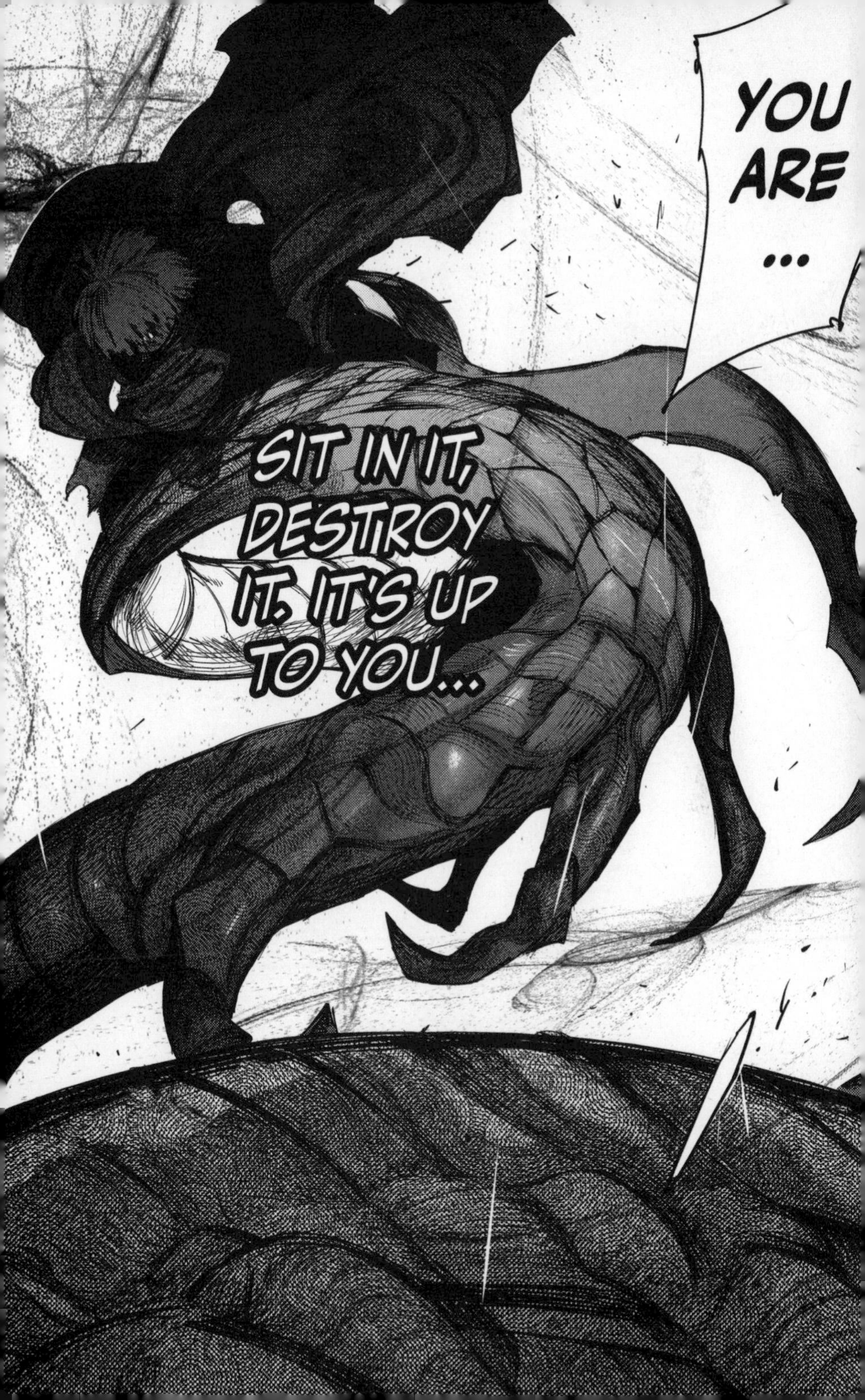
YOU ARE ...
SIT IN IT, DESTROY IT, IT'S UP TO YOU...

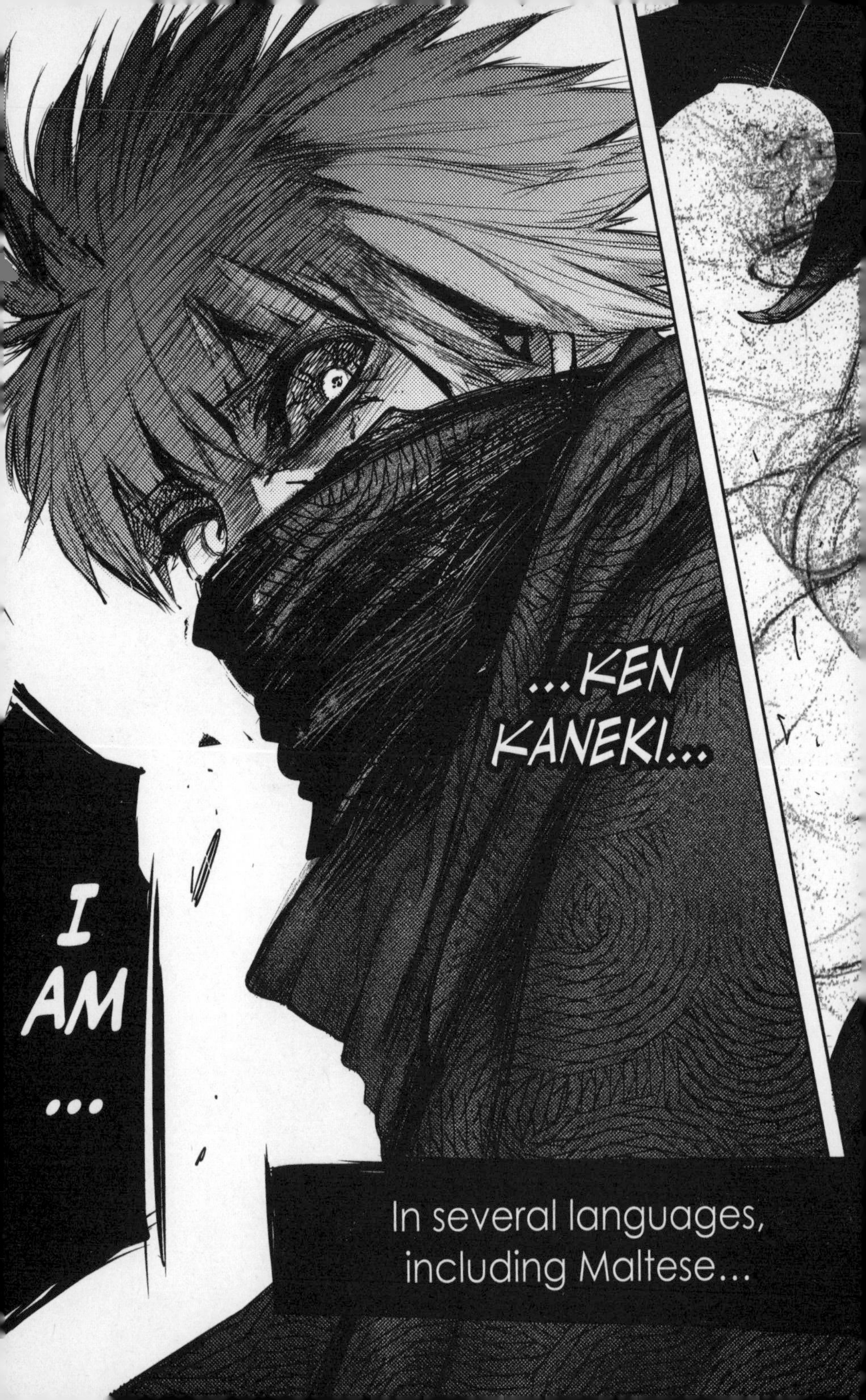
...KEN KANEKI...
I AM ...
In several languages, including Maltese...

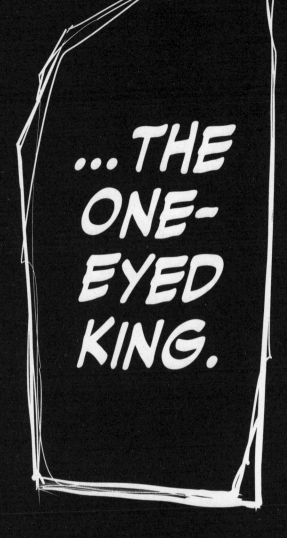

...THE ONE-EYED KING.

...*re* means "king."

To be continued in Tokyo Ghoul:re vol. 9

Spot the Difference At the beach! (find 5)

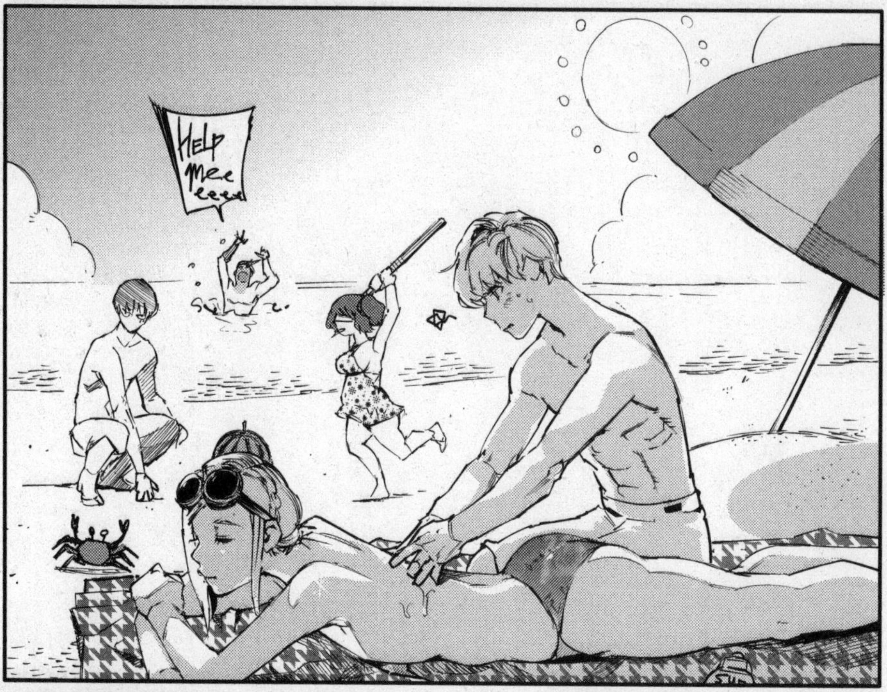
HELP meeeeee

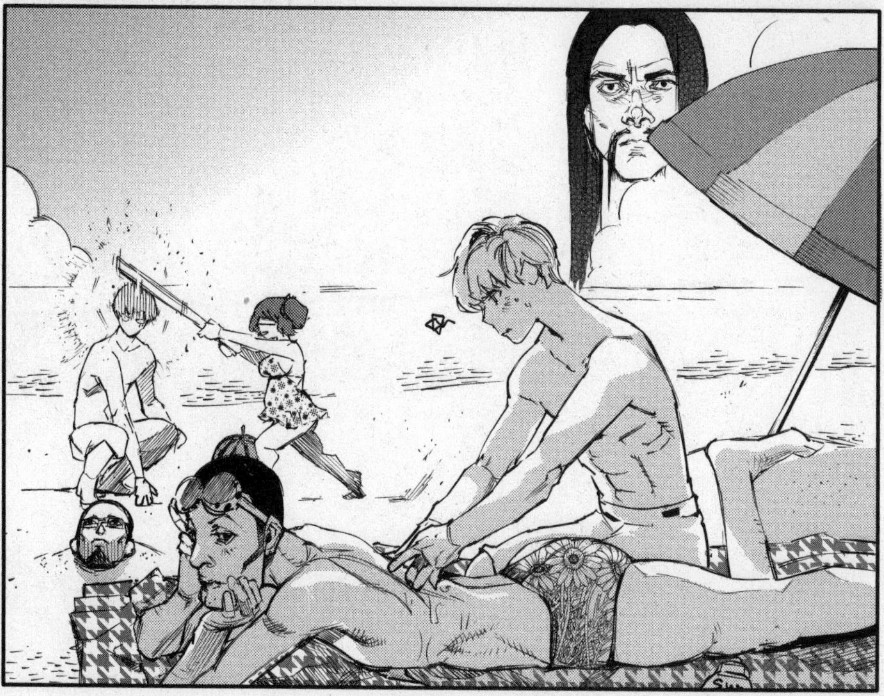

Answers 1. Haise is rubbing Nico's surprisingly smooth back. 2. Urie later loses consciousness. 3. Matsuri is buried. 4. Nobody could save Tsukiyama. 5. Shachi is overlooking them all.

Spot the Difference At the special investigators' meeting! (find 5)

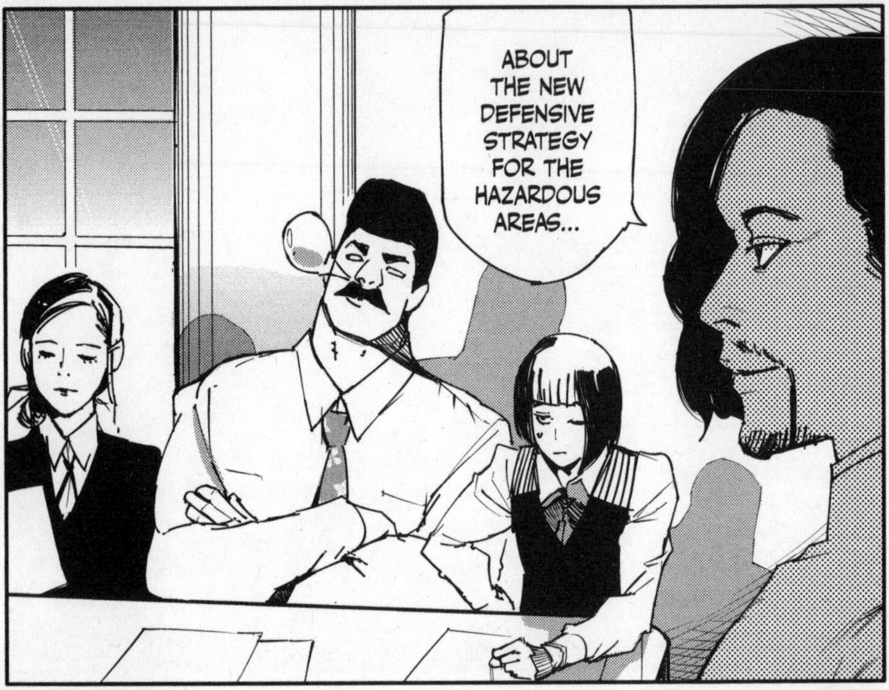
ABOUT THE NEW DEFENSIVE STRATEGY FOR THE HAZARDOUS AREAS...

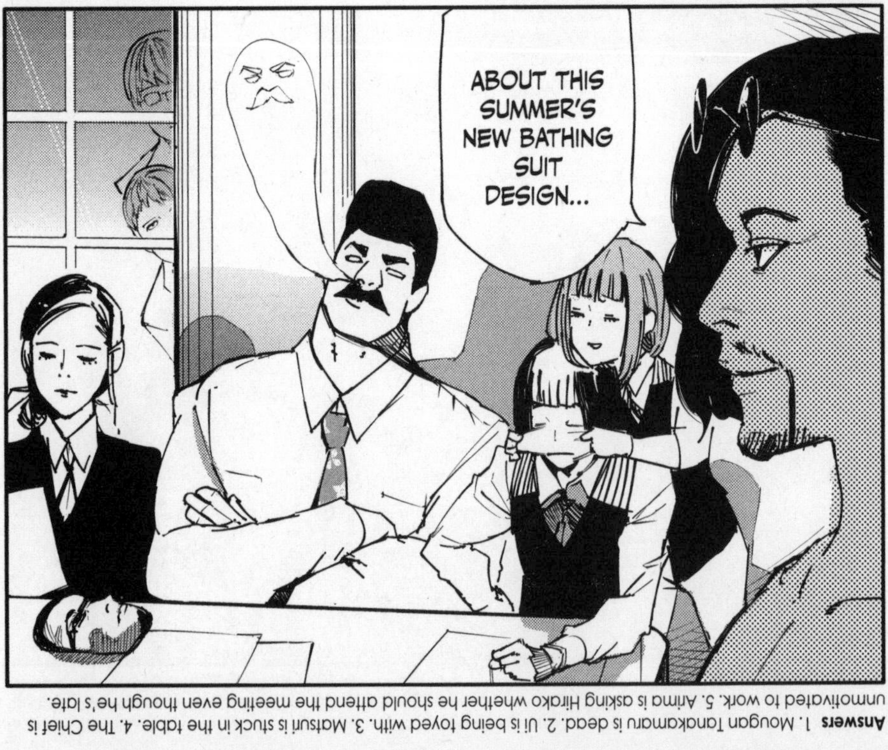
ABOUT THIS SUMMER'S NEW BATHING SUIT DESIGN...

Answers 1. Mougan Tanakamaru is dead. 2. Ui is being toyed with. 3. Matsuri is stuck in the table. 4. The Chief is unmotivated to work. 5. Arima is asking Hirako whether he should attend the meeting even though he's late.

Spot the Difference With pudding at a restaurant! (find 5)

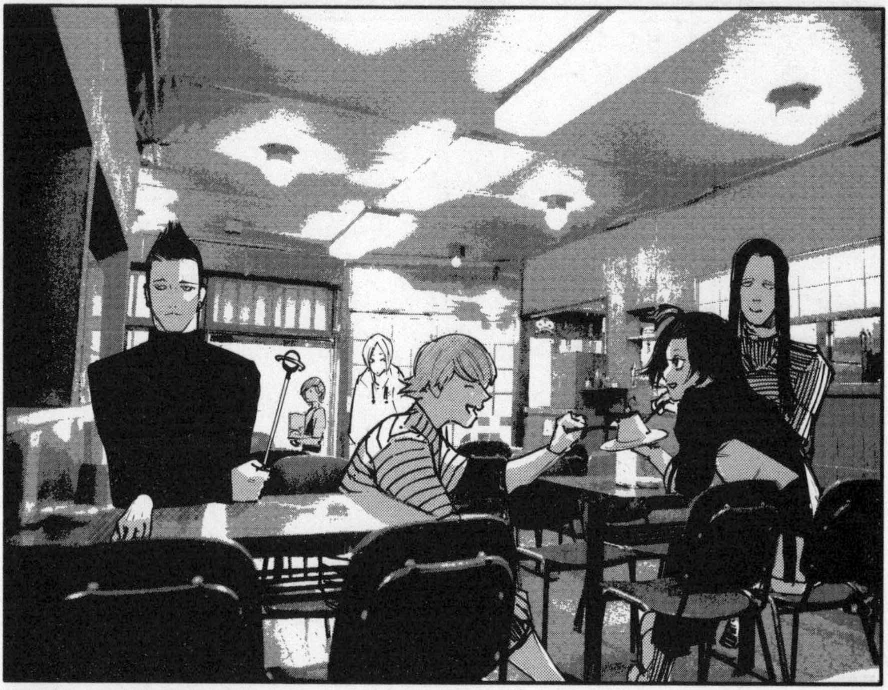

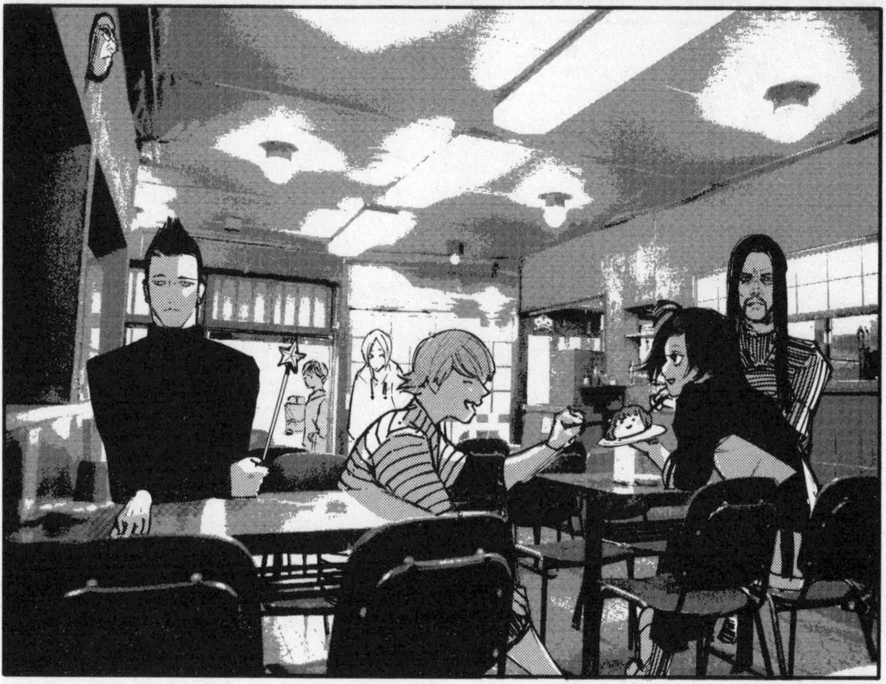

Answers 1. Juzo and Mizuro are eating a Saiko cake. 2. Mikage is extracting the universe's energy from a different source. 3. Matsuri is stuck in the wall. 4. Person passing by window changed from Touka to Haise. 5. Shachi is pretending to be Abara, but nobody notices.

Spot the Difference At Aogiri free time! (find 5)

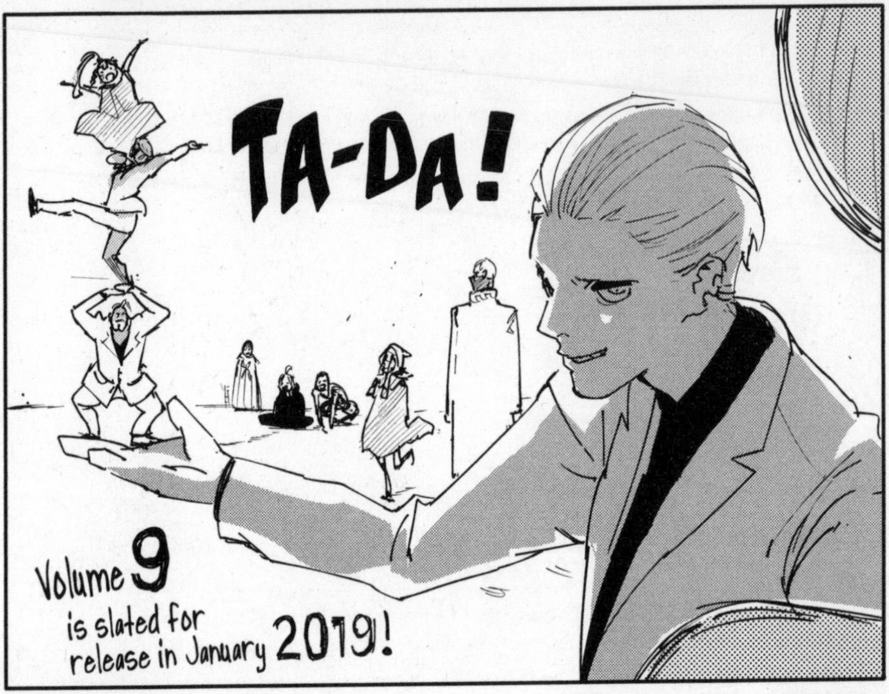
TA-DA!
Volume 9
is slated for
release in January 2019!

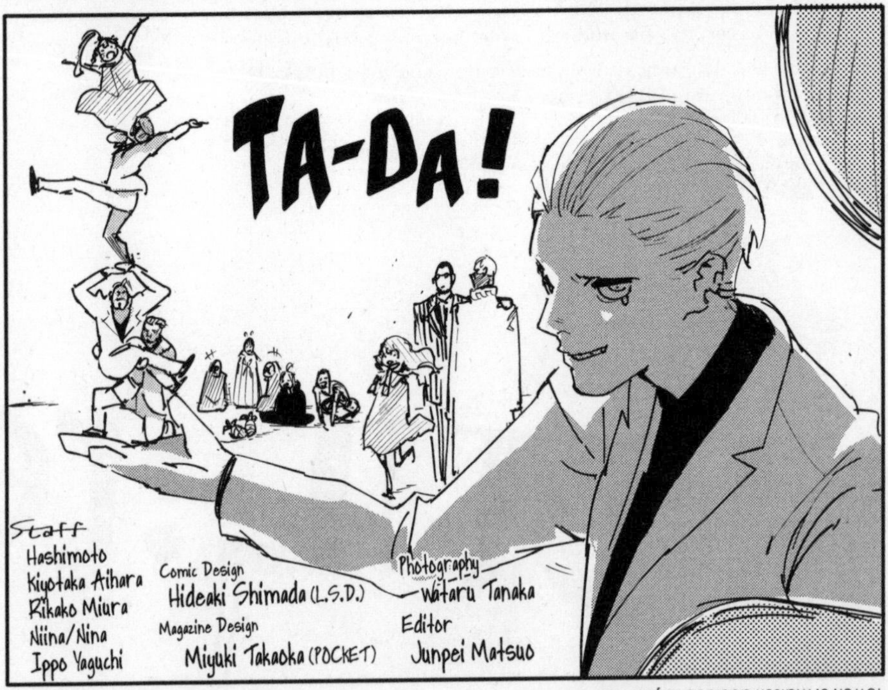
TA-DA!
Staff
Hashimoto
Kiyotaka Aihara
Rikako Miura
Niina/Nina
Ippo Yaguchi
Comic Design
Hideaki Shimada (L.S.D.)
Magazine Design
Miyuki Takaoka (POCKET)
Photography
Wataru Tanaka
Editor
Junpei Matsuo

Answers 1. Eto forgot to wrap herself up in bandages. 2. Freshly picked pineapples. 3. The Bin Brothers are enjoying themselves next to the Grave Robber. 4. Naki is crying because Yamori is the lowest level of the tower. 5. Matsuri decided to join them.

Kiyoko Aura
安浦 清子(あうら きよこ)   Special Investigator (Class 44)

- DOB: 11/19 ♀ • Blood type: B • Height/weight: 165cm/57kg
- Quinque: Zebizu (Ukaku – Rate/S+)

The sole female special investigator. She was a classmate of Akira Mado's mother, Kasuka, and is the aunt of Shinsanpei Aura from the Qs Squad.

A dual-Quinque wielder. Through her guidance, the technique was passed on to Kureo Mado, Kisho Arima and Keijin Nakarai.

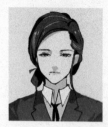

Mougan Tanakamaru
田中丸 望元 (たなかまる もうがん)   Special Investigator (Class 46)

- Age: 49 (DOB: 5/31) ♂ • Blood type: O • Height/weight: 192cm/111kg
- Quinque: Higher Mind/Angel Beat (Ukaku – Rate/SS)

His family runs a temple and he is highly sensitive to spirits, claiming to have had numerous paranormal experiences. This made him resistant to taking over his family's temple and led to him becoming a Ghoul investigator.

He may or may not have whined about seeing the spirits of Ghouls to Marude and other investigators.

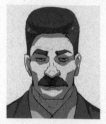

*Ages are from the start of the year.

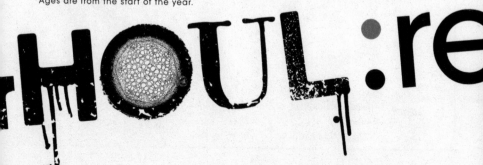

Kisho Arima

有馬 貴将 (ありま きしょう)

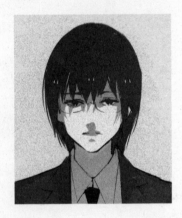

Special Investigator (Class 59)
Hakubi Garden

- Age: 15 (DOB 12/20) ♂ • Blood type: ? • Height/weight: 164cm/52kg

Stats are from date of enlistment.

A legendary Ghoul investigator. Holds the records for most eradications and most medals received. Feared by Ghouls as the White Reaper.

Remarkably successful in developing recruits, including Take Hirako, Kori Ui, Akira Mado, children in Hakubi Garden and Haise Sasaki.

Regarded as the ultimate investigator, but he was defeated and killed by the One-Eyed King at Cochlea.

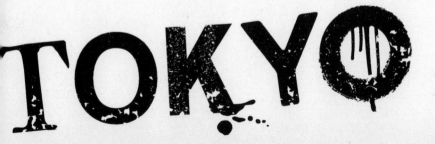

TOKYO

HOUL:re

SUI ISHIDA is the author of the immensely popular *Tokyo Ghoul* and several *Tokyo Ghoul* one-shots, including one that won second place in the *Weekly Young Jump* 113th Grand Prix award in 2010. *Tokyo Ghoul:re* is the sequel to *Tokyo Ghoul*.

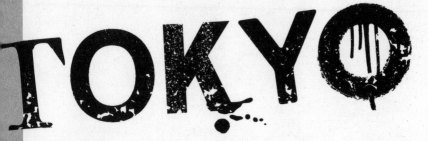

Story and art by
SUI ISHIDA

TOKYO GHOUL:RE © 2014 by Sui Ishida
All rights reserved.
First published in Japan in 2014 by SHUEISHA Inc., Tokyo.
English translation rights arranged by SHUEISHA Inc.

Translation Joe Yamazaki
Touch-Up Art & Lettering Vanessa Satone
Design Shawn Carrico
Editor Pancha Diaz

Printed in the U.S.A.

Published by VIZ Media, LLC
P.O. Box 77010
San Francisco, CA 94107

10 9 8 7 6 5 4 3 2 1
First printing, December 2018

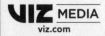

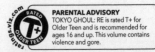

PARENTAL ADVISORY
TOKYO GHOUL: RE is rated T+ for
Older Teen and is recommended for
ages 16 and up. This volume contains
violence and gore.

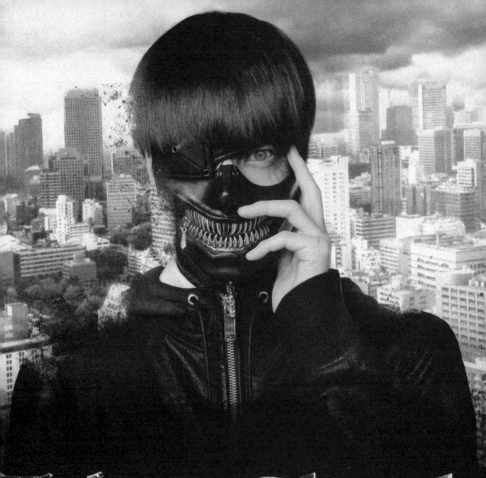

Tokyo Ghoul

YOU'VE READ THE MANGA
NOW WATCH THE
LIVE-ACTION MOVIE!

OWN IT NOW ON BLU-RAY, DVD & DIGITAL HD

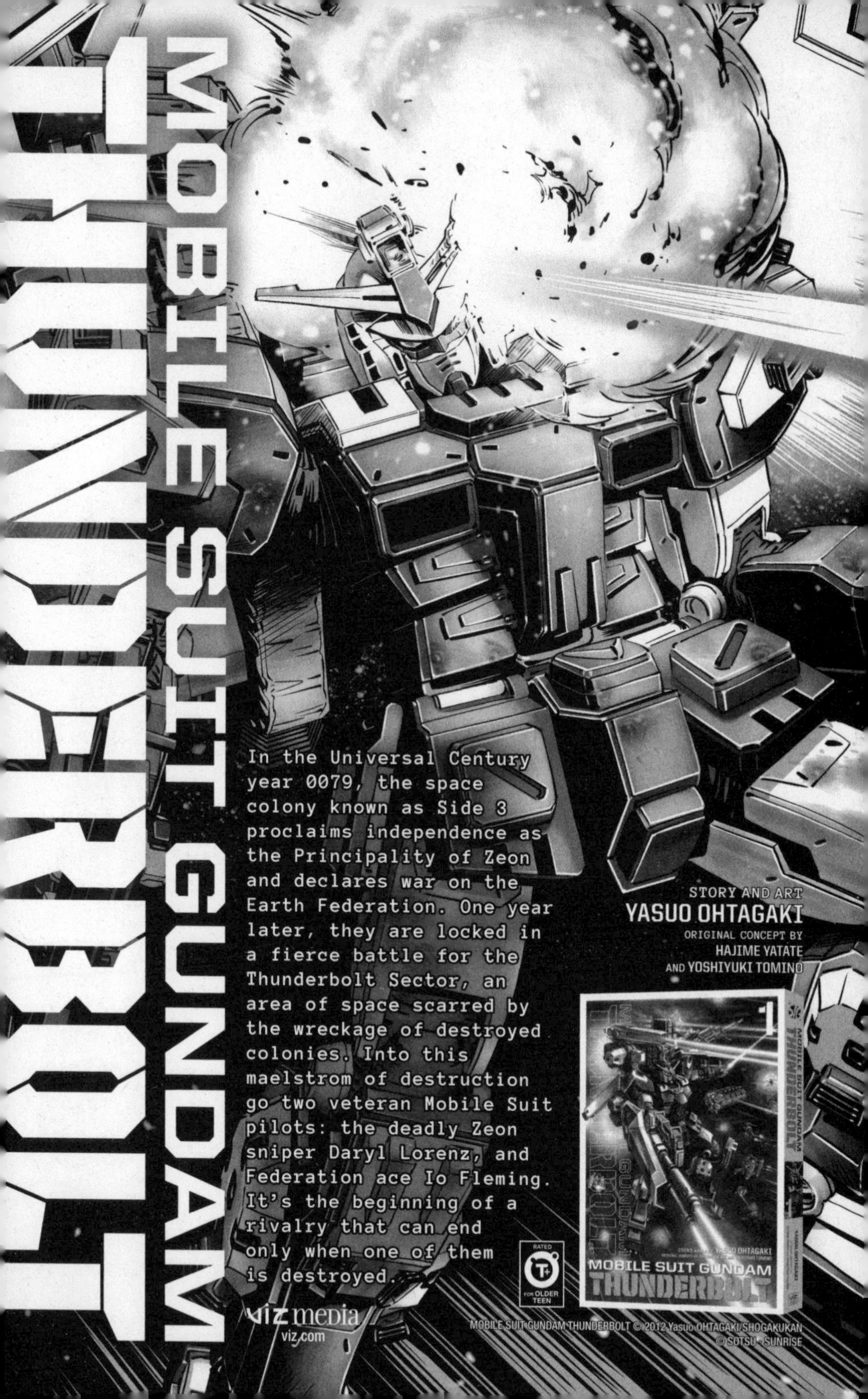
MOBILE SUIT GUNDAM
THUNDERBOLT
In the Universal Century year 0079, the space colony known as Side 3 proclaims independence as the Principality of Zeon and declares war on the Earth Federation. One year later, they are locked in a fierce battle for the Thunderbolt Sector, an area of space scarred by the wreckage of destroyed colonies. Into this maelstrom of destruction go two veteran Mobile Suit pilots: the deadly Zeon sniper Daryl Lorenz, and Federation ace Io Fleming. It's the beginning of a rivalry that can end only when one of them is destroyed.
STORY AND ART
YASUO OHTAGAKI
ORIGINAL CONCEPT BY
HAJIME YATATE
AND YOSHIYUKI TOMINO
MOBILE SUIT GUNDAM
THUNDERBOLT
1
RATED T+ FOR OLDER TEEN
viz media
viz.com
MOBILE SUIT GUNDAM THUNDERBOLT © 2012 Yasuo OHTAGAKI/SHOGAKUKAN
© SOTSU · SUNRISE

UZUMAKI

Story and Art by **JUNJI ITO**

SPIRALS... THIS TOWN IS CONTAMINATED WITH SPIRALS...

Kurouzu-cho, a small fogbound town on the coast of Japan, is cursed. According to Shuichi Saito, the withdrawn boyfriend of teenager Kirie Goshima, their town is haunted not by a person or being but by a pattern: uzumaki, the spiral, the hypnotic secret shape of the world. It manifests itself in everything from seashells and whirlpools in water to the spiral marks on people's bodies, the insane obsessions of Shuichi's father and the voice from the cochlea in our inner ear. As the madness spreads, the inhabitants of Kurouzu-cho are pulled ever deeper into a whirlpool from which there is no return!

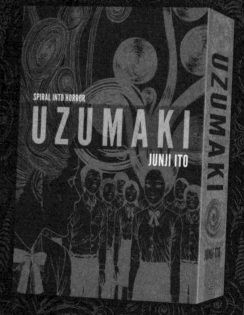

A masterpiece of horror manga, now available in a
DELUXE HARDCOVER EDITION!

TOKYO GHOUL:re

This is the last page.
TOKYO GHOUL:re reads right to left.